Stephanie Harvey & Anne Goudvis

Strategies That Work

second edition

Teaching Comprehension
for Understanding
and Engagement

Stenhouse Publishers
Portland, Maine

Pembroke Publishers Limited
Markham, Ontario

Stenhouse Publishers
www.stenhouse.com

Pembroke Publishers Limited
www.pembroke.com

Cover:
Cover image of *The Journey That Saved Curious George* by
Louise Borden, illustrated by Allan Drummond; published by
Houghton Mifflin Company. Illustration copyright © 2005 by
Allan Drummond.
Jacket image from LITTLE MAMA FORGETS by Robin Cruise,
illustrated by Stacey Dressen-McQueen. Reprinted by permis-
sion of Farrar, Straus and Giroux, LLC.
National Geographic Explorer. Jan/Feb 2006. © 2006 National
Geographic Society. Used by permission.
Page 56: From "Interrogating Texts: 6 Reading Habits to Develop
in Your First Year at Harvard." Copyright © 2007 President and
Fellows of Harvard College. http://hcl.harvard.edu/
researchguides/lamont_handouts/interrogatingtexts.html.
Used by permission.
Page 63: "This Is Cruising" by Kevin Keating. Copyright © 1998.
Hemispheres Magazine, March.
Page 89: "Testing, Testing." Copyright © 2002. TIME FOR KIDS
(January 25). TIME FOR KIDS is a registered trademark of
Time Inc. Reprinted by permission. Photographs by Tim
Sloan/AFP/Getty Images and Jonathan Selig/Getty Images.
Reprinted by permission.
Page 128. "Sea Otters Take a Dip." From *National Geographic for
Kids.* September 2001. Used by permission.
Page 170: "Should Cities Sue Gunmakers?" From JUNIOR
SCHOLASTIC, February 8, 1999. Copyright © 1999 by
Scholastic Inc. Reprinted by permission of Scholastic Inc.

Page 183: "In Sickness and In Health." Copyright © 1998. *Kids
Discover Magazine,* April. Reprinted by permission.
Page 192–193: "Moonstruck Scientists Count 63 and Rising" by
Robert S. Boyd. © McClatchy-Tribune Information Services. All
Rights Reserved. Reprinted with permission.
Pages 239–250: Adapted with permission from *Comprehension
Toolkit* by Stephanie Harvey and Anne Goudvis. Copyright ©
2005 by Stephanie Harvey and Anne Goudvis. Published by
Heinemann, a division of Reed Elsevier, Inc., Portsmouth, NH.
All rights reserved.
Pages 251–252: Reprinted with permission from *Comprehension
Toolkit* by Stephanie Harvey and Anne Goudvis. Copyright ©
2005 by Stephanie Harvey and Anne Goudvis. Published by
Heinemann, a division of Reed Elsevier, Inc., Portsmouth, NH.
All rights reserved.
Pages 300–303: *From My Freedom Trip: A Child's Escape from
North Korea* by Frances Park and Ginger Park, illustrated by
Debra Reid Jenkins (Caroline House, and imprint of Boyds
Mills Press, 1998). Reprinted with the permission of Boyds
Mills Press, Inc. Text copyright © 1998 by Frances Park and
Ginger Park; Illustrations copyright © 1998 by Debra Reid
Jenkins.

Library of Congress Cataloging-in-Publication Data
Harvey, Stephanie.
    Strategies that work: teaching comprehension for under-
standing and engagement / Stephanie Harvey, Anne Goudvis.—
2nd ed.
        p. cm.
    Includes bibliographical references and index.
    ISBN-13: 978-1-57110-481-6 (alk. paper)
    ISBN-10: 1-57110-481-X (alk. paper)
    1. Reading comprehension. 2. Reading (Elementary) 3.
Thought and thinking—Study and teaching (Elementary) 4.
Children—Books and reading. I. Goudvis, Anne. II. Title.

LB1573.7.H37 2007
372.47—dc22

                                                    2006103358

Cover and interior design by Martha Drury
Cover photograph by Jay York

Manufactured in the United States of America on acid-free paper
13 12 11 10 09 08 07   9 8 7 6 5 4 3 2

For David Pearson, whose lifelong commitment and dedication to the cause of education has inspired so many of us.

Contents

Part II Strategy Lessons

Part III Comprehension Across the Curriculum

Part IV Resources That Support Strategy Instruction

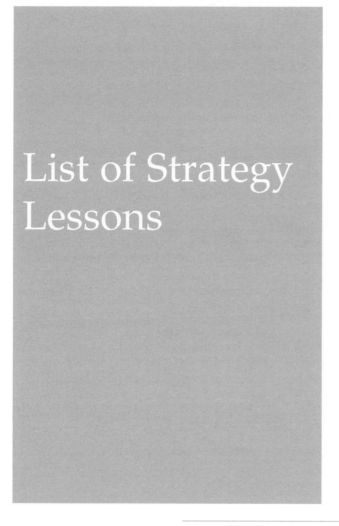

List of Strategy Lessons

Chapter 7: Activating and Connecting to Background Knowledge

Chapter 8: Questioning

Chapter 10: Determining Importance in Text

Foreword

When I was in elementary school I might have been categorized as a "dreamer reader." I remember reading *T Model Tommy*, by Stephen W. Meader, when I was in sixth grade. As I recall, the book was about a young enterprising boy who parlayed owning a small truck into a growing business enterprise. I immediately wanted to live the life of Tommy and start my own business. I read along, living through the characters, and would soon be lost in a reverie that had little to do with the text at hand.

When I came to my reading group, however, I lacked precision in answering precise questions about the text. For most of my life I've viewed myself as a defective reader. In one sense I was a problem reader, since I couldn't match my meaning with the original text required for discussion. I needed teachers who had read this book by Stephanie Harvey and Anne Goudvis.

Strategies That Work taps into the urge of all children to make sense of the world around them through reading. The authors make complicated theories of comprehension accessible to teachers. They never diverge from their focus of showing what reading is for along with the strategies of how to make connections between texts, lives, learning to read fiction, nonfiction, and all the genres. Each strategy is designed to open up new worlds for the child. In this case, reading is for living, a lifetime of enjoyment, and significant intellectual engagement with a fascinating world through people and books.

This is a book written by readers, for teachers of reading, whose children will become readers. The authors' enthusiasm leaps off the page as they demonstrate their own strategies for reading through actual books and texts. Several of the books they use in the strategy lessons appealed to me, and I started a list of these titles. The list exploded when I reached the wonderful resource section. Be prepared to have pencil and paper handy to jot down titles of must-read books. You're going to need them!

While reading *Strategies* I was struck by how distant most texts about teaching reading are from the act of reading itself. Other texts are steeped in comprehension strategies and skill lessons but rarely show the author in action with specific texts in the classroom. Our authors never get off the subject of showing how they think when they read with real texts so that teachers and children can do the same. Written and spoken examples of student thinking fill this book. This evidence of student thinking informs and guides the instruction in *Strategies That Work*.

We can't tell children how to read; we simply have to show them. We learn with the authors how to show children to make connections, synthesize, and approach new genres. The authors teach reading from the inside out. That is, they are already in the middle of reading a book by sharing the love of the book, how to read it, and how to develop lifetime strategies. I think of David McCulloch's statement that when he was teaching history at Cornell he was not satisfied until each student had fallen in love with history. He soon realized that unless the student was on a quest to discover some aspect of history that meant something to her, she wouldn't fall in love with the subject. Our authors show both teachers and children coming inside the process and developing a love affair with books.

Donald Graves

Acknowledgments

Education is a collective and collaborative effort. This book, as well as its predecessor, is no exception. We want to take a moment to acknowledge the many people with whom we have worked over the years and who have influenced our thinking and teaching in so many ways.

Our teaching careers began in the classroom, and to this day, we are teachers first and foremost. We honor all teachers. We know how hard they work, and we applaud them. We owe a special thanks to the teachers, librarians, and administrators who welcomed us into their lively schools and rich classrooms to teach and learn with them.

We continue to marvel at kids in classrooms around the country and their amazing thinking. We simply can't learn enough from them and are grateful for our time together.

For many years, we worked together as reading and writing staff developers at the Denver-based Public Education and Business Coalition. The PEBC originated a reading comprehension project that translated research findings into classroom practice. With colleagues at the PEBC, we spent many hours gathered around the table sharing stories about kids, reading articles, and discussing ways to transform teaching and learning. We relish those years and owe a debt of gratitude to our PEBC friends and colleagues.

We also want to thank our professors, teachers, and mentors, many of them giants in the field of literacy. Reading their work and listening to them at conferences has stretched our thinking and inspired us to keep writing.

Several people deserve our thanks for their wise guidance throughout the writing of this second edition. We begin with our editor and dear friend Philippa Stratton, who once again, despite the burgeoning word count, always kept the big picture in mind, yet never failed to roll up her sleeves and dig in whenever the need arose. Smokey Daniels read every word of this book in drafts, providing just the nudge we needed as he responded with humor and insight. Smoke, we owe you! Liz Stedem, our good friend and colleague, once again combined her phenomenal writing style with her knowledge of children's literature to annotate numerous new books for our updated bibliographies. Kelly Clarke artfully crafted the anchor charts in Appendix E. Martha, Erin, Jay, Dan, and the rest of the energetic Stenhouse crew designed and produced this book with the creative flair we have come to know and trust.

We chose to dedicate this book to P. David Pearson because it is grounded in his wisdom and life's work. As a researcher with a practitioner's knowledge of children—how they learn, how they think, and how they understand—David's research context has always been real classrooms in real schools and is based on a profound respect for the contributions of teachers and kids. We are deeply indebted to David for bridging the worlds of the researcher and the classroom as we continue to learn from him.

Once again, above all, we thank our families for their encouragement as well as their welcome distractions. We really couldn't do this time and again without them. And last but not least, we are still speaking and high-fiving each other. No small feat after so many years and so many words!

Introduction to the Second Edition

The process of reading is not a half sleep, but, in highest sense, an exercise, a gymnast's struggle; that the reader is to do something for himself, must be on the alert, must himself or herself construct indeed the poem, argument, history, metaphysical essay—the text furnishing the hints, the clue, the start or frame-work.

Walt Whitman

When we wrote the first edition of this book, we wanted to grapple with Whitman's jungle gym of thoughts, words, and ideas about reading. We are still following clues on the pathway to meaning and remain insatiably curious about kids' thinking. We love to hear about their reading—their questions, reactions, interpretations, opinions, inferences, arguments, and celebrations. Much of what we have learned about teaching reading comes from our conversations with children about their reading, their learning, and their lives. They are our most profound inspiration.

Kids continue to inspire us, of course. However, it's the teachers over the years who have come up to us to share their thinking, their books bursting with sticky notes, who have really moved us to write this second edition. We never cease to be amazed at how much we learn from educators as we work side by side in their classrooms, converse in workshops, meet with study groups, and engage in email exchanges. This new edition is a reflection of our collective thinking. Books offer little without readers. And the educators who have read our books have made all the difference, pushing our thinking, challenging our ideas, and asking us questions. So much of what we write about here comes from what they have taught us and what we have learned in the seven years since we wrote the first edition.

In that vein, we have been surprised and delighted by the warm response to our work, which stands on the shoulders of a number of wonderful researchers and practitioners in the field. The sheer number of teachers and schools who have taken this work and run with it is humbling. Teachers' determination to make sure their kids understand what they read and construct meaning is heartening in this age of short answers and multiple-choice questions.

As the practice of teaching reading comprehension continues to grow by leaps and bounds, we feel an ongoing responsibility to refine and improve our thinking. In that vein, we have noticed some problematic issues that continue to crop up as we work to implement comprehension instruction. Like everything in education, the challenge is to get beyond a surface level of understanding. If not, comprehension instruction can become routine and perfunctory. This can happen when we teach strategies merely for strategies' sake. It is not about how many connections our kids can make or how many questions they can ask. The purpose of comprehension instruction is to teach strategies as tools to expand and deepen understanding. We best do this by avoiding a lockstep sequence and teaching kids a repertoire of strategies they can use flexibly in many circumstances and with a variety of texts. So our thinking continues to change and evolve. This second edition reflects both the old and the new, what we still believe and what we have learned.

So What's New?

Much has occurred with comprehension instruction since we wrote the first edition of this book. Numerous books have been published on the topic. More teachers are teaching comprehension than ever before. Kids around the country can articulate how comprehension strategies help them understand what they read. And new research on reading comprehension abounds. Some of this edition is entirely new— new chapters and a new section. Some parts of the book have been reorganized and rearranged. Other parts remain relatively intact, but even in those, we have rewritten and revised, so that they reflect new stories, new research, new learning, and new thinking.

Active Literacy

One new thread that runs through this edition is our notion of Active Literacy. When we walk into an active literacy classroom, we know it. Two kids pore over a *Time for Kids* magazine article about TV-Turn-Off Week and jot their thinking in the margins. A small book club meets in the reading corner and debates current issues in immigration. A teacher confers with a group of second-grade kids who are sprawled on the floor researching earthquakes and recording their inferences on a large chart. Three other children draw a large diagram of an avalanche careening down a mountain. We don't save active literacy merely for the literacy block. No matter what time of the day or what subject, kids are actively engaged in doing the work. Great thinking happens in every context and in every content area.

When we began to see the enthusiasm generated around reading and thinking strategies, there was a quantum leap in our kids' eagerness to talk about, write about, sketch, and react to their reading on an almost constant basis. We advocated book clubs and lit circles in our first edition and still do. Now we expect kids to read, write, talk, listen, and investigate their way through the day and across the curriculum. Interacting with text and with each other is paramount.

The Title and Organization

This active engagement is reflected in a change in the subtitle. *Strategies That Work*, the primary title, remains. But we have changed *Teaching Comprehension to Enhance Understanding* to *Teaching Comprehension for Understanding and Engagement*. This has been one of our major *Aha*'s over the past seven years. No doubt comprehension instruction enhances readers' understanding. But what we have noticed repeatedly is how connected and switched on kids are when they really think about their reading.

This new edition of *Strategies That Work* is organized around four sections. The five chapters in Part I highlight what comprehension is and how we teach it. We include the principles that guide our practice as well as the recent research that underlies comprehension instruction. Part II is a practical chapter. It includes lessons and practices that we use when teaching comprehension. Part III emphasizes how we integrate comprehension instruction across the curriculum and the school day. Part IV is a resource of appendices to support teachers as they plan and design comprehension instruction.

Twenty New Lessons

Nothing colors our reading more than what we bring to it. We understand so much more about what we read if we know something about it beforehand. P. David Pearson suggests that learning happens when today's new knowledge becomes tomorrow's background knowledge (Pearson 1995). So we particularly emphasize connecting the new to the known in this second edition of *Strategies That Work*. We highlight the relationship of activating background knowledge to all the strategies we describe in this book. For instance, we often ask questions about what we *don't know* to try to fill in gaps in our background knowledge. When we infer, we take what we *know* and combine it with clues in the text. In order to determine importance, we make a decision about what we *think* is most important to remember. And when we synthesize information, we add to or change what we *already know*.

Our first edition of *Strategies That Work* has been a practical resource for teachers to use in their classrooms every day. We have added twenty new lessons and kept the old favorites, except for a few that relied on text currently out of print. We hope you enjoy the new ones. Most of them emphasize the central role of background knowledge in all of the thinking we do as we read. We want to stress that the lessons and practices describe some of the many possibilities for teaching reading comprehension and are generic. We use sticky notes to code our thinking about any strategy and any text. We use two- and three-column "think sheets" for inferring, connecting, asking questions, or any other strategy. We also adapt most of these lessons to different age groups and kids with a variety of learning needs. Just because we feature the lesson with a sixth-grade group doesn't mean that it wouldn't be equally effective if adapted for a group of second graders.

We have also changed the title of two of the comprehension lesson chapters in Part II. We call Chapter 7 (formerly Chapter 6, "Making Connections") "Activating and Connecting to Background Knowledge" to reflect our new focus on the role background knowledge plays when reading for understanding. We have changed the title of Chapter 11 (formerly Chapter 10,

"Synthesizing Information") to "Summarizing and Synthesizing Information." People ask us all the time about the difference between summarizing and synthesizing. A fair question. From our perspective, summarizing is primarily about retelling the information and putting it into our own words. Synthesizing happens when we integrate the information with our thinking and shape it into our own thought. So we really need to be able to summarize information in order to synthesize it. In this chapter, we include lessons on both summarizing and synthesizing and have made a clearer distinction between the two.

New Chapters

In this edition, we have added two chapters that reflect our focus on active literacy. In Part I, we offer a new chapter called "Tools for Active Literacy: The Nuts and Bolts of Comprehension Instruction." Here we expand on ways to engage our kids in interactive literacy, focusing on ways to turn and talk to each other, hold a discussion, and write about their thinking. We also expand on a range of options for explicit instruction and highlight the language we use for teaching and learning.

In Part II, we have added a new chapter called "Monitoring Comprehension: The Inner Conversation." When proficient readers read, they have an inner conversation with the writer and the text. It's as if they are talking to the text while reading. For instance, when a reader is confused, she might hear a voice in her head say, "Huh I don't get this part," or when she meets new information, she might hear, "Wow I never knew that before." This inner conversation is what active literacy looks like when the reader is reading silently. By paying attention to this inner voice, readers create meaning and understand what they read. They talk back to the text and have a dialogue with the author. They respond with delight, wonder, even outrage. They question the text, argue with the author, and connect to their own experience.

Recent work describes monitoring as much more than a single strategy (Baker 2002). It's really more of a thinking disposition. We teach kids to be disposed to consider and leave tracks of their thinking as they read. In the years since we wrote *Strategies That Work*, we began to see that teaching kids to monitor their understanding before focusing on specific strategies made all of the difference. As kids become aware of their thinking as they read, monitoring their comprehension, they soon notice how a question, an inference, or a connection helps them construct meaning. In this chapter, we have written five monitoring lessons that we believe are well worth teaching to launch comprehension instruction.

A New Section: Comprehension Across the Curriculum

What's next in comprehension instruction? That's the question we have been asked over and over again for the past few years. For us, it is all about merging comprehension instruction with content teaching and learning. As seventh graders read their history textbooks, they record their facts, questions, and responses about the American Revolution. As kindergartners observe photographs of Arctic animals, they sketch new learning on sticky notes and place them on the images. When kids read their textbooks or practice test reading, they bracket the information in a section and write the gist in the margins. Comprehension instruction needs to happen across the curriculum, throughout the day, and throughout the year.

If there is one place where we really need to use comprehension strategies, it is to learn new information and challenging content. P. David Pearson and researchers at the Lawrence Hall of Science at the University of California at Berkeley suggest that "reading and writing are tools, not goals" (2006). In this way, literacy is in the service of learning in the disciplines—biology, history, geography, physics, and so forth—and research backs this up. A recent study at Berkeley found that kids who received instruction that included both first-hand experiences and focused content reading outperformed kids who received only one of these methods (Barber, Catz, and Arya 2006).

Content matters! Big time. We agree with David Perkins when he says, "Knowledge does not just sit there, it functions richly in people's lives to help them understand and deal with the world" (2006). To give content the attention it deserves, we have created an entirely new section in this second edition with four distinct chapters where we show how we integrate comprehension and content instruction across the curriculum and throughout the year.

- *Chapter 12 "Content Literacy: Reading for Understanding in Social Studies and Science."* History, science, geography, the arts, and other subjects present opportunities to teach kids about the big wide world. When we engage students in content literacy, they learn information and ways of thinking in a variety of disciplines. The goal of content literacy is for kids to actively use thinking strategies as tools for understanding content. This chapter shows how we teach kids to merge their thinking with content to learn, understand, and remember it.
- *Chapter 13 "Topic Studies: A Framework for Research and Exploration."* Central to our idea of content literacy is the notion of inquiry and investigation. When we plan instruction in the content areas, we organize teaching and learning around what we call topic studies. Topic studies are curricular units that systematically incorporate reading and thinking strategies. In this chapter, we share a four-part framework for organizing a topic study and explain how we work with teachers and librarians to apply this framework in the content areas.
- *Chapter 14 "Reading to Understand Textbooks."* We acknowledge that textbooks are a staple of the curriculum. But if we are going to ask children to read them, we must show them how. The content overload and hard-to-read writing style make textbooks one of the toughest genres. Kids need a lot of help reading their textbooks. The more difficult the text, the more kids need explicit comprehension instruction to navigate it and the more interactive their reading must be. We share a variety of strategies and practices for tackling textbook reading in an active way.
- *Chapter 15 "The Genre of Test Reading."* We never would have dreamed that this edition would include a chapter on test reading. But times have changed since the first edition, and tests are everywhere. We still believe that good comprehension instruction combined with having kids read extensively is the best way to grow powerful, lifelong readers. But we also understand that preparing for these tests in a thoughtful way can be helpful. So we offer a chapter recognizing that test reading is a genre in and of

itself, and we need to teach it as such. We adapted much of this chapter from *The Comprehension Toolkit: Language and Lessons for Active Literacy*, our practical resource for reading and understanding informational text (2005).

Appendixes

Part IV of this book includes a resource of bibliographies for classroom instruction. Kids need books they can sink their teeth into. If students are to acquire and actually use knowledge, they need books full of substantive and engaging information. The information woven through the texts, both fiction and nonfiction, builds students' knowledge and heightens their curiosity so they want to find out more. The appendixes, a popular feature of the first edition, have been updated as follows:

- Appendix A includes an extensive list of trade books arranged by subject areas, primarily social studies and science topics with many published since 2000. Additionally we have updated text sets grouped around the arts, sports, and literacy. And since we have had so many requests for short pieces, we have added to our collections of short text. Text really matters. Despite the growing page count of this new edition, we simply couldn't resist including these trade and picture books. The explosion in children's nonfiction publishing over the past five years gives us a myriad of options for teaching science and social studies. In the first edition, we included an appendix that arranged text sets by strategy. In this edition, we have merged that appendix into our new trade book appendix, because readers activate a repertoire of strategies with any book they read. We connect and infer in all text we read. It feels artificial to recommend a book "only" for questioning. To support teachers as they plan, we have addressed how we choose text for strategy instruction in Chapter 5, our revised "Text Matters" chapter.
- Appendix B presents a list of magazines and websites especially selected for young people.
- Appendix C contains a list of professional journals that review children's books for classroom use.
- Appendix D offers an assessment interview between Anne and some students at Columbine Elementary in Boulder, Colorado. As she interviews them, Anne scripts the children's language to record their thinking and reflect on what she learns from it. She uses the book *My Freedom Trip* by Frances and Ginger Park to assess how effectively these students use comprehension strategies to better understand text.
- Appendix E features seven anchor charts, one for each strategy explored in Part II. These charts are representative of various strategy charts teachers and kids co-construct to connect past teaching and learning to future teaching and learning.

Assessment

Our teaching has one purpose—to foster understanding and learning over time. Every time we teach a lesson, we assess kids' thinking and their understanding of what we have taught. Our concern here is that we cannot see the forest for the trees when it comes to assessment. In the current climate, it often seems that we are asked to spend so much time testing students that we have less and less time to teach them. But assessment is not a four-letter word, not when it's authentic anyway. Authentic assessment is a continuous operation that is at the heart of teaching and learning. We assess 24/7 and use authentic assessments such as evidence of kids' work and thinking to guide our teaching and move kids forward.

We have added a section on assessment in Chapter 3, placing it up front where it belongs. Additionally, at the end of each lesson chapter in Part II, we have suggested learning goals and ways to assess evidence of kids' thinking. We share examples of their work and a running commentary of what we notice about their learning and progress. In addition, we offer some suggestions for differentiating instruction. Kids' written and oral responses provide a window into their thinking. Nothing is more important than learning about our students' thinking. Their responses give them a chance to weigh in with reactions, opinions, and personal connections, and through their responses we are able to assess their understanding, learn more about them as readers, and respond with appropriate instruction.

So enough with the preliminaries. We read for many reasons. The ideas in this book hover in that twilight area between reader and text, that elusive space where meaning takes shape and personal insight takes root. We read to connect the text to our lives, to let our imagination carry us away, to hear the sound of narrative language, to explore age-old themes, to glean information, and to acquire knowledge. Reading and learning is far more than sitting passively with a book in hand. Engaged readers interact with text, other ideas, and other people. Reading prompts thinking and even spurs action. Eleanor Roosevelt says it better than we ever could:

> *Every effort must be made in childhood to teach the young to use their own minds. For one thing is sure: if they don't make up their own minds, someone will do it for them. (Beane 2005)*

Above all, readers need to think when they read. If readers swallow everything they read or hear whole, we've got a problem. In schools across the country, kids brim with curiosity, questions, and opinions. Schools need to be havens for thinking; classrooms, incubators for deep thought. Thinking thrives when readers connect to books and to each other. We hope kids' thinking shines through here.

Part I

The Foundation of Meaning

Chapter 1

Reading Is Thinking

Thirty sixth graders crowd onto a woven area rug in the reading corner. A brass floor lamp casts a warm, amber glow onto their faces. Steph takes a seat in the rocking chair in front of them. "Today, I am going to read you a picture book called *Up North at the Cabin*, by Marsha Wilson Chall. I wish I had written it. I'll tell you why. This book reminds me exactly of my own childhood. It is the story of a young girl about your age who left the city every summer to spend time in a cabin on a lake in Minnesota. Minnesota is called the land of ten thousand lakes. I grew up in the neighboring state of Wisconsin. We had our share of lakes, too," Steph tells them as she points out the location of these two upper-midwestern states on the wall map.

"Writers write best about things they know and care about," Steph says. She reads from the inside flap that the author spent her summers on northern lakes and was inspired by her own experience as a child and later on as a mother when she returned to this cabin with her own children. "I was a kid who loved summer," Steph says while a dozen heads nod in agreement. "Like the young girl in the book, I spent summers on a lake where we fished, swam, water-skied, hiked, and canoed." Steph mentions how fortunate she feels that Marsha Chall wrote a book with which she identifies so closely. "Have you ever read a book that reminds you of your own life?" she asks. Hands wave wildly as kids share their favorites.

"*Koala Lou*" (Fox 1988), Shelby blurts out. "I have a whole bunch of brothers and sisters, and sometimes I get really jealous of them, just like Koala Lou did."

"*I Hate English!*" (Levine 1989), Jen-Li chimes in. "I couldn't understand a word of English when I first came from Korea. School was really hard. I know exactly how that girl felt."

Steph points out that Shelby and Jen-Li have made a connection between books and their lives. "If we connect to a book, we usually can't put it down. Good readers make connections between the texts they read and their own lives. Let's try something. I am going to read you *Up North at the Cabin*. As I read the words, I am going to show you the thinking that is going on in my head. I'll use these sticky notes to jot that thinking down and mark a connection. I'll mark the sticky note with the code T-S for text-to-self connection because it reminds me in some way of my own life and prior experience. Then I'll place the sticky note on the appropriate passage or picture. I'll let it stick out of the book a little, like a bookmark, so I can find it easily if I want to come back to it later on."

Steph reads through the book page by page sharing her thinking about waterskiing, the local bait shop, pruney fingers from too much swimming, and portaging canoes. She marks the text and illustrations with sticky notes coded T-S and jots down a few words such as, "Sometimes we even used peanut butter for bait when we ran out of night crawlers" or "Boy, was I mad when my dad made me carry that canoe."

When she comes to a page that shows the main character in an orange canvas life jacket with two white cotton closures, she laughs and stops to share a brief story. "I can't help but think of my mom when I see this orange life jacket. There were five of us kids, and we lived right on the edge of the water. When we were toddlers, my mom was wracked with worry that one of us might fall into the lake and drown. Her solution: the day we started to walk, she wrapped us in those orange life jackets. We wore them everywhere. We ate our cereal in them. We watched TV in them. Sometimes, we even slept in them. We looked like five little bulldozers!" Two kids in front grab the book to take a closer look at the tell-tale life jacket.

"How embarrassing," Josh murmurs.

"You'd better believe it. But I think my mom was onto something. We learned to swim quicker than any kids around just to get rid of those goofy life jackets!"

When Steph finishes reading out loud, she encourages kids to find a book they connect with and to use sticky notes to mark their text-to-self connections and jot down their thinking. We urge teachers to do the same. Find one of those books you really connect to. Unless you are one of Steph's life-jacket-bound siblings or a Wisconsin ice fisherman, it may not be *Up North at the Cabin*. Read it to your students, sharing your connections as you read. When we connect our past experience to new information, we are more apt to engage in the reading as well as understand it. There is nothing more powerful than a literacy teacher sharing her passion for reading, writing, and thinking.

The Reader Writes the Story

Reading out loud and showing how readers think when they read is central to the instruction we share in this book. When we read, thoughts fill our mind. We might make connections to our own life, as Steph did. We might have a question or an inference. It is not enough to merely think these thoughts. Strategic readers address their thinking in an inner conversation that helps them make sense of what they read. They search for the answers to their questions. They attempt to better understand the text through their connections to the characters, the events, and the issues.

Readers take the written word and construct meaning based on their own thoughts, knowledge, and experiences. The reader is part writer. The novelist E. L. Doctorow says, "Any book you pick up, if it's good, is a printed circuit for your own life to flow through—so when you read a book, you are engaged in the events of the mind of the writer. You are bringing your own creative faculties into sync. You're imagining the words, the sounds of the words, and you are thinking of the various characters in terms of people you've known—not in terms of the writer's experience, but your own" (Plimpton 1988).

Active readers interact with the text they read. Getting readers to think when they read, to develop an awareness of their thinking, and to actively use the knowledge they glean are the primary goals of the comprehension instruction outlined in this book. In this way, reading shapes and even changes thinking.

When we walk into classrooms, we often begin by asking kids to describe reading for us. "What is reading?" we ask. A variety of answers bursts forth, and we record these on a chart. "Figuring out the words," "spelling the words," "knowing the letters" are common responses. Fourth grader DeCoven answered that "reading is thinking." He went on to explain that "when you read, you have to figure out the words and what they mean. Sometimes it's easy. Sometimes it's hard." DeCoven hit the target. He understood that reading is about more than decoding words.

Reading encompasses both decoding and the making of meaning. The first entry on the word *read* in *Webster's New World Dictionary* (1991) defines reading as "getting the meaning of something written by using the eyes to interpret its characters." We're inclined to add "by using the brain" to that definition. Reading demands a two-pronged attack. It involves cracking the alphabetic code to determine the words and thinking about those words to construct meaning. Ask your students to define reading. Keep a chart posted in the room with their responses. The nature of their answers may evolve as your class begins to explore thinking when reading and as you provide explicit instruction in comprehension that helps readers better understand what they read.

Comprehension as a Means to Understanding

Teachers have never been under more pressure. Pressure to perform. Pressure to cover the curriculum. Pressure to meet standards. Pressure to ensure high scores on standardized tests. The political climate surrounding education is more demanding than ever before. Teachers are overwhelmed with state mandates, tests, and rubrics for every task. With all these expectations, one might ask why take the time to teach comprehension at all? "I already have to teach kids to decode words, spell them, learn vocabulary, and respond in writing. And now you're asking me to teach one more thing?" is a common refrain.

The truth is, we sympathize. It has never been tougher to be a teacher. But after many years of studying and teaching reading comprehension, we are convinced that comprehension instruction is not just one more thing. In fact, when it comes to reading, it's the most important thing. If the purpose for reading is anything other than understanding, why read at all? Researchers Linda Fielding and P. David Pearson describe the shift in our thinking about comprehension: "Once thought of as the natural result of decoding plus oral language, comprehension is now viewed as a much more complex process involving knowledge, experience, thinking, and teaching" (1994).

Why the shift? In 1979, Dolores Durkin jolted the reading world when she concluded, after many hours of observation in classrooms, that the questions in basal readers and on worksheets were the primary focus of comprehension instruction in classrooms. Teachers thought they were providing instruction in comprehension through the use of story questions. Durkin suggested that teachers were assessing rather than teaching students to better comprehend what they read.

Research on and ideas for teaching reading comprehension have exploded in the almost thirty years since Durkin's study. Comprehension instruction is ubiquitous in schools across the country. We recognize that there are a myriad of ways to teach what we label as "comprehension," and, moreover, we understand that there is no one right way to go about it. But we have found that teaching the reading/thinking strategies described in this book is an effective way to help students engage in and understand what they read.

Central to all of the recent research is the idea that comprehension strategies are a means to an end, not an end in themselves. Teaching strategies for strategies' sake is simply not the point. According to Sinatra, Brown, and Reynolds, "Comprehension strategies are no more than tools that readers employ in the service of constructing meaning from text" (Block and Pressley 2002). So our goal when we work with teachers and students in classrooms is to explicitly teach a repertoire of thinking strategies that are used to further the cause of understanding and engagement.

Constructing Meaning as the Goal of Comprehension

We believe that constructing meaning is the goal of comprehension. We want students to

- Monitor understanding
- Enhance understanding
- Acquire and actively use knowledge
- Develop insight

When we began our teaching careers, we typically checked children's story comprehension by evaluating their answers to oral or written questions. Dolores Durkin might have completed her comprehension studies in our classrooms! Initially, comprehension for us was about literal understanding of stories and narrative text. And, of course, this remains one goal of reading comprehension instruction. But this is not the only goal. True comprehension goes beyond literal understanding and involves the reader's interaction with text. If students are to become thoughtful, insightful readers, they must merge their thinking with the text and extend their thinking beyond a superficial understanding.

As we read the research about reading, we also noticed that strategies such as determining importance or synthesizing information helped students as they read for information, particularly in social studies and science content areas. Comprehension came to mean more than merely literal story understanding. A new definition of understanding involves acquiring knowledge as

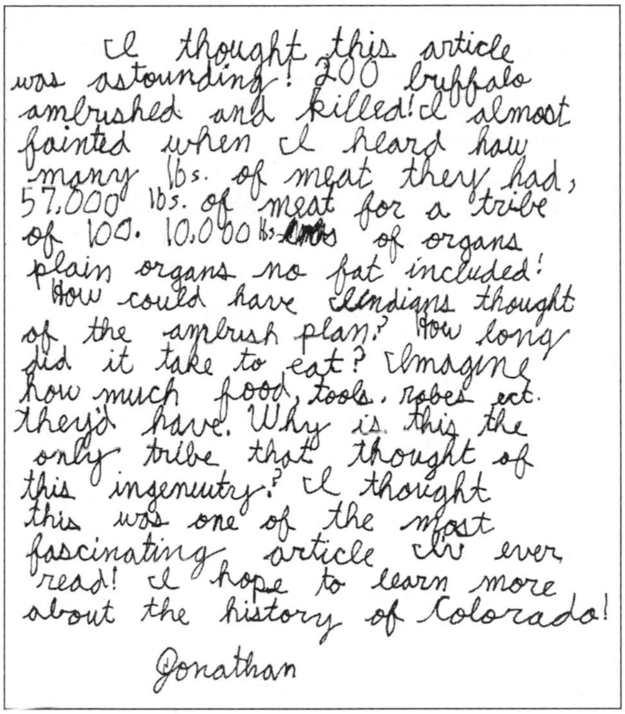

I thought this article was astounding! 200 buffalo ambushed and killed! I almost fainted when I heard how many lbs. of meat they had, 57,000 lbs. of meat for a tribe of 100. 10,000 lbs. of organs plain organs no fat included! How could have Indians thought of the ambush plan? How long did it take to eat? Imagine how much food, tools, robes ect. they'd have. Why is this the only tribe that thought of this ingenuity? I thought this was one of the most fascinating article I'v ever read! I hope to learn more about the history of Colorado!

Jonathan

Figure 1.1 Jonathan's Response to "The Great Buffalo Hunt"

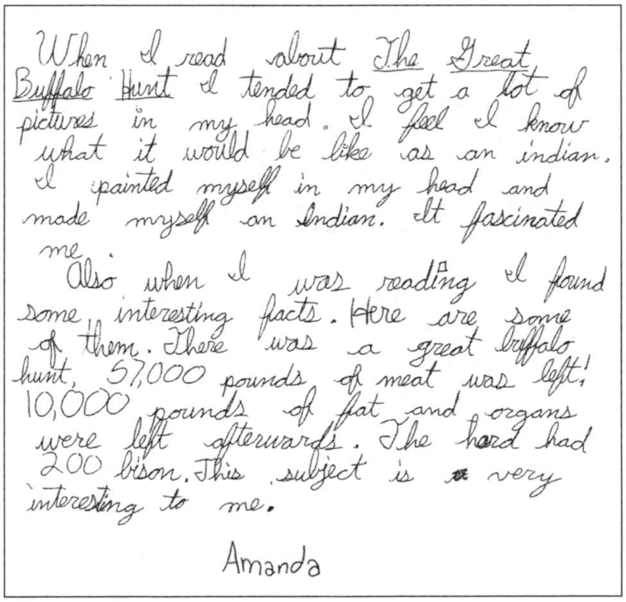

When I read about The Great Buffalo Hunt I tended to get a lot of pictures in my head. I feel I know what it would be like as an indian. I painted myself in my head and made myself an Indian. It fascinated me.
Also when I was reading I found some interesting facts. Here are some of them. There was a great buffalo hunt, 57,000 pounds of meat was left! 10,000 pounds of fat and organs were left afterwards. The hard had 200 bison. This subject is a very interesting to me.

Amanda

Figure 1.2 Amanda's Response to "The Great Buffalo Hunt"

well. Isabel Beck and others define a constructivist view of understanding as "being able to explain information, connect it to previous knowledge, and use information" (1997).

Comprehension means that readers think not only about what they are reading but about what they are learning. When readers construct meaning, they are building their store of knowledge. But along with knowledge must come understanding. Professor Howard Gardner, known for his theories on multiple intelligences, states simply, "The purpose of education is to enhance understanding" (1991).

By enhancing understanding, we mean that readers go beyond the literal meaning of a story or text. A reader who understands may glean the message in a folk tale, form a new opinion from an editorial, develop a deeper understanding of issues when reading a feature article. Acquiring information allows us to gain knowledge about the world and ourselves in relation to it. We build up our store of knowledge not so much for its own sake but in order to develop insight. With insight, we think more deeply and critically. We question, interpret, and evaluate what we read. In this way, reading can change thinking (Harvey 1998).

Content or Process: Why Not Both?

In light of our view of reading, we believe that the national content/process debate, still raging at present, is a smokescreen. Why argue that teaching content (what students learn) is more important than teaching process (how students learn), or vice versa? You can't think about nothing. We believe that we must teach our students to think when they read so they *can* access information and learn, understand, and remember what they read.

When we use the term *constructing meaning*, we refer to building knowledge and promoting understanding. We all remember times when we've had to work hard to gain meaning or when a startling piece of information or outrageous opinion has jolted our thinking. Meaning doesn't arrive fully dressed on a platter. Readers make meaning. But they can't do it alone. Our students need to be transformed by great literature (Harwayne 1992) as well as be given opportunities to explore their passions, interests, and questions to bring the world into focus (Harvey 1998).

In Mary Buerger's fourth-grade classroom, student responses to a Colorado history lesson illustrate how acquiring knowledge and enhancing understanding go hand in hand. While reading a nonfiction trade book called

It Happened in Colorado (Crutchfield 1993), Jonathan conveys a sense of astonishment and wonder when he responds to a gripping vignette on ancient buffalo hunting (see Figure 1.1). His classmate Amanda reveals both knowledge and understanding in her response to the same piece (see Figure 1.2). Amanda imagines herself "in the hunt" and responds in a very personal way. Both she and Jonathan acquire factual information as they read. Amanda uses the strategy of visualizing to better understand what she is reading, while Jonathan can't resist asking piercing questions and making inferences about the entire scenario. More than anything else, by making connections, questioning, inferring, creating mind pictures, and so on, Jonathan and Amanda are constructing meaning.

Active Literacy

Active literacy is the means to deeper understanding and diverse, flexible thinking. Reading, writing, drawing, talking, listening, and investigating are the cornerstones of active literacy, and comprehension instruction is more effective when it takes place within an active literacy framework. Classrooms that promote active literacy fairly burst with enthusiastic and engaged learners. Teachers aren't the only ones doing the talking. Kids weigh in with their opinions, thoughts, and ideas. They talk to each other, have inner conversations with the text, leave tracks of their thinking, and converse in book clubs and lit circles. They can't get away with being passive participants when they are the ones doing the thinking. In classrooms that nurture thinking, kids are actively questioning, connecting, inferring, discussing, debating, and inquiring throughout the school day and across the school year. We can't read kids' minds but one way to open a window into their understanding is to show them how to surface their thinking by talking and writing about it.

Stories from kids, teachers, and parents convey how using comprehension strategies has changed them as readers. One father of a third grader, who had participated in a parent-child book club, commented that none of his high school friends would believe that he belonged to a book club where he read books with his daughter. "I dropped out of high school, reading was such a chore for me. I wish I'd learned to read like this in school. I might have graduated," he told us. His experience captures the power of these strategies to engage readers in reading and thinking. Stories such as this one reiterate how effective comprehension instruction can be to help readers understand and enjoy reading.

Strategies That Work

For many years educators studied struggling readers for clues about the best ways to teach reading. Research in reading comprehension took a different tack in the 1980s when researchers identified and systematically investigated the thinking strategies that proficient readers used to understand what they read. Building on this work, researchers then explored ways to teach these strategies to children. Pearson, Dole, Duffy, and Roehler (1992) summarized the strategies that active, thoughtful readers use when constructing meaning from text. They found that proficient readers

- Search for connections between what they know and the new information they encounter in the texts they read
- Ask questions of themselves, the authors they encounter, and the texts they read
- Draw inferences during and after reading
- Distinguish important from less important ideas in text
- Are adept at synthesizing information within and across texts and reading experiences
- Monitor the adequacy of their understanding and repair faulty comprehension

Pressley (1976) and Keene and Zimmermann (1997) added sensory imaging to this list of comprehension strategies. Proficient readers visualize and create images using the different senses to better understand what they read.

Activating Background Knowledge and Making Connections: A Bridge from the New to the Known

Whether we are questioning, inferring, or synthesizing, our background knowledge is the foundation of our thinking. We simply can't understand what we read without thinking about what we already know.

In the 1980s cognitive psychologists devised the term *schema theory* to explain how our previous experiences, knowledge, emotions, and understandings have a major effect on what and how we learn (Anderson and Pearson 1984). Our schema—the sum total of our background knowledge and experience—is what each of us brings to our reading. When we apply our background knowledge as we read, we guide students to make connections between their experiences, their knowledge about the world, and the text they read. Connecting what readers know to new information is the core of learning and understanding.

When students have had an experience similar to that of a character in a story, they are more likely to understand the character's motives, thoughts, and feelings. And when readers have an abundance of background knowledge about a specific content area, they understand more completely the new information they read. Additionally, when readers have a general understanding of different genres of text, they comprehend more completely.

Questioning: The Strategy That Propels Readers Forward

Very young children brim with questions. If we didn't delight so in their youthful enthusiasm, they might drive us crazy with the sheer number that burst forth. Primary teachers know this. Kindergartners blurt out questions fast and furiously, often without raising a hand. Why is the moon out during the day? How do birds fly? Do animals talk to each other? Where did the cowboys go? Sadly, by fifth grade, kids' questions practically disappear. Schools do not foster questions. Schools demand answers—answers to teachers' questions, answers to literal questions on tests, and answers to math problems many kids can do but can't explain. For too many years, schools have focused on answers to the exclusion of questions.

Questions are at the heart of teaching and learning. Human beings are driven to make sense of their world. Questions open the doors to understanding. Questioning is the strategy that propels readers forward. When readers have questions, they are less likely to abandon the text. Proficient readers ask questions before, during, and after reading. They question the content, the author, the events, the issues, and the ideas in the text. We need to celebrate kids' questions and help facilitate their answers.

Making Inferences: Reading Between the Lines

Human beings infer in many realms. We make inferences about expressions, body language, and tone as well as text. Inferential thinking serves people well in all walks of life. Inferring involves drawing a conclusion or making an interpretation that is not explicitly stated in the text. Writers don't spill their thoughts onto the page, they leak them slowly, one idea at a time, until the reader can make an educated guess or an appropriate inference about an underlying theme in the text or a prediction about what is to come. Inferring relates to the notion of reading between the lines. According to the writer Susan Hall, "Inferring allows readers to make their own discoveries without the direct comment of the author" (1990).

Readers infer when they take what they already know, their background knowledge, and merge it with clues in the text to draw a conclusion, surface a theme, predict an outcome, arrive at a big idea, and so forth. If readers don't infer, they will not grasp the deeper essence of texts they read. Sometimes readers' questions are only answered through an inference. The more information readers acquire, the more likely they will make a reasonable inference.

Visualizing: Becoming Wordstruck

In his book *Wordstruck*, Robert MacNeil remembers being overwhelmed with the images and feelings—the sights, sounds, touches, and tastes—that words conjured up in his mind. On a cold night in Nova Scotia, Robert Louis Stevenson's poem "Windy Nights" brought images to MacNeil's young mind of his father, a Canadian naval officer, at sea in a gale.If only all of our students could be as riveted by the printed word. Visualizing is the reading world's term for describing what Robert MacNeil does as a reader. Like E. L. Doctorow, MacNeil's love for and understanding of language allow him to paint a picture of the story in his mind. It is almost as if he produces the text as a full-blown theatrical experience.

Visualizing is all about inferring meaning, which is why we combine these two strategies into one chapter in Part II of this book. When readers visualize, they are actually constructing meaning by creating mental images. We've found that when we create scenarios and pictures in our minds while reading, our level of engagement increases and our attention doesn't flag. Younger children seem particularly able to visualize to support understanding as they listen to and read stories, often "living through or living in" the stories they read (Miller and Goudvis 1999). Teaching children to construct their own mental images when reading nonfiction helps them stop, think about, and understand the information. And sharing the movie that rolls on in our mind while reading fiction will help readers get much more out of the story, more or less "becoming the book" as Jeff Wilhelm suggests in *"You Gotta Be the Book"* (1996).

Determining Importance: Distilling the Essence of Text

We'd like to think that the days of underlining or checking off the main idea are over. Unfortunately, comprehension exercises and test questions still require students to choose one main idea. Indeed, in artificially constructed paragraphs such as those we see on standardized tests, often there is only one main idea. However, determining essential ideas in authentic text such as a piece of historical fiction, a newspaper editorial, or a nonfiction trade book may not be so easy.

What we determine to be important in text depends on our purpose for reading it. When we read fiction, we focus on the character's actions, motives, and problems that contribute to the overall themes. If the reader has had experiences similar to those of the main character, the reader is likely to enjoy a richer, more fulfilling reading experience. Nonfiction presents its own issues. When we read nonfiction, we are reading to learn and remember information. We can't possibly remember every isolated fact, nor should we. We need to focus on important information and merge it with what we already know to expand our understanding of the topic. One good reason to determine important ideas is that they are the ones we want to remember.

Summarizing and Synthesizing Information: The Evolution of Thought

As readers move through text, thinking evolves. They add new information to what they already know and construct meaning as they go. Summarizing is about retelling the information and paraphrasing it . When readers summarize, they need to sift and sort through large amounts of information to extract essential ideas. Synthesizing happens when we merge the information with our thinking and shape it into our own thought. As readers distill text information into a few important ideas or larger concepts, they might form a particular opinion or a fresh perspective that leads to new insight.

When readers synthesize information, they see the bigger picture as they read. It is not enough to simply recall or restate the facts. As they move from summarizing to synthesizing the information, readers integrate the new information with their existing knowledge. Sometimes, they add new information to their store of knowledge, developing thinking and learning more in the process. Other times, readers change thinking based on their reading, gaining an entirely new perspective. Either way, when readers synthesize, they reach a more complete understanding.

Our information-rich society requires us to sift though ever-increasing amounts of data to make sense of them and act. We couldn't possibly remember all the information that appears on our radar screen each day. Summarizing and synthesizing allow us to make sense of important information, get the gist, and move on.

Using Comprehension Strategies in Our Own Reading

We became convinced that this repertoire of comprehension strategies—activating and connecting to background knowledge, asking questions, making inferences, visualizing, determining importance, and summarizing and synthesizing information—was powerful when we began to consciously apply the strategies in our own reading. We can safely say that we are better readers today than we were before we studied comprehension instruction. And this is something, considering we're at that stage in life where we can't remember who we're calling half the time when we pick up the phone!

Thinking about how we use strategies ourselves provides the best foundation for understanding how to teach comprehension. For instance, when Anne read *Into Thin Air*, by Jon Krakauer, the gripping story of tragedy striking expert and novice mountain climbers alike as they tried to conquer Everest, she found herself trying to visualize what was going on by creating a mental map of who was where on the mountain. This proved a tough task, but visualizing in this way prevented her from becoming hopelessly confused about the different clients, guides, and climbing teams all trying to reach the summit in the face of a raging blizzard. Because of Krakauer's riveting images and considerable skill as a writer, Anne's lack of background knowledge of mountain topography and technical climbing terms wasn't a huge disadvantage. She had little trouble understanding the terrible dilemmas that arose for people when fate, heroism, and hubris combined to cause a tragic loss of life.

Anne found *Into Thin Air* to be one of those books you just can't put down. Krakauer's vivid writing drew Anne into the text to the point that she felt like she was trudging up Mt. Everest herself. When we began to ask children to visualize, make connections, and tell us what they wondered about, we noticed increased interest and engagement on their part. We sensed that using these strategies encouraged children to think more carefully about their reading, just as Anne had done.

As we explored our own process as readers and listened to our students, they taught us the power of these strategies. Their commitment to making meaning soared when they began to understand that their own interpretations and ideas mattered. "Can we please read now?" became the anthem in many classrooms where we worked. Kids couldn't wait to get on with reading once they began to interact with the text.

Explicit Instruction: Showing Kids How vs. Telling Them What to Do

Much of our responsibility when teaching reading is to make what is implicit, explicit. Explicit instruction means that we show learners how we think when we read, as Steph did when reading *Up North at the Cabin*. We explicitly teach reading comprehension strategies so that readers can use them to construct meaning. We are likely to teach a strategy by modeling the strategy for the class; guiding students in its practice in large groups, small groups, and pairs; and providing large blocks of time for students to read independently and practice using and applying strategies. This is what Pearson and Gallagher (1983) call the Gradual Release of Responsibility framework for instruction. (See Chapter 3.)

In our work, we make a distinction between what might be called "mentioning" and explicit instruction. From our perspective, mentioning is similar to the education we received in the 1950s; the teacher stood at the head of the class, read a lengthy set of directions, and assigned a variety of tasks. Questions were more likely to be used to clarify procedures than to enhance understanding. In many classrooms, assigning was the norm; teaching was conspicuously absent. We advocate more teaching, less assigning.

We want readers to use comprehension strategies flexibly, seamlessly, and independently. No one envisions readers lying in bed with a great book and having to get up, find a pencil, and jot a question on a sticky note. All of our instruction is geared toward children's using these strategies independently and applying them if and when they enhance understanding.

Like writing, reading is an act of composition (Pearson and Tierney 1984). When we write, we compose thoughts on paper. When we read, we compose meaning in our minds. Thoughtful, active readers use the text to stimulate their own thinking and to engage with the mind of the writer. Readers construct and maintain understanding by merging their thinking with the text. They have an ongoing inner conversation with the author as they read, a dialogue of sorts where the reader engages with and talks back to the writer throughout their reading.

In an interview with George Plimpton, E. L. Doctorow said,

I really started to think of myself as a writer when I was about nine. Whenever I read anything I seemed to identify as much with the act of composition as with the story. I seemed to have two minds: I would love the story and want to know what happened next, but at the same time I would somehow be aware of what was being done on the page. I identified myself as a kind of younger brother to the writer. I was on hand to help him figure things out. So you see, I didn't actually have to write a thing, because the act of reading was my writing. I thought of myself as a writer for years, before I got around to writing anything. It's to blur the distinction between reader and writer. As a child, I somehow drifted into this region where you are both reader and writer: I declared to myself that I was a writer. I wrote a lot of good books. I wrote Captain Blood *by Rafael Sabatini. That was one of my better efforts. (1988)*

Wouldn't you be thrilled if your students saw reading in this light? The comprehension strategies that we describe in this book, along with the powerful literature we recommend, help readers construct their own meaning and interact with the text to enhance understanding and engage their minds.

Chapter 2

Reading Is Strategic

Steph slid her chair up next to Alverro to confer with him. A second grader, he was reading Diana Short Yurkovic's *Meet Me at the Water Hole*, a nonfiction emergent-reading book filled with captivating photographs and interesting cutouts to stimulate thinking. He turned to a picture of a baby giraffe drinking at the water hole and began to read the one sentence of text that constituted the entire page: "When a baby giraffe is born, it is already six feet tall." Stunning information, to say the least!

Alverro read easily through the first clause and then stumbled on the word *already*. He tried a number of decoding strategies to figure it out, including parsing the word, going back and rereading, and reading ahead. After several tries, he got it. He read *already*. His teacher beamed, deservedly so. She had dedicated considerable time to teaching Alverro those very decoding strategies. And now here he was, using them to crack the code independently without teacher intervention.

When Alverro reached the end of the sentence, however, he went right on to the next page without taking even a moment to ponder the remarkable fact about giraffe birth size.

"Whoa! Not so fast," Steph said. "What did you just read?"

He scrunched his nose and looked at her quizzically. "*Already*?" he asked.

"Besides that."

But he couldn't answer. He had no clue. He had committed himself single-mindedly to decoding the word *already* and had lost all track of meaning in the process. Worse, so pleased was he with his decoding triumph that he didn't realize that he had missed the meaning. Steph suggested he read the sentence again and think about what the words meant. As he did, his face lit up. He pointed to the life-size cutout of Michael Jordan in the corner of the room and made an authentic connection. "Wow, baby giraffes are almost as tall as Michael Jordan on the day they are born! That's incredible!" And he was right, of course; that is incredible.

Steph and Alverro talked about what had happened in his first reading of the sentence. Together they decided that from now on when he reached the bottom of the page, he would stop and think about what he had just read. The end of a page became a sort of red light for Alverro to remind him to think about what he was reading, before forging on through the text. Stopping to digest and synthesize information periodically helps readers construct meaning.

Alverro had successfully activated strategies to decode text but had difficulty figuring out the words and gaining meaning simultaneously. When readers focus solely on decoding, meaning takes a back seat. While Alverro struggled to figure out the word *already*, he simply couldn't pay attention to the overall meaning of the text. Readers have to learn that reading is an interactive process involving decoding words and constructing meaning. Teachers need to teach students like Alverro to become more active, strategic readers as well as proficient decoders.

The term *strategic reading* refers to thinking about reading in ways that enhance learning and understanding. The dictionary defines *strategic* as being "important or essential to a plan of action." Readers are strategic, and typically we think of strategic readers as proficient readers who have a plan of action that moves them towards their goal or purpose for reading. When we consider ways to teach kids to become more strategic as they read, we encourage what Perkins, Tishman, and Jay (1995) call a "strategic spirit." As teachers, we make sure that curiosity, engagement, and interest motivate kids to become not only better readers, but thoughtful, critical, and independent ones as well.

Research That Supports Comprehension Instruction

Studies cited in the National Reading Panel report (2000) as well as a burgeoning body of research reviews (Block and Pressley 2002; Block, Gambrell, and Pressley 2002; Ruddell and Unrau 2004) provide substantial evidence that explicit comprehension instruction improves students' understanding of texts they read in school. Some studies of comprehension strategy instruction have examined ways to teach specific strategies, such as questioning (Gavelek and Raphael 1985), drawing inferences (Hansen 1981), or creating text summaries (Brown and Day 1983). When researchers explicitly taught kids these comprehension-fostering strategies, kids not only learned to apply the strategies they were taught, but the instruction had positive effects on students' general comprehension as well.

More recent studies have described the effectiveness of transactional strategy instruction (Pressley 2002; Guthrie 2003). Rather than a single strategy focus, transactional strategy instruction teaches students a repertoire of strategies that they apply flexibly according to the demands of the reading tasks and texts they encounter. Pressley (2002) found that students who were taught a group of strategies performed better than those receiving more traditional instruction when asked to think aloud about and interpret texts. These findings seem to hold true for younger children (Pearson and Duke 2002) and for students learning information in content topics such as science (Reutzel, Smith, and Fawson 2006).

Research studies have also focused on teaching students thinking and learning routines that incorporate comprehension strategies as part of ongoing classroom instruction. Anne Marie Palincsar's original work in reciprocal teaching (Palincsar and Brown 1984) illustrates how comprehension strategy instruction improves students' learning from text. Teaching students to become more metacognitive with respect to their thinking about their reading has also proved effective. Block et al. (2002) focused on "process-based" comprehension instruction, teaching kids to articulate the processes they used to make meaning. She found that students' comprehension scores on both standardized and criterion-referenced measures improved. In summary, whether instruction is called transactional strategy instruction, multiple strategy instruction, or something else, Trabasso and Bouchard conclude:

> *There is very strong empirical, scientific evidence that the instruction of more than one strategy in a natural context leads to the acquisition and use of reading comprehension strategies and transfers to standardized comprehension tests. Multiple strategy instruction facilitates comprehension as evidenced by performance on tasks that involve memory, summarizing and identification of main ideas. (2002)*

This body of research gives practitioners recommendations for effective comprehension instruction. As you read this book, we hope you keep the following in mind. We are not researchers. We are practitioners. We have spent the past twenty years learning from and thinking about ways to apply research in our classroom practice. But don't take our word for it. We suggest you take a look at *Improving Comprehension Instruction: Rethinking Research, Theory and Classroom Practice* (Block, Gambrel, and Pressley 2002) and *Theoretical Models and Processes of Reading* (Ruddell and Unrau 2004). Important articles and resources include Nell Duke's article in *Reading Research Quarterly* entitled "3.6 Minutes per Day: The Scarcity of Informational Text in First Grade" and Ellin Oliver Keene's chapter "From Good to Memorable: Characteristics of Highly Effective Comprehension Instruction" (Block, Gambrell, and Pressley 2002). And don't forget our own DVD *What Every Teacher Should Know About Reading Comprehension* (2005), which includes a lengthy interview with David Pearson.

For practical teaching ideas, we constantly draw on a wide range of books including Richard Allington's *What Really Matters for Struggling Readers*; Brad Buhrow and Anne Upczak Garcia's *Ladybugs, Tornadoes, and Swirling Galaxies: English Language Learners Discover Their World Through Inquiry*; Harvey Daniels and Marilyn Bizar's *Teaching the Best Practice Way*; Ellin Oliver Keene and Susan Zimmermann's *Mosaic of Thought*; Debbie Miller's *Reading with Meaning*; Cris Tovani's *I Read It, but I Don't Get It*; and Karen Szymusiak and Franki Sibberson's *Beyond Leveled Books* and *Still Learning to Read*.

A final word: we cannot emphasize enough the need for kids to read extensively over time. Cunningham and Stanovich (2003) report that "the amount of print that children are exposed to has profound cognitive consequences. The act of reading itself serves to increase the achievement differences among children. If we want children to improve their fluency and vocabulary, we must get them to log many hours on the printed page." Readers get better at reading by reading. Reading volume is critical to reading progress (Allington 1994; Stanovich 2000). So we must never forget to build in time every day for independent reading.

Reading with a Purpose

When we were kids, we obediently kept our noses in our school books without knowing why we were reading or what we were expected to get out of it. We were passive readers, because we didn't believe that we had much to do with anything in the text or that our thoughts and opinions mattered. Our task seemed to be to answer end-of-chapter questions, make an outline, and remember the author's ideas and information just long enough for Friday's test. Thinking about what we were reading was beside the point. The truth is we weren't very engaged and remember very little, since we viewed ourselves as ancillary to the whole reading process. If only our colleague Cris Tovani had been one of our teachers. She reminds us to continually consider our purpose for reading and ask ourselves if our purpose is authentic. We teach kids to think about their purpose as well. If they can't tell us why they are reading something, we may all need to go back and reconsider what we are doing and why we are doing it. There is one purpose that never changes, however. The purpose of reading is always understanding.

From Metacognitive Knowledge to Monitoring Comprehension

Proficient readers, then, adapt strategies to their purposes for reading. But matching strategies to one's purpose requires metacognitive knowledge—an awareness and understanding of how one thinks and uses strategies during reading. For instance, when Amanda read and responded to the buffalo hunt passage, she purposefully created visual images in her mind to better understand what happened during the hunt (see Figure 1.2 in Chapter 1). According to Amanda, "I feel I know what it would be like as an Indian. I painted myself in my head and made myself an Indian." This strategy worked for Amanda. Not only did she begin to get a sense of what it might have been like to have been there; she remembered amazing facts as well. Jonathan's strategy of choice was questioning. He asked questions to clarify and reinforce what was to him incredible information (see Figure 1.1 in Chapter 1).

What Jonathan and Amanda were able to do as readers is what metacognitive knowledge is all about. They were aware and ready as readers to use strategies as tools for understanding unfamiliar information. They successfully linked their strategy knowledge with their purpose for reading. Once we've taught students a repertoire of strategies, it's important to keep track of how well they are using and applying them.

Perkins and Swartz (Perkins 1992) define four aspects of metacognitive knowledge that are helpful for understanding how learners adapt strategies to their purposes. These aspects illustrate how learners move from less to more sophisticated ways of monitoring their thinking and understanding. We have adapted these ideas to apply to readers and reading and identify four kinds of learners/readers here.

- Tacit learners/readers. These are readers who lack awareness of how they think when they read.
- Aware learners/readers. These are readers who realize when meaning has broken down or confusion has set in but who may not have sufficient strategies for fixing the problem.
- Strategic learners/readers. These are readers who use the thinking and comprehension strategies we describe as tools to enhance understanding and acquire knowledge. They are able to monitor and repair meaning when it is disrupted.
- Reflective learners/readers. These are the readers who are strategic about their thinking and are able to apply strategies flexibly depending on their goals or purposes for reading. They monitor their thinking and understanding and according to Perkins and Swartz, they also "reflect on their thinking and ponder and revise their use of strategies."

Based on these descriptions, we can see that Amanda and Jonathan, who were able to use visualizing and questioning to enhance their understanding of content, are well on their way to becoming strategic if not reflective learners/readers. Alverro, a second grader still learning to decode print, is an example of a tacit learner/reader, one who is not aware of his thinking while reading. When Steph intervened to help Alverro think about the content, she nudged him toward becoming a more aware or even a strategic reader, one who knows when meaning breaks down and has a strategy for repairing it.

A clear knowledge of comprehension strategies combined with an awareness of when and how to use them provides readers with an arsenal of tactics to ensure that they construct meaning as they read. Our goal in teaching comprehension strategies is to move readers like Alverro from the tacit level of understanding to a greater awareness of how to think while reading. And we need to challenge readers like Amanda and Jonathan to apply their strategy knowledge in progressively more difficult text and different genres.

We view monitoring as an overarching umbrella that encompasses the comprehension strategies we identify and more. In this way, questioning, connecting, reacting, inferring, and so forth are all different and related aspects of monitoring. When readers have the disposition to stay on top of their thinking as they read, they are better able to access the strategies that best suit their purpose. According to Paris, Lipson, and Wixon (1983), it isn't enough for students to simply understand a given strategy. They must know when, why, and how to use it. So we teach readers to be active, flexible thinkers who are capable of responding to a variety of reading texts, tasks, contexts, and purposes with a repertoire of strategies.

Monitoring Comprehension: The Inner Conversation

When readers read, they have an inner conversation with the text. They listen to the voice in their head speaking to them as they read, which allows them to construct meaning. Only when they are having an inner conversation will they notice when they stray from it. Both of us read before turning in for the night.

We mark the chapter and turn off the light. Or we wake up with lights blazing at 2:00 A.M., our glasses cocked, our books sprawled across our chests. But whichever the case, we've each had the same experience of picking up the book the next night, opening to the marked page, and having no clue what the last page or so was about. We know we read it, but we don't know what we read. We might scroll back a few paragraphs or might even flip back several pages to reconstruct meaning. The fact is that all readers space out when they read. Kids need to know this, or they risk feeling inadequate when it happens to them. We share these stories of our attention lapses with our students. When they learn that adult readers space out, too, they are less likely to brand themselves poor readers at such times.

We need to teach readers to be disposed to think about their reading as they read, moving towards becoming the strategic, reflective learners that Perkins and Swartz describe above. Once readers are made aware of their inner conversation, they tend to catch themselves quicker and repair meaning if there's a problem. So we teach all readers how to stay on top of their reading. Readers take a giant leap toward independence when they develop the ability to monitor their comprehension. When readers have the disposition to focus on their thinking while reading, they are able to use reading strategies flexibly to enhance understanding.

We teach readers to

- Become aware of their thinking as they read
- Monitor their understanding and keep track of meaning
- Listen to the voice in their head to make sense of the text
- Notice when they stray from thinking about the text
- Notice when meaning breaks down
- Detect obstacles and confusions that derail understanding
- Understand how a variety of strategies can help them repair meaning when it breaks down
- Know when, why, and how to apply specific strategies to maintain and further understanding

Proficient readers—adults and children alike—proceed on automatic pilot most of the time, until something doesn't make sense or a problem arises and understanding screeches to a halt. At that point, experienced readers slow down and reread, clarify confusions before they continue, and apply appropriate strategies to cruise on down the road. They might ask a question when they need more information. Perhaps they infer a theme from a character's actions. Or they might activate their background knowledge when reading an editorial and disagree with the author's premise.

Less proficient readers may be so focused on decoding that they can't give adequate attention to making meaning when they run into trouble. Just as Steph taught Alverro to stop and think about meaning, students need to be reminded to stop periodically in order to keep track of their understanding. Awareness and monitoring go hand in hand, enabling an active reader to constantly check for understanding.

Monitoring by itself, however, isn't enough. Just because readers realize there's a problem with comprehension doesn't mean they can solve it. Reflective, strategic readers know which strategies to activate when meaning is lost and how to match the appropriate strategy with their purpose for reading. Readers who monitor their understanding can access different strategies—asking questions, visualizing, or inferring—to construct meaning in the face of problems. A reader's repertoire of strategies needs to be flexible enough to solve comprehension problems with words, sentences, or overall meaning.

Leaving Tracks of Thinking

The Wisconsin that Steph described in Chapter 1 is Wisconsin in the heart of the summer. Wisconsin in the dead of winter is a different animal. One of Steph's annual winter childhood games will give you an idea; it involved counting the string of subzero highs each January in hopes of breaking the established record. But what northern Wisconsin lacked in Fahrenheit each winter, it made up for in beauty. The roof-top icicles, the frosty pines, and the drifting snow lent winter a luster one never forgets. Each morning after a fresh snow, northern Wisconsin kids would scan their backyards for critter tracks. They knew whose pawprints were whose, and they leapt out of bed at the crack of dawn to see who had trespassed during the night.

We tell kids these stories about fresh tracks in the snow, or in the sand for those who live near water. We explain that fresh tracks let us know who's been there, even after they've gone. In the same way as animals leave tracks of their presence, we want readers to "leave tracks of their thinking." It is impossible to know what readers are thinking when they read unless they tell us through conversation or written response. The reading comprehension instruction described in this book encourages students to mark and code text with thoughts and questions, to "leave tracks" so they can remember later what they were thinking as they read. Kids love the idea of making tracks in the margins, tracks on sticky notes, tracks in their journals. These written tracks help the reader monitor comprehension and enhance understanding. They also provide clues to the teacher about a reader's thinking, evidence that is difficult to ascertain without some form of oral or written response. (See Chapter 6 for lessons that show kids how to monitor their comprehension and leave tracks of their thinking.)

A Common Language for Teaching and Learning

When you really think about it, teaching boils down to two things, what we say and what we do. This book emphasizes what we say and do, the comprehension lessons we teach, the ways we engage kids, and the language we use to teach them. It can only be helpful for readers if we settle on a common language for teaching and talking about reading comprehension across grade levels in schools. It makes sense to develop clear explanations for each strategy that remain consistent from one grade level to another. When children come into the classroom knowing how to make connections, visualize, or determine important ideas, teachers don't have to reinvent the wheel each year.

We encourage teachers to work together to become conversant with a variety of comprehension strategies and decide as a group on the language that makes the most sense for their kids. For example, the terms *background knowledge, prior knowledge,* and *schema* actually represent three different ways of referring to a similar concept—the knowledge and experience that readers bring to the text. You will notice that we tend to use the term *background knowledge* in this book when referring to this idea. We want our kids to use language that is understandable outside of school as well as inside. So we do our best to avoid "educationese." Choose whatever terms make the most sense to you, but remember to talk with your colleagues to develop a consistent language of comprehension across grade levels. This way we won't confound kids with our ever-changing jargon.

The cumulative effect of teaching comprehension strategies from kindergarten through high school is powerful. When kindergartners who have learned to visualize hit first grade, they are more likely to activate that strategy when they hear the word again, see their teacher doing it, and try it themselves. Each year teachers build on strategies the kids already understand, emphasizing a common language and how to use strategies flexibly with a variety of texts. We can teach all of these strategies in developmentally appropriate ways to kids at all grade levels.

One caution on the language front, however. P. David Pearson, reading researcher and Dean of the Graduate School of Education at the University of California at Berkeley, reminds us that "just because readers say they are using a strategy to better understand what they read doesn't necessarily mean that they are. And conversely, just because students do not articulate the thinking behind the strategy doesn't mean they aren't using it to better understand what they read" (1995). In schools where we work, it is not unusual to hear one first grader turn to another and say, "I inferred that. . . ." Our initial inclination is to pat ourselves on the back for all the wonderful teaching we have done. But we hold our exuberance and check with that child to see if she really did make an inference. Or is she just playing with the new language or trying to impress the teacher? We determine whether readers are using strategies to better comprehend by having conversations with them, reading their written responses, and observing them closely.

Chapter 3

Effective Comprehension Instruction: Teaching, Tone, and Assessment

Anne closed Allan Baillie's *Rebel* after reading the last page out loud to a group of eighth graders. This clever picture book, about the courageous response of a group of rural Burmese peasants to a dictatorial military strongman, was one of her favorites. She glanced up at the clock and noticed the time slipping away. She really wanted to confer with the kids, and she couldn't wait to read their responses to this compelling story. Feeling pressed for time, she asked the kids to divide a sheet in half and mark one column What the Text Is About and the next column What the Text Makes Me Think About. She had found this form useful in the past to get at children's deeper thinking. Although she had never introduced the form to this group of kids, it appeared to be self-explanatory.

As the kids returned to their tables to respond on this form, Anne sat down at one table and began to confer with Jasmine. Others at the table soon joined in and a lively book discussion ensued. The kids brimmed with questions and comments. With Anne present, they talked about what really went on in the story, where it took place, who these people were, and why they were fighting.

As she began to construct meaning from the discussion, Jasmine wrote the following in the first column: "This was about some people in Burma who used to be free and now were under the control of a bad government and an even worse general. The people rebelled in a surprising way." "Great thinking," Anne commented to Jasmine. In the second column, Jasmine wrote that the book reminded her of stories her grandfather had told about Vietnam. Anne felt pleased with Jasmine's summary and viable connection. She left the table with Jasmine writing about her grandfather's Vietnam experience and her table group writing about all kinds of things.

The bell rang and Anne collected the forms as kids filed out the door. Her heart sank as she paged through them. With the exception of the kids at Jasmine's table and a few very prolific writers who always filled entire pages regardless of the instruction, most of the forms stared blankly at her, hardly a word written in either column. She knew the form couldn't be at fault; it had worked effectively in the past. As Anne pondered the disappointing results of her instruction, she realized that she had once again made a familiar mistake.

Almost every time she reflected on why a certain lesson had been ineffective, she concluded that it was because of a lack of explicit instruction. She either hadn't modeled explicitly enough what she was trying to do or she hadn't given her students enough time to practice what she had shown them. If she had modeled how to use this form on the overhead projector rather than giving a series of directions, she suspected, things would have gone quite differently.

The next time Anne saw Steph, she described the debacle. Steph could only smile knowingly. She herself had repeatedly told her own kids that it was okay to make a mistake as long as they didn't make the same mistake over and over. But when it came to delivering instruction, she, too, continued to make the same mistake over and over. Like Anne, whenever Steph cut corners on modeling, her instruction suffered.

Don't surrender to the clock. It takes time to show kids how, but it is time well spent. When it comes to instruction, it is nearly impossible to be too explicit. So much for making the same mistake over and over.

Effective Comprehension Instruction

Teaching kids to comprehend means we show them how to construct meaning when they read. Strategy instruction is all about teaching the reader not merely the reading. Comprehension instruction is most effective when teachers

- Teach with the end in mind
- Plan instruction that is responsive to the individual needs of students
- Model their own use of comprehension strategies over time
- Remind students that the purpose for using a strategy is to construct meaning and engage in the text
- Articulate how thinking helps readers better understand what they read
- View strategies as a means to an end with the goal of building a repertoire of thinking strategies
- Model their oral, written and artistic responses to the text
- Gradually release responsibility for using strategies to the students, always moving them toward independent reading and thinking
- Provide opportunities for guided and independent practice
- Show students how comprehension strategies apply in a variety of texts, genres, and contexts
- Help students notice how strategies intersect and work in conjunction with one another
- Build in large amounts of time for actual text reading by the students
- Make sure students have many opportunities to talk to each other about their reading
- Provide opportunities for students to respond by writing and drawing
- Take time to observe and confer directly with students and keep records of those observations and conferences to assess progress and inform instruction
- Use student work and talk to assess past instruction, guide future instruction, and assess and evaluate student performance.

The Gradual Release of Responsibility: Showing Kids How and Giving Them Time to Practice

For too long, we have been telling kids what to do rather than showing them how. Now the way we deliver effective instruction always involves modeling and/or guided practice in one form or another. We deliver instruction through the Gradual Release of Responsibility framework (Pearson and Gallagher 1983).

Staff developer Laura Benson visualizes gradual release in terms of learning to ride a bike. First, and in fact this is not a written part of the framework, the adult *carefully* watches the child approach the bike and make sense of it. This is the assessment piece, finding out what the child can and cannot do independently. Once we understand what is needed, we begin to show the learner how and scaffold his or her experience. So in this case, the child watches the adult ride a bike, which parallels the teacher's modeling. Next, the child rides the bike with training wheels, a metaphor for guided practice in pairs or small groups. Finally, the happy five-year-old sheds the training wheels and cruises down the street, illustrating how children perform the task independently and apply it in new situations (Harvey 1998). We work hard not to release our students too soon or, conversely, keep them trapped in our instruction to the point of boredom. This involves a delicate balance.

We've adapted the gradual release framework to include five components of comprehension strategy upon which we elaborate here.

Teacher Modeling
- The teacher explains the strategy.
- The teacher models how to effectively use the strategy to understand text.
- The teacher thinks aloud when reading to show thinking and strategy use.

Guided Practice
- The teacher purposefully guides a large-group conversation that engages students in a focused discussion that follows a line of thinking.
- The teacher and students practice the strategy together in a shared reading context reasoning through the text and co-constructing meaning through discussion.
- The teacher scaffolds the students' attempts and supports their thinking, giving specific feedback and making sure students understand the task.

Collaborative Practice
- Students share their thinking processes with each other during paired reading and small-group conversations.
- The teacher moves from group to group assessing and responding to students' needs.

Independent Practice

- After working with the teacher and with other students, the students try practicing the strategy on their own.
- The students receive regular feedback from the teacher and other students.

Application of the Strategy in Authentic Reading Situations

- Students use the strategy in authentic reading situations.
- Students use the strategy in a variety of different genres, settings, contexts, and disciplines. (Fielding and Pearson 1994; adapted by Harvey and Goudvis in 2005a)

In the past few years, we have come to understand that modeling should be short and sweet. Kids' waving hands and whispered comments have sent us this message loud and clear. If all we ever did was think out loud about a piece of text, kids wouldn't listen for long. So we model for a few minutes, just long enough to get our point across, and then quickly engage kids in guided practice. Most of our instructional time is spent in guided practice because that is where we can best support kids as they move towards independence. We ask kids to talk to each other frequently throughout the lesson, process the information, and share their thoughts and opinions. As soon as we sense they are ready, we send them off to practice collaboratively and/or independently.

Strategy Instruction: A Means to an End

Comprehension instruction is not about teaching strategies for strategies' sake. Nor is it about making sure that kids "master" the strategies. It *is* about teaching kids to use strategies purposefully to read any text for any reason, and to walk away from their reading experiences with new understanding that may generate still more learning. Comprehension strategies are interrelated, and we don't keep this a secret from kids. We show kids how strategies overlap and intersect. We demonstrate how readers weave them together for a more engaged, rewarding read. What counts is that kids use strategies to become readers with diverse ideas and opinions.

We frequently walk into classrooms and hear kids bursting with connections and questions. As the conversation continues, we sometimes find ourselves feeling a little queasy if it appears kids are using strategy language without understanding the thinking behind it. This suggests that they may not realize that the purpose of a strategy is to help their understanding. Comprehension strategies are not an end in themselves, but rather a means to understanding. Our classroom instruction must reflect this.

One at a Time? For How Long?

We are often asked, "Should I really teach the strategies one at a time?" Or, "I've been teaching inferring for seven weeks. When should I move on?"

The real question is whether or not we teach strategies in isolation and how long we focus on a particular strategy. The short answer is that we introduce the strategies one at a time but quickly move on to introduce additional strategies so that kids build a repertoire of strategies and use them flexibly to understand what they read. Otherwise, instruction may become all about the strategy rather than using the strategy as a tool for understanding. If kids only think about strategies in isolation, they tend to think about how many questions they can come up with rather than how their questions foster understanding. The last thing we want is for strategy use to become rigid and rote.

That said, there's a big difference between introducing and teaching kids strategies for the first time versus how they will eventually use a repertoire of strategies to construct meaning. For practical purposes, when we first teach a strategy, we model the strategy on its own so we don't confuse kids. If we were to introduce all the strategies at once, kids simply couldn't handle all the information. When we launch a strategy, we clearly explain and demonstrate how we use it to better understand what we read. For instance, we show kids how we think when we ask a question and how that question helps us to make meaning. Then we give kids time to practice with their peers and on their own.

But we don't wait very long to let kids know that readers don't use strategies in isolation. Why would we teach them to only ask questions throughout an entire book or just make connections as they read a poem? Readers weave a variety of strategies together to make sense of text. Comprehension strategies work in concert. Once kids ask a question, an inference is never far behind. So when we hear kids making inferences before we've introduced inferring, we celebrate their great thinking. "Oh oh! No inferring today. Remember we are working on questioning right now!" is not a refrain we hope to hear. The last thing we want to do is limit kids' thinking, directing them away from one strategy because we happen to be teaching another.

In *The Comprehension Toolkit*, a resource we created for comprehension instruction with informational text (2005), we share lessons that demonstrate how the strategies build on each other over time as well as a range of options for teaching comprehension strategies. Time frames vary, but in our opinion it makes sense to introduce all of the comprehension strategies described in this book within a reasonably short time period. For instance, we might introduce and explore many strategies within the first few months of school. Even as we introduce a new strategy, kids keep using the strategies already in their repertoire and we keep coming back to them. That is the point. We don't introduce a strategy and never mention it again. We continue to model, introduce, and use various comprehension strategies throughout the year and across the curriculum. We teach and reinforce the strategies in all curricular areas, including science, social studies, and mathematics. Comprehension instruction is cumulative and recursive.

Is There a Sequence?

One question that crops up more than any other is, "In what order should I teach the strategies?" Although we are convinced that there is no one sequence for strategy instruction, we have come to believe that teaching kids to monitor their comprehension comes first. We begin by explicitly teaching students to think about their reading and leave tracks of their thinking.

For clarity's sake, we introduce specific strategies in each chapter. But we do not believe there is any one sequence for teaching comprehension strategies. What matters is that children use them flexibly according to the demands of the texts and the tasks they encounter. For instance, we view activating background knowledge as a foundational strategy, because it is something kids need to do from the get-go. It is likely they will need to to be taught to notice new information and learning before they can determine important information. On the other hand, we may want to teach kids to infer the meaning of unfamiliar words on the first day of school because they're reading a textbook with a ton of unfamiliar concepts and need to know how. So rather than following a prescribed sequence, we consider what our kids need to learn, what they are reading, and which strategies will best facilitate their learning.

Above all, we take our cue from the kids. So as you read this book, let your kids lead the way. Maybe you go through the strategy chapters in order, or maybe not. Perhaps your fourth graders learned as much as they ever needed to know about making connections in the primary grades, so skip the connections chapter. After all, if we find ourselves teaching connections year after year after year, Houston, we've got a problem! So as you use the lessons in the second part of this book, we suggest dipping in and out of the strategy chapters on an as-needed basis. Our goal is to teach a repertoire of strategies to further engagement and understanding.

Setting the Tone: Building a Literate Community

In a thinking classroom, literacy is an active process. Teachers set a tone that values student curiosity and thinking and respects all voices and visions. We work hard to build a community of thinkers, expressers, listeners, and learners, a community where kids and teachers care and wonder about each other's interests and ideas and take time to talk about them, think about them, and explore them. Some of the principles that guide our practice follow. We elaborate on many of these in Chapter 4.

Foster passion and curiosity. Einstein said, "I have no special talent. I am only passionately curious." An interesting assessment considering the source. It was his passion and curiosity that led to his discoveries. Passion is contagious. So we share our own. Students enter our classrooms brimming with curiosity, and we want school to encourage rather than squelch it.

An environment that values collaborative learning and thinking. In classrooms that promote thinking, students and teachers co-construct meaning in large groups, small groups, and conferences; through discussions, book groups, and partner work. Everyone gets a chance to weigh in with meaning.

Large blocks of time for extended reading and writing. The importance of independent reading cannot be stressed too much. Reading volume is a strong indicator of reading achievement (Cunningham and Stanovich 2003). The more we read, the better we read. And the same goes for writing. If we want students to get better at reading and writing, they need to read and write a lot and think about what they are reading and writing. If we only went to a piano lesson on Monday and never sat down to practice the rest of the week, we wouldn't get any better.

We need to build in time for readers to read on their own and practice using strategies in self-selected text that they can and want to read. Richard Allington (1994) notes that higher achieving students spend much more time reading than their lower achieving counterparts, providing evidence that time spent in independent reading makes a difference. Reading actually makes you smarter (Stanovich 2000), and our kids need to know this. In Chapter 5, "Text Matters," we talk about how to get our kids to read a lot, and in Appendix A, we suggest a plethora of books to pique their interest.

Explicit instruction. Showing our thinking and modeling the mental processes we go through when we read give students an idea of what thoughtful readers do. In this way, we make our thinking visible for all of our kids. We explicitly teach reading comprehension strategies by demonstrating them for students in large-group instruction, in small-group instruction, and in conferences, and we give kids plenty of time to practice.

Language matters. What we say and how we say it makes a difference for our kids. Using respectful language that values kids' thinking sets a tone that encourages their participation and their trust. When we begin to hear kids using and understanding language that we have shared through instruction, we know that our kids are learning in ways that matter. Language shapes and expands thinking.

Authentic response. In active literacy classrooms, students have opportunities to respond to reading in a variety of ways. Talking, writing, and drawing in response to reading give kids an opportunity to make their thinking visible.

Responsive teaching and differentiated instruction. One size does not fit all. Responsive teaching is intentional, flexible, and adaptive. We have an instructional plan in mind, but we know that kids differ, so we plan instruction that responds to individual needs and interests. We design our instruction to support students with varying reading proficiencies, learning styles, and language backgrounds. For more information on ways to differentiate instruction for kids with special needs, pick up a recent favorite of ours, Patrick Schwarz's *From Disability to Possibility* (2006).

Text matters. Surround your students with text of every conceivable genre, style, form, and topic. Richard Allington reminds us that when teachers use a "multi-source, multi-genre curriculum" (1994), instruction tends to be more thoughtful and effective. And we'd add multimedia as well. Fill bookshelves and book baskets with books on every level and every imaginable topic for independent reading. Remember to share magazines and newspapers as well. When rooms burst with a vast array of print, kids pick it up. For more on this, see Chapter 5, "Text Matters."

Room arrangement matters. Long gone are classrooms characterized by desks in rows and no talking. It's nearly impossible to participate in the discussion if all you see is the back of someone else's head. In classrooms that value thinking, kids sit at tables or desks in clusters so that they can easily talk to one another and collaborate. We provide instruction in a comfortable meeting place where kids, no matter their age, sit up close in front of the teacher so they easily focus on the instruction and listen to and interact with one another. We also create quiet spaces and nooks and crannies for kids to read independently or work in small groups. When we create our classroom spaces, we keep bookstores or libraries in mind. If it's within your district guidelines, seek out area rugs, pillows, lamps, perhaps a couch. And don't forget the walls. Trade in the Teacher's Helper bulletin boards for co-constructed anchor charts and examples of students' work and thinking. Kids thrive in intimate, comfortable surroundings.

Accessible resources. In classrooms that value thinking, resources that support literacy are easily accessible. Books, although we love them, aren't the only resources. Overhead projectors and oversized charts for explicit instruction and recording kids' thinking are essential. Transparencies and transparency pens can't be overlooked. Clipboards act as portable desks so kids can sit up close to the teacher and respond. Pads of sticky notes top the supply list. Notebooks and journals fill student cubbies and desks.

Teachers may sigh at this extensive list of resources in this era of ever-dwindling funds. These days of diminishing resources require a creative response. Use your budget to get whatever you can and use your brain to get the rest. Head to the school or public library, and check out as many books as they will part with. Wander around garage sales, used-book sales, and bargain sections of bookstores. Introduce yourself to local businesses. Business-school partnerships are increasingly common and productive. And don't forget about grants. You may just have to add "grant writer" to your list of job titles. But it can pay off, big time!

Teaching Comprehension in the Reading Workshop

Strategic reading takes hold in classrooms that value student thinking. In our work in classrooms, we've noticed that the classroom context makes all the difference for effective strategy instruction. The comprehension instruction described in this book is a natural compliment to the workshop model. Our notion of workshop has expanded in recent years so that we now include science workshop, history workshop, and researcher's workshop as well as reading and writing workshop. Kids read a variety of genres, texts, and topics in these workshops. They read poetry and literature to enhance their understanding and love of reading. They engage in something we call "real-world reading," which is the nonfiction reading that resembles reading adults do each day—newspapers, magazines, essays, editorials, and so forth. And they do a great deal of focused content reading to investigate topics of study in science and social studies.

In the workshop, the teacher models a whole-group strategy lesson and then gives students large blocks of time to read and to practice the strategy in small groups, pairs, or independently. During this time, the teacher moves about the room, slides her chair up next to readers, and confers with them about their reading. Sometimes the teacher meets with small, flexible groups to provide additional needs-based instruction. Often at the end of the workshop, the whole group comes together to share their learning.

The workshop model emphasizes choice in book selection. Reading researcher Richard Allington recommends that readers choose much of what they read. We know that readers get better at reading when they choose books they can and want to read. Kids can choose from any book under the sun or they can choose from a number of options the teacher offers. Allington refers to this as "managed choice" (1994). For instance, a language arts teacher may offer several books from which kids choose and form literature circles. A social studies teacher may offer a dozen picture books on the Civil War to build background knowledge of the topic. We need to fill our rooms with terrific books at every level, on every conceivable topic, to ensure that kids get their hands on books they want to read. In Chapter 5, we describe how we choose books and how we help students choose their own books to read independently when practicing various comprehension strategies.

For a more in-depth discussion of reading workshops, see Shelley Harwayne's *Lifetime Guarantees* and Regie Routman's *Reading Essentials*. Each of these books describes the components of a successful reading workshop where student ideas and thoughts carry weight. To explain reading workshop to parents, we recommend *7 Keys to Comprehension* by Susan Zimmermann and Chryse Hutchins (2003).

But it is important to keep in mind that comprehension strategy instruction can and should be taught in any classroom context and with many different materials. Some teachers use a four-block instructional model, others organize their teaching around guided reading and balanced literacy. Some use published anthologies, basal readers, or scripted programs. But whatever resources or structures you choose, kids need comprehension instruction to read, write, and talk about their thinking. And they need to learn reading strategies that support them to understand what they read.

Assessing Comprehension: Teaching with the End in Mind

Reading assessments, like rodents, run rampant. DIBELS, DRAs, IRIs, SATs, ACTs. You name it, kids have taken it and sometimes for hours and hours on end. Unfortunately, in this era of No Child Left Behind, test preparation is becoming the default curriculum. Assessment is not only about what our kids do, but also about how effective our instruction has been. When we reflect on evidence of their learning and understanding, we revise and shape our subsequent instruction. Authentic assessment provides us with three very important pieces of information which guide our instruction. Assessment informs us about

1. *Our students' learning and progress.* By looking carefully at our kids' work and listening to their words and thoughts, we derive an authentic understanding of how they are doing and what they have learned or not learned.

2. *Past instruction.* What kids learn depends on how well we have taught it. If kids don't get it, we need to rethink our instruction and change it accordingly. If most of the class doesn't get it, it is our responsibility. If 25 percent of the class doesn't get it, it is still our responsibility. And if one child doesn't get it, it remains our responsibility. It's not about teaching the same lesson over and over again, because that doesn't work. We need to redesign our lessons keeping in mind what we have learned from our kids and letting that information guide our instruction.

3. *Future instruction.* Responsive teaching and assessment go hand in hand. Based on what we see in students' work, the evidence of their understanding, we design subsequent instruction that is tailored to what they need. We plan our next steps based on what we notice in their work that needs attention and elaboration. Kids all have different needs. Some are quickly ready for independent practice. Others need more time, support, and guided practice. We may convene a small group or we may confer individually depending on need.

Finding Out What Students Are Thinking

When we lead a discussion, we notice and evaluate children's responses. When we look over their written responses after class, as Anne did after reading *Rebel* out loud, we learn what we have to teach or reteach the next day. Small-group sessions such as book groups or study groups provide opportunities for students to practice comprehension strategies on their own.

The only way we can confidently assess our students' comprehension is when they share their thinking with us. Readers reveal their comprehension by responding to text, not by answering a litany of literal questions at the end of the chapter on rocks and minerals. Personal responses to reading give us a window into students' minds. We connect with their thinking when we know what's going on for them as they read.

All the lessons, discussions, responses, and study groups described in this book have one purpose: to move kids toward independence as readers. What ultimately matters is that students internalize comprehension strategies that promote understanding. When we listen to kids, ask them questions, and watch them closely, we learn not only what they understand, but also what they don't understand. We can begin to see how we can design instruction that is responsive to what they need to learn.

We find out if readers are understanding what they read in the following ways.

We listen to kids. We can't stress enough how much we learn about kids' reading and thinking by simply listening closely to what they say. If we listen, they will talk. Sometimes kids might say, "I made a connection" or "I'm inferring." Using the language isn't enough, however. We check to see that there is substance underlying their statements.

We read kids' work. We read their responses closely, looking for evidence that they are constructing meaning. And we use these responses to design future instruction.

We confer with kids. The reading conference provides an ideal opportunity to talk one on one with students and help them sort out their thinking and come to a deeper understanding of how reading strategies support comprehension. Sometimes, discovering what readers are thinking only takes asking them. Those natural talkers are only too happy to fill you in on their thinking. Those more reticent kids may surprise you and open up, too, if you only ask.

We listen in on conversations. Even though we were both taught that eavesdropping is rude, we know that it's invaluable when trying to find out what kids are thinking about their reading. Listening in on conversations kids have with one another during reading workshop is a surefire way to get at their honest thinking. We hear what kids are really thinking when we listen in on them.

We observe behavior and expressions. A scrunched-up nose, a raised eyebrow, or a quizzical look lets us know what a reader is thinking. We watch kids carefully and notice their expressions while they read to give us a glimpse into their thinking.

We chart responses. We record what kids say in class discussions on anchor charts. This holds their thinking and makes it visible, public, and permanent. Students can refer to the charts during discussions or use them as guides when crafting their own responses.

We keep anecdotal records of conferences and conversations. In classrooms where we work, teachers keep track of student thinking by taking notes of interactions they have with students and reviewing them regularly. Many teachers have three-ring binders with a tab for each student. Behind the tabs, teachers mark the date and record notes about individual students' reading, writing, and thinking.

We script what kids say, recording their comments and questions. Teachers we work with move about the classroom with clipboards, keeping track of kids' comments by scripting what they say. Later on after school, teachers take a look at these notes and reflect on them to determine if students are understanding what they read and flexibly using strategies where needed.

Occasionally, we make a point of sitting down with a couple of kids to assess their ongoing comprehension of a story or a piece of short nonfiction text. We document how kids use comprehension strategies in an authentic situation via what we call an assessment interview. Assessment interviews of this type are similar to conferences but are longer in duration, more thorough, and less frequent. They give us an opportunity to see how kids process and reason through the text as we record their thinking for the purpose of later reflection. To get a clear picture of how an assessment interview unfolds and of how we draw conclusions from it, see Appendix D for an example of one that Anne conducted with three fourth graders as they read *My Freedom Trip* by Frances and Ginger Park.

The chapters in Part II of this book include comprehension lessons arranged by strategy. At the end of each of these chapters, we share some student work accompanied by our running commentary. We show and explain how we look at the work and think about it to assess how our kids are doing and where they need to go next.

What About Grades? Moving from Assessment to Evaluation

There is no need to grade students on what they know when they walk in the door. We need to grade them on what they learn from what we have taught. When we give students grades to evaluate them, we make sure the grades are based on evidence gleaned from ongoing and authentic assessment. This is how assessment informs evaluation. When we assess our kids' progress, we look for a demonstration of understanding. Work samples, student talk, and artifacts are the evidence we use to assess their learning. Grades are all about evaluating what kids have learned through practice. We evaluate and give grades only after students have had a lot of time to practice and internalize the strategies and skills we have taught. We base our grades on a substantial body of evidence that stands as proof of kids' learning.

Regurgitating answers to end-of-chapter questions does not give us enough evidence to accurately evaluate what kids know and what they have learned. Likewise for fill-in-the-blank worksheets and literal comprehension questions. Grading a stack of worksheets and packets doesn't provide us with information about authentic learning. So we look at constructed and more open-ended responses that require kids to show us their thinking and learning. This evidence comes in the form of responses on sticky notes, two- and three-column think sheets, short and longer summary responses, notes from discussions, thoughtful illustrations, journal and notebook entries.

We constantly check what kids are doing against what we have taught them and the outcomes we hope to achieve. We review and save work that demonstrates understanding as well as work that doesn't, and we design instruction accordingly.

After students have had plenty of practice and we have collected a good deal of their work, we grade them, holding them accountable for what they have learned. Much of our grading is done using rubrics that directly correspond with and measure what we have taught. So in the end, we evaluate students to measure their learning, to "grade" their understanding, and to satisfy the norms of school and society.

Out of the Pens of Kids

We are often asked what comprehension strategies do for kids. How they help kids understand what they read. How they help kids engage in their reading. So we go straight to the kids and ask them. After all who knows better than the kids if and how comprehension strategies help them understand and engage in what they read? Students love to share their ideas and talk about their thinking.

Fifth-grade teacher Eleanor Wright sees merit in having her students write about how strategies help them comprehend text. In her response, Amy writes about how visualizing helps her "get it" when she reads: "I had lots of trouble with reading. I mean I can read but I didn't get the book. Now, I have a film through my head like I am actually there in the book." Skilynn shows how she stops and thinks about her reading for a minute or two before going on—synthesizing, if you will:

> *This year I have been going home and reading for at least 30 minutes and I love it! Ever since we started the sticky notes, it has really been making me think a minute or two to understand what the book is about. When I go home, I always go back and look at my questions to see if I can answer them yet. I usually can.*

And Cassie, finally, has an outlet for those pent-up thoughts and feelings (see Figure 3.1). Eleanor was amazed by these responses. She was delighted that her students were so engaged in reading. The strategies helped them move between their lives and books in meaningful ways, and Eleanor had a thorough understanding of what they were thinking and learning.

When we write our questions, we "think" – the reason why I say think in " " is you're teaching us how we really are supposed to "think" about – and when we ask questions we are going beyond and we are really expressing what we wonder. Most of us had those thoughts in us, but we were never given the opportunity to express those trapped-in feelings we had. We had them in us all along, and you let them out. I would have to say that I think that 5th grade is the grade I must need to know for the coming years.

Cassie

Figure 3.1 Cassie's Thoughts on How
Reading Comprehension Instruction
Helped Her

Chapter 4

Tools for Active Literacy: The Nuts and Bolts of Comprehension Instruction

We've often heard our colleague Cris Tovani say that schools should not be places where old people go every day to do the work for young people. Isn't it interesting how when the bell rings at 3:00 P.M. on Friday afternoon, the kids bound out of the room like so many Bambis, as we teachers drag our exhausted rear ends out the door. The kids should be dead tired, and we should be ready for a 5:00 P.M. power yoga class!

Seriously, teachers are working too hard on stuff kids should be doing themselves. All of our teaching and learning should move learners toward independence. No one learns to function and think independently by listening to someone else talk all day. Kids don't learn much when the teacher does most of the work. Readers get better at reading and thinking by doing the reading and thinking. And learners learn more by doing the work!

If we want kids to do the work and engage their minds in the learning, we need to give them interesting texts and tasks that challenge them and stimulate their thinking. We need to build in an abundance of time for students to read extensively, talk about their learning, write about their learning, do research, conduct investigations, and share their learning and thinking with others. This is what we mean when we talk about *active literacy*. In classrooms framed around *active literacy*, kids are doing interesting work, delving into important issues and ideas, asking questions, researching answers, and doing investigations.

This new chapter is designed to share the teaching and learning tools, the nuts and bolts of comprehension, that we use to help learners think about what they are reading and work out their thinking to construct meaning.

The Importance of Language

Explicit instruction is all about what we say and what we do. Language is the driving force behind the instructional approaches described here. We use language to explain and prompt thinking. Peter Johnston, in his book *Choice Words: How Our Language Affects Children's Learning* (2004), advocates using language that encourages a constellation of diverse responses and ideas. Open-ended questions such as Why do you think this? What makes you say that? How did you come up with this? Can you say a little more about that? lead to meaningful conversations where kids take an active role. Asking open-ended questions that prompt thinking goes a long way towards developing thoughtful, independent thinkers and learners.

Language has the power to give rise to exciting, vibrant classrooms with eager learners or, conversely, to spawn deadly dull classrooms full of bored kids. The choice is ours. Research has shown that the most effective instruction is conversational rather than didactic in nature (Allington and Johnston 2002). When we engage kids in natural conversations about ideas, issues, and topics they care about, learning takes a front seat. When we merely emphasize directions or procedures and engage in endless recitation, learning never has a chance. In addition, the language we use can create a climate that encourages kids' participation or shuts them down. We all remember times in school where we were so embarrassed by a teacher's comment that we were afraid to utter a word. We also relish the memory of classrooms that nudged us into lively conversations where we knew our thinking mattered.

We want our kids to adopt and adapt our teaching language as their learning language. When we teach explicitly, we use a common language for reading and thinking that kids take on as their own. When we begin to hear them articulating the language that we have shared through instruction, it's a good indication that they are thinking about their reading and their learning.

Options for Explicit Instruction

We use a vast array of options for explicit instruction. In one lesson, we might think aloud as we read a picture book and ask kids to notice what we were doing as a reader. In another, we might think through a feature article on the overhead projector and ask kids to interact with the text. As a matter of fact, many of the instructional approaches we describe involve thinking aloud in one form or another. Our definition of thinking aloud means that we peel back the layers of our thinking, show kids how we approach text, and make visible how understanding happens in a variety of reading contexts. To demystify the comprehension process, we share the thoughts we have as we read, surfacing our own inner conversation with the text so kids can do so independently.

We mix and match a variety of instructional techniques to reach all kids and keep them engaged. Sometimes we do an interactive read-aloud, sometimes a text lift. Other times we lead a group discussion. Variety is the spice of life! We design instruction that will keep our kids interested and matches the task at hand. And we focus on what we need to teach and what our kids need to learn. Not only do we share our thinking and how we make sense of text during whole-group instruction, we also remember to teach explicitly, modeling our thinking, when meeting with small groups in guided practice as well as when we confer with individuals.

This section describes a range of options for "showing kids how" through explicit instruction. Explicit instruction is not just about modeling. Opportunities for explicit instruction also occur during guided practice, collaborative practice, and independent practice. Each of the strategy lessons in Part II of this book incorporates one or more of these explicit instructional approaches to teaching comprehension.

- Think-alouds
- Read-alouds
- Interactive read-alouds
- Lifting text
- Guided discussion
- Anchor lessons and anchor charts
- Rereading for deeper meaning
- Sharing our own literacy by modeling with adult literature

Thinking Aloud

The detailed process of making our thinking public by showing students how we construct meaning is called "think aloud" (Davey 1983). The think-aloud shows kids how skillful readers think—how we activate our background knowledge, ask questions, draw conclusions. Steph demonstrated one way to think aloud during her *Up North at the Cabin* mini-lesson. She simply showed students what she was thinking as she read and wrote a comment or two leaving tracks of her thinking. Think-alouds are central to comprehension instruction. It is often by seeing us model our thinking that kids are best able to understand what they need to do as independent readers.

Some think-alouds demonstrate all aspects of the inner conversation we have as we read—our reactions, our questions, our connections, and so on. Others are strategy specific. When we teach kids to wonder and ask questions initially, we focus mostly on the questions we have and the thinking behind them so our students know when, why, and how we ask questions. As a matter of fact whenever we launch a new strategy, we make very explicit the kind of thinking that underlies it.

Too often, we model for our kids without letting them in on the purpose of our demonstration. To counter that, before we begin the lesson, we ask our kids to watch us carefully as we model our thinking and notice what we do as readers. After our demonstration, we ask them to share what they noticed us doing. This focuses their attention, gives them an opportunity to participate, and increases their engagement.

Tips for Thinking Aloud
Share aspects of the inner conversation. To give kids an understanding of how we monitor ongoing comprehension, we share the many thoughts, reactions, connections, confusions, questions that crop up as we read. "In this book, *Gleam and Glow*, I think it would be really scary to have your dad off fighting in a war somewhere like the father in this story is doing." We also share how our attention can flag and our thoughts can stray from the text so that kids will see

how we get ourselves back on track. We jot down our thoughts on sticky notes or in the margins to leave tracks of our thinking and stay on top of meaning.

Share how we activate and connect background knowledge. We show kids how we merge what we already know with new information we encounter as we read. " I knew that sharks have big teeth, but they are even bigger than I thought they were. Wow!" We also show how our thinking changes as we read. "I always thought that sharks like to eat people, but now I know that they are very picky eaters."

Share our questions. We demonstrate how questions engage us in thinking about the text, how we read with a question in mind noting that some are answered in the text and others are not. We might ask one question and then show how it leads to others. "Why are the sea otters disappearing? Is there not enough food? Is a predator killing them? Is the water polluted?" In this way, we demonstrate how our questions can lead to a line of thinking that we can follow as we read.

Share our inferences. We model how we can infer in a variety of ways. We share how we infer the meaning of unfamiliar words and concepts using the context. We show how we infer themes in fiction. We show how we use illustrations, photos, and features to draw conclusions in nonfiction. "It says the radio guys on the Titanic were weary. I'm inferring it means they were tired because the next sentence says they had been up all night."

Verbalize confusing points and demonstrate fix-up strategies. We monitor ongoing comprehension and show our reaction when meaning breaks down. "Huh? I don't get this part. This doesn't make sense." And we also show how we use fix-up strategies like rereading or reading on to clarify confusion. After rereading, we might say, "Oh now I get it. I missed that the first time I read."

Share how we sort and sift information to determine important ideas. We can't remember all of the details when we read. So we model how we pick out the information we want to remember. "Boy, there are a lot of details here about photosynthesis. But what's really important is how plants use sunlight to make their food. I can tell that because the writer talks a lot about the sunlight and its relationship to plants."

Reading Aloud

Jim Trelease, author of *The Read-Aloud Handbook*, says that the purpose of literature is to provide meaning in our lives. He believes that literature is the most important medium because it "brings us closest to the human heart" (2006). He states that reading aloud serves to "reassure, entertain, inform, explain, arouse curiosity and inspire our kids."

We wholeheartedly agree. Some of our best moments have come from reading aloud or being read to. Steph first encountered Dr. Seuss in kindergarten when Miss Buehler read *The 500 Hats of Bartholomew Cubbins*. Anne remembers reading E. B. White's *Charlotte's Web* to her five-year-old daughter, Allison, and finding herself unable to continue through the tears when Charlotte died. The recent proliferation of books on tape illustrates our love affair with oral reading. Suddenly, we endure traffic jams with a smile, as we listen to an author like Frank McCourt regale us with compelling stories.

Thoughtful teachers everywhere dedicate time each day to read out loud to their students in all genres and content areas. When teaching reading comprehension, we do a good deal of instruction via reading aloud. But we need to remember that if we only read aloud for the purpose of instruction, we will ruin reading aloud. We need to read aloud every day for the sheer joy of it!

Interactive Reading Aloud

When teaching comprehension, we also read aloud for the purpose of instruction in what we call an interactive read-aloud. An interactive read-aloud is all about listening comprehension. The kids do not have a copy of the text. The teacher reads the text and guides the instruction while the students listen, talk to each other, and jot down their thinking about the text. Interactive reading aloud can reflect the overall inner conversation that readers have when they read, or it can be strategy specific. For example, in an interactive read-aloud meant to teach a specific strategy, we might model only our questions to give kids practice asking questions or we can read aloud a trade book that builds kids' background knowledge in an upcoming social studies topic. The bottom line is that with this process, decoding doesn't interfere with understanding. All kids are free to listen, think about the ideas, talk to each other, and use strategies to understand the text.

We keep in mind, however, that interactive reading aloud does not improve fluency because the kids are not doing the reading. Kids only become more fluent by reading in text they are able to read. Interactive reading aloud is a process to enhance comprehension. After this experience, kids transfer the process into their independent reading. And that is when they work on both fluency and comprehension!

Steps for Interactive Reading Aloud

Activating background knowledge. We build and activate background knowledge about the text by asking kids to turn and talk about what they already know about the topic at hand. Then we allow a minute to share some of this information. This engages our kids and prepares them to listen.

Modeling. We read through the text and model our thinking as we read—our inner conversation, a strategy, our confusions—the lesson focus. Then we stop and record our thinking on sticky notes, a chart, a think sheet, a journal. After kids have observed us modeling, we stop and ask them to share what they noticed us doing as a reader. As they share their thoughts, we record their thinking on a note pad to transfer to a chart later on.

Guided practice. After modeling, we read a bit more and then encourage kids to turn to each other and talk about their thinking and jot down a note or two. We continue reading, stopping frequently to jot down kids' thinking and giving them time to write their responses and talk to each other.

Sharing thinking. To wrap up the lesson, we bring the kids together and return to the focus of the lesson. Perhaps we talk about how a strategy helped our understanding as well as the bigger ideas in the text that were discussed throughout the lesson or any new insights that occurred through the guided discussion.

Lifting Text

We frequently use the overhead projector to model instruction through close readings of short text. We lift a piece of text, make a transparency of it, distribute a copy to each student in the class, and place it on the overhead projector. Kids are gathered up near the projector, and they each have a copy of the text so we can read it together. We need our students to be up close and personal, clipboards in hand, during our mini-lesson as we read through the text, stop to point out how we use a strategy, and invite them to add their own responses. We reason through the text together (Anderson et al. 1992). We might lift a newspaper article or the first page of a chapter from a social studies textbook and spend a few minutes showing students how we figure out unfamiliar words and navigate the text features. It is a thoughtful rehearsal that anticipates obstacles students might encounter in advance, so kids better understand the content when they read.

Charts and Big Books are also favored friends of teachers who model instruction through text lifts. We lift text and copy it onto charts to give kids a shared reading experience through the use of enlarged text. We might use such a chart when we teach inferring in poetry to young children, rewriting a poem on large chart paper and then encouraging kids to come up and code this enlarged version of the text. They can write their inferences in markers right next to the words that prompted their thinking. Or students might place a sticky note on the text and illustrations of a Big Book to share their questions, inferences, or connections. In this way, children's thinking is visible for all to see, providing an explicit and permanent example.

Guided Discussion: Developing a Line of Thinking

When Anne models her own thinking in front of kids, she has difficulty restraining the children's participation. She knows it is necessary to show her thinking first and give children clear, explicit language for talking about their reading before they join in. But ignoring dozens of waving hands is nearly impossible for her. Thank goodness, because the insights and ideas that children bring to the discussion strengthen our teaching and their learning. After Anne has launched a lesson by modeling her thinking for a few minutes, she moves quickly into guided practice and invites the kids to join her in the discussion. This invitation seldom goes unanswered, since most of the children are chomping at the bit. Active participation in the discussion is essential if students are to construct meaning.

But the discussion need not be a free-for-all. During guided discussion, with the whole group gathered together, we facilitate a conversation focused on a topic, issue, theme, or idea. Together we develop a line of thinking by listening to each other and building on each other's comments. We listen carefully to what kids say. As they talk, we may restate their responses for emphasis or to clear up misconceptions. Rather than dominating the discussion by doing all the talking ourselves, we facilitate a discussion that weaves together the kids' ideas and comments into a coherent conversation. We help to shape their responses into a line of thinking that moves the discussion forward.

To do this, we might share some information or ideas from a text we are reading or one of the kids might launch the discussion with a question or an idea of his or her own. Regardless, we ask kids to turn and talk about the topic or issue for a minute or two. After they have processed the information, they share their responses. Our role is to teach them to listen to what everyone has to say and build on each other's thinking. When kids make a thoughtful comment, we pick up on it and the discussion may head in that direction. We also show kids how to gear their comments to the ideas under discussion so they will avoid going off on a tangent or making unrelated comments. We explicitly teach them to listen and speak to previous comments, "piggybacking" off of one another and asking follow-up questions. In this way, they learn from the ideas of others and add to the collective thinking. The discussion goes somewhere. It's got momentum.

In essence, we are teaching the art of conversation. We think this is guided practice at its best. When children have opportunities to share their thinking with peers, kids pay attention. This joint thinking allows students to respond to and follow the conversation to a logical conclusion enhancing understanding for the whole group.

Anchor Lessons and Anchor Charts

We try to provide students with anchor experiences when we deliver instruction in reading comprehension. We identify and choose our most effective mini-lessons as anchors for students to remember what they learned and to better understand it. After Steph read *Up North at the Cabin*, the sixth graders searched for books they were able to identify with and then coded their own connections. The next time Steph talked about making personal connections with that group of kids, she referred back to that lesson and reminded them, "Remember when I read that book about the girl in the cabin in Minnesota, which reminded me so much of my own life, and then you chose books of special importance to you and marked your own connections? Try to find some places in today's reading where you connect to the text like that." Steph's reading *Up North at the Cabin* became an anchor lesson for kids to return to and activate their prior knowledge independently at a later date. Anchor charts provide a record of our instruction. We co-construct anchor charts to record kids' thinking about a text, lesson, or strategy so that we can return to it to remember the process. Anchor charts make both the teacher's and the students' thinking visible and concrete. These charts connect past teaching and learning to future teaching and learning, serving as reminders of what has come before so that kids can better understand what comes next. Anchor charts are not written in stone. We often add to and elaborate upon them. Teachers and students can make use of several different kinds of anchor charts.

Strategy charts. During an interactive read-aloud, we co-construct charts incorporating points we want to teach as well as the children's comments and insights. We record their questions, inferences, and connections. We capture the language that demonstrates strategic thinking so that kids know when, how, and why to use a strategy in their reading and can refer to the chart for support.

Content charts. Content matters. These anchor charts record the interesting and important information that readers discover when reading. Sometimes we record new learning, how our thinking has evolved and changed, or new information we have acquired during a content area study.

Genre charts. As kids read in a particular genre and discuss what they know about it, we capture their thoughts in writing. So we might co-construct a chart about the features of nonfiction or the elements of fiction, which we post for all to see and remember.

One thing we have noticed is that it can be cumbersome to create a full-fledged anchor chart smack in the middle of a mini-lesson. There is a difference between an anchor chart as we have described above and a lesson chart that we write quickly as we teach, capturing a bit of kids' thinking and supporting them when they go off to practice. Later, to hold thinking over time, we can construct a more carefully composed and elaborate anchor chart that kids can refer to again and again for guidance.

Rereading for Deeper Meaning

Oscar Wilde once said, "If one cannot enjoy reading a book over and over again, there is no use in reading it at all" (Charlton 1991). Too often, we mistakenly think that once children have listened to a book one time, we're done with it. In truth, the more children hear or read a story, the better they comprehend it and the more they love it. Yet perhaps we don't remember our own teachers ever reading the same book to us more than once and so we assume that once is enough.

Educator Debbie Miller recommends reading books aloud several times to help children gain meaning. Debbie points out that young children often get little meaning from hearing a book only once. She appears in our video series *Strategy Instruction in Action* (2001) and does a think-aloud with Sherry Garland's *The Lotus Seed.* As Debbie read the text for the first time, the kids had many questions that she recorded on a chart. Then when she read it the second time, they began to sort out their questions into those that were answered and those that were not. After the second reading, they were able to focus on the bigger ideas in the story and the deeper questions. Without a second or third reading, a basic understanding of the text might have eluded many of them.

After reading a book like *The Lotus Seed* once to first graders, some teachers might assume that it is too difficult for them to understand, and they might not think to read it again. However, with more time, support, and discussion, kids have a better shot at understanding it.

Sharing Our Own Literacy

For many years, Don Graves has said that those of us who teach reading must be readers ourselves. As readers, we experience the hoops and hurdles as well as the joys and insights that come with reading, and we can share the struggles as well as the victories with our students. When teachers model their own reading process using their own reading material, kids take note.

When Steph's son, Alex, was in the first grade, he received reading support from Laura Benson, the school reading specialist. Alex, it seemed, was far more interested in discussing ideas and thinking than he was in learning to decode words. A thoughtful teacher, Laura understood the role that interest plays in reading, and she conceived ways to hook Alex on the written as well as the spoken word. A voracious reader to this day, Alex credits the day in first grade when Laura brought in an excerpt from Pat Conroy's *Prince of Tides* as the day reading became important to him. No one had ever shared adult text with him before, and he's never forgotten it.

We bring in magazines, book club books, newspaper articles, essays, and poetry, all sorts of adult real-world reading material to share with kids and model our own reading process. We might have a lot of questions about a new novel so we read a paragraph and show that even though we are proficient readers we still have questions when we read. If we have trouble staying on track with meaning in an article on a topic that is not of great interest to us, we show kids how we refocus our thinking to understand it. We also share books that we are totally passionate about so that our kids can see the importance of reading in our daily lives.

As the custodians of reading instruction, teachers must be readers first. Of all professionals who read, teachers must top the list. Ellin Oliver Keene and Susan Zimmermann drive this point home in their book *Mosaic of Thought* (1997). They remind us that we need to understand reading comprehension strategies ourselves and notice how they play out in our own reading before we can successfully teach them to children.

Beyond Dioramas: Responding to Reading

Lucy Calkins, professor at Teachers College, Columbia University, notes that when she finishes a book late at night in bed, she doesn't grab her husband by the arm and say, "Oh, I just can't wait to get downstairs and make a diorama." We understand. For too many years, kids in classrooms all over the United States have been asked to do a laundry list of activities when they finish reading books. You know the ones—dioramas, shadow boxes, word jumbles, word searches, and so on. Reading response is more than these. Authentic responses don't have to be so contrived or complicated. As our colleague Harvey "Smokey" Daniels suggests, "Why can't kids do what real life-long readers do when they finish a great book? Talk about it and then get another book."

In one way or another, every lesson described in this book focuses on student response. Be they oral or written, simple or sophisticated, responses tell us what children are thinking and learning. They let us know if our kids are engaged with reading or are tuning out from boredom. Once students respond to a text, we have some evidence to go on. We have an inkling about whether their understanding is in the ballpark or off the mark. And usually we know a whole lot more. Kids in active literacy classrooms are only too happy to share their thoughts and opinions about their reading.

Diverse, open-ended responses tell us the most about what children understand or don't understand when they read. The two most common forms of response are oral and written, and many of the responses in this book fall into these two categories. We caution, however, not to neglect other less obvious forms, such as artistic or musical response. Visualizing lends itself to artistic response. Why not ask a less verbal, artistic child to sketch or draw his or her response? Inferring lends itself to some more offbeat responses, such as charades and drama. But these responses are more than mere activities; they show us how kids use a variety of strategies to construct meaning and what their reading means to them.

Where do our ideas for different response options come from? Mostly from the children. For instance, as we teach a lesson on questioning to first graders, we often notice they have many more questions than we can reasonably record on a class chart. We may decide then and there to turn the kids loose to record their questions in their own notebooks. For us, one measure of classroom success relates to diversity in work product. Kids differ. Their work should, too. Careful observation of children, their interests, and their needs as learners is the best guide to developing different response options. We share ideas for talking and writing about reading in the following sections.

Talking About Reading

Literacy floats on a sea of talk (Britton 1970). We often tell teachers that their kids simply need to talk more. They look at us dumbfounded. "Just shoot me!" they say. "That's all our kids do is talk." And we understand what they mean, having been there ourselves. But we are not talking about idle conversation here. Allington and Johnston (2002) found that in high-achieving classrooms, kids spent significant amounts of time engaged in discussions about their reading and learning. Classrooms that promote active literacy reverberate with what Allington describes as "purposeful talk"—conversations and discussions that further thinking. As a matter of fact, purposeful student-to-student talk is probably the most underrepresented teaching and learning practice that we can think of. We work hard to increase the amount of purposeful talk in our classrooms, because there is no better way to understand what we read than simply to talk about it. Not dioramas but conversations. Much of the oral responding that we describe in this book falls into the category of "purposeful talk."

Structures That Encourage Purposeful Talk
Purposeful talk doesn't just happen. In fact, purposeful talk is wasted if no one is listening. Active listening is at the heart of thoughtful conversation and discussion. To make sure kids understand how to engage in thoughtful conversations, listening and talking to each other, we model a variety of different discussion structures. Whether it's turning and talking during a mini-lesson or jigsawing the text in small groups, we make sure all kids understand what is expected of them as they talk to each other. Some of the discussion structures that encourage purposeful talk are described here.

Turn and talk. In whole-group instruction we stop every few minutes and ask kids to share their thinking with each other by turning and talking to a peer sitting next to them. The purpose of this is threefold: to process information, to enhance understanding, and to maximize engagement. Turning and talking gives all children, not only the most vocal ones, a chance to participate in the conversation and construct meaning. Less vocal kids have a chance to first rehearse their thinking and feel more confident to share it. This discussion structure is particularly useful for students who are just learning the language. To see what this looks like in the classroom, check out our video *Read, Write, and Talk* (2005b), which features kids turning and talking throughout the lesson and practice.

Paired reading. We often recommend that students team up with work buddies or partners during collaborative practice. Paired reading has a variety of goals. Kids may be paired around a common interest, question, or topic of study. Sometimes we assign these pairs with a specific goal in mind. Sometimes kids choose their own partners. And they change partners frequently so that all students get to know each other as readers. This is not simply about pairing more and less developed readers, we just need to make sure that everyone has access to the information. Regardless, we teach our kids that the listener has the most important job: pay attention, think about, and respond to what the partner is reading.

Jigsaw discussions. When we ask kids to jigsaw text, they work in small groups to read a particular section of a piece or to read one of several articles on a similar theme or topic. Jigsawing is both authentic and engaging because kids assume the responsibility for reading a small amount of text carefully and then teaching what they have learned to others. When kids are the teachers, they are motivated to understand and talk about the information. We make sure that each section of an individual piece of text stands alone so they can understand what they are reading without benefit of previous sections of the text.

Book clubs and literature circles. In these groups, students read the same text and meet together to discuss and respond to it much the same way that adults meet in monthly book clubs to talk about a book they have read. When students talk in these informal peer groups, the goal is to get away from a one-right-answer, one-interpretation discussion of the book. The authentic conversations that occur encourage participants to express their opinions, raise questions and issues, and connect the text to their own lives. We highly recommend Harvey Daniels's book *Literature Circles* (2001), which describes this process in depth and offers practical suggestions for practice and implementation.

Study groups. In these groups, students work together to build knowledge about a common topic of interest. These topics may emerge from a facet of the curriculum or simply from student interest. Participants often begin this inquiry by asking questions that propel research efforts. The many different types of texts that address the topic allow readers of differing proficiency to participate because they can search for text they are able to read and we can help them find some as well.

Small-group shares.
- *Pair shares.* After the teacher models a strategy, children get in pairs and are encouraged to go back and work through text, talk about it, and respond together.
- *Small informal discussion groups.* Similar to pair shares. Three to five students discuss and reason through a piece of text together.
- *Compass-group four-way shares.* Compass-group sharing and responding is a structure that helps teachers manage classroom talk and gives equal access to everyone. Four kids sit either on the floor or at tables at the points of a compass, one in the north position, one in east, one in south, and one in west. With groups bunched throughout the room, the teacher announces north's turn. After a few minutes, the teacher suggests that north conclude, and that east begin, and on through the four points. In this way, each child will have had a turn to share and respond for several minutes. The teacher can wander and eavesdrop, comfortable in the knowledge that this process helps to make sure that even the most reticent talkers have a chance to respond (Harvey 1998).

A Word About Sharing

Gone are the days when a child sat in the author's chair and read a never-ending story to an audience who was mostly staring off into space. We are much more intentional about sharing than we used to be. We want kids to learn from the sharing session and find it engaging. So we offer a wide range of options for sharing learning, and we create authentic learning opportunities for everyone during the sharing. As you can see from the above options, sharing does not always have to involve the whole group. Children can share in partners, in small groups, and with other classes. When kids share in a whole group, we usually link their responses to the teaching, having them reflect on a new strategy or on the content they have learned.

Kids love taking their thinking public, and we all benefit when students make their thinking visible. So we create a respectful environment where everyone feels comfortable when sharing. We teach them how to interact with each other, and we model ways to have an inclusive conversation. We show them how to respectfully invite each other to share—looking their classmate in the eye, using their name, and speaking in polite language, saying something like "Josephine, would you like to share?" And Josephine replies, "Yes, thank you." Or kids may pass but when they do, they respond by saying "No, thank you."

Writing About Reading

Many of us remember how we highlighted our texts with abandon, went back to study for the test, were blinded by yellow, and had no idea why we highlighted in the first place. Active literacy, by its very definition, requires readers to merge their thinking with the information. Annotating in the margins and jotting thinking on sticky notes gives readers a place to hold their thinking and work through it as well. Recently we came across a document that Harvard University sends incoming freshmen to prepare them for academic life. "Interrogating Texts: 6 Reading Habits to Develop in Your First Year at

Harvard" describes how students are expected to read while at Harvard. The suggestions include previewing, annotating, summarizing and analyzing, looking for patterns, contextualizing, and comparing and contrasting. All these techniques contribute to thoughtful reading. But we wanted particularly to share what Harvard says about annotating here, because we have a feeling it may sound very familiar.

From start to finish, make your reading of any text thinking-intensive.
- *First of all: throw away the highlighter in favor of a pen or pencil. Highlighting can actually distract from the business of learning and dilute your comprehension. It only seems like an active reading strategy; in actual fact, it can lull you into a dangerous passivity.*
- *Mark up the margins of your text with WORDS: ideas that occur to you, notes about things that seem important to you, reminders of how issues in a text may connect with class discussion or course themes. This kind of interaction keeps you conscious of the REASON you are reading and the PURPOSES your instructor has in mind. Later in the term, when you are reviewing for a test or project, your marginalia will be useful memory triggers.*
- *Develop your own symbol system: asterisk a key idea, for example, or use an exclamation point for the surprising, absurd, bizarre. . . . Like your marginalia, your hieroglyphs can help you reconstruct the important observations that you made at an earlier time. And they will be indispensable when you return to a text later in the term, in search of a passage, an idea for a topic, or while preparing for an exam or project.*
- *Get in the habit of hearing yourself ask questions—"what does this mean?" "why is he or she drawing that conclusion?" "why is the class reading this text?" etc. Write the questions down (in your margins, at the beginning or end of the reading, in a notebook, or elsewhere). They are reminders of the unfinished business you still have with a text: something to ask during class discussion, or to come to terms with on your own, once you've had a chance to digest the material further, or have done further reading. (Harvard College Library 2007)*

Highlighting can actually "lull you into a dangerous passivity." Who knew?! The people who wrote this document could have read the book you are holding in your hands! But we doubt it. What we do suspect is that they read the research on reading comprehension. Just as teachers all over the country know, kids need to think when they read and jot that thinking down in order to construct meaning and better understand. To read this article in full, head to http://hcl.harvard.edu/research/guides/lamont_handouts/interrogatingtexts.html.

Whereas talk is likely the most immediate way to respond to reading, writing allows readers to really work out their thinking in relation to the text. Most skillful adult readers have developed a way of marking important parts of the text they encounter. When readers jot notes while reading, leaving tracks of their thinking, they are able to clarify confusion, record their questions, answer questions, notice the craft, and so forth.

Text coding. We use text codes as a shorthand way to capture our thinking as we read. We develop a variety of codes with our students, and they go on to create their own. Text coding keeps the reading process interactive and reminds us that reading is active thinking. We often post them in our classroom on an anchor chart for handy reference, using an asterisk for a key idea, an exclamation point for surprising information, and so on. Kids add their own codes on a regular basis; for example, S for *Shocking* was a code that Jake came up with when reading a piece about hurricanes. We don't hand out a canned list of text codes, because kids are unlikely to use them if they have no owner-ship. We co-construct an anchor chart of the codes and find that kids are much more interested in using them after having helped create them. Some codes that students and teachers have created follow, but this is by no means a com-plete list.

- R, reminds me of
- T-T, Text to text connection
- L, New learning
- ?, Question
- *, Key idea
- ☼, A lightbulb for new idea
- !, Surprising information
- I, Inference

A word of caution here. Occasionally students will mention that coding text while reading interferes with their train of thought. If that is the case, we suggest that the student read through a section first and then take a few moments to record thoughts and questions on sticky notes. The purpose of text coding is to enhance our students' understanding, not to break their concentra-tion and disrupt meaning.

Margin notes. It's not enough to simply code the text with an R or highlight in yellow. Highlighting all on its own is not active reading. Readers need to mark up the margins of text with words, to remind themselves why they highlighted or underlined. So along with the text codes, highlighting, bracketing, circling, and underlining, we teach kids to make brief margin notes that explain the thinking behind those codes, what was actually going on in their heads when they coded the text.

Sticky notes. Since we can't always write directly on the text, we are grateful for the mistake that resulted in the invention of sticky notes. Stickies are ubiq-uitous in classrooms today to help kids hold their thinking while reading. And we can't think of a better use of them. To keep track of thinking when reading, kids can write short notes or even use some of the above codes on their sticky notes. Over time we've noticed that where kids might write only a sentence or two on a full piece of paper, they will scrunch many ideas on to a small sticky note. Go figure! What matters here is that these notes give kids an easy, accessi-ble way to monitor their comprehension and leave a record that helps us assess their understanding.

Teachers sometimes ask us, What do you do with all the sticky notes? And our instant answer is that we read them, or at least most of them. From reading them, we can learn about what our kids know, what they have learned, and about their reading process. Sticky notes also guide us as we plan future instruction. We encourage kids to place them in their reading notebooks to inform parent conferences and evaluation efforts. Additionally, these brief notes can give students ideas for longer written responses and may even become a time line of their thinking and a record of their evolution of thought.

Think sheets. We use a variety of scaffolds and forms so that kids can think about their ideas and record their own responses and opinions. Think sheets include graphic organizers, double- and triple-column forms, response starters, webs, mind maps, and more. We make a distinction between fill-in-the-blank worksheets, those staples of traditional schooling that keep kids busy, and think sheets. Any form that encourages kids to construct meaning, write down their thinking, and merge it with the new information meets our definition of a think sheet. Think sheets are open-ended forms that invite students to think deeply and widely about their own questions, opinions, reactions, inferences, connections. In addition, these scaffolds allow kids to work out their thinking through writing during and after reading.

Response journals, lit logs, notebooks, wonder books, and more. We never tire of reading these entries because they give kids lots of latitude for creating their own responses. And we are always curious to know what kids will think of next. They write, draw, sketch, paste in artifacts, and so forth as they explore their thinking in relation to reading. Their entries can often spur longer, more extensive writing, such as poems, stories, and essays. Check out Aimee Buckner's *Notebook Know-How* (2005) to get a good idea of ways to inspire your kids to respond in notebooks.

Other responses. Artistic, dramatic, musical, numerical, scientific, historical, economic. You get the idea. If we only stick to oral and written responses, that future Georgia O'Keeffe or Leonardo DiCaprio may never emerge. We work with kids to develop the broadest spectrum of meaningful responses. But *meaningful* is the key word here. We want to remember to keep these responses authentic and not have kids responding just for the sake of it.

Aesthetic Reading and Efferent Reading

The famous reading theorist Louise Rosenblatt ([1938] 1996) talks about two distinct reading stances, efferent reading and aesthetic reading. Efferent reading is reading to learn. When we read efferently, we are reading to "take away" pieces of information or to synthesize big ideas. It is the stance we take when we are reading informational text. There is often too much information for a reader to take in without stopping and thinking. We read nonfiction in fits and starts, as if we are watching a slide show where we see a hurricane swirling over the ocean and we simply have to stop and respond right then and there. In classrooms where we work, nonfiction texts burst with sticky notes and text codes. When readers read nonfiction, they need to read it with a pencil gripped tightly in hand. We teach nonfiction readers to stop, think, and react as they read. Annotating informational text gives readers the best shot at learning, understanding, and remembering what they read.

The fiction and literature reading we do is what Rosenblatt refers to as aesthetic reading: "In aesthetic reading, the reader's attention is centered directly on what he is living through during his relationship with that particular text" ([1938] 1996). When reading fiction, it's practically a goal to get lost in the read and find ourselves in the story. We imagine ourselves running through the rain forest right alongside of the character. It's highly unlikely that we would stop and write a note about it in the midst of a gripping narrative or a suspenseful mystery. We suggest that kids keep a pad of sticky notes and pencil close at hand when they read literature to support them if and when they need it. But we do not recommend that they constantly pick up the pencil and jot their thinking if it interferes with their reading.

It is all about our purpose for reading. Kids might stop and jot in fiction when they need to sort out meaning, when they are confused, or when they have a question that they want to keep in mind. They might write a comment on a sticky note to hold their thinking for a book club discussion. And when we launch a strategy, we encourage kids to notice their thinking a little more acutely and apply the strategy that we have just taught by jotting down their questions, their inferences, and so forth. But writing about reading should enhance engagement and understanding, not interrupt it and bring it to a halt. So we encourage readers to jot down their thinking during narrative reading whenever *they* need to. Since we need to see their thinking, we encourage kids to write their thinking in lit logs or notebooks after they have finished reading, so they have more time to explore their thinking. In this way, writing about reading can inform and deepen understanding

Chapter 5

Text Matters: Choice Makes a Difference

Winston Churchill once said, "If you cannot read all of your books, at any rate handle, or as it were fondle them—peer into them, let them fall open where they will, read from the first sentence that arrests the eye, set them back on the shelves with your own hands, arrange them on your own plan so that you at least know where they are. Let them be your friends; let them at any rate be your acquaintance" (Gilbar 1990). We know from whence Mr. Churchill spoke. At last count, between the two of us, we had nearly two dozen books on our nightstands of which we had not read a word. But we have held them, flipped through them, and introduced ourselves to them. The pile, however, just seems to grow. So we hold Churchill's words dear, and dream of when we might have time to read them all. This holds true for our children's book reading as well.

Each year, huge numbers of children's books roll off the presses. The sheer number boggles the mind: nearly 5,500 new books for young people in 2005 alone (Bowker 2006); at that rate, approximately 55,000 to come in the next decade. We can't read them all; we can't even meet them all. So how do we get to know more books and get them into the hands of kids? Share those books you love with your colleagues. Spend some time each week talking about books. Your repertoire of picture books, trade books, chapter books, and collections will grow with each conversation. Get up close and personal with the library. School librarians and children's librarians in public libraries have the most in-depth knowledge of children's literature of anyone we know. They regularly read and review publications such as *Horn Book Magazine* and *Book Links*, both of which include extensive reviews of children's books on every conceivable theme and topic. (See Appendix C for a list of journals that review children's books.)

"Read widely and wildly," suggests literacy educator Shelley Harwayne. The mini-lessons in this book incorporate a wide range of genres, including realistic fiction, historical fiction, nonfiction, and poetry. Kids love to read in every genre. Not surprisingly, though, we have yet to run into a kid who can't put down his social studies textbook. It's the compelling text in Kathleen Krull's *Harvesting Hope: The Story of Cesar Chavez*, the realistic fiction of a changing era in the South in Jacqueline Woodson's *The Other Side*, and the beautiful poetry of Naomi Shihab Nye's *19 Varieties of Gazelle* that hook our kids. We need to fill our classrooms with text of every shape, size, and topic.

We wrote this book, in part, to ease the job of choosing from among so many books. In that vein, we have included an extensive annotated list of picture books, trade books, and subject area texts that has been updated from the first edition of this book. (See Appendix A.) We hope this is helpful. But we know that you may find your favorite picture book missing from this list. We simply couldn't list them all, so by all means improve this list by adding those books you dearly love.

Text Matters

Down with innocuous text! Alfred Tatum, author of *Teaching Reading to Black Adolescent Males* (2005), suggests that literacy holds power for young black men when it relates to their lives and concerns, when it is authentic, and when it raises issues that matter to them. We believe this holds true for *all* of us. Text matters—a lot.

If children are not reading engaging, interesting, thought-provoking text, why bother? A steady diet of textbooks and worksheets would be enough to turn anyone off to reading. So we surround kids with text that includes a variety of perspectives, opinions, ideas, issues, and concepts to read about, write about, and talk about. When students read and respond to text that provokes thinking, they are much more likely to become active, engaged readers. We flood our classrooms with text of all different types and on tons of topics, so we have a better shot at reaching all of our kids. How we choose text and how kids choose their own makes a difference in their literate lives.

Many of the lessons in the upcoming chapters use text that we've chosen because it furthers the purpose of the lesson. It is important, however, to keep in mind that these lessons can be done with many different texts—long, short, fiction, nonfiction, poetry, and so on. *Strategies That Work* is all about teaching the reader not merely the reading. Choose those books that serve your purpose or that you love, and teach with those.

This chapter shares our thoughts about the need for using a variety of short text forms for literacy teaching and learning, such as picture books, trade books, magazines, and newspaper articles. It also describes ways to support teachers in choosing the best possible text for instruction. Last but not even close to least, it shares how teachers can teach their kids to select books they can and want to read. When kids read text at their level and of interest to them, they are more likely to further their understanding and have a great read. Choice makes a difference for both teachers and kids.

A Case for Short Text

We often ask teachers to write down the different types of reading they've done over the past few weeks. Usually, they mention newspapers, magazines, letters, manuals, cookbooks, brochures, reports, newsletters, and so on. Many also have a novel or a long nonfiction trade book going, but about 80 percent of the reading they report is of the short-text variety. This is true of adults in general. Yet this is typically reversed in schools, where about 80 percent of the reading kids do is long text. We are convinced that school reading should more closely reflect the reading done outside of school. Since much of the reading our students will do as adults will be short, we advocate more short-text instruction in school. As an added bonus, we have found short text very effective for teaching comprehension.

Short text is, in a word, short! The length of short text makes it more accessible than full-length novels or textbooks. The term *short text* can refer to a picture book. But it can also describe a favorite poem used for teaching inferring, an essay for modeling how to determine an opinion or perspective, a magazine article on a current event, or a short story such as Sandra Cisneros's "Eleven" (1991), which brings forth a barrage of students' memories of their own embarrassing moments. Well-written short text gives kids an opportunity to read a piece quickly, dig into the themes and respond to them.

We choose short text for the purpose of comprehension instruction for the following reasons:

- It is easily read out loud, which gives everyone in the room a common literary experience and builds classroom community.
- It is often well crafted, with vivid language and striking illustrations or photographs.
- It provides an intense focus on issues of critical importance to readers of all ages.
- It is authentic and prepares children for the reading they will encounter outside of school.
- It is self-contained and provides a complete set of thoughts, ideas, and information for the entire group to mull over.
- It is easily reread to clarify confusion and better construct meaning.
- It is accessible to readers of many different learning styles and ages.
- It allows even very young children to engage in critical and interpretive thinking regardless of their decoding capability. Ideas about the reading are easily shared and discussed.
- It provides ample opportunities for modeling and thinking aloud.
- Teachers can provide students with anchor experiences through short-text reading that students can call upon later to help comprehend longer or more difficult text.
- Picture books and many short-text forms cover an extraordinary range of topics, ideas, and issues.

Collecting Short Text

In these days of ever-changing airline regulations, Steph still tries to lug a bag the size of a small Buick onto every flight. One time, she reached the gate and was asked to check her bag. She did so quickly and without regret, until she sat down in the plane and realized that she had inadvertently checked all of her reading material. Four hours without print! For someone who reads at red lights, this was just short of disastrous.

After several minutes of watching the oxygen-mask demonstration, memorizing the emergency exits, listening to the cockpit on the headset, and clicking her tongue, she reached into the seat pocket in front of her and pulled out *Hemispheres Magazine*, the United Airlines in-flight magazine. Although she flew regularly, she had never opened one before, and her expectations were less than sky high. She turned to an article on cruising, which began as follows:

> *When I was young and slippery as a sea squirt, I spent a sun-splashed summer polishing brass for the glory of waterborne commerce. In those long glorious sea days, we glided into tropical ports—dead slow—in the early morning, the sea like melted glass, the ship causing barely a ripple. You could feel the faint beat of the engines and hear the steady wash of creaming water alongside. The anchor chain went out, the bridge telegraphed "finished with engines" and we looked wonder of wonders on a foreign land. My old cargo line called at dusty little coffee ports, but they were Paris, London and Rome to me. I thought then that traveling by ship was the best way to see the world. I still do. (Keating 1998)*

They say necessity is the mother of invention. If Steph hadn't mistakenly checked her reading material, she would have missed this stunning text. Compelling short text is everywhere. We just need to live in a way that lets us find it. Pore over newspapers, magazines, travel books, brochures, and picture books. The next time you read an article, a poem, or a short story that really grabs you, think about why. Don't just toss it away. Clip it and file it even if you don't know exactly how you will use it. In all likelihood, you will find a place for it in your teaching sooner or later. When we collect and save short text, we consider the following:

Purpose. When we create instruction around picture books and other short text, we need to be clear about what we want children to learn from the particular experience. Do we want to model a specific strategy or build background knowledge on a particular topic? Sometimes a thoughtful picture book may be the best way to launch a discussion about a pressing issue like racism or an unfamiliar topic like the Great Depression. The clearer we are about our instructional focus, the easier it is to match books with our teaching goals.

Audience. The interests, ages, and learning needs of our students are paramount in choosing texts for teaching. Awareness of our students' backgrounds and experiences is essential if we are to select books for them that, as librarian Fran Jenner says, "touch their souls." First-grade students in a Denver classroom read, debated, and loved Mary Hoffman's *Amazing Grace* until the book fell apart. A replacement copy was a small price to pay for these children's strong and personal connections to the book.

Genre. Teachers in literature-based classrooms have always focused on genre studies in folk tales, fairy tales, realistic fiction, historical fiction, and so on, as a mainstay of their reading instruction. We choose a variety of genres in short-text form, including poetry, short stories, essays, letters, feature articles, and columns, to expose our students to the different characteristics of each form. The recent explosion in nonfiction trade book publishing has made it possible to teach almost any genre or topic with picture books and other nonfiction text. Trade books haven't yet replaced textbooks as a staple in classrooms, although we long for the day that they do!

Topic. We always make sure that kids have opportunities to choose any book for investigation and independent reading. But we also collect books in relation to a specific topic or curricular focus. In science and social studies, kids do not all have to read the same textbook, nor should they. Topic-specific text sets, often kept in baskets or special shelves made up of nonfiction trade books, picture books, magazines, and newspaper articles, build kids' background knowledge and provide additional opportunities to explore, learn more about the topic, and share information. The time we spend collecting these texts is worth it, because it allows us to differentiate instruction and gear our teaching to students' needs and interests.

Writing quality. We look for vivid writing like that in the cruising article from *Hemispheres Magazine*. A *Denver Post* article that has always appealed to us described a phantom snowstorm as follows: "The forecast for Friday promised much of Colorado a full-fledged affair with the snow, but all the storm could muster was a cheap kiss on the cheek. An overnight snowstorm that swirled its way into the state barely flirted with the metro area but dumped up to 10 inches in parts of southeast Colorado" (Esquibel 1999). What a charming metaphor!

Text structure and features. We clip different short-text forms that showcase a variety of structures and features. We find articles that are framed around a specific text structure, such as compare and contrast, and look at them closely to better recognize and understand the structure the next time we meet it. We look for pieces containing features and visuals, such as headings, bold print, charts, and graphs, so that we can show authentic examples of these and discover their purpose.

When choosing short text, we need to be thoughtful consumers of fiction and nonfiction. We might ask, Is the writing well crafted? Does a story strike our imagination, allow for interpretation, and make us think? Is a nonfiction text logically organized and easy to understand? Is the language clear and vivid? Does the author's choice of information and presentation pique our interest in a subject?

Choosing Short Text for Comprehension Instruction

Certain genres and forms lend themselves to teaching certain strategies. Realistic fiction and memoirs often spur connections and questions in readers. Poetry often stimulates visualizing and inferential thinking. We frequently choose nonfiction pieces to teach determining importance and synthesizing information. Certain authors, too, cause us to activate one strategy or another. Eve Bunting's picture books often leave us asking questions. We might rely on inferring when we read a book by Chris Van Allsburg such as *The Stranger*, the mysterious story of a wanderer who may be Jack Frost. And we have found that books by Jonathan London and Steve Jenkins are great for teaching visualizing. We recognize that all text, genre, and forms foster a wide range of thinking, but we find that some lend themselves to a particular strategy or two for the purpose of instruction.

Here are some brief guidelines for finding texts that support the teaching of specific strategies.

- Activating and connecting to background knowledge: We choose text that kids are likely to have some prior knowledge about on topics such as pets, family, common childhood experiences, school, and so forth. When kids read text on topics that are familiar to them, they are more likely to connect new information to what they already know in order to construct meaning.
- Questioning: We choose text that sparks wonder and inquiry. Text and topics for which readers lack schema often spur them to ask questions.
- Inferring: We choose text that is ambiguous and nudges the reader to think about what they know and merge their thinking with clues in the text to make an inference or draw a conclusion.
- Visualizing: We choose text in which the writer paints pictures with the words and uses active verbs and specific nouns to show rather than merely tell the story or information.

And we choose from among a variety of texts when teaching readers to monitor their comprehension, determine importance, and summarize and synthesize, because we apply these strategies whenever we read. Above all, we keep in mind that we teach our kids to use a repertoire of comprehension strategies actively and flexibly in every text they read. See Appendix A, our annotated trade book bibliography, where we often suggest what we would emphasize when teaching with a particular book.

Magazines, Newspapers, and Web Reading

We are constantly on the lookout for well-crafted, interesting short text for the purpose of teaching comprehension. Magazines and newspapers are full of useful and compelling information, but we sometimes forget to share them in school. *Kids Discover, Time for Kids,* and *WR News* (formerly *Weekly Reader*) all feature strong writing, interesting content, and an abundance of text and visual features such as photographs, illustrations, graphs, diagrams, and maps. Trade magazines lend themselves to teaching comprehension in both the science and social studies content areas. Articles from *Ranger Rick, National Geographic Explorer, Click,* and *Ask* have helped us model how to ask questions as we begin animal research. *Cobblestone: The History Magazine for Young People*; *Faces: People, Places, and Cultures*; and *Appleseeds* are particularly good magazines for addressing social studies content. They rarely fail as sources of information and strong models for writing.

The many forms in magazines and newspapers, including essays, editorials, feature articles, sports stories, and business updates, give kids in the class the widest range of possibilities for finding and reading interesting text. And more and more frequently much of our reading and research comes from the Web. Internet articles give us the most current and up-to-date information. We need to pack our classrooms with magazines, newspapers, and Web reading as well as with books. Short texts often rescue us from turning a mini-lesson into what we sheepishly call a maxi-lesson. When we use just a little bit of text for a demonstration, students can get the point, teachers can stick to the point, and everyone can get on with what's most important: students reading and practicing on their own. (See Appendix B for a list of magazines, newspapers, and websites, all of which provide valuable reading opportunities.)

The Possibilities of Picture Books

Picture books offer certain unique advantages when we deliver instruction. Of all literature that lends itself to reading comprehension strategy instruction, picture books top the list. Why?

We believe that interest is essential to comprehension. If we read material that doesn't engage us, we probably won't remember much. Engagement leads to remembering what is read, acquiring knowledge, and enhancing understanding. Picture books, both fiction and nonfiction, are more likely to hold our attention and engage us than dry, formulaic text. There's nothing like a striking photograph of the flukes of a killer whale jutting out from a sky-blue sea to capture a reader's interest. Readers are more likely to comprehend material that interests them and that is written in a compelling way.

Picture books have been a prominent feature of elementary classrooms for decades. Elementary teachers the world over share compelling picture books with kids. But elementary kids can't have all the fun! There is a picture book for every reader and a reader for every picture book. The wide range of themes, issues, words, and ideas reach out into classrooms like tentacles drawing in each member, regardless of the different learning styles, ages, reading levels, or prior experiences. We need to think about *all* the students who can benefit from picture books. The teachers portrayed in this book use picture books with the broadest spectrum of students.

Picture Books with Older Kids

High school teacher Cris Tovani surprised a group of visiting teachers when she read aloud a picture book to her college-bound, twelfth-grade world literature students. The book, *Rose Blanche* by Roberto Innocenti, set during World War II, recounts the story of a young German girl who passes a concentration camp on the way to school each day. Her daily journey leads her from curiosity to sympathy to action. "I never think to read picture books to my high school kids," one teacher whispered to another.

"Nor I," her teammate said, nodding in agreement.

Cris's students were mesmerized. Several dried their eyes as she read. The power of well-written picture books cannot be overestimated. Traditionally viewed as a genre reserved solely for younger children, picture books lend themselves to comprehension strategy instruction and guided discussion at every grade level. Older kids may balk when you first share picture books with them. Comments such as "Why are you reading those baby books?" will dissipate, however, when you share powerful picture books that are filled with sophisticated content best suited to older students.

Picture Books with Young Children

Don't readers need to be able to decode before they can comprehend? is a question we are frequently asked. We have found that we can begin teaching comprehension in preschool and kindergarten even though we recognize that young children are mostly nonreaders at this age. But teaching reading comprehension is mostly about teaching thinking. We can teach readers strategies for thinking through listening and viewing the illustrations as well as through reading.

Books written with emergent readers in mind focus primarily on the decoding aspect of reading. Short words, repeated phrases, and patterns are great for decoding and enjoying the sound of language but offer little to prompt thinking. When we read out loud to kids, we expose them to more sophisticated text that requires them to think. We eliminate the barriers that face young readers who can't decode text yet. Steph has read *Up North at the Cabin* to kindergartners as well as to eighth graders.

Picture Books with Reluctant Readers

There are no better print materials to use with reluctant readers than picture books. The pictures complement the text to help less proficient readers access meaning. The topics, ideas, and issues are often sophisticated and prompt stimulating discussion. Readers can choose from many different levels and genres on a single topic. The shorter form is less intimidating than longer chapter books.

Nonfiction picture books, in particular, convey fascinating information through the use of vivid photographs, illustrations, and features such as bold print, italics, captions, and diagrams that support reluctant readers in their quest to gain information and understand the text. We can teach the meaning of these features and help readers use them to better understand. One distinct advantage of nonfiction literature is that it doesn't have to be read sequentially to get needed information. We can teach reluctant readers to use the table of contents to search for the content that is most interesting to them or the section that will best serve their purpose.

But sometimes reluctant intermediate and middle school readers are more reticent to choose picture books than their proficient reader counterparts. They believe that reading picture books will further identify them as unsuccessful readers. We need to promote picture books by reading them out loud, both fiction and nonfiction. Book choice is contagious. If we read picture books and share our passion for them, kids will choose them, too. In classrooms where proficient readers and their teachers choose compelling picture books, reluctant readers climb aboard.

Picture Books with Linguistically Diverse Learners

For kids who are learning English, any text with pictures can be a lifeline. When kids are able to view the illustrations and photographs in relation to the language, they have a better shot at making sense of the ideas, story lines, and information in the text. Sometimes kids from other countries lack the background knowledge about topics that we frequently study in school. Picture books in science and social studies build background and make the content comprehensible for English language learners. Big books, posters, cut-up calendars, realia and photographs from magazines and newspapers are essential

DVD

materials for teaching kids with limited English proficiency. An added bonus is that any materials and resources that make information and concepts more concrete enhance learning for everyone. Adding these visuals into our daily lessons makes a huge difference in kids' interest, engagement, and understanding. See our video *Reading the World: Content Comprehension with Linguistically Diverse Learners* (2005) for additional ideas for teaching English language learners.

Additionally, we frequently choose picture books that our kids can connect with. At Denver's Horace Mann Middle School, many of the kids come from Mexico. They arrive daily and begin to make their way in a new world of English, strange food, unfamiliar teachers, and fat textbooks. Using picture books with ESL students can ease life in this new world, particularly if the books relate to their past experiences.

Kristi Sutherland, an enthusiastic first-year teacher, had reported an extreme lack of interest in reading on the part of many of the kids in her seventh-grade room. She knew that for her students to engage in reading, they must connect the text to their lives and activate their prior knowledge. She also knew that many of them had rich lives back in Mexico, but they were reluctant to share their past experiences for a variety of cultural, personal, and practical reasons. Kristi felt that their rich experiences were undervalued in this new American culture.

Steph and Kristi looked long and hard before discovering Eve Bunting's *Going Home*, a book that told the story of a family living in Los Angeles who returned to their hometown in Mexico at Christmastime. When the teachers finished reading the story, the middle schoolers swarmed around the book. Kristi commented that kids who had never responded to a book seemed to be overjoyed with this one. Kristi recognized and valued all of her kids' prior experiences, both in Mexico and in Denver. And she knew that building on their past experiences would enhance their understanding.

Teachers often tell us that they understand the need to activate children's prior knowledge and experience when they teach, but that some of their kids, particularly those from more impoverished neighborhoods, "don't have any prior knowledge" to activate. It's true that some kids come to school with more experience with books than others. But all kids bring a wealth of life experience that we can build on to enhance understanding, even though much of that prior knowledge may lie outside the realm of books.

Kristi and the seventh graders at Horace Mann teach us one of the most important lessons. Classrooms where children's personal histories are valued serve as learning communities that respect differences. Before teachers can create a climate of mutual respect, they must help kids understand and value their differences. Sharing books that kids connect with sparks their interest in reading and builds community.

Picture Books to Build Background Knowledge and Teach Content

It's no secret that trade books are extraordinarily effective for teaching content. In many of the schools we know, teachers and librarians find picture books like Patricia Polacco's *Pink and Say*, Ann Turner's *Nettie's Trip South*, and Stewart Lees's *Runaway Jack* essential for beginning a study of the Civil War. Biographies like Pam Ryan Munoz's *When Marian Sang*, the story of the famous opera singer, Marian Anderson, or Joseph Bruchac's *Squanto's Journey*, a narrative about the surprising life of Squanto and the first Thanksgiving, encourage us to read and write about people in history. Thoughtful picture books about ecological topics, such as Jane Yolen's *Letting Swift River Go* or Emily Arnold McCully's *Squirrel and John Muir*, are ideal for launching a study of environmental concerns. Building text sets in a particular topic or genre is a good start, but focusing on content alone isn't enough.

Teaching students to read text strategically sharpens and enhances their understanding of the content. At the same time, we can bring up issues, problems, and concerns without deluging students with facts and information. Unlike longer nonfiction or reference materials, picture books and other short texts focus our attention on one issue or topic at a time. Curricular stalwarts such as history and geography benefit from an ever-growing collection of picture books covering every conceivable time period and culture. Using picture books, children can investigate topics as diverse as the predatory patterns of great white sharks and the contemporary settlement at Dharamsala, the refuge in India where Tibetans strive to preserve their culture. And science trade books provide ample opportunity for children to ask and answer many of the questions they have about the natural world.

Picture Books That Challenge Kids to Think

Just as we read difficult books ourselves, it's important to share books that are a stretch for children. We usually find that if a book is clearly and engagingly written, young children can follow intricate plot lines and understand complex characterization. In fact, books with more ambiguity and mystery about them are sometimes more likely to hold our students' attention and prompt questions and inferences. We've noticed that stories and narratives set in strange cultures or unfamiliar historical periods often result in more rather than less interest. Stories in familiar circumstances with straightforward characters and obvious plots require less of students in the strategic thinking department.

Nonfiction books are often challenging to read and filled with sophisticated information that kids love. Students are fascinated by books on unfamiliar but compelling topics, such as *Rosa* by Nikki Giovanni; *Luba: The Angel of Bergen-Belsen*, as told to Michelle McCann, and *Woody Guthrie: Poet of the People* by Bonnie Christiansen—all books about remarkable people in difficult circumstances. We know many kids who would rather read nonfiction than a riveting mystery or adventure story and have learned over and over never to underestimate what kids can understand when motivated to do so.

Choosing Picture Books Just Because We Love Them

We remember the words of the writer C. S. Lewis when we choose books for reading and instruction: "No book is really worth reading at the age of ten which is not equally (and often far more) worth reading at the age of fifty" (Cullinan 1981). When we find a book that inspires our teaching, we can hardly wait to see how children will respond to it. We are hopeful that it will engage them. The best reason of all to read a picture book to a group of students is simply because you love it. Anne and her colleague Nancy Burton made frequent trips to a local bookstore to purchase books for their classroom library. One day they became so engrossed in choosing books that they never noticed when an over-efficient bookstore employee unloaded the mountain of books they had stacked in their cart. Thinking no one in their right mind would buy that many books, she had quietly reshelved each one of them. So, unless you live next door to the public library, beware. Children's books can be habit-forming.

Enthusiasm for books is contagious. Sometimes we become so focused on a theme or curricular topic that we put off sharing our favorites. Big mistake! Steph still often reads Margaret Wise Brown's *The Sailor Dog* to kids regardless of their age. It was the first book she ever really read, and she can't not share it with kids because it means so much to her. Kids pick up on this. Invariably, the moment she closes the book, they leap up and grab for it en masse, even eighth graders. We also choose books we have always wanted to read but have never gotten around to. Anne has a list of several dozen. Once in a while, she picks one up and reads it to the kids. In this way, they learn about the book together, which gives everyone a fresh, authentic experience.

Sharing our thoughts about why we love a book allows students to get to know us better and shows them how discerning we are about what we read. Children in classrooms where everyone talks about books, teachers included, aren't afraid to venture their thoughts about a book. There's no better way to encourage readers than to ask them to contribute their favorites to a classroom text set. And students can't resist becoming engaged when we consistently ask them to voice their honest opinions.

Beyond Picture Books: Choosing Longer Text

Many of the texts that launch the lessons in this book are short—picture books, magazine articles, poems, and so forth. Don't get us wrong. We love long text, too, and most of our kids are reading chapter books and other longer forms as well as short pieces. As we work with book clubs and literature circles or when everyone in the class has a different novel going, we remind our kids of the many lessons we have done with short text so they will apply what they learned to their ongoing independent reading in longer text.

Our kids read long chapter books and love them. And they also read lengthy nonfiction—anthologies, trade books, even textbooks. They may not read these books cover to cover, but they get important information from them. Books like Phillip Hoose's *We Were There Too*, a compelling compendium of vignettes of children in American history that engages kids who are surprised at the roles kids played in history, and Joy Hakim's series on history (A History of US) and on science (The Story of Science) are among our favorites for getting essential content information written in an interesting way. So as you work with the strategies in Part II of this book, think of ways to apply them in longer text.

Children's Choices: Helping Students Choose Text

Kids must be reading texts they can and want to read if they are to successfully read, think, and get something meaningful from text. The reading workshop model described in Chapter 3 includes large uninterrupted blocks of time for readers to engage in text reading. During these reading blocks, students read independently and activate strategies to comprehend text. The teachers portrayed in this book understand that kids are more likely to become engaged in reading if they choose their own books. This is easier said than done. Many readers abandon books they can't read or find boring. Sometimes a very compelling book is too difficult.

Teachers can suggest ways to support students in book choice and can explicitly teach students how to choose books they want to read as well as books they are able to read. Teachers recognize that the reader faces a number of considerations when deciding what to read.

Choosing Books for Readability: Easy, Just Right, and Challenge Books

Many teachers encourage readers to choose a book according to how hard or easy it is to read. Readability is an important factor when readers choose books if our goal is to get better at reading. We encourage young readers to think about the level of a book. We talk to them about three kinds of books according to readability: easy, just right, and challenge books (Hagerty 1992). We model each of these categories by showing young readers how we choose books ourselves from a readability standpoint. Our kids often don't realize that adults can't read everything. They seem to believe that grown-ups have already learned all there is to know about reading. We are here to fill them in on that closely guarded secret: Adults continue to learn to read throughout their lives, and even sophisticated adult readers encounter text that challenges them.

To model this, we bring in three books that we consider easy, just right, and challenging. Steph shares Dave Barry's *Best Travel Guide Ever* as an easy book she reads over and over. She loves his sense of humor and connects much of what he writes to her own zany household. She explains that for her the book practically reads itself. She can read all of the words, and she understands all of the ideas. Next, we share a book that we find extremely challenging. For Steph, it might be a book about physics such as Stephen Hawking's *A Brief History of Time*. She explains that she has always been interested in physics and physicists, although she's never taken a course in physics and wasn't particularly good at math. She has started this book several times, but she doesn't understand quite a few of the words and many of the ideas, probably because of her lack of prior knowledge.

And then there is the just-right book. Just like baby bear's chair, this book fits like a glove. We can read most of the words and understand most of the ideas, but not every one necessarily. For Steph and Anne, it might be the novel or biography they keep on their nightstand, their favorite new professional book, or the *New Yorker* magazine. A just-right book challenges us to think but doesn't frustrate us when we read it.

We let kids know that reading is a bit like eating. If we only eat ice cream, we won't stay healthy, and if we only choose easy books, we won't get better at reading. Yet everyone needs a little ice cream now and then, and everyone needs a respite from difficult text, a moment to enjoy a good laugh from the comics or a Dave Barry column.

Similarly, if we only choose books that are too hard, we are likely to abandon them out of boredom or frustration. Some books are emotionally more rugged than others. Justin, a fourth grader, was reading *Bridge to Terabithia* by

Katherine Paterson in his book club. He was completely captured by the book but nevertheless suggested to the group, "Since we are reading such a sad book in November, we'd better read a funny one in December." A constant diet of sad books can be a downer for kids. We have to vary our diets both in eating and reading. Just as we generally try to choose healthy balanced meals, we can strive to choose just-right books most of the time.

As our demonstration nears an end, we reiterate that if we only choose easy or challenging books, we won't get better at reading. We close this mini-lesson by creating a chart together with the kids and then posting it in the room for all to see. The one that follows ends with a quote from Sam, a Denver fifth grader.

- *Easy books.* An easy book is a book in which you can read every word and understand every idea.
- *Challenge books.* A challenging book is a book where there are many words you can't read and many ideas you can't understand.
- *Just-right books.* A just-right book is a book where you can read most of the words, but not all, and you can understand most of the ideas, but not all.

"It is fine to read easy books sometimes and challenging books sometimes, but most of the time we try to choose books that are just right for us. That way we'll get better at reading."

One thing we share with our students is an exciting outcome of classifying books into these three categories: as we grow as readers, books that were once challenging suddenly seem just right and eventually even become easy. These easy, just right, and challenging designations can help readers recognize reading improvement.

Choosing Books for Purpose and Interest

Readability is only one factor in book choice. Teachers need to think beyond readability alone when helping students consider book choice. The subject, the author, the content, and the reasons to read all come into play when choosing books.

Teacher and author Cris Tovani believes that we must explicitly show our students how to choose a book based on three criteria. She asks her students to consider the following when they select a book:

- Purpose
- Interest
- Readability

Cris demonstrates this by asking young readers to list some different purposes they have for reading, and she records their responses on a chart. Their purposes include

- School assignments
- To find out information
- Entertainment
- To read instructions

Dear Ms. Urtz,
I'm reading about Misakes That Worked, and let me tell you, it is so funny!! I'll tell you about them Like did, you know that fuge was spossed to be carmel when it was made? And it got it's name from the lady who made it? She said "fuge," Because she wanted it to be carmel and saying "fuge "would be like saying "darn" or "shat"! ha! ha! Soon, I will read "Ocean Life but Mistakes that Worked is too interesting to just stop in the middle of. Well, I've got to read it so BYYYYE!

(Adding on) Sincerly, Julia

My favorite of Mistakes that Worked is potatoe chips. I know you have already read it, but isn't it SO fun- ny? I hope you liked it. BYYYYE (again)

Figure 5.1 Julia's Letter About *Mistakes That Worked*

- To cook something
- Just for fun

Cris emphasizes that these are but a few of the many purposes for reading and that purpose affects our book selection. She encourages the students to add more purposes to the chart whenever they arise.

Joaquin, a seventh grader at Horace Mann Middle School in Denver, noted that one of his purposes for reading was to put his little sister to sleep at night. Cris asked him if he chose easy or hard books to do that. He said easy books, so his five-year-old sister could understand them. And as for interest, he said he might choose *Cinderella* because princesses were a big deal to his sister. In other words, his primary purpose in this instance was reading to his little sister. Help your students think of the many purposes for reading. Hopefully, they won't forget enjoyment. If they neglect to mention it, add it, or any other purpose you deem worthy, to the list.

Of course, we read out of interest. Nothing compels readers more than their personal interest in a piece of text. We have noticed that readers can read more difficult books if they are interested in the material. It is why textbooks are so tough for students to read. They are frequently written in a dull, dry, uninteresting way, making reading more challenging.

Interest is central to book choice for readers of every age. Text that addresses a reader's interest promotes engaged reading. Julia was so engaged in reading *Mistakes That Worked*, Charlotte Foltz Jones's book about inventions like Post-it notes that came about serendipitously, that she simply couldn't put it down. Her enthusiasm burst forth in a letter to Mary Buerger, her fourth-grade teacher, in which she mentioned that she would soon get back to a science book titled *Ocean Life* but not until she finished *Mistakes That Worked* (see Figure 5.1). For personal reading, adults primarily choose books based on their interests. Why expect kids to be any different?

Helping Kids Select Books to Read

To scaffold book selection, we ask kids how they choose a book. What exactly do they do when they reach for a book on the shelf? We record their responses on a chart in hopes that some of these suggestions will be contagious. The kids in Leslie Blaumann's class compiled the following list for how they choose books:

- Reading the back
- Reading the flap
- Reading the first page—an interesting lead can reel us in
- Reading the first few pages

- Reading the table of contents
- The title
- The length
- The level
- Flipping through the pages
- Reading the last page
- The pictures
- The cover
- The author
- The subject
- The series
- The genre
- Recommendation

All of these are helpful suggestions, but Leslie understands that if she merely copied this list each year and posted it, the kids in her class would likely ignore it. This list makes sense to them because they create it based on their own needs and practices.

Don't be afraid to weigh in here, however. You, too, are a member of the learning community in your classroom. Leslie recognized that she generally chose a book based on the recommendation of someone close to her. Recommendation never made the original list. So Leslie added it to the list. She wanted her students to know that in her experience the books she enjoyed most were those recommended by her friends and family, who know her and tend to suggest books they know would capture her interest. And in truth you even read such a book differently, sticking with it longer than you might otherwise if you had picked it yourself. You might think, well if my best friend thought it was so good, maybe I better hang in there a little longer.

Kids need to keep you apprised of their interests so that you can fill the room with books they will read. Post a chart where kids can record their interests and, more specifically, some books they would like to see in the classroom. That way, when teachers order books or head off to libraries, garage sales, and bookstores, they can look for those special books that kids in their classrooms yearn for.

Part II

Strategy Lessons

Chapter 6

Monitoring Comprehension: The Inner Conversation

"So tell me something. How many of you have ever found yourself reading something but thinking about something else?" Steph asked a group of seventh graders gathered in front of her during the last period of the day. The entire class shot their hands into the air. "Wow, all of you. Okay, take a minute and think about a time this has happened to you. Then turn and talk to a partner about what you were reading and what you were thinking about." The room exploded with chatter as kids shared their thinking. Apparently, this was routine stuff for them. After several minutes, Steph asked if anyone wanted to share his or her experience.

"It happened to me last period in science," Taunia ventured. "We were reading about atoms in the textbook, but I was thinking about something else."

"So what were you thinking about?" Steph asked. Taunia explained that Friday would bring the first middle school dance of the year and she and her mom had made a deal that if she did all of her chores that week, her mom would buy her a top that she had picked out at TJ Maxx the previous weekend. Today was the day, so she was focused on that top. Her main concern was whether it would still be there, since she knew that many of the items at TJ Maxx were one of a kind. However, she had taken action to increase her chances of securing that top. She had moved it from the girl's junior department to men's coats, hiding it deep in the middle of the size 46 rack. Now that's strategic!

If only all of our kids were as strategic about their reading as Taunia was about her outfit for the dance. Sometimes reading goes smoothly, and sometimes it doesn't. Sometimes readers can't get enough of a topic. Other times they could care less about it. Sometimes a lack of background knowledge interferes with reading and understanding. Other times a compelling topic engages readers throughout the text. Sometimes readers proceed seamlessly; other times they stumble because the text is too hard. And sometimes, they lose focus as Taunia did and don't even notice that they are no longer thinking about the words and ideas in the text.

Surprisingly, Taunia reported that she was able to answer the questions at the end of the atoms chapter, not because she understood what she read, but because all of the answers were in bold print. So she just skimmed the bold print answers and matched them to the questions they fit, another strategic act on Taunia's part. We want our kids to do more than skim bold print to discover answers. We want them to merge their thinking with the text information, building knowledge as they go. And we want them to stay engaged in their reading and be stimulated by their thinking.

In the lessons described in this chapter, we use explicit language that relates directly to monitoring comprehension. As you do these lessons, we suspect you'll hear your kids tell you that they need to stop, think, and react to the information, or that they have strayed from their inner conversation. We teach the language and lessons of monitoring so that our kids can monitor meaning, articulate their thinking, and become strategic readers who develop new insights.

Strategy Lessons: Monitoring Comprehension

Following the Inner Conversation

New

Purpose: Listening to the inner voice and leaving tracks of thinking
Resource: *Gleam and Glow,* by Eve Bunting
Responses: Sticky notes on a piece of paper on clipboards

Reading comprehension is an ongoing process of evolving thinking. When readers read and construct meaning, they carry on an inner conversation with the text. They hear a voice in their head speaking to them as they read—a voice that questions, connects, laughs, cries. This inner conversation helps readers monitor their comprehension and keeps them engaged in the story, concept, information, and ideas, allowing them to build their understanding as they go. Once we have modeled the inner conversation, readers will more seamlessly activate a particular strategy, such as questioning, connecting, or determining importance, when they read because they are more likely to notice and consider their thinking.

Interactive Reading Aloud
Steph launched this lesson on the inner conversation with a group of eighth graders at Horace Mann Middle School in San Diego. Most of the kids in the class were immigrants from a variety of countries around the world, including Somalia, Sudan, Cambodia, and Mexico. Steph chose to use Eve Bunting's picture book *Gleam and Glow*, a gripping fictionalized account of a true story from the war in Bosnia. In this story, a family is separated by the ravages of war and eventually reunited in a refugee camp. Steph knew that many of the kids in this class could readily relate to this story having been immigrants themselves, some even having lived in refugee camps at one time or another. So she purposely chose this book since the kids would likely connect to it. This lesson is part of our video series *Strategic Thinking* (2004).

DVD

Throughout the story the two young protagonists never forget the two pet fish, Gleam and Glow, who they were forced to leave behind, but who, amid the great destruction of war, survive and flourish in a pond behind the family's former home. Despite the loss of material possessions

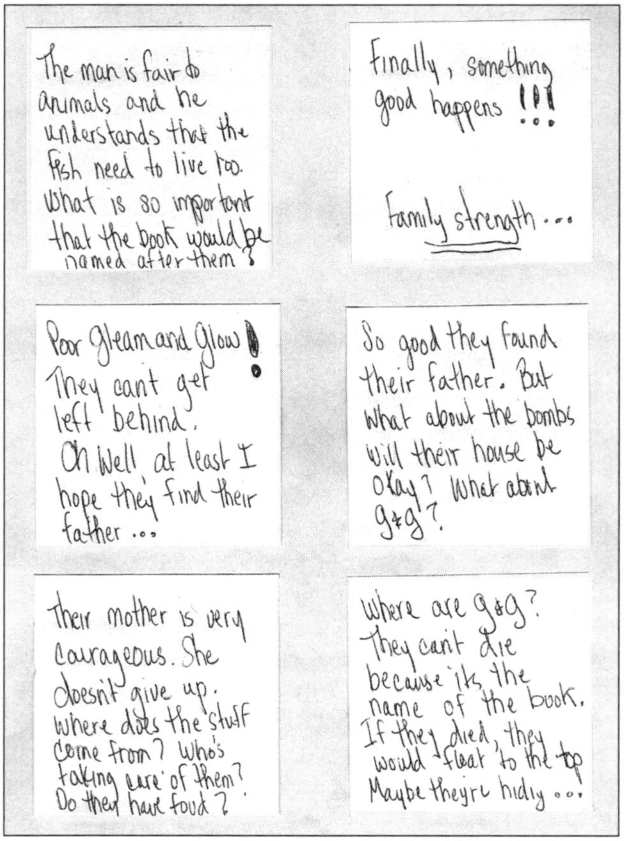

Figure 6.1 Sticky Notes on *Gleam and Glow*

and the disintegration of their former way of life, the family survives and emerges stronger than ever, which in many ways parallels the story of the two fish, Gleam and Glow. In the end, the story remains one of determination, hope, and survival.

With the kids gathered in front of her, Steph began by saying, "Nothing is more important during reading than the reader's thinking. I have chosen this book because it makes me think about so many things. When readers pay attention and think about the words and ideas in the text, they carry on an inner conversation with the text. It is a quiet conversation that happens in the reader's head."

She then gave some examples of the kinds of things readers hear in their heads as they read. "When I read and pay attention, I hear a voice in my head that says different things to me. For instance, when I am confused I might hear something like *Huh, I don't get this part.* And when I read on, I might hear something like *Oh, now I get it.* Or when I meet new information, I might hear something like *Wow, I never knew that before.* This is the inner conversation that I have with the writer as I read. While I am reading to you, I want you to think about and notice what you hear in your inner conversation."

Steph then modeled her thinking with the first page of *Gleam and Glow*. As she did, she pointed out her connections, questions, and reactions and jotted her thoughts on sticky notes showing how she left tracks of her thinking.

Next Steph continued to read the story, engaging the kids in guided practice. Sometimes she simply asked them to turn and talk about their thinking. This is an open-ended thinking prompt that we encourage teachers to ask frequently. Other times, she asked a more specific thinking prompt, such as, "Turn and talk about the mom in this story. What are you thinking about her role in this story?" This more specific thinking prompt gets kids to talk about a certain aspect of the story that may help them focus on a specific theme. What is important here is that she varied the thinking prompts from open ended to specific and gave kids a lot of time to interact with the text.

At the end of the story, kids got into groups of four and used their sticky notes responses to fuel a discussion of the story as Steph moved around between the groups and listened in on them. Upon conclusion of the lesson, Steph asked them to share some of what they learned about monitoring comprehension and the inner conversation as well as their thoughts on the story. See Figure 6.1. (See additional examples of their inner conversations on sticky notes in the assessment section at the end of this chapter.)

New

Noticing When We Stray from the Inner Conversation

Purpose: Monitoring the inner voice to focus thinking and "fix up" comprehension
Resource: A piece of adult text
Response: Two-column chart titled Why Meaning Breaks Down/What to Do About It

Only when readers listen to their inner voice will they notice when they stray from an active inner conversation with the text. In truth, it is natural for our minds to wander when we read.

An idea in the text may trigger a personal connection and suddenly we have no idea what we are reading about, but we can remember our first prom with clarity! Or we come to a part where we lack the background knowledge needed to process and understand; meaning breaks down and we find ourselves thinking of something else. Perhaps we are thinking about our to-do list and we simply can't concentrate on our reading no matter how hard we try. When we teach our kids to listen to the inner conversation and notice when they stray, they are more likely to catch their wandering minds sooner, stop, and refocus before they become completely befuddled.

Share stories with your kids of times you found your mind wandering when reading or of times when the text was simply too dense for you to comprehend. One time, Steph brought in Azar Nafisi's *Reading Lolita in Tehran* to model how she found herself straying from an inner conversation when reading. The book follows the story of an English professor in Iran who led a secretive women's book group that studied books by authors including F. Scott Fitzgerald, Vladimir Nabokov, Jane Austen, and Henry James. When Steph got to the section on Henry James, her attention really began to flag because she had never read James and knew so little about him and his work. As she read, she kept hearing herself say, *Huh? I don't get this part.* She tried to go back, but lost meaning as her mind kept drifting off. She discovered when reading this section that if she were going to understand it, she needed to read the words more closely, rereading frequently. In most of the book, she could read quickly, sometimes skipping words and scanning the text, because she had enough background knowledge to make sense without reading every word. But not with James.

Bring in a text of your own where you have noticed meaning break down and you have struggled to pay attention and understand. Show the kids how you notice yourself straying from an engaged read and what you do to get back on top of meaning. Construct an anchor chart with the kids. Share a couple of reasons that meaning breaks down for you as Steph did and write them on the chart. Then ask kids to turn and talk about what causes them to lose focus when they read and discuss what to do about it in partners, having them share their responses. You'll see some amazing ideas that we really need to take to heart when teaching reading! A co-constructed chart with a group of fifth graders follows.

Monitoring Comprehension

Why Meaning Breaks Down	*What to Do About It*
Fatigue (Steph)	Reread to construct meaning.
	Put the book down when too tired.
Not enough background knowledge (Steph)	Focus and read words more carefully than usual.
Thirst	Get up and get a drink of water.
Stress	Talk to a teacher or friend about what's on your mind.
Don't like the book	Choose another book.
Too hard	Think about what you know and try to connect it to new information.
Boring	Choose another book if possible or talk to someone who finds the topic interesting.

(See a student example of a co-constructed anchor chart like this in the assessment section of this chapter.)

One caveat. As adult readers, understanding what we read is often automatic. That automaticity makes it difficult for us to experience what less developed readers go through every day to make sense of text. Try this on your own: Choose a challenging piece of text, one that is difficult for you to understand, and then try to peel back the layers of your own process as you read it, thinking about what you do to stay on top of meaning, monitor understanding, and make sense of your reading. You will notice yourself listening to the voice in your head and noticing when meaning breaks down, going back and rereading to clarify understanding. Paying attention to your own reading process as you navigate difficult text will give you a heads up on what's happening to your kids when they find themselves in similar situations. There is no better way to help our kids read than to think about our own reading process and consider what we do to repair meaning when it breaks down.

Knowing When You Know and Knowing When You Don't Know

Purpose: Monitoring comprehension to clarify confusion or answer questions about the text
Resources: Any number of picture books and magazines selected by the students
Responses: Sticky notes coded Huh? for confused or with a light bulb for the reader's illumination

A useful technique for monitoring comprehension involves the code Huh? We have noticed that when kids become confused by their reading or when they have a question, they are likely to stop, scrunch up their noses, and say Huh? as Steph did as she read *Reading Lolita in Tehran.*

We can't stress how important it is for teachers to realize when kids are confused and to help them do something about it. We encourage kids to code a sticky note Huh? and place it at the point of confusion in the text. We model this ourselves, sharing the language we hear in our heads when we are confused by the text and we write Huh? on the top half of the sticky note, leaving the bottom half blank.

As kids continue reading or rereading to clarify meaning, they often clear up their confusion or find the answer in the text. At this point, we encourage them to move their original sticky note to the place where their confusion is clarified or their question is answered. There, hot on the heels of Huh?, we encourage them to sketch a light bulb on the bottom half of the sticky note to signal their new understanding or to write the answer to their question. This coding technique supports their effort to monitor their comprehension and stay on track with their thinking.

Noticing and Exploring Thinking

New

Purpose: Listening to the inner voice and responding to the text
Resource: *Little Mama Forgets,* by Robin Cruise
Responses: Large sticky notes and an anchor chart marked What the Story Makes Me Think About

Monitoring comprehension is about more than simply following along with thinking. Monitoring happens when readers pay attention to their own thinking and explore it.

All of the lessons in this book promote active literacy. In some lessons, we have kids write as we read. In others, they write after they read. In many, they turn and talk while we read out loud. Sometimes they just read, read, read! In this lesson, we simply read a book without saying a word—that's right, no thinking aloud! Then we ask kids to write down their thinking *after* we read, share their writing with a partner, and have a conversation.

Liz, a second-grade teacher, chose Robin Cruise's *Little Mama Forgets*, the poignant story of a little girl and her beloved grandmother who is suffering age-related memory loss. In this book, the author explores the tender relationship between these two characters changing places as it were, the girl growing up and the grandmother forgetting more each day. Liz suspected that this text would remind kids of their own grandparents, other elderly people in their lives, or various family stories they had heard. She introduced the book by telling the story of her own adored grandfather, who became more forgetful as he grew old. She mentioned that this story reminded her of that relationship. Liz read the book aloud straight through. When she finished she gave them each a large sticky note and explained that she didn't want them to retell the story, but rather to write down what the story made them think about, their thoughts and reactions, their inner conversation.

After kids jotted down their thinking, Liz asked them to turn to a partner and read what they wrote as well as talk about it. When kids finished their conversations, some shared their thinking with the whole group. To conclude, Liz collected the sticky notes and, with the kids' permission, put them all up on the chart titled What Little Mama Forgets Makes Me Think About. This became a wonderful anchor lesson and anchor chart to remind the kids to focus on their thinking when they read, not merely on the details, the plot, or the sequence of events of the story.

Read, Write, and Talk

New

Purpose: Teaching readers to stop, think, and react to informational text
Resource: *Time for Kids* article "Could You Survive a Week Without TV?"
Response: Jotting thinking in the margins

Reading is a social act. We all love to talk about what we read: sharing the latest novel with a friend, reacting to an outrageous editorial with a colleague, or exploring a picture book with a child. Read, Write, and Talk is a practice that gives readers an opportunity to think, record their thoughts, and then talk about their reading. We model our own inner conversation with the text and jot down our thoughts in the margins of a piece of text and then give kids a chance to try it on their own. We explain that when readers read informational text, it is a good idea to stop and jot down their thinking while they read so that they can add

Figure 6.2 Student Responses to an Article and Their Talk with a Partner

TV Too much violence
TV makes children aggresive

I learned some background knowledge.

I thought it was worth while Because it was interesting to see what other people had to say, and what they thought was cool.

I couldn't belive that 93,000 tigers died in 94 years! Also it's very cool that ever tige has different stripes.

People are actually supporting tests & I'm thinking if they were ever kids once

My conversation with Emma was very useful because we talked about How UNFAIR it is to test. she made me think about stuff I never realized when I read the article

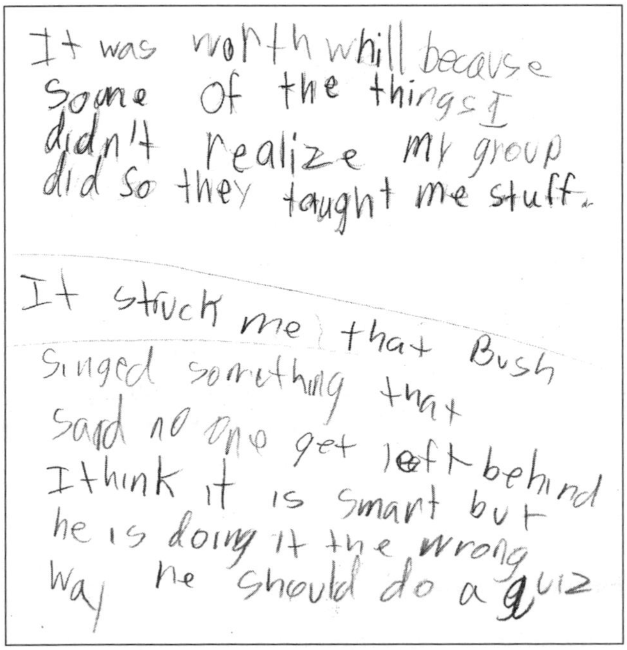

It was worth whill because some of the things I didn't realize my group did so they taught me stuff.

It struck me that Bush singed something that said no one get left behind I think it is smart but he is doing it the wrong way he should do a quiz

Figure 6.2 Student Responses to an Article and Their Talk with a Partner *(continued)*

to their store of knowledge, remember the information, and better learn and understand it. We teach kids to merge their thinking with the text by stopping, thinking, and reacting to the information—STR for short. When they finish reading, they can find someone who read the same piece and use their margin notes to talk further about their reading. When kids notice their thinking while they read and engage in purposeful talk afterwards, they comprehend more completely and think beyond the text.

Steph launched Read, Write, and Talk with a group of fourth graders, using an article from *Time for Kids* titled "Could You Survive a Week Without TV?" She modeled her own thinking, remembering to stop, think, and react to information as she read. In this way, she hoped that the kids would get an explicit idea of her thinking process—how she merged her thinking with the information by jotting down her connections, questions, and reactions.

After modeling her thinking by interacting with the text for a few paragraphs, Steph invited the kids to jot down their thinking on their own copies of the article during guided practice. She continued to read but stopped every few moments and asked them to jot their reactions in the margins and turn and talk to each other about their thinking. When she finished reading, Steph asked the kids to flip over their papers and write down three things: (1) something they learned that they think is important to remember; (2) how talking to a partner helped them understand what they read; (3) any lingering questions that they still had. The kids shared their responses with the whole group and talked about how stopping, thinking, and reacting helped them understand what they read and if and how talking to a partner added to the experience.

After we do this together as a class, we suggest kids try it on their own. We usually offer a choice of three pieces at different levels and on different topics and ask kids to read a piece, jot down their thinking, and then find someone who read the same article and have a conversation with them. Some of their responses to different articles are shown in Figure 6.2. (See additional examples of kids' thinking tracks in the assessment section at the end of this chapter.) Read, Write, and Talk is not a lesson, but rather a practice that we implement with science, social studies, mathematics, and even textbooks. It sets up a way to interact with text and with each other. For further information about how to launch this practice, see our video *Read, Write, and Talk* (2005b).

Monitoring comprehension is above all about engagement. When readers interact with the text, they are more apt to stay on top of meaning as they read. When readers are passive, not much happens and meaning eludes them. *Passive* may mean that readers are not interested in the text, find the text to be too difficult, or have insufficient background knowledge to understand. Whatever the reason, the result is that passive readers stray from an engaged read and lose track of meaning. Active reading is a dynamic process that puts the reader at the helm.

Teaching with the End in Mind: Assessing What We've Taught

Monitoring Comprehension

Based on the lessons in this chapter, we look for evidence that

1. *Students follow their inner conversation and leave tracks of their thinking.* We look for evidence of the reader's thinking, including their reactions, questions, connections, and inferences.
2. *Students notice when they stray from the inner conversation and repair comprehension—use fix-up strategies.* We look for evidence that the reader understood why meaning breaks down and how to go about repairing understanding.
3. *Students stop, think, and react to information as they read.* We look for evidence that the reader is stopping frequently, thinking about the information, and jotting down thoughts and reactions.

Suggestions for Differentiation

Monitoring at this point is very open-ended. We are not assuming that all kids know about or understand the importance of questioning or inferring. So we are really looking for the disposition to think about and react to what the reader hears and reads.

When modeling an interactive read-aloud, the teacher is doing much of the reading and the kids are listening. All kids are free to think about the ideas, because coding doesn't interfere. In this way, all kids can access the text. We ask kids to leave tracks of their thinking. Those who are less developed writers are encouraged to draw a picture or use a short code to represent their thinking. We also encourage kids to turn and talk to each other before writing to hone their ideas and rehearse what they are going to write down or share. Those who are unable to write at all can still construct and share meaning by talking to someone about their thinking. When we confer with kids, we realize that English language learners may be able to say more about their thinking and reactions than they are able to write. So we make sure that we talk with them a great deal to give them an ongoing opportunity to sort out and share their thinking.

For younger kids or English language learners, we might make a large copy of the text and together we monitor our thinking and chart our response right on the text. The poster-size text becomes an anchor chart that guides kids as they do their own reading and practice monitoring their own comprehension. If kids seem to be monitoring and using a number of strategies, such as questioning, connecting, and inferring, we review these and quickly move on to teaching a more sophisticated strategy.

Monitoring Comprehension Assessment Commentary

Sticky notes from an interacitve read-aloud with *Gleam and Glow* from the lesson "Following the Inner Conversation"

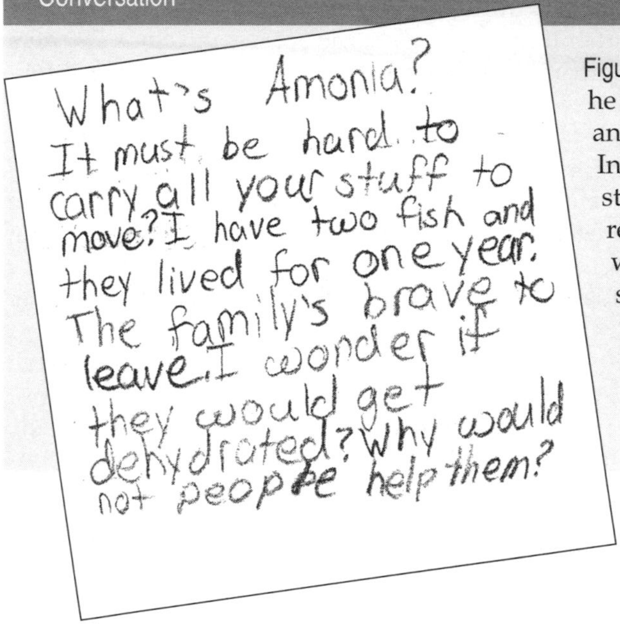

What's Amonia?
It must be hard to carry all your stuff to move? I have two fish and they lived for one year. The family's brave to leave. I wonder if they would get dehydrated? Why would not people help them?

Figure 6.3 When this child asks, "What is ammonia?" he is aware that he doesn't understand something, and we can tell he is monitoring his comprehension. In truth, we see a likely misconception; the girl in the story had *pneumonia*. We would stop and help the reader sort out the difference between the two words, but we would also let him know that by stopping and asking a question, he is doing exactly what we want him to. Additionally, we can see him inserting himself into the story with an inference, "it must be hard . . . ," and a connection to his own fish as well as more questions.

Figure 6.4 Here we see a drawing of a father leaving. We did not explicitly model drawing, but this student chose to illustrate his reaction, which is a terrific example of an authentic response to literature.

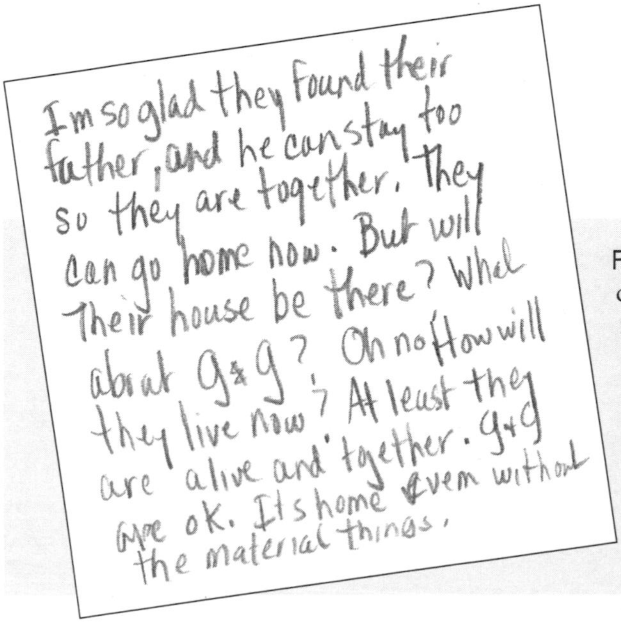

The father is leaving   Jim

I'm so glad they found their father, and he can stay too so they are together. They can go home now. But will their house be there? What about G&G? Oh no How will they live now? At least they are alive and together. G&G are ok. It's home even without the material things.

Figure 6.5 On this note, we get a running commentary. Some kids are ready to write as we read; others need us to stop more frequently so they can collect their thoughts and jot them down. This child is really listening to her inner conversation when she says, "Oh no, how will they live now?" after seeing that their house has burned down. And she comes up with her own synthesis in the last line: "It's home even without the material things."

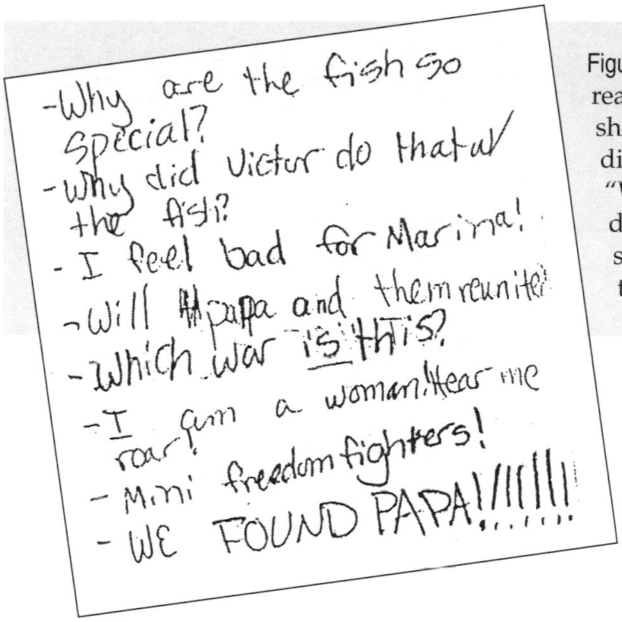

-Why are the fish so special?
-Why did Victor do that w/ the fish?
- I feel bad for Marina!
-Will papa and them reunite?
-Which war IS THIS?
-I am a woman.Hear me roar!
- Mini freedom fighters!
- WE FOUND PAPA!!!!!!!!!

Figure 6.6 This reader asks questions, expresses reactions, and shows her personality, especially when she says, "I am woman, hear me roar!" But the diagnostic words come at the end when she writes, "We found papa!" Notice the use of pronouns. She did not say, "They found their dad." Instead, she saw herself in the story at that point, which is one of those moments we live for as teachers.

Figures 6.7a and 6.7b This child is diagnosed with a processing deficit. He goes to the learning lab several days a week, and on two other days the special ed teacher comes into the classroom. He couldn't have read the book on his own, but he can think at the highest levels as is evidenced from his notes. On the first sticky note, he reacts to the fact that the family's house was burned to the ground with the question, "Why did they burn the houses?" and follows that up with perhaps the most important question of anyone in the class, "How could people do such a thing?" He also nails a parallel theme on the second sticky note, where he notices that Gleam and Glow survived just like the humans in the story. Many kids in the class did not recognize this, but interactive reading aloud levels the playing field and gives everyone a chance to weigh in with their thinking.

Ⓠ why did they bren Ⓠ the houses?
How could people do such a thing?

Ⓢ there alive!
Ⓢ there gest like humens.

Think sheet for noticing when meaning breaks down and how to fix up comprehension; Mathias used this in his own independent reading of *Gleam and Glow*

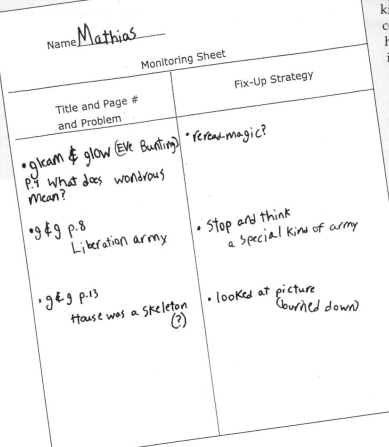

Figure 6.8 This think sheet supports kids to monitor and repair their comprehension as they read. Mathias has used a few fix-up strategies, including rereading, stopping and thinking, and looking at the picture. This think sheet scaffolds understanding and help kids remember to choose from a repertoire of strategies when meaning breaks down.

Figure 6.9
Sometimes we have kids jot their
thinking right on the text as Elizabeth did on her
independent reading of an article on testing. Her evolving thinking is
apparent when she reads that soon every third grader will face these tests, and she reacts by
writing *Glad I'm in fifth*. But as she reads on, she finds that older kids will also need to take these
tests and responds with *Darn!* We can see how she stops, thinks, and reacts to the information as she
reads. We look for questions, connections, and reactions. And we want to see thoughts in the
margins next to underlined portions, so the reader can go back and remember why he or she
underlined in the first place.

Chapter 7

Activating and Connecting to Background Knowledge: A Bridge from the New to the Known

A group of second graders swarmed around Anne as she read William Steig's delightful picture book *Amos and Boris*, the story of a friendship between a whale and a mouse, and the predicament they face when the whale becomes stranded on the beach. Amos, a tiny mouse, figures out how to get his gigantic friend Boris back into the ocean where he belongs. As they listened to a number of picture books by William Steig, the kids added more information to their store of background knowledge about his books, and they began to see a variety of connections. Rashid noticed that most of the characters were animals that could talk. Julianna observed that all the characters seemed to encounter difficult problems over the course of the story. The more these second graders read William Steig's books, the more they came to expect certain themes, humor, and ideas to emerge.

As serendipity would have it, the night after Anne read *Amos and Boris* to this group, she heard a remarkable story on National Public Radio of a whale marooned on a Texas beach. The local citizens of the town had turned out in shifts over a twenty-four-hour period to spray the whale with water in an attempt to keep it wet and alive till a helicopter could rescue it. Having once gone on a whale-watching expedition off the coast of California, Anne was drawn to the NPR story. When she woke up the next morning, all she could think about was that unfortunate whale, and she wondered if it had survived the night. The minute she arrived at school, she rushed off to the library to search the Internet for a news update. Much to her delight, the whale was still alive, so she took copies of the news bulletin to the classroom.

As the children listened to the unfolding news story, the discussion turned to the similarities between the stranded whale in Texas and Boris's quandary in the story. Several students coded the news transcripts with connections they noticed between Boris and the stranded Texas whale, and later that day a small group found the sad news online that the whale had died. Two children wrote the following brief news account noting the difference in the two endings: "Boris lived, but the Texas whale died. Sometimes stories have a happy ending.

Sometimes real stories don't." Some students were so interested in this event that they continued to seek and find information about the plight of stranded whales and why whales beach themselves in the first place.

The background knowledge we bring to our reading colors every aspect of our learning and understanding. If readers have nothing to hook new information to, it's pretty hard to construct meaning. When we have a lot of background knowledge in a topic, we are much more likely to understand the text. When we have background knowledge of a certain writing style or structure, we more easily make sense of it. But when we know little about a topic or are unfamiliar with the format, we often find ourselves mired in confusion.

Making connections to personal experience facilitates understanding. The kids connected Boris to the Texas whale to better understand its plight. They knew that William Steig's animal characters would figure their way out of predicaments. They looked forward to Steig's humorous writing style, coming to expect laughter when they pulled his books off the shelf. Our prior experience and background knowledge fuel the connections we make. Books, discussions, experiences, newscasts, magazines, the Internet, and even nightly dinner-table conversations all forge connections that lead to new insight. We teach kids to activate their background knowledge and think about their connections so that they read in ways that let them discover these threads.

Connecting the New to the Known

When we begin strategy instruction with children, stories close to their own lives and experiences are helpful for introducing new ways of thinking about reading. Readers naturally make connections between books and their own lives. Once they have heard a wealth of stories and narratives, they begin to connect themes, characters, and issues from one book to another. When children understand how to connect the texts they read to their lives, they begin to make connections to the larger world. This nudges them into thinking about bigger, more expansive issues beyond their universe of home, school, and neighborhood.

Our suggestions for strategy lessons move from close to home to more global issues or cultures and places further removed from most children's lives. Although some lessons emphasize understanding literature and others focus on building background knowledge in a particular topic or genre, all have a common purpose: to use our personal and collective experience to construct meaning. Toward the end of this chapter, we address some issues that sometimes crop up when teaching readers to activate their background knowledge and make connections. The purpose of making connections is to enhance understanding not derail it. There are a number of pitfalls that cause kids to stumble when making connections. So we attempt to sort out some of the obstacles to understanding that can occur when kids make perfunctory connections.

Strategy Lessons: Activating and Connecting to Background Knowledge

Beginning to Make Connections: It Reminds Me of . . .

Purpose: Thinking aloud to introduce connection making

Resource: The story "Slower Than the Rest" in *Every Living Thing*, a collection of short stories by Cynthia Rylant

Responses: Coding the text R for remind; listing connections on a large chart and a two-column form headed What the Story Is About/What It Reminds Me Of

Slower Than the Rest," a short story about a boy who rescues a turtle that subsequently becomes his constant companion, is one of our favorites for teaching readers to think about the connections they make to their own lives and to the larger world. The story draws comparisons between the slow turtle and the little boy, Leo, who attends special education classes at school and frequently feels "slower than the rest" himself. Leo's self-esteem soars when he shares his knowledge about and love for his turtle at school, much to the delight and acclaim of his teachers and peers.

When we begin teaching connection-making in reading, we often share realistic fiction or a memoir, because these genres are likely to bring up thoughts and ideas that are close to the reader's own experience. "It reminds me of . . ." is a common refrain from even very young children in classrooms that feature literature that is close to kids' lives. "Slower Than the Rest" is a good example of a story most kids can relate to.

At first, we design very simple codes to describe our thinking. For example, whenever we read parts that remind us of our own lives, thoughts, or experiences, we stop, think out loud, and code the text R for reminds me of. . . . Then we write a few words on the sticky note that explain the incident, thought, or feeling. Of all connection-making codes, this is the simplest. The word *remind* makes sense to most kids, and they understand the notion of being reminded of something when they read.

As students join in and share their own connections, we might list them on a large chart. This chart sometimes evolves into a list of topics for writing personal narrative pieces, in which students expand on their individual connections to write stories from their personal experience. As we continue exploring the notion of connecting the story to our own lives, we may model a simple two-column form. What the Story Is About/What It Reminds Me Of encourages students to summarize the story in the first column and respond to a memory, some prior knowledge, or a past experience in the second.

With "Slower Than the Rest," the connections run the gamut from "I have a pet iguana" and "I had a turtle once, too" to the more sophisticated, poignant connection that Randall, a reticent fourth grader, shared: "It reminds me of how I feel just like Leo sometimes, especially when Mrs. Steadly [the special education teacher] comes to get me." He went on to say that he always wondered what the rest of the class was doing while he was out of the room. A lively conversation ensued that enhanced the understanding of the rest of the students, who became more aware of what it was like to feel just a little different.

New

Making Connections Between Small Poems and Our Lives

Purpose: Illustrating and writing connections to our lives
Resource: *Sol a Sol,* by Lori Carlson, poems in English and Spanish
Responses: Kids read, make connections, and write short pieces about their lives and experiences.

Lori Carlson's *Sol a Sol* is an engaging book of short poems about everyday events and happenings that all kids can relate to. Written in both English and Spanish and with vibrant illustrations, these poems are great models for kids' writing: they are short, full of action, and accessible. Centered on family life and everyday activities, the poems include topics such as riding bikes, rolling back the rug and dancing after dinner, making tortillas, cats, grandmothers, and gazing at the sky and counting the stars. After we read some of these poems aloud, we create a "snippet," a short free-verse poem, together. The kids turn and talk about their own ideas for snippets and then they are off—responding, connecting, drawing, and writing about their own lives. We often introduce making connections by eliciting kids' own personal snippets, showing them how we can draw and write down "just a piece of our experience." We often read, talk about, and write these experiences at the beginning of the year. It's a great way for new classmates to get to know each other and to share a small part of their lives with others. See Figure 7.1 for two examples of these snippets.

Figure 7.1 Students Get to Know Each Other by Sharing Snippets Such as These

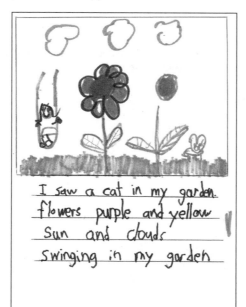

I saw a cat in my garden.
flowers purple and yellow
Sun and clouds
Swinging in my garden

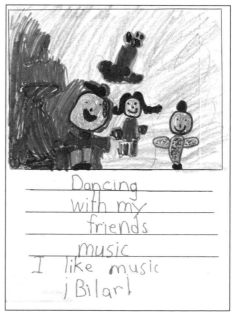

Dancing
with my
friends
music
I like music
¡Bilar!

Text-to-Self Connections: Relating the Characters to Ourselves

Purpose: Linking the text to our life
Resources: Picture books by Kevin Henkes, including *Owen, Chrysanthemum,* and *Julius, the Baby of the World*
Response: Coding the text T-S for text-to-self connections

When Kelly Clarke and Melissa Oviatt introduced a Kevin Henkes author study at the beginning of the year, children found it easy to make text-to-self connections with these books, whose characters were about the same age as they were and had similar problems and experiences. They were drawn to characters like Owen, who won't give up his ragged old blanket, or Chrysanthemum, whose mouthful of a name is problematic for a kindergartner. Melissa and Kelly chose these narratives because they suspected their first graders would relate to them.

Just as Steph did in her *Up North at the Cabin* think-aloud described in Chapter 1, Kelly and Melissa modeled their own text-to-self connections for the kids as they read the Kevin Henkes's stories aloud, coding the text T-S and writing a few words about their own connections to their past experiences. As they modeled text-to-self coding for these first graders, Gerald waved his hand wildly in the air and asked, "What is text?" Kelly and Melissa thanked Gerald for his right-on question and explained that text is any print that is written down—a book, a newspaper, a poem, a magazine article, and so on. These first graders had to understand the meaning of the word *text* before they could begin to comprehend the term *text-to-self connection*. Once again, we are reminded that we can't be too explicit!

As the children listened to a variety of Henkes stories, they began to make text-to-text connections as well. They noted similarities between characters and their predicaments in Henkes's books. One wise first grader noted that Lily in *Julius, the Baby of the World* was every bit as stubborn about accepting the new baby in the family as Owen was about giving up his blanket. Melissa quickly labeled that comment a text-to-text connection, pointing out that we make connections between the characters in different stories.

Having made strong connections between the characters in the stories and their own lives, and having learned some language for connection making, these first graders had a greater understanding of Henkes's narratives. In fact, when kids made meaningful connections to the characters, problems, and events, they seemed to gain some insight into the story as a whole.

Distracting Connections

New

Purpose: Teaching readers to identify distracting connections and fix up meaning
Resource: Any text or part of a text that triggers a connection that leads the reader astray
Response: Conversation

If we are going to teach our kids to make connections as they read, we must teach them about a type of connection that we have come to call the distracting connection. Distracting connections actually cause our minds to wander from the text and disrupt meaning. This happens when a point in the text triggers a thought and the next thing we know we are thinking about that thought rather than constructing meaning from the text. There is nothing wrong with indulging a particular connection for a moment or two. The problem is continuing to read while doing it!

We teach the notion of distracting connections by modeling how it happens to us so kids will come to recognize when it happens to them. For Steph, it happens when she meets the term *Fourth of July*. She grew up in a town in central Wisconsin where nothing happened for 364 days a year, but the Fourth of July was unbelievable—the bike parade, the fireworks, the carnival that came to town. To this day, whenever she comes to the words *Fourth of July* as she reads, no matter what the context, she is back there in the Wisconsin of her youth, celebrating that memorable holiday.

To teach distracting connections, Steph models with a bit of text that mentions the Fourth of July. When she comes to those words, she stops and shares those vivid Fourth of July images.

After a paragraph or two, she stops reading again and explains that she can't understand anything she just read, because she is still thinking about the Fourth of July. She explains distracting connections and then models how to go back to the point in the text where she got off track, in this case to the words *Fourth of July*. She consciously refocuses her thinking and begins reading from that point. After reading a few paragraphs, she stops and shares what she just read, showing that she understands the text now, because she successfully pushed the Fourth of July out of her mind and focused on the ideas in the text.

Find a topic or an idea in a piece of text that triggers another thought and causes you to stray from meaning as you read. The sky is the limit. Steph knows a teacher who comes across the word *fishing* and he is out of there. Another sees the word *golf* and she is on the fifteenth hole at Pebble Beach! Then do as Steph did and model the idea of the distracting connection for your kids so that they can recognize and repair meaning themselves when it happens to them.

Text-to-Text Connections: Finding Common Themes in Author Studies

Purpose: Connecting big ideas and themes across texts
Resources: Picture books by Eve Bunting, including *Smoky Night, The Wall, A Day's Work, Fly Away Home*
Response: Coding the text T-T for text-to-text connections

Anne Ertmann's third graders were engaged in a study of Eve Bunting's picture books. As they pored over books such as *Smoky Night*, an account of the Los Angeles riots; *The Wall*, a book about the Vietnam Veterans Memorial; and *A Day's Work*, a story about a boy and his Mexican immigrant grandfather who were day laborers, the kids realized that Bunting writes about serious topics.

That wasn't all they noticed. Anne Ertmann and her students were avid writers who were studying leads in writing and experimenting with different ways to begin their own personal narratives. One day, while meeting with his Eve Bunting book club group, Gregory suggested that the group look at how Eve Bunting begins her stories and list some of the leads. As the children discussed what they had found, Lauren flipped to the end of *Fly Away Home*, Bunting's book about a father and child who are homeless and take shelter in an airport. "Wait a minute," she exclaimed. "Eve Bunting doesn't really tell us what happens at the end of this book, to the boy and his dad."

"Yeah," Josh chimed in. "At the end of *Fly Away Home* I still had a lot of questions about what would happen."

"She leaves us up in the air a lot," ventured Sara. "Sometimes there isn't really an ending."

No one told these kids what to think about Eve Bunting. They came up with their own ways of understanding and interpreting the text. They moved from studying leads to delving into endings in the most natural way. Their teacher had prepared them to think beyond the obvious by teaching them to "read like writers." Another group of children might well have come up with equally thoughtful but quite different observations about Eve Bunting's books.

Generally, kids start by making text-to-text connections to more obvious elements of stories, such as characters or problems. Some text-to-text connections, in order of increasing sophistication, might include

- Comparing characters, their personalities, and actions
- Comparing story events and plot lines

- Comparing lessons, themes, or messages in stories
- Finding common themes, writing style, or perspectives in the work of a single author
- Comparing the treatment of common themes by different authors
- Comparing different versions of familiar stories

Noticing and Thinking About New Learning

New

Purpose: Merging thinking with new information
Resource: *Avalanche*, by Stephen Kramer
Response: Sticky notes

When readers read nonfiction, they are reading to learn new information. Noticing and thinking about new learning is one of the first lessons we teach to support nonfiction readers in gaining information and acquiring knowledge. When we encounter new information, we are likely to hear a voice in our head that says something like, *Wow, I never knew that before* or *Hmmm, interesting. . . .* A compelling book such as Stephen Kramer's *Avalanche* engages kids easily and encourages them to listen to their inner voices and merge their thinking with the text. In addition, the book is so jam packed with information that every student will likely learn something new.

Figure 7.2 On Sticky Notes Like These, Students Record New Learning and Their Reactions to What They Learn

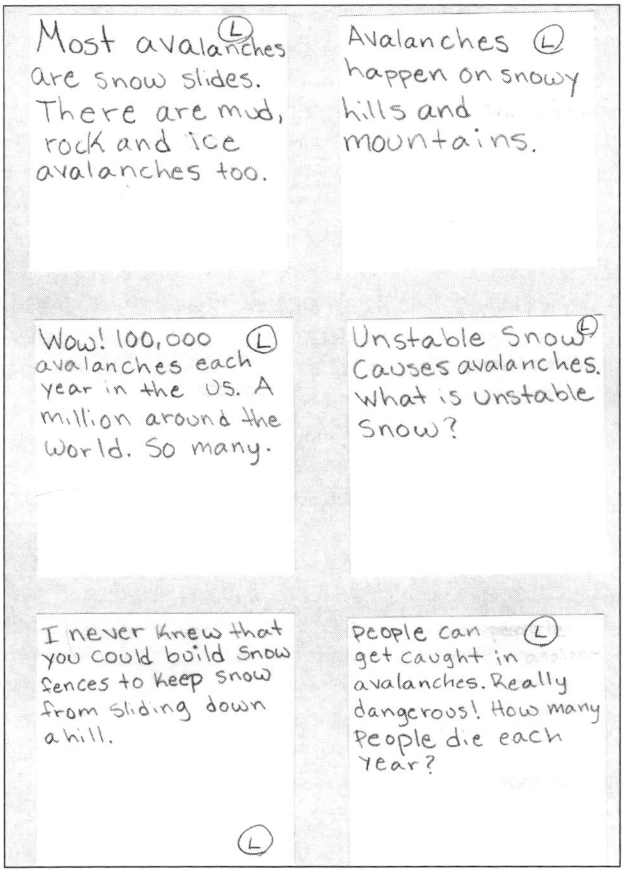

Most avalanches are snow slides. There are mud, rock and ice avalanches too. (L)

Avalanches happen on snowy hills and mountains. (L)

Wow! 100,000 avalanches each year in the US. A million around the world. So many. (L)

Unstable Snow Causes avalanches. What is Unstable snow? (L)

I never knew that you could build snow fences to keep snow from sliding down a hill.

People can get caught in avalanches. Really dangerous! How many People die each Year? (L)

(L)

Steph launched this lesson with fifth graders by modeling the voice she hears in her head when she meets new information. She explained to the kids that it is not enough to simply regurgitate facts when we read but that we have to listen to our inner conversation and merge our thinking with the text in order to learn, understand, and remember the information.

As she read the text, she thought aloud, sharing the voice she heard in her head when she met new information. For instance, on page ten of the text, she read that anything that slides down a mountain or a hillside—rocks, ice, mud—can be called an avalanche. She stopped and said to the class, "I never knew that anything that slid down the side of a mountain could be called an avalanche. I thought avalanches had to be made of snow. I'm going to jot this new learning on a sticky note because that is surprising, new information to me. Then I'm going to mark this sticky note with an L for *learn* and write *Wow! I never knew there were different types of avalanches*. I'll place this note on the page near where I read the information so I can find it easily if I need to."

Steph continued reading and sharing new information she met as she read, marking sticky notes with an L, merging her thinking with the information, and jotting down the new learning to better remember it. After she read a page or two, she engaged the kids in the process. They were bunched up in front of her on the floor with clipboards with a blank page covered with six 3" x 3" sticky notes. When they heard new information about avalanches, they jotted down a word or two from their inner conversation along with the new information. When Steph stopped reading the text, she sent the kids off to practice independently in text at their level and on a topic of their choice. At the end of the workshop time, the kids formed a circle and shared some of the new learning they encountered in their own texts. Figure 7.2 shows one student's page of new learning.

Above all, we must be teaching readers to merge their thinking with text information, to stop, think, and react to the information throughout the read. When readers interact with text in this way, they are likely to remember the information way beyond Friday's quiz. To see a similiar lesson in action, check out our DVD *Think Nonfiction! Modeling Reading and Research* (2003).

Rethinking Misconceptions: New Information Changes Thinking

New

Purpose: Linking what we know to what we learn
Resources: *Why Do My Feet Fall Asleep? And Other Questions About the Circulatory System,* by Sharon Cromwell, and other health books
Response: Chart titled Questions/What We Think We Know/New Learning

Most kids are curious about how their bodies work. They wonder why they sneeze, get a stomachache, or shiver in the cold. But we've noticed that kids, understandably, have a lot of misconceptions about body systems such as the digestive system or the circulatory system. We know it can be difficult to "replace" limited or incorrect knowledge with more accurate information, so we explicitly teach kids to leave their misconceptions behind and be open to learning new information.

Anne and teacher Carole Suderman worked with third graders to think and talk about what they already knew about the circulatory system, starting with questions from the book *Why Do My Feet Fall Asleep?* Anne and Carole recorded the kids' prior knowledge about these questions on a chart (see Figure 7.3).

They reminded the kids that they were writing down "what *we think* we know" to prepare kids to let go of some of their prior misconceptions. Anne and Carole suggested that the kids "get their brains ready to take in some new information." As Carole and Anne read the text out loud, they modeled how their thinking changed when they encountered new and more accurate information. They signaled their new learning by prefacing it with language including, "Now I know that . . ." or "Wow, I just learned . . ." or "Now I get it. . . ."

As Jordan looked at the chart that compared kids' initial knowledge with their new learning, she piped up, "I get it! We can cross out the old information and write down what's new." Carole and Anne congratulated her on her suggestion, adding that this would help everyone focus in on new and more accurate information.

Anne and Carole sent the kids off to read for new and more accurate information that answered their questions. When the class regrouped to share new learning and discuss how their thinking changed, Anne and Carole celebrated when they heard kids using language that signaled new learning. Some kids had crossed out their previous thinking, others were more reticent to rethink their misconceptions. When misconceptions lingered, Anne and Carole knew that they'd need to spend more time explaining and discussing the sophisticated information presented in the book. But as the chart in Figure 7.3 demonstrates, the kids were well on their way to learning new—and more accurate—information!

The Circulatory System

Questions	What We Think We Know	New Learning
Why does my heart beat?	"Your heart beats." "If your heart isn't beating you aren't alive."	"Your heart helps you with your blood, it goes to each part of your body."
Why do I have blood?	"If you don't have blood you would die." "If you didn't have blood you would be like a balloon, like a basketball."	"Blood helps you fight your sickness." "We have blood so that it can carry oxygen around your body so it can help you breathe." "I learned that there are different blood cells that do different things."
Why do I shiver when I get cold?	"You shiver because your blood is cold."	"Because you are trying to keep yourself warm, this is why we shiver." "I learned when you shiver you warm up." "Now I know, when you get the shivers you get warm for a little bit."
What makes bruises "black and blue"?	"Your skin turns purple and black." "There is a black spot on your leg when you fall down."	"I get it, there's a bruise because it is bleeding under your skin."
Why do I sweat when my body gets hot?	"Because you are HOT when you run!" "When you sweat, water comes out of you."	"We sweat because it cools our body down."

Figure 7.3 Questions/What We Think We Know/New Learning

Building Background Knowledge to Teach Specific Content

Purpose: Collecting information to build a store of knowledge about a content area
Resources: Assorted books on Africa, including Gray and Dupasquier's *A Country Far Away*
Responses: Large chart and fact sheet

Kindergarten teacher Paige Inman's goal was to explore the continent of Africa with her students. Asking children what they already knew about Africa allowed Paige to discover that, in fact, they knew very little. With librarian Jeanine Gordon, Paige found and read lots of books about Africa to the children to build their background knowledge. They discussed pictures and photographs, and asked questions. These five-year-olds were amazed at some of the information they unearthed. As the children asked questions, Paige wrote each on a sticky note and placed them on a chart for all to see. As the number of questions grew, she helped the children sort their questions into categories like food, homes, wildlife, games, and customs.

Figure 7.4 Tiffany's Response to the Africa Fact Sheet

An African Fact
by Tiffany

ButtRFI Lv IN The LNGL.

After much discussion, Paige asked her students to write what they knew. Using an African fact sheet, the children used their knowledge of letter-sound relationships and invented spelling to write what was memorable. Tiffany shares her new information about African butterflies on her fact sheet (see Figure 7.4). The children's enthusiasm for their work illustrated what Paige had most encouraged in these beginning researchers: a sense of curiosity and a willingness to investigate life in another culture.

At the conclusion of this project, Paige had learned a lot from her kindergartners. She now viewed them as veritable sponges soaking up information about Africa. They continued to wonder out loud about a culture quite different from their own. And once her kids heard a fact, they seldom forgot it. It's not often we start from scratch to build background knowledge about a topic. But when we do, sharing information and encouraging student questions is the simplest route to teaching content.

Building Background Knowledge Based on Personal and Text-to-World Connections

Purpose: Sharing connections to build historical understanding
Resource: Sherry Garland's picture book *The Lotus Seed*
Responses: Coding the text T-W for text-to-world connections; listing student connections on a large chart

As we introduce new topics or issues, we observe students struggling to understand unfamiliar ideas and information. Students who have background knowledge about a topic have a real advantage because they can connect the new information they encounter to what they already know. Our responsibility is to help build students' background knowledge so that they can read independently to gain new information. Encouraging students to make text-to-world connections supports our efforts to teach students about social studies and science concepts and topics.

Intermediate teacher Tim Downing introduced his fourth and fifth graders to Sherry Garland's picture book *The Lotus Seed*, the story of a refugee family fleeing their homeland during the Vietnam War. This story is about a young woman who took a lotus seed with her to remember her country and culture as she journeyed to a new life in the United States. As Tim's class studied the United States in the twentieth century, this piece of historical fiction added to their knowledge of the time period. Tim asked the students to focus on text-to-self and text-to-world connections as they read. As the students shared copies of the book, jotting down their thoughts on sticky notes, Anne wondered whether they would have many connections. Most elementary students she'd worked with had little knowledge about, let alone personal connections to, the Vietnam War. However, as she conferred with pairs during reading time, she noticed the response on Jimmy's sticky note: "My uncle fought in Vietnam and he told me all about it."

When the students shared their connections later, Jimmy elaborated on his T-S connection, telling his classmates that his uncle had fought in Vietnam. Sylvia looked puzzled. As she studied a *Lotus Seed* illustration of bombs falling on a rice paddy, she asked incredulously, "You mean, we were the ones bombing Vietnam?" Jimmy explained that probably the people in the picture were North Vietnamese and that U.S. planes may have been doing the bombing. At that point, Rory chimed in with his text-to-world connection and his summary of the war, saying "the North Vietnamese were fighting for communism and the South Vietnamese were fighting for freedom."

Jimmy's personal connections and Rory's knowledge about the Vietnam War added to their classmates' background knowledge of events and issues. Later, Tim and Anne charted the students' responses to display their thinking and used this as a springboard to build on kids' knowledge of this time period. In this lesson, not all of the students were able to make connections like Jimmy and Rory. The chart served as a continuing reminder to the children of ways to link text to their own lives and the larger world. When kids share their background knowledge and connections, other kids listen and learn from them.

Building Background Knowledge for Literary Elements

Poetry has its white space, fiction its characters, and nonfiction its bold print. In fact, every literary genre or form has certain features that define it. When we explore fiction, we teach our students about character, setting, problem, and solution. When we investigate nonfiction, we share expository text structures such as "compare and contrast" and "cause and effect." We teach visual and text features so that students will have the background knowledge to better comprehend a specific genre or form when they read and write.

Text-to-self, text-to-text, and text-to-world connections are content-based connections. Readers also make connections to the nature of text and the literary features. Once they become aware of these elements, readers know what to expect when they read a novel, pick up the newspaper, follow a manual, or glance at an advertisement. We design instruction around the following elements so that readers will see the connections and better comprehend what they read.

Genre. Nonfiction, fiction, poetry, and so on vary. With exposure, readers become familiar with the special characteristics and conventions of each genre.

Format. Readers learn the differences among picture books, novels, nonfiction trade books, and so on. They rely on these differences to better understand what they read.

Form. Readers learn to distinguish among essays, editorials, manuals, feature articles, and so on. This awareness heightens their understanding when they read different forms.

Author. Readers learn that certain authors carry similar themes, issues, and topics throughout their writing. Readers come to expect these.

Text structure. Readers recognize the differences between narrative and expository text and other structures. They learn the characteristics of each to better comprehend.

Signal words. Readers learn to identify certain words that signal them about what's to come. For example, *but* suggests a coming change, *in other words* is followed by a definition, and *most important* means exactly that. (See the signal word section in Chapter 15.)

Writing style. Readers notice the various writing styles of different authors, develop an appreciation of them, and begin to make connections between them.

Literary features. Readers learn to search for themes, identify problems, and recognize settings when they read. They develop background knowledge for these features of text. When readers think about connections they make to the features or nature of text, they might code them LC for literary connection. For instance, when they recognize the white space in a poem from having seen the same feature before, they might code it LC to help them think about the purpose of white space in poetry. They could do the same with boldface print or italics in nonfiction. The more they understand about the nature of text, the better they will comprehend it.

See Chapter 10 for more about nonfiction features.

Tangential Connections: Pitfalls to Understanding

Once children understand the concept of making connections, there seems to be no stopping them. They link books, experiences, and ideas in delightful ways. In classrooms where teachers teach kids to think about their background knowledge and then build in time to practice strategy application, kids fill their pages with sticky notes coded R, T-S, T-T, and T-W. The truth is, however, we've encountered a number of pitfalls on the connections path. Sometimes, kids make tangential connections rather than meaningful ones. We need to keep a watchful eye out for tangential connections that do not enhance understanding. The lesson on distracting connections in this chapter addresses one of the obstacles we have to overcome when teaching kids to make connections. Some others follow here.

"Connections in Common"

Sometimes when we ask kids to share a connection they have, they burst forth with comments such as "The book mentioned San Diego and I've been to San Diego"; or, "The character is a boy and I'm a boy"; or, even better, "The coolest character's name is Jasmine and my name is Jasmine!" Some kids might make a connection between the fact that there is a grandfather in Eve Bunting's *A Day's Work* and that they have one, too. A more meaningful connection would involve the relationship between the grandfather and the boy. The primary reason for a reader to make connections is to enhance understanding, and it is highly unlikely that sharing a name with the main character or noting that you, too, have a grandfather will do that. To be honest, these situations make us uncomfortable and present a bit of a dilemma. As teachers who believe that nothing matters more than the reader's thinking, it's tough to tell a reader these connections are unimportant since they are a part of the reader's thinking. And yet these connections are unlikely to add to understanding.

We've come to call these connections "connections in common." For instance, if you share a name, birthplace, or relative with a character, you have that in common. And although these connections in common do not lead to understanding, they very well may lead to engagement, because kids like to read about characters with the same name or who have been places they have been, and so forth. So these connections in common may in fact be important to the reader but not important to understanding the text. To help the reader decide, we use a three-column form headed My Connection/Important to Me/Important to Understanding the Text. Kids record their connection in the first column and then decide if it is important to the reader or important to understanding. In this way, we are not telling the reader that their thinking doesn't matter, but rather that their thinking matters a great deal and that it is their responsibility to decide about the relative importance of their connection.

Will Any Connection Do?

We watch carefully for authentic connections that support understanding. Kids are terrific teacher-pleasers and may think that any connection is better than no connection at all. Sometimes, particularly when kids are new to the practice, they go overboard making connections just for the sake of it. Younger kids often get so excited about writing on sticky notes that they write down just about anything that comes to their mind. "It reminds me of when I went down on a sinking ship," third grader Jake wrote while reading Robert Ballard's *Exploring the Titanic*. When his teacher quizzed him privately about this connection, he sheepishly admitted that he had never really been on a ship at all, much less a sinking one!

After the untimely death of a class pet, Michelle Meyer read her first-grade class *The Tenth Good Thing About Barney*, Judith Viorst's picture book about the death of a beloved pet and the family's attempt to gain closure after the incident. After reading the story, Michelle encouraged the kids to write down their connections in their notebooks. Katie was clearly moved by the story and wrote prolifically about her similar past experience (see Figure 7.5). And although Daniel wrote less, a smile crept across Michelle's face as his honesty burst through (see Figure 7.6). Sharing Daniel's connection with the class as well as Katie's shows how Michelle values authentic, honest connections.

Figure 7.5 Katie's Connection Response to *The Tenth Good Thing About Barney*

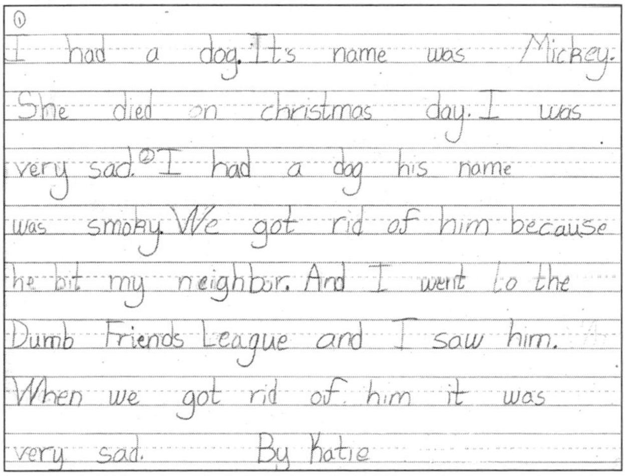
① I had a dog. It's name was Mickey. She died on christmas day. I was very sad. ② I had a dog his name was smoky. We got rid of him because he bit my neighbor. And I went to the Dumb Friends League and I saw him. When we got rid of him it was very sad. By Katie

Figure 7.6 Daniel's Connection Response to *The Tenth Good Thing About Barney*

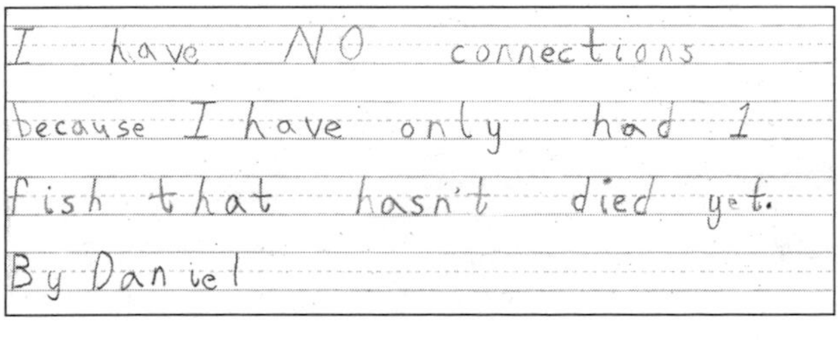
I have NO connections because I have only had 1 fish that hasn't died yet. By Daniel

Which Connection Is It Anyway?

Alexandra, a fifth grader, was reading *When Jessie Came Across the Sea*, Amy Hest's story of a young Jewish girl at the turn of the twentieth century who was chosen by the local rabbi to emigrate to America from Eastern Europe but was forced to leave her beloved grandmother behind. When Alexandra came to a passage that said, "The ship docked at Ellis Island. Wait on line. Inspections. Wait on line. Papers. Wait on line. Questions. Wait on line." she stopped, coded the passage T-S, and wrote "I've been to Ellis Island," referring to a trip she'd made with her parents the previous summer.

But she had trouble moving on from there because she also began to think about the history of Ellis Island and the difficulty some people faced while waiting in line or being told to turn back. She knew that even today immigrants sometimes have a tough time at the border and are denied entry. Connecting immigration today with immigration during the heyday of Ellis Island caused her to recode the passage T-W to note a text-to-world connection that said, "Life is very hard for immigrants."

Either code works. As Alexandra reread the passage, her contemplation about Ellis Island drove her to a deeper, more meaningful connection. But we don't want kids, or teachers for that matter, to get hung up on which code belongs where. The purpose of making connections and coding the text is to monitor comprehension and enhance understanding. Alexandra was definitely doing those things.

How Does That Connection Help You Understand?

One day Steph conferred with Allison, a seventh grader reading *Mirette on the High Wire* by Emily Arnold McCully, the story of a brave little girl who helps an aging tightrope walker overcome his fear. She noticed Allison's sticky note coded R that said, "I get really scared in high places just like Bellini does."

"Tell me about that," Steph nudged.

"Oh, I don't know. I just get scared looking down from tall buildings or standing on the edge of a cliff," Allison explained.

"That's interesting. So how does that connection help you understand the story?" Steph asked.

"I don't know," Allison replied. She hadn't even thought about it because she was so busy reading and writing down her connections.

"It seems to me that you have a leg up on understanding the character of Bellini because you, too, have a fear of heights. You bring your own experience to the character, and you know better how that character feels and even how he might react. Better than me, for instance, because although I have plenty of fears, height isn't one of them," Steph said.

Steph and Allison agreed that the next time Allison made a connection, she would stop and ask herself how the connection helped her understand the story. Although children may initially have trouble articulating more significant connections, with teacher and peer modeling and plenty of time they gradually begin to refine and limit their connections to those that deepen their understanding and engagement.

Teaching with the End in Mind: Assessing What We've Taught

Activating and Connecting to Background Knowledge

Based on the lessons in this chapter, we look for evidence that

1. *Students make connections to their own lives to further their understanding of events, characters, problems, and ideas in realistic fiction.* We look for responses that illustrate insight into characters' problems, actions, and motives or that demonstrate that kids have understood ways to meaningfully connect to books.
2. *Students make connections to stories, short pieces, or poems. They demonstrate these connections through responses including their personal narratives, poems, and illustrations.* We look for responses that show rather than merely tell. (We also check to see that illustrations and writing are complementary.)
3. *Students record "what we think we know" about a topic, add to their learning, and share it on sticky notes and two-column forms as they read informational text.* We look for evidence of text-to-text and text-to-world connections, as well as evidence that students have merged their thinking with new information.

Suggestions for Differentiation

Reading picture books with clear illustrations that complement the vocabulary and language of the text builds kids' background knowledge and scaffolds their understanding as they learn about new topics. When introducing a new subject or topic, we take a few minutes to make sure kids link the text's language and vocabulary with the illustrations so that children learning English, especially, won't be lost as they listen to the story.

As one class launched their study of pioneers and the journey west with *Red Flower Goes West*, by Ann Turner, Anne wanted to make sure all the kids understood vocabulary words and ideas, including *pioneers, covered wagon, oxen,* and *crossing the river*. She decided to put up pictures of these terms on a chart and work with the class to label them. This would support some of the English language learners, but Anne also wanted to make this time worthwhile for kids who already had some background knowledge of this topic. So she asked the kids to turn and talk about what they already knew about pioneer times and going west in a covered wagon. They wrote down and illustrated their background knowledge and put it up on the chart as well.

Before beginning to read the book, the kids quickly shared their information and illustrations. Children who were new to these words and ideas could refer to the pictures and labels as they listened to the story. Kids who had some background knowledge were enthusiastic about teaching others what they already knew. In short, this preview engaged kids and got them "warmed up" and ready to participate in the interactive read-aloud.

Activating and Connecting to Background Knowledge Assessment Commentary

Independent reading sticky notes from the "Text-to-Self Connections" lesson, using Kevin Henkes's books

In Lilly's purple plastic Purse, she was rude to her teacher and in Julius The baby of the world Lilly was rude to her baby brother. T-T Jordan H.

Sheila Rae got scared when she got lost coming home from school and Lilly go+ T-T scared when she had a dream about Julius eating her. Jordan H.

Figure 7.7 These notes show how a child compared the characters in three stories. When kids make these connections, they arrive at a fuller understanding of characters and themes.

Figure 7.8 When kids first begin to make connections, we often let them tell us what they are thinking, and we record their words as they draw. In this particular case, we can see that perhaps this child did not understand what it is to make a connection, but she clearly understood the character's problem and summarized it. So we would meet with her and celebrate her understanding of the character, but push her thinking further and show her how to think about her own connection to the story.

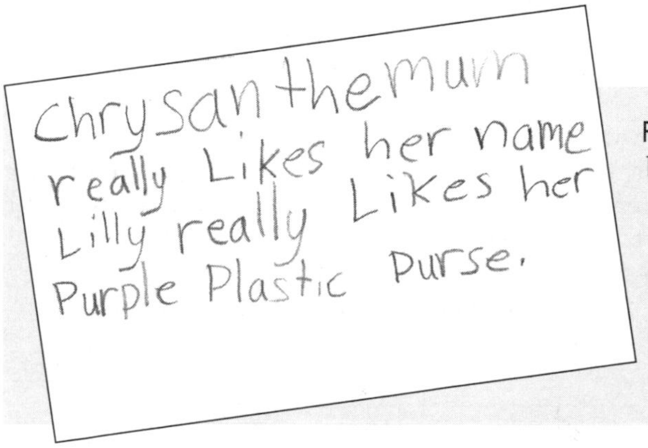

She went to school and kids made fun of her because she was named for a flower!

chrysanthemum

chrysanthemum really Likes her name Lilly really Likes her Purple Plastic Purse.

Figure 7.9 This child has made a surface connection between two characters in two different stories by noticing how much Chrysanthemum liked her name and how much Lilly liked her purse. We would confer with him and ask him to tell us more about his thinking and how this connection might help him understand the story, showing him how if he was unable to express this.

Independent reading sticky notes from the lesson "Noticing and Thinking About New Learning," which uses Stephen Kramer's *Avalanche*

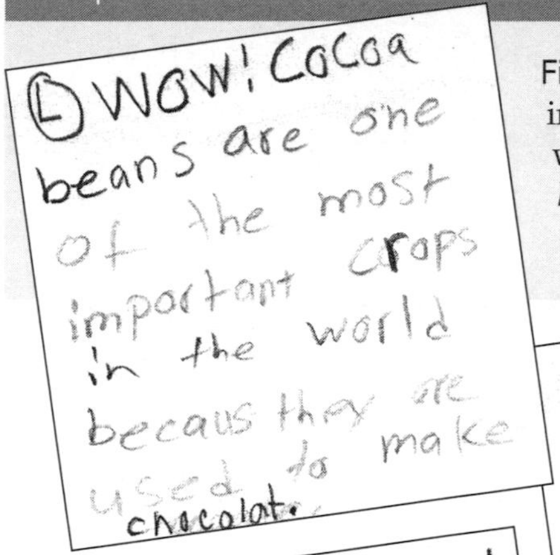

(L) WOW! Cocoa beans are one of the most important crops in the world becaus they are used to make chocolat.

Figure 7.10a–d These sticky notes show how readers recorded new information and merged their thinking with it. The readers used words like *Wow, Oh my gosh, News to me, I didn't know,* or *I never knew* to shape the new information into their own thought. That is exactly what we are shooting for when we teach this lesson.

(L) Shrubs are a short word for bushy plants News to me!

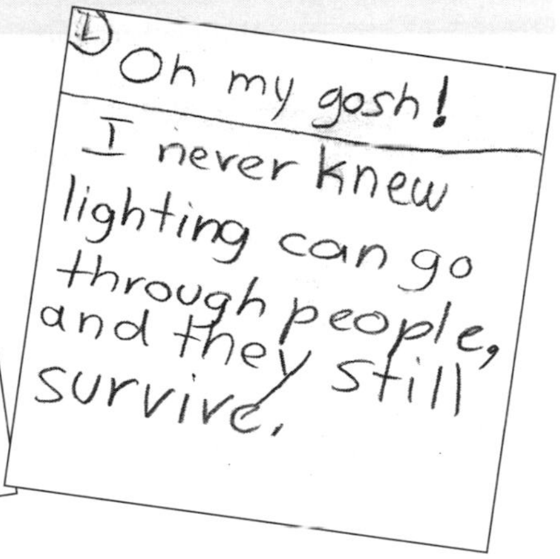

(L) Oh my gosh! I never knew lighting can go through people, and they still survive.

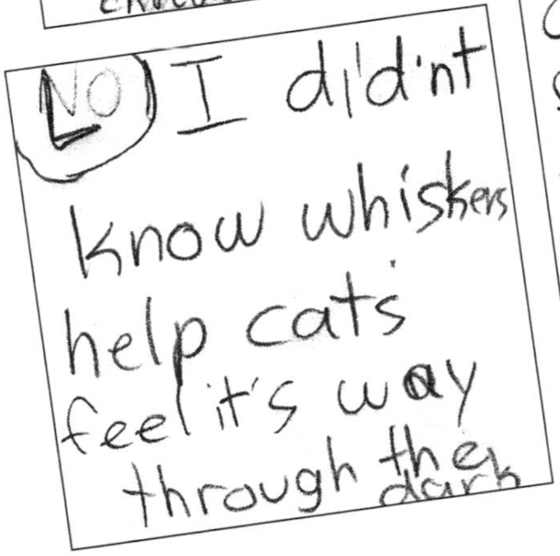

(NO)(L) I did'nt know whiskers help cats feel it's way through the dark

Figure 7.11a–b These two sticky notes were done by a student who was reading a book about the sun. We can see that she cleared up some big misconceptions by stopping and thinking about the information. She used to think the sun was solid and not a star, but after the reading, she changed her thinking. She still has a lot to learn about the sun, but it is likely she will never forget this information since she thought of it herself and really "owns" the new thinking. We are thrilled when kids clear up their own misconceptions through reading!

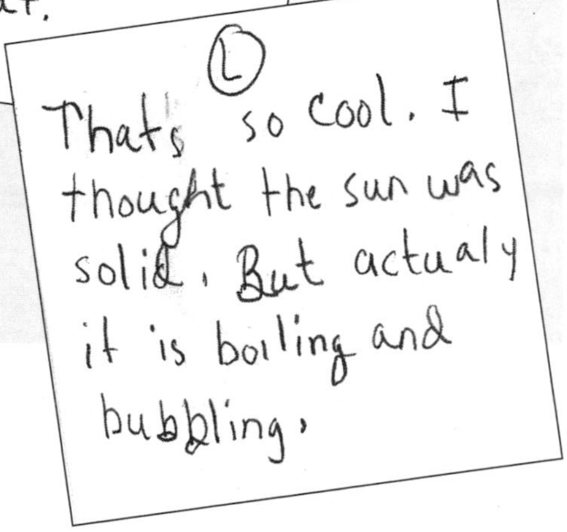

(L) Wait but how could the sun be a star because stars come out at night I never knew that.

(L) That's so cool. I thought the sun was solid. But actualy it is boiling and bubbling.

Notes that do not demonstrate understanding and need clarification and intervention

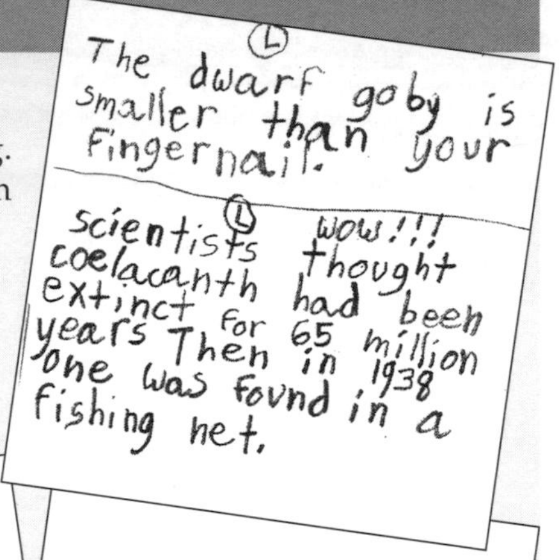

Figure 7.12a–c The first sticky note is copied directly out of the text. This is very common when kids first begin to jot down new learning. We would form a small group with anyone who copied directly from the text and show how we merge our own thinking with the information, using starters such as *I never knew, I didn't know, I learned.* That would be the first step in supporting kids to put the information into their own words and shape their own thought.

The second sticky note merely says WOW! No content here. We would meet with kids who do this and ask "What is so Wow?" And then we would encourage them to write that information.

The third sticky note is one of our all time favorite misconceptions! It is likely this reader actually knows that it was Neil and not Lance Armstrong who went to the moon, but we need to check it out. Reading kids' sticky notes is one of the quickest and best ways to clear up misconceptions.

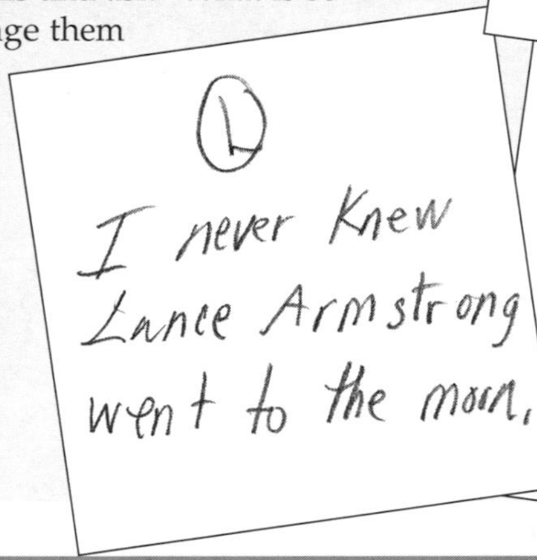

The dwarf goby is smaller than your fingernail.

scientists wow!!! coelacanth thought extinct had been years for 65 million Then in 1938 one was found in a fishing net.

I never knew Lance Armstrong went to the moon.

Wow!

A collection of responses to *The Lotus Seed* done after the lesson "Building Background Knowledge Based on Personal and Text-to-World Connections"

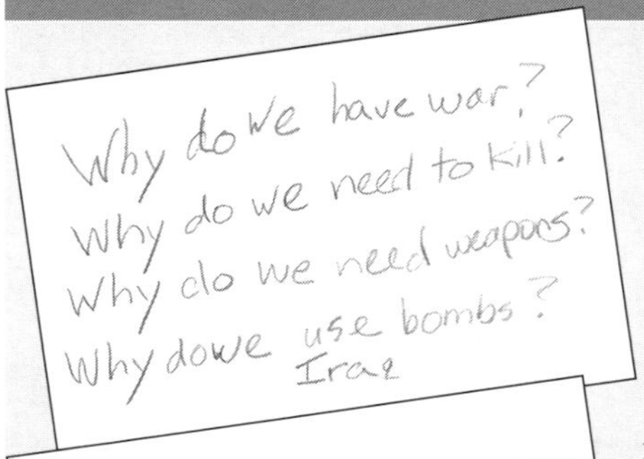

Figure 7.13a–d Kids responded independently with text-to-world connections on war themes that emerged after reading this book. One child asked searching questions about the Iraq War and wars in general. Several others questioned information about the war in the story that the book left unanswered. Another child described the tragedy of families who are victims of war. As they talked about these issues, a small group of children recognized their common themes and combined their notes to make a powerful statement about war and its devastating effects.

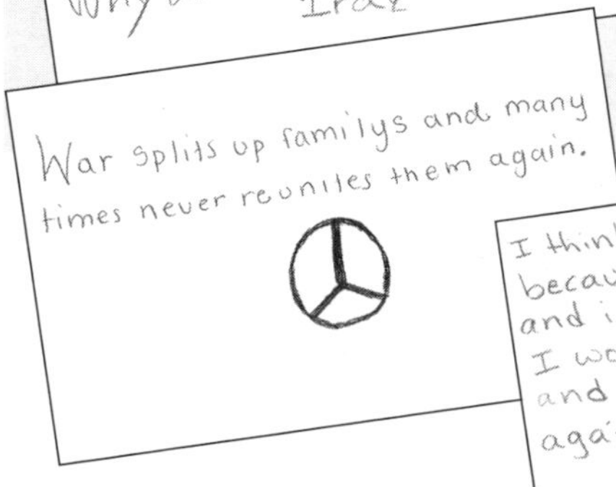

Why do we have war? Why do we need to kill? Why do we need weapons? Why do we use bombs? Iraq

War splits up familys and many times never reunites them again.

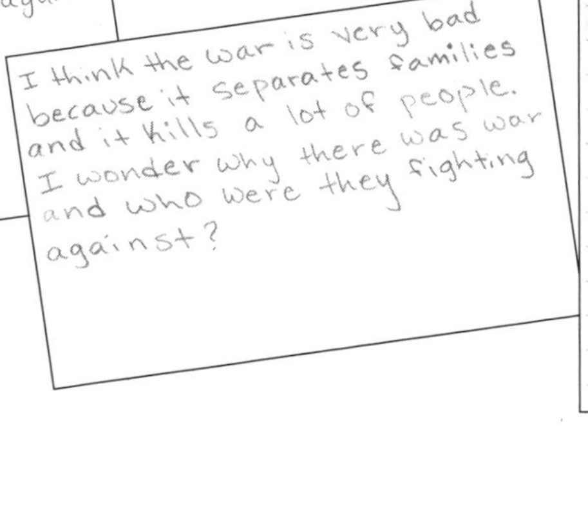

I think the war is very bad because it separates families and it kills a lot of people. I wonder why there was war and who were they fighting against?

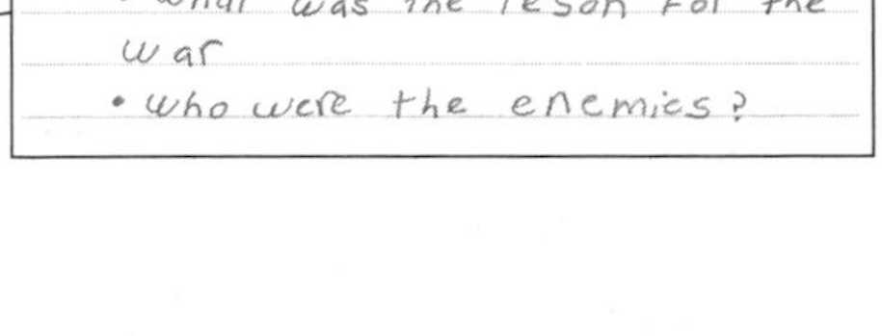

I think Bà was very, very strong to leave her husband and go to a country half way across the world. I had some questions about the war, here they are:
• Who was the war against.
• What happened to Bà's husband.
• What was the reson for the war
• Who were the enemies?

Chapter 8

Questioning: The Strategy That Propels Readers Forward

Curiosity spawns questions. Questions are the master key to understanding. Questions clarify confusion. Questions stimulate research efforts. Questions propel us forward and take us deeper into reading. Human beings are driven to find answers and make sense of the world. The Nobel prize–winning physicist Richard Feynman referred to this need as his "puzzle drive" (Feynman 1985). He couldn't *not* search for answers to those things that confounded him, those things he didn't understand.

Teachers portrayed in this book encourage this same puzzle drive in their students. Matt, a space lover, began writing what he knew and was learning about his favorite topic. But his curiosity got the better of him, and halfway into a letter to his teacher his questions burst forth and hijacked his response (see Figure 8.1). Matt reminds us that good questions spring from background knowledge. Matt knew about and loved space; hence he could ask terrific questions. It's tough to ask a substantive question about something we know or care nothing about.

As adult readers, we question all the time, often without even thinking about it. When we first began to pay attention to our thinking as we read, we were stunned at the number of questions we had, many of which were inspired by relatively small amounts of text. Kids don't grow up knowing that good readers ask questions. In fact, schools often appear more interested in answers than in questions. So now we teach kids to think about their questions before, during, and after reading. We encourage them to stop, think, and record their questions throughout the reading process. And we always remember to ask them if they have any lingering questions after they read. Those are the most important questions, the ones the reader has.

Our students need to know that their questions matter. They need to see us asking questions as well as answering them. Asking questions engages us and keeps us reading. A reader with no questions might just as well abandon the book. When our students ask questions and search for answers, we know that they are monitoring comprehension and interacting with the text to construct meaning, which is exactly what we hope for in developing readers.

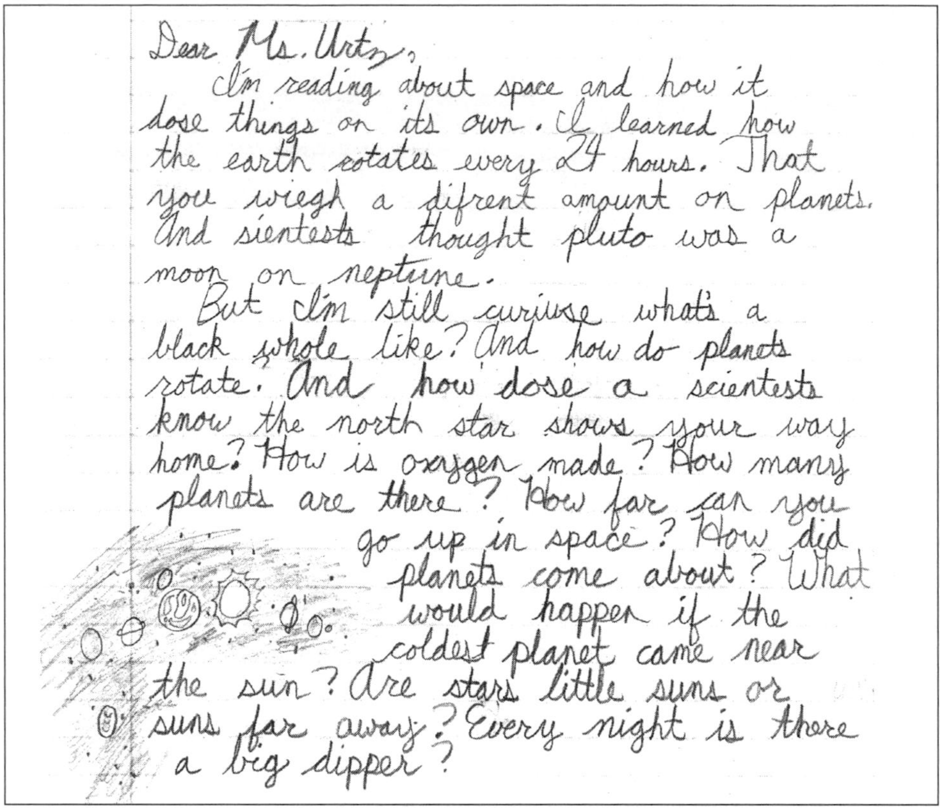

Figure 8.1 Matt's Response, Full of Questions

Dear Ms. Urtz,
    I'm reading about space and how it dose things on its own. I learned how the earth rotates every 24 hours. That you wiegh a difrent amount on planets. And sientests thought pluto was a moon on neptune.
    But I'm still curiuse whats a black whole like? And how do planets rotate. And how dose a scientests know the north star shows your way home? How is oxygen made? How many planets are there? How far can you go up in space? How did planets come about? What would happen if the coldest planet came near the sun? Are stars little suns or suns far away? Every night is there a big dipper?

Strategy Lessons: Questioning

Share Your Questions About Your Own Reading

Purpose: Using adult text to show the questions we have when we read
Resource: The novel *The God of Small Things*, by Arundhati Roy
Responses: Sticky notes coded with ?; follow-up group discussion

The next time you read a piece of adult text, pay close attention to the questions that surface and share those questions with your kids. Let them know that all readers—even adults—have questions. When introducing questioning to a group of sixth graders, Steph shared an excerpt from the novel *The God of Small Things* by Arundhati Roy, a book she loved despite her many questions and frequent confusion about it.

She gathered the kids in front of her and talked about how the text raised questions for her. She wrote her questions on sticky notes, placed them next to the passages that spurred them, and coded them with ?. She pointed out that some of her questions were answered in the text and others were not. She explained that her sticky note marked with "I love the title, but why is it called *The God of Small Things*?" was not addressed until quite late in the book. Her question "What is a paravan?" was answered several paragraphs further on: it is a member of the untouchable caste in India. When she read the answer, she moved her sticky note to the spot where the question was answered, wrote the answer on the sticky note, and recoded it A for answered.

Sometimes she was mired in confusion. In those cases, she coded a sticky note Huh? to note that meaning had broken down for her. This code signaled her to reread or read a few sentences ahead to try to make sense of the text before going on.

At the conclusion of this mini-lesson, Steph invited the kids to talk about questioning in reading. Robbie commented that he never knew a teacher could have so many questions about her reading. He seemed to be saying, "If she can have questions, so can I."

The More We Learn, the More We Wonder

New

Purpose: Wondering as we learn new information
Resources: Books on topic of study, in this case, Antarctic animals
Responses: Gather information, record it, and wonder about it

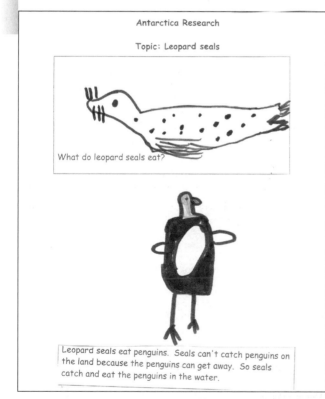

Figure 8.2 Students Present Their Questions and the Answers They Find by Reading

By the end of the year, Kristen Elder-Rubino's kindergartners knew how to do research. They'd studied African people, cultures, and animals. They'd explored photographs, artifacts, and books. So when Kristen asked them if they were interested in another adventure, this time to the vast, frigid continent of Antarctica, they were ready to put on their mittens!

As the kids learned information through videos, photographs, picture books, and other sources about life in this inhospitable climate, they asked a lot of questions. Questions are natural for curious five-year-olds, but for the entire year Kristen had encouraged the kids to stop, think, and wonder about what they were learning.

After Kristen modeled ways to record information and questions on an I Learned/I Wonder chart, the resulting list of questions demonstrated that thinking and wondering had become second nature to her students. As the kids worked with Kristin and librarian Nell Box in small groups to do animal research, Nell used this same format to record their thinking. Frankie, Eduardo, and Leah, who were researching leopard seals, learned that leopard seals eat penguins, and Nell recorded this information for them. A picture of a swimming leopard seal capturing a fleeing penguin confirmed that leopard seals catch penguins in the water, and they recorded this information on their chart, too. But then they noticed a picture of a leopard seal on the ice, with a few penguins standing some distance away. Leah offered, "I learned leopard seals and penguins are on the ice." Of course, a question was not far behind. "Wow," Frankie wondered, "is that leopard seal going to catch those penguins?"

I Learned	I Wonder
Leopard seals eat penguins.	Do they eat the feet?
Leopard seals catch penguins in the water.	Can penguins swim faster than leopard seals?
The leopard seals and penguins are on the ice.	Is that leopard seal going to catch those penguins?

Frankie was still thinking about that question when he noticed a caption under the picture of the leopard seal and penguins on the ice. After the group read the information, Frankie responded, "I get it. When they are on the ice, leopard seals can't move very fast. So they can't catch the penguins." When Frankie shared his Antarctica research, he noticed the concerned looks on his classmates' faces. "Don't worry," he said. "Penguins are safe when they're on the ice." (See Figure 8.2.) These kindergartners do a great deal of talking as they think through, draw, and begin to write down the information they are learning. Learning new information, wondering about it, and answering their questions prepares them for more independent research in first grade.

Some Questions Are Answered, Others Are Not

Purpose: Beginning questioning; listing and categorizing questions to promote understanding
Resource: The picture book *Charlie Anderson*, by Barbara Abercrombie
Responses: Chart with list of kids' questions; codes for categories of questions, including A for answered, BK for background knowledge, I for inferred, D for discussion, RS for research, C or Huh? for confused

When we begin teaching the strategy of questioning, we simply share the questions we have before, during, and after reading, and talk about them. All written text gives rise to questions, but sometimes we find a book that spurs questions from start to finish. Barbara Abercrombie's *Charlie Anderson* is just such a book. It tells the story of a cat who moves surreptitiously between two homes, living with one family by day and another by night, unbeknownst to the two separate owners. This story line parallels the lives of the two young characters, Sarah and her sister, Elizabeth, who move between their divorced parents' homes, as many kids do. This is a terrific book for kids who share this lifestyle. In fact, we have noticed that kids who spend their time in two different homes are more likely to pick up on the parallel theme. Alternatively, many young kids never even notice the divorce angle but seem to enjoy the simple story of a mysterious cat who disappears each night and returns home each morning.

Listing Questions
For all kids, however, we have found this to be a useful book to teach questioning, since they brim with questions when they read it. Second-grade teacher Mary Lawlor read *Charlie Anderson* to her class. The text is sparse, with fewer than five or six sentences per page. When she reached the end of each page, she solicited kids' questions. A parent volunteer recorded their questions on a piece of chart paper as Mary read. Their numerous questions emerged from the cover illustration and the prereading discussion as well as from the text and pictures during the reading. At the end of the story, the chart included the following list of questions:

Why is the book called Charlie Anderson?—A
Who is that cat in the yard?—A
Why was the door open just a crack?
Do cats really like French fries?
Where does the cat go every morning?—A
Are these girls twins?
Does Sarah get jealous that he likes Elizabeth's bed best?
Why did he get fatter and fatter every day?—A
Did they miss Charlie when they went to their dad's on the weekends?

Do they like their dad's house better?
Why didn't Charlie come home one night?—A
Is he going to be all right?—A
How come Anderson looks just like Charlie?—A
Which family does Charlie like better?

As Mary read through the questions, she asked the kids to come up and put an A for answered next to the questions that were explicitly answered in the text. After reviewing and coding the questions, the class discussed them. In most cases, the unanswered questions were the more intriguing ones, the questions that dug toward deeper themes and bigger ideas. The question about where the girls preferred to live sparked a lively conversation. We have discovered that unanswered questions often stimulate the most stirring discussions.

Categorizing Questions

We can start helping kids categorize questions in primary grades. As we move up through grade levels, we can add different categories of questions. Some question categories and corresponding codes include

- Questions that are answered in the text—A
- Questions that are answered from someone's background knowledge—BK
- Questions whose answers can be inferred from the text—I
- Questions that can be answered by further discussion—D
- Questions that require further research to be answered—RS
- Questions that signal confusion—Huh? or C

The endearing question about whether cats eat French fries would likely require further research, although someone may have the background knowledge to provide an answer. As we look at the questions, we can work together as a class to code them. After kids have had some time to practice together, they practice on their own in their independent reading. See some examples of questions that kids explored during independent reading in the assessment section of this chapter.

Gaining Information Through Questioning

Purpose: Writing in Wonder Books (nonfiction notebooks that support inquiry) to explore thinking and wondering
Resources: Wonder Books and assorted nonfiction trade books
Responses: Written question lists; two-column note form headed Questions/Facts

Fifth-grade teacher Eleanor Wright begins the year by sharing her own questions, those things she wonders about and longs to explore further. Kids are encouraged to share their questions in notebooks reserved for wonder and exploration. Eleanor asks her students to choose at least three things they wonder about. Cassie is nothing if not curious! Eleanor asks Cassie's permission to make an overhead transparency of her question list to share with the class (see Figure 8.3). Eleanor understands that questions are contagious and that kids who are struggling to come up with a question may just catch the wonder bug from Cassie. In classrooms that value wonder, kids come up with terrific questions.

In Mary Buerger's fourth-grade classroom, questions abound. Kids refer to their nonfiction notebooks as Wonder Books, and they explore questions on topics of interest, questions from

Figure 8.3 Cassie's List of Questions

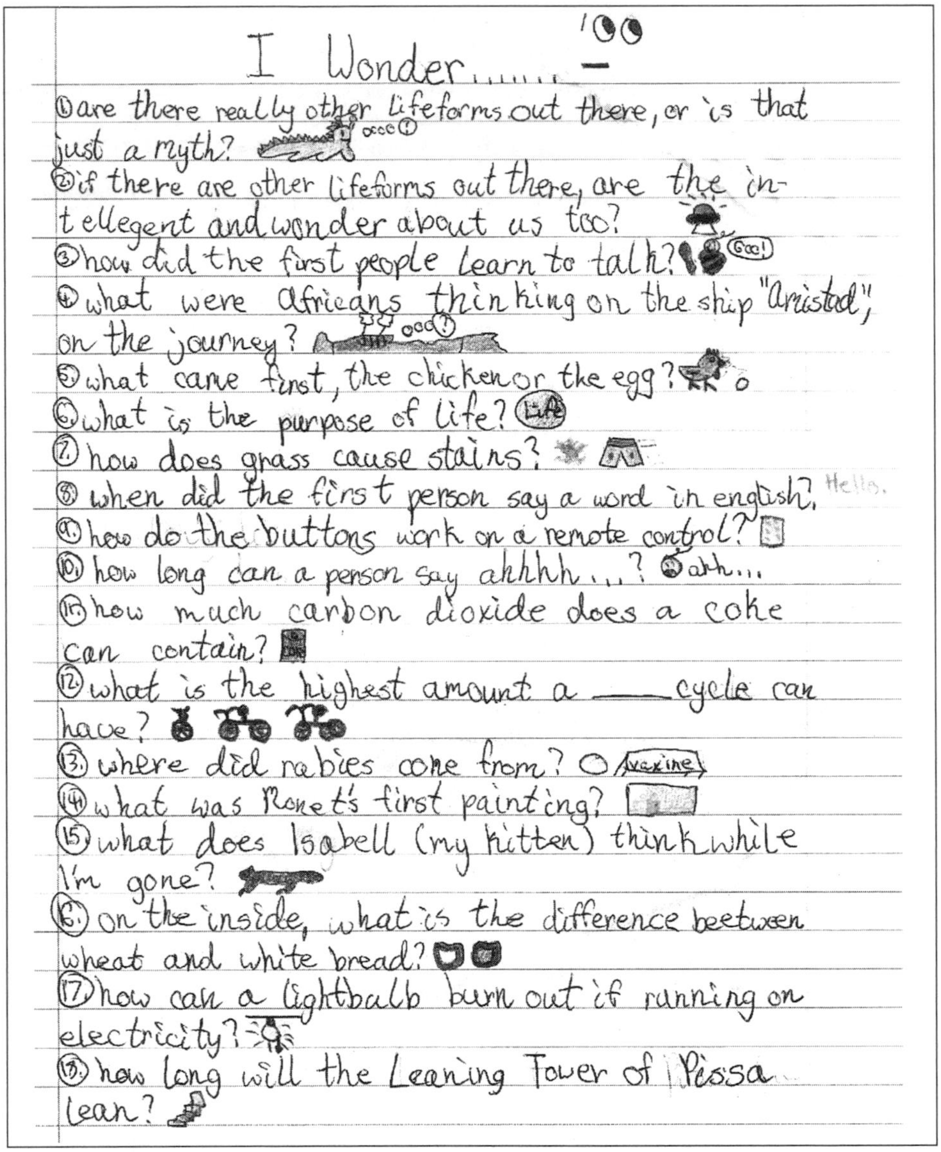

I Wonder.......

1. are there really other lifeforms out there, or is that just a myth?
2. if there are other lifeforms out there, are the intellegent and wonder about us too?
3. how did the first people learn to talk?
4. what were Africans thinking on the ship "Aristad", on the journey?
5. what came first, the chicken or the egg?
6. what is the purpose of life?
7. how does grass cause stains?
8. when did the first person say a word in english?
9. how do the buttons work on a remote control?
10. how long can a person say ahhhh...?
11. how much carbon dioxide does a coke can contain?
12. what is the highest amount a ___ cycle can have?
13. where did rabies come from?
14. what was Monet's first painting?
15. what does Isabell (my kitten) think while I'm gone?
16. on the inside, what is the difference beetween wheat and white bread?
17. how can a lightbulb burn out if running on electricity?
18. how long will the Leaning Tower of Pissa lean?

their reading, and questions for research. Most begin by simply listing a wide range of topics they wonder about, as Jonathan did when he wrote the following in his Wonder Book:

Anacondas. How can an anaconda squeeze so tight when it looks all fat and lazy and isn't all bulked up like Arnold Schwarzenegger?

Hurricanes. How do they form? What season? Where?

Spinal cord. How can breaking your spinal cord paralyze or kill you?

Allergic reactions. How can a bee sting kill a person? How can nuts make you all puffed up? How come hair and fur make you sneeze a lot?

Monkeys and gibbons. How do they have such good balance? How can they stand on a branch that is so thin or swing on branches with speed and not hit another branch or fall off?

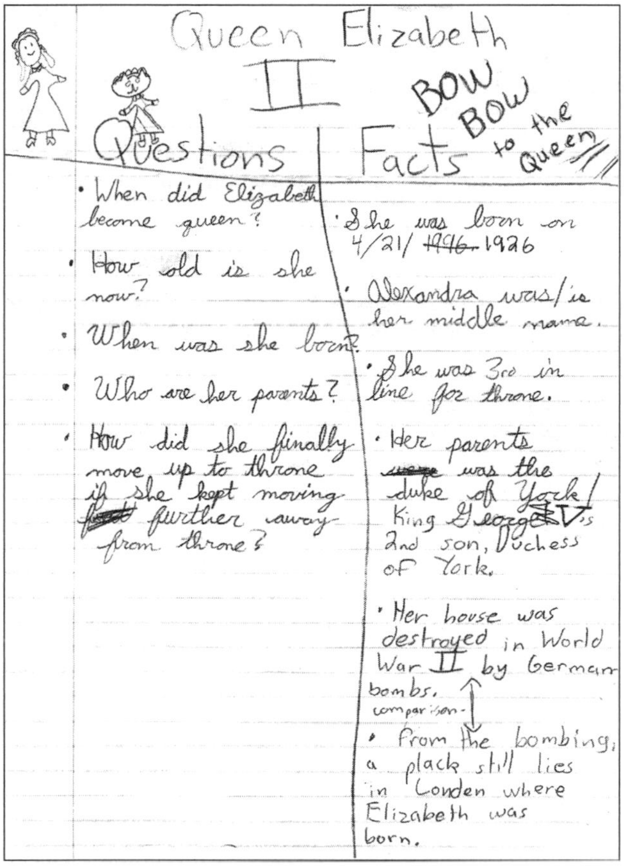
Queen Elizabeth II

Questions | Facts

BOW BOW to the Queen

• When did Elizabeth become queen?
• How old is she now?
• When was she born?
• Who are her parents?
• How did she finally move up to throne if she kept moving further away from throne?

• She was born on 4/21/ ~~1996~~ 1926
• Alexandra was/is her middle name.
• She was 3rd in line for throne.
• Her parents ~~were~~ was the duke of York/King George V's 2nd son, Duchess of York.
• Her house was destroyed in World War II by German bombs.
comparison
• From the bombing, a plack still lies in London where Elizabeth was born.

Figure 8.4 Amanda's Questions and Answers in Two-Column Format

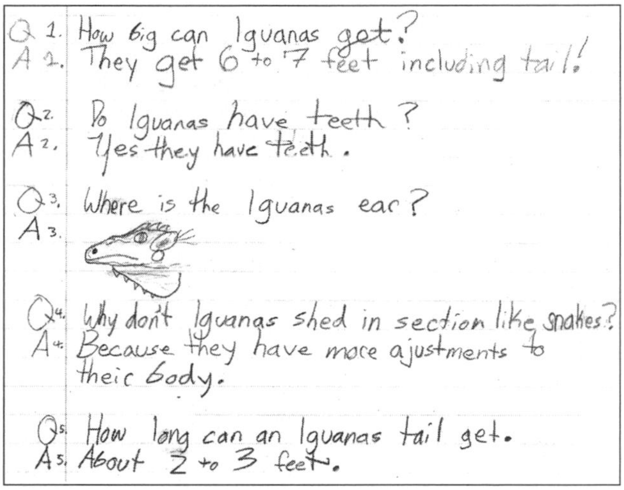
Q 1. How big can Iguanas get?
A 1. They get 6 to 7 feet including tail!
Q 2. Do Iguanas have teeth?
A 2. Yes they have teeth.
Q 3. Where is the Iguanas ear?
A 3.
Q 4. Why don't Iguanas shed in section like snakes?
A 4. Because they have more ajustments to their body.
Q 5. How long can an Iguanas tail get.
A 5. About 2 to 3 feet.

Figure 8.5 Matthew's Questions and Answers

Matt's curiosity grew as he investigated space. In a letter he wrote to Mary, he burst with questions (see Figure 8.1). When Mary talked to Matt, she found that his questions were especially useful to help him narrow the broad topic of space. We have found that the easiest way to guide students to focus research topics and pare them down is through their questions.

As kids read books on a specific topic, they acquire information and record new questions in their Wonder Books. Some code their questions on sticky notes. Some simply list their questions in their Wonder Books. Others record them in a variety of two- and three-column note forms (see the anchor chart in Appendix E). Mary teaches the class to use a two-column form headed Questions/Facts. Amanda chose it to record questions and facts as she did research on Queen Elizabeth II (see Figure 8.4). Others chose listing, webbing, or mapping to record questions and new information. Matthew recorded his questions and left room to answer them as he read (see Figure 8.5).

In sum, Eleanor and Mary expose their students to a variety of possibilities for asking questions, organizing thinking, and responding in writing. In addition, the kids come through with a wide range of original ideas and forms for sharing their own questions. Mary and Eleanor frequently ask the kids' permission to make transparencies of these organizational forms to share on the overhead projector. These teachers know that ten-year-olds often learn best from each other, so they invite kids up to teach other class members how to use these forms. For more information on Wonder Books and inquiry-based learning, see *Nonfiction Matters: Reading, Writing, and Research in Grades 3–8* (Harvey 1998).

Thick and Thin Questions

Purpose: Differentiating between large global questions and smaller clarification questions in a content area
Resources: Science textbook, nonfiction trade books
Responses: Thick questions on the front of 3" x 3" sticky notes, thin questions on the front of sticky flags; attempted answers on the reverse sides of the sticky notes and flags

Horace Mann Middle School teacher Margaret Bobb uses many different types of texts to teach seventh-grade physical science: newspaper and magazine articles, trade books, and, yes, the dreaded science textbook. She knows that textbooks don't usually go deep enough to give kids the background they need to understand important science topics, so she surrounds her kids with science print of every type. But she also knows that her students will be steeped in textbooks for at least five more years, and she would be doing them a disservice if she ignored teaching them how to read these bastions of American secondary education.

A technique she uses that helps her students sift large global questions from smaller clarification questions is the thick and thin question approach. Thick questions in Margaret's class are those that address large, universal concepts and often begin with Why? How come? I wonder? Or they address large content areas, such as What is photosynthesis? The answers to these questions are often long and involved, and require further discussion and research.

Thin questions are those primarily asked to clarify confusion, understand words, or access objective content. Questions that can be answered with a number or with a simple yes or no fit into this category. How many moons does Neptune have? is an example of a thin question. The answers are typically shorter than those for thick questions.

Kids in Margaret's classroom code for thick and thin questions in trade books as well as in textbooks. As they read, they code for thick and thin questions with different-sized sticky notes. For thick questions, they use the 3" x 3" sticky notes, mark them with the word *Thick*, and write the question on the front. For thin questions, they use the skinny, sticky flags with room only for small questions. In both cases, Margaret encourages her students to take a stab at the answer on the back of the sticky note. They may have no ideas about the answer, which is fine. But if they do, they can attempt an explanation on the reverse side of the sticky note.

Margaret has noticed that the visual marker of 3" x 3" sticky notes for thick questions and small sticky flags for thin questions has an immediate impact and helps students categorize questions more quickly than before. In the content areas particularly, these question categories, which separate broad concepts from smaller issues of clarification, seem to guide students to organize their thinking.

New

Reading to Answer a Question

Purpose: Reading to answer specific questions
Resources: A variety of nonfiction books on Plains Indians
Response: Writing a short summary

When Carole Suderman brought her third graders together to discuss what they had learned about Native Americans during their study of early Colorado history, she asked the kids if they had any lingering questions. The kids had spent some weeks studying the Plains Indian way of life, especially during the time when they depended on the buffalo for their food, clothing, shelter, tools, and other needs. Charlie thought for a minute and raised his hand.

"I wonder," he said, "whatever happened to the Plains Indians?" Charlie's question prompted a flood of questions from the other kids. "Did they disappear when all the buffalo got killed?" "Where did the Native Americans go if they didn't live on the plains anymore?" "Did the settlers live on the Indian's land without asking permission?" Often, we notice that the more kids learn, the more questions they have. Charlie and the other kids were eager to pursue these lingering questions. So Carole and the kids hightailed it down the hall to meet with librarian Nell Box and enlist her help as the kids read to find some answers.

They began by putting Charlie's question squarely in the center of a large piece of paper. As the kids shared their additional questions, Nell and Carole listed them, and then the group searched the library for books that might contain some answers. First, Nell and Carole modeled how to check for relevant information in a book, skimming the table of contents and the index for key words related to a particular question. Next, they read aloud several promising subtitles and sections of texts to show kids how they found the information in the text that answered a question. Then, Nell and Carole demonstrated how to read and paraphrase the information, write up a short paragraph to summarize the information, and add it to the chart. Finally, the kids went off to try this same process with their own questions.

When they came back together, the kids placed their answers on the large paper. Some kids found information about the diseases that settlers brought to the plains and which killed many of the native people. Other kids wrote about the over-hunting of the buffalo and how this destroyed the Plains Indians' source of food, shelter, and tools, effectively forcing those remaining tribes and nations to find their way to reservations. (See examples of their work in the assessment section of this chapter.) After reading and writing the answers to their questions, the kids came together to summarize and share what they had learned. During the share session, Irania raised her hand. "So what's happening to the Plains Indians right now?" Carole and Nell looked knowingly at each other and then smiled at Irania's next question—"Can I go back to the library to find out?"

Reading with a Question in Mind

New

Purpose: Taking notes on information to expand thinking and answer questions
Resource: "What's the Fuss About Frogs?" an article in *Odyssey* magazine by Laurie Ann Toupin (2002)
Response: A two-column think sheet headed Notes/Thinking

As readers read informational text, they are frequently overwhelmed by the sheer volume of information. Modeling how we read with a question in mind is one way to help readers cut through the dense text and zero in on important information. Steph joined Jeff Osberg's science class to help his eighth graders read with a question in mind, take notes on related information, and merge their thinking with it as they engaged in a study of global warming. Steph brought in an article titled "What's the Fuss About Frogs?" from *Odyssey*, a science-oriented magazine for intermediate and middle grade kids. The article explored the recent decline in amphibian populations throughout the world, some possible reasons for their disappearance, and some suggestions about what can be done about it.

Steph passed out the article and a think sheet headed Notes/Thinking and asked the kids to skim it and then turn and talk about what they knew about this topic and what they wondered about. A number of them shared that they noticed that frogs were disappearing and wondered why. Several inferred that their disappearance might be related to global warming, which they had been studying. After several shared their thinking, Steph explained that readers can sometimes better understand what they read and pick out the most salient information if they read with a question in mind. So she wrote the question, Why are these frogs disappearing? in the Thinking column. The kids, with their think sheets on clipboards, jotted that question down as well.

Steph explained that as she read, she would keep her question in mind and jot down information that related to that question in the Notes column. In addition, she shared that simply jotting the facts by themselves was not enough and that readers need to merge their thinking with information to make sense of it. So as she read the first few paragraphs of the article, she took notes on the information that related to her original question in the Notes column and merged her thinking in the Thinking column. Through her reading, she discovered that all amphibians are in great decline, that they are an important food source, that they slow the greenhouse effect by eating insects that normally contribute to decomposition, and that they are the canaries in the ecological coal mine.

As she modeled, she didn't write just any fact in the Notes column, but only information that related directly to her question. In this way, the process of note taking didn't become cumbersome and unwieldy, but instead contributed to her understanding. She also showed how she used the Thinking column to help her when she became confused. She would simply jot down the page number and paragraph that didn't make sense so she could clarify the confusion later on. She shared how sometimes one question leads to another. As she read, she noted several questions in the thinking column including a big one, Why does it matter if amphibians are declining? From that point on, she kept that question in mind as well as her original question. Her Notes/Thinking two-column form follows here:

Notes	**Thinking**
All forms of amphibians are in decline, not just frogs	Why are these frogs disappearing?
Frogs, toads, newts, salamanders, and caecilians are all amphibians	Don't get this part—what is decomposition? (p. 15 3rd ppg)
Slows down greenhouse effect	Why does it matter if amphibians are declining?
Because they are the canaries in the ecological coal mine	Miners used to take canaries into coal mines to test the air and if the canaries died, it meant they had to get out right away

After modeling and engaging the kids in guided practice, Steph reminded them once again that the Notes column was to jot down information related to their question and the Thinking column was a place for them to "work out their thinking" and try to make sense of the new information. Then she sent them off to try this with a partner, having them take turns reading and talking about the section they read, keeping the big question in mind and filling in the think sheet in response to their question. Shoko's think sheet is shown in Figure 8.6. Her last comment in the Thinking column illustrates how she merged her thoughts with the information and expanded her thinking after reading.

Figure 8.6 Shoko's Think Sheet About Frogs

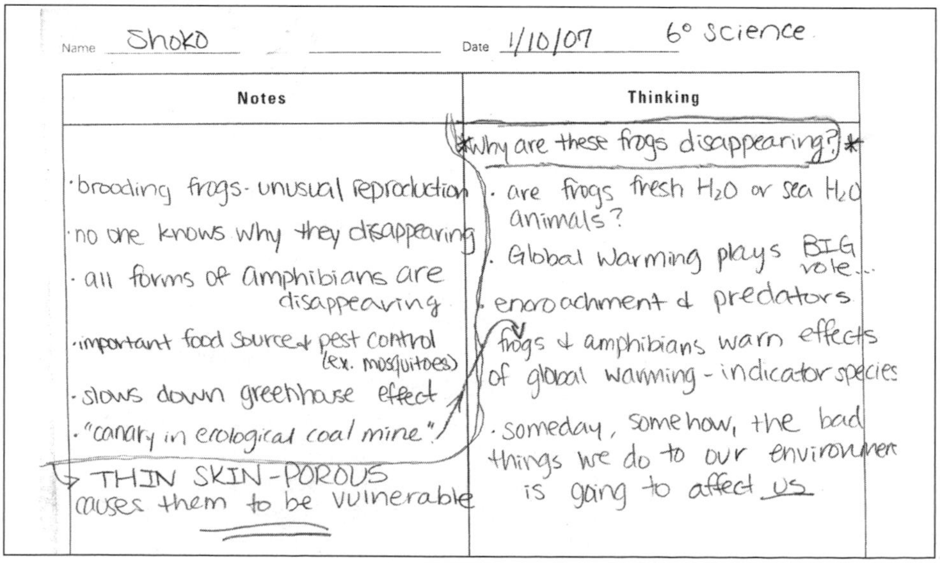

Name Shoko Date 1/10/07 6° Science

Notes	Thinking
	Why are these frogs disappearing?
· brooding frogs - unusual reproduction	· are frogs fresh H_2O or sea H_2O animals?
· no one knows why they disappearing	· Global Warming plays BIG role...
· all forms of amphibians are disappearing	· encroachment & predators
· important food source & pest control (ex. mosquitoes)	frogs & amphibians warn effects of global warming - indicator species
· slows down greenhouse effect	· someday, somehow, the bad things we do to our environment is going to affect us
· "canary in ecological coal mine."	
THIN SKIN - POROUS causes them to be vulnerable	

Questioning That Leads to Inferential Thinking

Purpose: Making meaning through asking questions
Resource: Langston Hughes's poem "Dreams"
Response: Chart of questions students ask about the poem

Poetry, with its images and metaphors, provides students with ample opportunities to exercise their powers of interpretation. When planning a lesson on questioning with poetry, Anne chose Langston Hughes's poem "Dreams" because it is one of her favorites. She wondered if it might prove a little too abstract for third graders. But if she'd learned anything in her years of teaching, it was to never underestimate the kids' potential.

Hughes's poem uses the metaphors of "a broken-winged bird" and "a barren field" to describe what life would be like without hope. His first line, "Hold fast to dreams," could be a message to the reader to remain hopeful in the face of adversity. Anne knew more about Langston Hughes's difficult life than these third graders, and she wondered if their lack of background knowledge would hinder their understanding.

Anne copied the poem on a large chart and placed it on an easel set up in front of the kids. When the students started thinking out loud about the poem, they used the questioning strategy to help them better understand it. They had experience with questioning, and the poem evoked many questions.

This lesson was a guided conversation. Anne began by modeling her own struggle to understand the poem by asking a few questions. Sharing her own doubts and questions about the meaning of the poem opened up the opportunity for the kids to risk sharing their own interpretations and inferences. Their questions were quite sophisticated and attempted to unlock the poem's meaning. As the class read the poem out loud together, Anne wrote their questions on the chart next to the place in the poem where they asked them or at the end of the text for less specific questions.

What does "Hold fast to dreams" mean?
Could "Life is a broken-winged bird" mean that life is sad and miserable?
When dreams go, do you die?
The poet seems to want to hold on to his dreams. Is he hopeful or sad?
Is this about a dream, like a sleeping dream?
What's a barren field?
Why is nothing growing?
Could the author or poet be thinking of dying?
Did his wish come true?
Was this a broken dream of the author?
Did he have a hope that didn't come true?
When did he write this?
Does he mean that if we don't have dreams, we don't have hope?

The children's questions ranged from the literal What's a barren field? to thoughtful inferences about the poet's feelings, such as Was this a broken dream of the author? Rather than stopping to answer each question as it was asked, Anne and the students continued reading the poem, returning later to look again at the questions. The questions served as prompts to the interpretation of the poem and inferences about its meaning. Students didn't always agree. Some argued over whether the poem's message was ultimately hopeful or discouraging. Two students offered to find out more about Langston Hughes in the hope that learning something about his life would help them resolve this difference of opinion. In this lesson, the kids asked more questions than they answered, and they learned that there are no absolute answers when interpreting poetry. But in the end their questions took them deeper into the poem and inspired a thoughtful conversation.

Although the lesson ended without a comfortable sense of closure, the students now viewed questions in a new way. Questions didn't always have to be answered. Questions prompted their inferences and guided their interpretations. Questions opened their minds.

Responding to "Beyond-the-Line" Questions in Literature

New

Purpose: Extending and deepening thinking in response to inferential questions
Resource: *Journey,* by Patricia MacLachlan
Response: Written responses demonstrating inferential thinking

Intermediate teacher Tiffany Boyd knows that thoughtful conversations about literature don't just happen. She teaches her kids ways to share their questions and interpretations as they debate and discuss in book clubs. At the beginning of the year, Tiffany and her kids read a variety of short stories and chapter books together so that children have plenty of opportunities to respond in thoughtful ways that fuel lively discussions. Tiffany teaches her students to ask questions that encourage discussion and keep their book club conversations stimulating.

To make sure that kids ask genuine questions, Tiffany teaches them about what she calls "beyond-the-line" questions. Beyond-the-line questions are those that can't be answered with a one- or two-word response or by referring to one or two lines of the text for a simple, straightforward answer. Instead, these inferential questions arise when the text is ambiguous; when characters, events, and issues in the story prompt a variety of interpretations; and when the reader needs to read between the lines to gain a fuller understanding. Often, readers need to pull evidence and ideas from several parts of the text to answer these beyond-the-line questions.

To model how to ask beyond-the-line questions, Tiffany chose the book *Journey*, by Patricia MacLachlan. It begins when Journey's restless mother disappears, leaving him and his sister Cat with their grandparents. Full of the difficulties and issues of a family coming apart, the book is about Journey's struggle to come to terms with his mother's leaving. As his grandparents hold things together and do their best to recreate a family life, Journey learns important and hard-won lessons. As kids navigate the symbolism and metaphors, they think deeply to figure out the family mysteries that unfold over the course of the story.

Tiffany launches the first discussion with her beyond-the-line question: "Cat and Journey are dealing with Mama leaving in really different ways. How is each one handling this? I'm thinking about how I deal with things that are hard to face." She shares her written response with the kids to demonstrate how she works out her thinking about the first part of the story. (See Figure 8.7.)

Figure 8.7 Tiffany Wrote Out and Shared Her Thinking with a Beyond-the-Line Question

"BTLQ"

Journey — Beyond the Line Question

BTLQ: Describe how Cat and Journey are dealing with Mama leaving differently. How do you deal with things that are hard to face?

Answer:
Journey is thinking about how all of this affects him. He is being very thoughtful and introspective. He seems kind of stuck and needs to dwell on it for a while. Cat wants to keep busy. She is getting rid of things — her flute, camera, sweatshirt and she appears to be trying to make a fresh start.

When something is hard for me to deal with, sometimes I'm like Journey, I just want to go to bed and hope everything will be okay when I wake up. Sometimes I'm like Cat, I keep moving and try not to think about the thing that is hard.

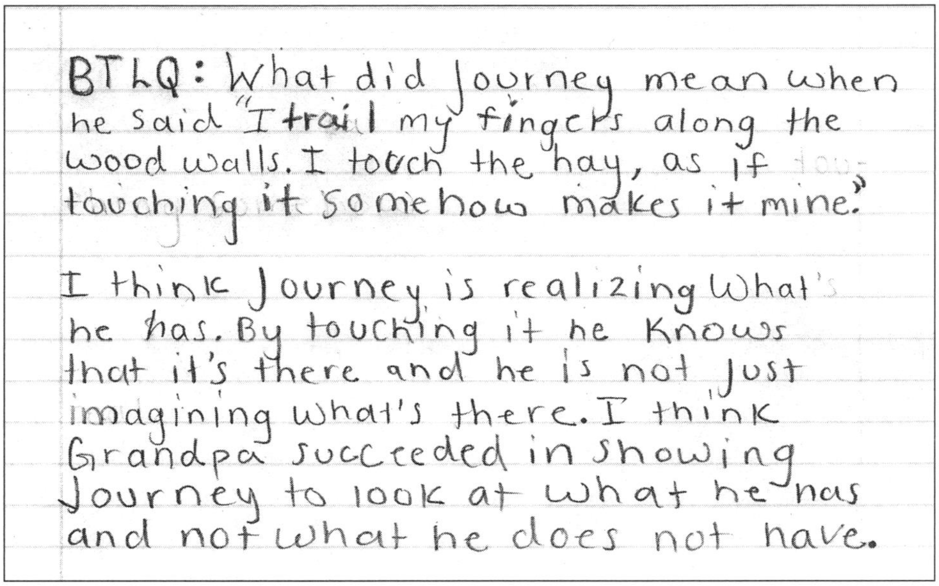

Figure 8.8 Samantha's Beyond-the-Line
Question and Response

BTLQ: What did Journey mean when he said "I trail my fingers along the wood walls. I touch the hay, as if touching it somehow makes it mine."

I think Journey is realizing what's he has. By touching it he knows that it's there and he is not just imagining what's there. I think Grandpa succeeded in showing Journey to look at what he has and not what he does not have.

Samantha also shares her thinking about her own beyond-the-line question. (See Figure 8.8.)

As the kids fit the pieces of the puzzle together toward the end of the story, not all of them feel a sense of closure. This is not a story with a clear resolution, and the kids still have more to talk about. What drives their thinking and discussion are the beyond-the-line questions that are open-ended and lead to multiple interpretations.

Using Question Webs to Expand Thinking

Purpose: Organizing content knowledge to answer a specific question
Resources: Civil War picture books and young adult magazines (see Appendix A for Civil War text sets and Appendix B for magazines)
Response: Question web

We are always searching for different ways to help students make meaning through questioning. It is not easy for children to pick out essential questions from a long list of unrelated questions. One way we have found to highlight the most essential questions is to construct a question web. Similar in form to other semantic webs, a question web differs in that it has a question at its center. The lines that emanate from the center are used to add information that relates in some way to the question, with the ultimate goal of building an answer from all of the various bits of information. Kids can use question webs individually to answer specific questions when reading. Or, additionally, question webs have proven useful for small groups studying a content area.

As kids study a specific content area, small research teams can explore a common question of their choice and construct meaning through a question web. One such informational study group was doing research on the Civil War. After reading a wide variety of picture books and young adult magazines on the Civil War, one member raised the question, Why was it called the Underground Railroad? No one was completely sure. From that point on, members of the

Figure 8.9 Question Web About the Civil War

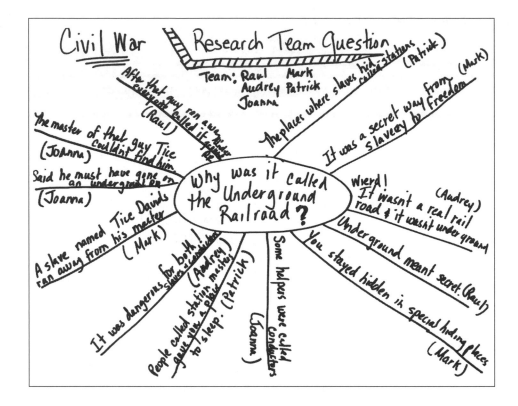

research team read to answer that question and added pertinent information to the question web as they came upon it in their reading. They drew their web on a large piece of butcher paper and added new web lines when they found new information. By the end of the inquiry, they had amassed enough information to answer the question. (See Figure 8.9.)

Researchable Questions

Many of kids' questions have an important purpose—to seek out information. Busching and Slesinger, in *It's Our World, Too: Socially Responsive Learners in Middle School Language Arts* (2002), make a useful distinction between "focused" and "unfocused" information-seeking questions. Unfocused information-seeking questions, they suggest, occur when students are puzzled or confused and need additional background information to make sense of things. Focused information-seeking questions are posed to fill in specific information about a particular topic. These initial questions may lead to bigger questions that ask why or how.

Once their interest is piqued, kids want more information, and we give them the opportunity to explore all manner of information-seeking questions. Charlie's question, Whatever happened to the Plains Indians? is a good example of a researchable question that got the whole class involved. The kids who created the web based on the question, Why was it called the Underground

Railroad? worked as a team to organize questions to find out additional information. Regardless of the source, we encourage any and all questions that spur kids to think more deeply about their learning.

Lingering Questions

Whenever kids finish reading, listening to, or thinking about something they've read, we ask them to jot down any remaining questions they still have. These lingering questions extend their understanding beyond the text. Some lingering questions come up when there is no clear resolution to a story and the reader is left up in the air. Sometimes a good story requires the reader to draw his or her own conclusions about what happened or consider varying interpretations of the characters' actions and the unfolding events. When readers finish a book like *Journey* or *Charlie Anderson*, questions may remain. These lingering questions encourage kids to consider the many possibilities raised by an ambiguous ending. It's these kinds of questions that prompt discussion and debate or keep us up at night pondering the twist at the end of a great novel.

Kids also ask lingering questions in science, social studies, and history. It is these questions that often become researchable questions. Students may come up with important questions as they read magazines and newspapers about current events. Sometimes, these significant questions spur kids to ask why or how questions that may not be answered by simply amassing more information. Lingering questions in history move into the realm of speculation—what-if questions that consider how things might have turned out differently. Or lingering questions can extend a child's understanding of a topic or issue, as he or she grapples with new ideas or empathizes with different perspectives. When reading about an Afghan refugee child and her difficult life in a war-torn country, Megan asked, "I wonder what it would feel like to live where there is a war going on." Megan's empathy for a young girl in difficult circumstances pushed her thinking further. Second graders read newspaper accounts of the recent hurricanes, and as the enormity and tragic nature of the events sank in, they asked, "How could we help the victims of Hurricane Katrina?" (See Chapter 13.) In response to their question, they brainstormed things they could do to help. We encourage kids to engage in further conversation about a great read or take action in response to compelling information, so we constantly model and encourage kids to ask and consider lingering questions.

Authentic Questions or Assessment Questions

When we were in school, the teachers asked the questions, and we supplied the answers, or tried to anyway, whether we knew them or not. The teachers knew the answers to the long list of questions they asked or that appeared at the end of the story in our basal readers. Teachers asked these questions to check on us, to see whether we had done the homework, read the chapter, or memorized our facts. Those were the only questions we remember in school. Our own questions, important or not, were reserved for recess, walking home after school, or the dinner table that night. School was not to be mucked up with a lot of tangential kid questions.

Fortunately, in the classrooms portrayed in this book, authentic student questions are encouraged and valued. Authentic questions, whether asked by students or teachers,

- Prompt thinking
- Don't always have one right answer
- May have many answers
- Cause us to ponder and wonder
- Dispel or clarify confusion
- Challenge us to rethink our opinions
- Lead us to seek out further information
- Are subject to discussion, debate, and conversation
- May require further research

Many tasks we ask kids to do in schools involve what we have to come call *assessment questions*. Assessment questions are questions that we teachers know the answers to and that we ask primarily to check or monitor our students' knowledge. Now, before launching a full frontal attack on assessment questions, we recognize that we are teachers and that we have both the right and the responsibility to ask assessment questions to monitor our kids' progress. Asking assessment questions represents one way to measure academic growth. But do we need to ask so many? Right now, most of the questions asked in schools fall into the assessment category. Curiosity-driven questions are still rare in classrooms. We need to balance this by allowing more time for kids and teachers to ask and explore authentic questions.

We explain the difference between authentic questions and assessment questions to the kids. Why fake it? When we ask assessment questions, we might tell our students, "This is an assessment question. I know the answer. Here comes the question." With younger primary kids, we might call these *checking questions*. "I know the answer to this question. I'm asking it to check and see if you do." When we consider authentic questions, our response is something like, "I don't know the answer, but let's see if we can find out."

Peter Johnston (2004) lists a number of ways that teachers can ask students authentic questions that prompt thinking. Authentic questions are typically open-ended and encourage divergent thinking rather than one right answer. Some that we use frequently include

- What makes you think that?
- Why do you say that?
- Can you elaborate on that?
- Can you tell me more about your thinking?
- How did you come up with that?

When all is said and done, these kinds of questions have an authentic feel. We ask these kinds of questions to probe and find out about what kids are thinking not to check whether or not they did their homework. Authentic ques-

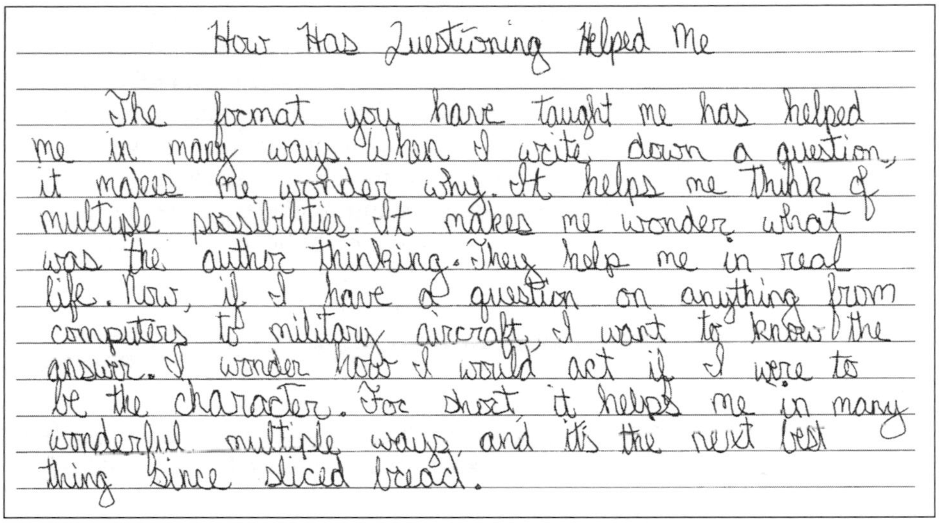

Figure 8.10 Brandon's Opinion About the Questioning Strategy

How Has Questioning Helped Me

The format you have taught me has helped me in many ways. When I write down a question, it makes me wonder why. It helps me think of multiple possibilities. It makes me wonder what was the author thinking. They help me in real life. Now, if I have a question on anything from computers to military aircraft, I want to know the answer. I wonder how I would act if I were to be the character. For short it helps me in many wonderful multiple ways, and its the next best thing since sliced bread.

tions such as these, whether asked by kids or adults, are more likely to encourage new thinking and prompt new insight. In his enthusiastic response to his teacher Eleanor Wright, fifth grader Brandon reminds us how questioning helps him in both reading and life (see Figure 8.10). We think that's terrific!

Teaching with the End in Mind: Assessing What We've Taught

Questioning

Based on the lessons in this chapter, we look for evidence that

1. *Students stop, ask questions, and wonder about their reading.* We look for evidence that students are stopping to think about their reading and record their questions.
2. *Students ask questions to clarify confusion.* We look for evidence that students are monitoring their understanding and stop and ask a question when they are confused.
3. *Students read to gain information and answer questions.* We look for evidence that students are reading with a question in mind and noting when they find information that answers it.
4. *Students consider lingering questions to expand thinking.* We look for evidence that students are asking inferential and interpretive questions that encourage discussion and debate.

Suggestions for Differentiation

Anchor charts make comprehension strategies concrete and can be invaluable for our English language learners and children just learning to read. We keep anchor charts of kids' questions about a text, a topic, an issue, and so forth posted on the walls and refer back to them frequently. In addition to written questions from both the teachers and the kids, we encourage kids to illustrate their questions with a visual image that helps them keep their question in mind. They also write or illustrate answers as they find them.

Another anchor chart that we co-construct focuses on how questioning helps us understand and ways kids can use questions in their reading. For instance, the chart might begin with a statement such as "We ask questions to . . ." and go on to finish the statement with "make sense of what we read," "find information," and "answer our wonders." Kids then draw themselves on large sticky notes doing these things—answering questions, finding information, and so on—and place their pictures on the appropriate place on the chart.

We can create anchor charts such as these for a variety of strategies. Incorporating drawing is one of the best ways to make kids' thinking visible and to support those who need additional help with reading.

Questioning Assessment Commentary

Stopping to wonder and think about pictures and information with the lesson "The More We Learn, the More We Wonder"

As young children learn from pictures and listen to the teacher reading informational text, they often stop, think, and wonder about the information.

Figure 8.11 In this series of drawings, a young child draws and writes in her own invented spelling the questions she asked as she learned about penguins. Among her questions were, *I wonder why penguins fall down, I wonder why the egg is on his feet, I wonder if they eat fish,* and *I wonder what else they eat.* Our next step would be to teach her to keep her questions in mind as she continues to learn about penguins. In this way, she could find answers to her questions.

Figure 8.12 As kids learn more information, they sometimes find the answers to their questions. Young children's drawings often illustrate very specific information that we need to talk to them about in order to see if they are making sense. This question and its answer are part of a kindergarten class's research on Antarctica. We recorded and typed the child's language and she illustrated the information. In this case the drawings accurately depict both the question and the answer.

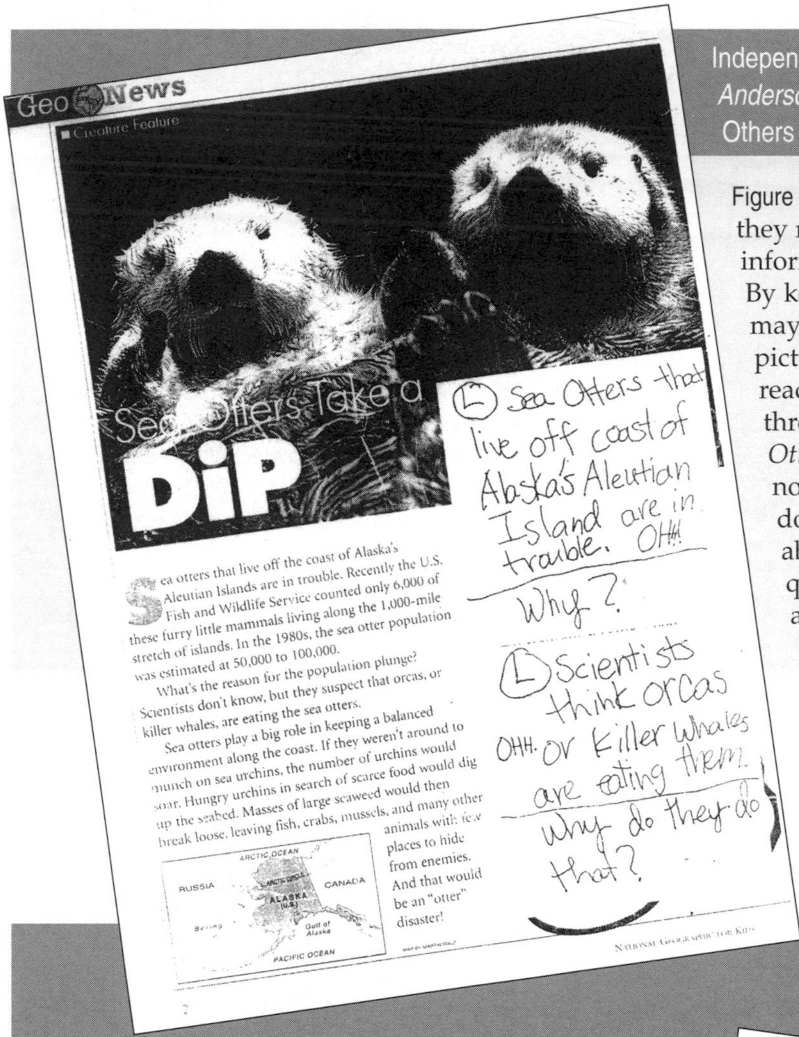

GeoNews

Creature Feature

Sea Otters Take a DiP

Sea otters that live off the coast of Alaska's Aleutian Islands are in trouble. Recently the U.S. Fish and Wildlife Service counted only 6,000 of these furry little mammals living along the 1,000-mile stretch of islands. In the 1980s, the sea otter population was estimated at 50,000 to 100,000.

What's the reason for the population plunge? Scientists don't know, but they suspect that orcas, or killer whales, are eating the sea otters.

Sea otters play a big role in keeping a balanced environment along the coast. If they weren't around to munch on sea urchins, the number of urchins would soar. Hungry urchins in search of scarce food would dig up the seabed. Masses of large seaweed would then break loose, leaving fish, crabs, mussels, and many other animals with few places to hide from enemies. And that would be an "otter" disaster!

Independent reading after the lesson with *Charlie Anderson*, "Some Questions Are Answered, Others Are Not"

Figure 8.13 Readers wonder about what they read, but they also read to gain information and answer their questions. By keeping their questions in mind, they may answer them and see the larger picture develop. We have noticed that readers can develop a line of thinking through their questions. Here in *Sea Otters Take a Dip*, we have two sticky notes that show the reader jotting down new information and wondering about it. Because she keeps her question in mind, she notices the answer and follows a line of thinking.

Researching answers to questions with the lesson "Reading to Answer a Question"

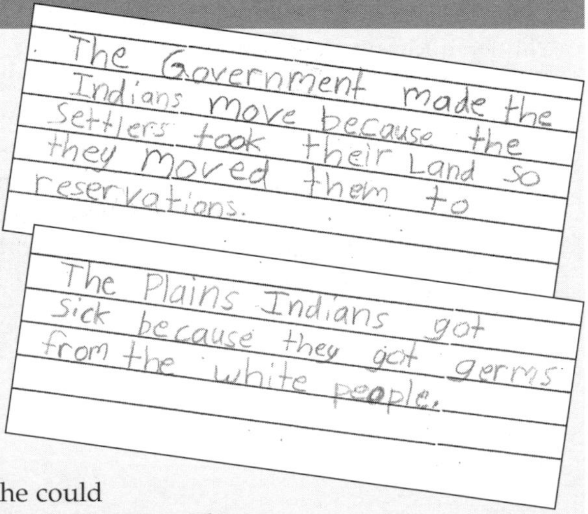

When kids have lingering questions, we take the time to read to answer them. Charlie's question, "Whatever happened to the Plains Indians?" provided an opportunity for kids to extend their thinking about this topic.

Figure 8.14 When kids read to answer their questions, they often come up with information that answers the question but may need additional explanation to clarify the answer. This response summarizes information that answers the question, but in order to make sure the child understands the information he's found, we would confer and discuss what he means by "the government" and see if he could tell us what happened as the Native Americans moved to reservations. Then we would work with him to elaborate on his answer to the question.

Figure 8.15 When we do research with the whole class, it's all about differentiation. This response clearly describes what happened when the Plains Indians caught diseases from settlers. An English language learner, this child's illustration of an Indian in poor health lying on buffalo robes demonstrates her understanding.

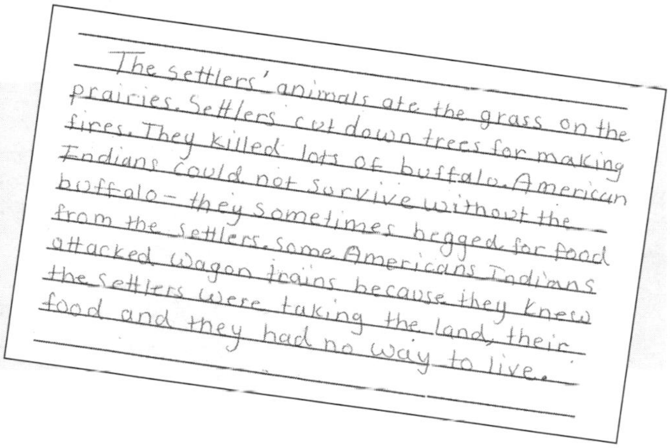

Figure 8.16 This detailed answer summarizes many aspects of what happened as settlers moved west. The child synthesized information from several sources and wove it together to explain what happened to the Indians as well as why they began to try to defend their lands from settlement.

> The settlers' animals ate the grass on the prairies. Settlers cut down trees for making fires. They killed lots of buffalo. American Indians could not survive without the buffalo — they sometimes begged for food from the settlers. Some Americans Indians attacked wagon trains because they knew the settlers were taking the land, their food and they had no way to live.

Figure 8.17 This illustration succinctly sums up what happened to the Plains Indians over time. Incorporating many of his peers' responses, this child asked to put his response at the end of the class chart—a thoughtful synthesis of everyone's learning.

Chapter 9

Visualizing and Inferring: Making What's Implicit Explicit

One day Steph walked into a staff developers' meeting and mentioned that she was in search of a fresh, new picture book to teach visualizing. Our colleague and friend Chryse Hutchins suggested Estelle Condra's *See the Ocean*, a beautiful book filled with stunning watercolor illustrations, striking poetic words, and a moving narrative.

It is the tale of a little girl who travels to a beach house with her parents and her brothers each summer. As we read through the story, we soon notice that something is different about Nellie. She never begs to sit near the window in the car, she describes the ocean as an old white-bearded man, and she asks her parents endless questions. Near the end, we discover that she is blind. As Steph read through it, she, too, had endless questions.

"I wonder why Chryse recommended this for visualizing?" she asked Anne the next day. "I think it's perfect for questioning." Anne read it and commented that she thought it was just what she was looking for to teach inferring. When we talked with Chryse later, she said that from her perspective, the poetic language, metaphoric writing, and stunning imagery best lent itself to teaching visualizing.

Different readers rely on different strategies to help them gain better understanding. We mention this because, as we have said, well-crafted picture books can be used to teach and practice just about any strategy. To gain understanding of *See the Ocean*, readers are likely to activate several strategies, including visualizing, questioning, and inferring.

Many teachers we know introduce this book after their students have spent considerable time practicing different strategies. They encourage their kids to think about which strategies they are using to make sense of *See the Ocean* and to mark sticky notes with whatever strategy seems to help them gain meaning. Veronica's sticky notes show how this eighth grader activates all three of these strategies and more as she reads and thinks through *See the Ocean* (see Figure 9.1). These sticky notes provide strong evidence of her flexibility with strategy use. She activates multiple strategies to comprehend.

We discuss visualizing and inferring in one chapter because they are closely related. Visualizing strengthens our inferential thinking. When we

Figure 9.1 Veronica's Sticky Note Responses for *See the Ocean*

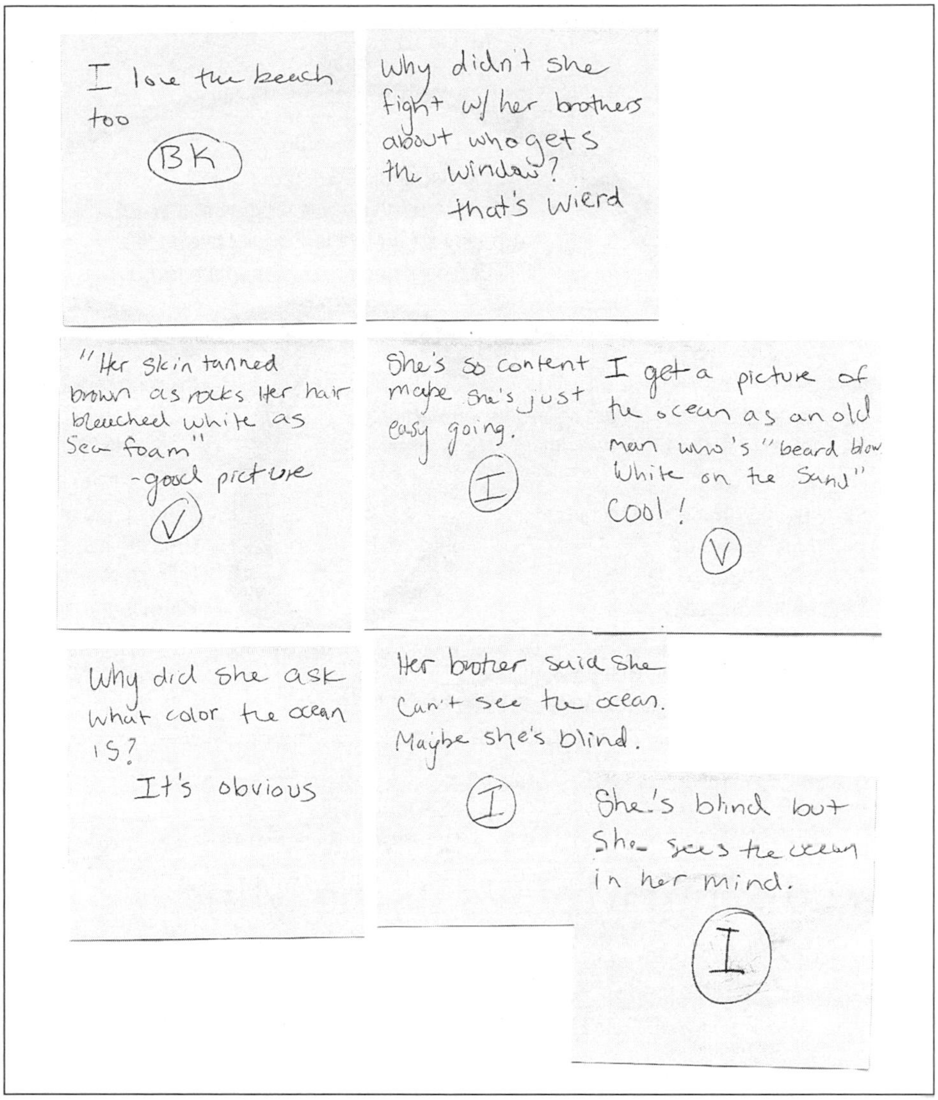

visualize, we are in fact inferring, but with mental images rather than words and thoughts. Visualizing and inferring don't occur in isolation. Strategies interweave. Inferring involves merging background knowledge with text clues to come up with an idea that is not explicitly stated in the text. Inferring is the proverbial reading between the lines.

A variety of mental processes occur under the umbrella of inferential thinking. When we teach kids to infer, we might teach them to draw conclusions or make predictions. Inferring may involve using the context to figure out the meaning of an unfamiliar word or noticing a character's actions to surface a theme. Our colleague Judy Wallis created a visual that describes the multifaceted nature of inferential thinking. She chose an umbrella to represent the many aspects of inferring. We have adapted it here as a way of showing the different ways readers use inferential thinking to enhance understanding. (See Figure 9.2.)

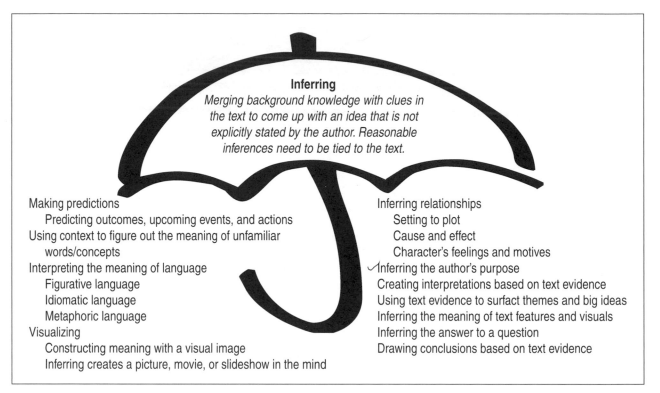

Figure 9.2 The Inferring Umbrella

Visualizing: Movies in the Mind

Visualizing brings joy to reading. When we visualize, we create pictures in our minds that belong to us and no one else. As more and more books are routinely churned into movies, we are not surprised that most people prefer the book over the movie, kids included. One problem inherent in transforming text to film is that Hollywood routinely takes a four-hundred-and-fifty-page novel and converts it into a one-hundred-page script. Not surprisingly, depth and texture suffer. Another common complaint relates to the characters. Steph could never sit back and enjoy the film *Seven Years in Tibet*, based on one of her favorite books by Heinrich Harrer, because Brad Pitt, no matter how cute he was, did not jibe with her image of the book's protagonist.

Some years ago, a short-lived program about Beverly Cleary's beloved character Ramona hit TV. Kids were outraged. Each had clear, yet very different, pictures of Ramona in mind. Not one we spoke to could relate to the televised image of Ramona. When we visualize, we create our own movies in our minds. We become attached to the characters we visualize. Visualizing personalizes reading, keeps us engaged, and often prevents us from abandoning a book prematurely. When we introduce visualizing, we are likely to facilitate a conversation about books and movie adaptations in an attempt to make the strategy concrete. Kids relate and quickly weigh in with their own opinions.

Strategy Lessons: Visualizing

Visualizing with Wordless Picture Books

Purpose: Visualizing to fill in missing information
Resource: *Good Dog Carl*, by Alexandra Day
Response: Drawing what you visualize

We teach visualizing in many different ways, but one surprising way is through wordless picture books. One might think that when a book has only pictures with no written text, visualizing is rendered unnecessary. Not so. We take the clues revealed in the illustrations and combine them with the missing pictures we create in our minds to make meaning.

Alexandra Day's picture books about Carl, the baby-sitting rottweiler, are wonderful examples of wordless books that kids love and that we can use for the purpose of teaching visualizing. *Good Dog Carl* tells the story of a household adventure in which Carl leads the baby on a romp through the house while the mother is out shopping.

Midway through the book, we find a picture of the baby sitting in front of a laundry chute with Carl standing right behind her. The very next page (picture) shows Carl dashing down the stairs. The kids' expressions are priceless. Many erupt with laughter. We ask them what they visualize between the two pictures and then have them draw, write, or talk about their response. Angie Carey's first-grade class visualized an array of scenarios, including the baby falling down the laundry chute, the baby sliding down on purpose, and Carl pushing the baby down.

Cristina and Max had different mental pictures, but both had the baby headed down the chute, which is exactly what happened one way or another. Cristina visualized an elaborate floor plan of the house in relation to the laundry chute (see Figure 9.3). Max created a less complicated image but used the phrase "shot down the shoot" to convey how the baby got down (see

Figure 9.3 Cristina's Response to *Good Dog Carl*

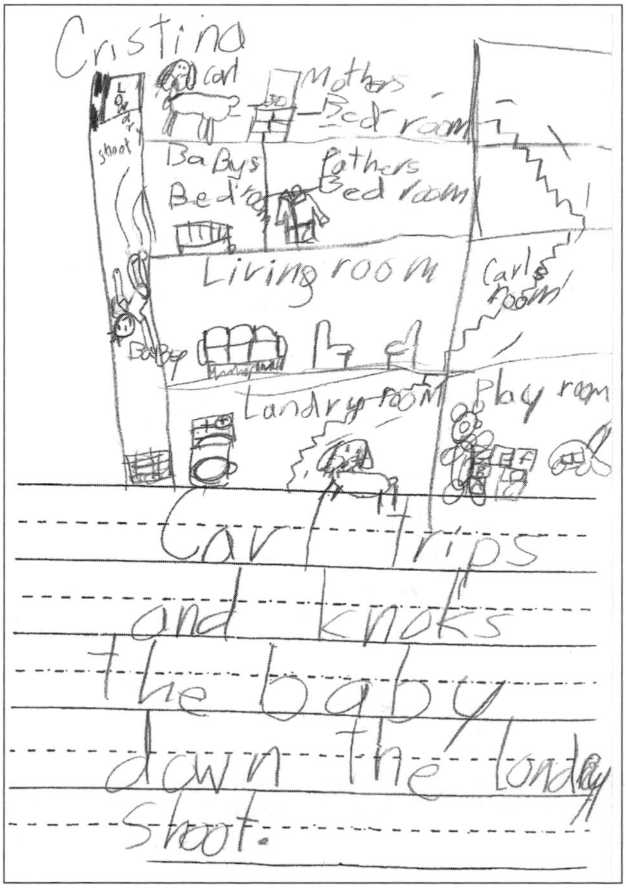

Figure 9.4 Max's Response to *Good Dog Carl*

Figure 9.4). As with all comprehension strategies, we bring our schema to our mental images to make sense of things. Both Cristina's and Max's images make perfect sense.

We can alert ourselves to misconceptions by looking at student work. For instance, if a drawing had the baby sprouting wings and flying into the clouds, we would talk to the child about whether that was reasonable given the context of the story. We don't want kids to go too far afield because the purpose of visualizing is to help them better understand the actual text. One student in Angie's class drew a picture of Carl carrying the baby down the stairs. While this was closer to reality than a baby sprouting wings, it was still a misconception. The first picture clearly showed the baby at the edge of the laundry chute followed by the next picture of Carl running down the stairs, no baby on his back. In either case, we would confer with the child to help clear up any misconceptions.

Visualizing with wordless books helps readers build meaning as they go. Visualizing with text does the same thing. This lesson might become an anchor to help kids remember how visualizing helps them better comprehend. Although the examples here are from first graders, we have used wordless picture books for teaching visualizing with older kids as well, to give them a concrete sense of the strategy and how it works. They are frequently amazed at how their notion of visualizing is clarified when we show them wordless picture books.

Visualizing from a Vivid Piece of Text

Purpose:　Merging prior experience and the text to create visual images
Resource:　The lead to Chapter 3, "Escape," in *Charlotte's Web*, by E. B. White
Response:　Drawing visual images with small groups

We work on and practice strategies with small groups. A group of six fourth graders had chosen to read E. B. White's *Charlotte's Web* in their book club. Steph saw this as a great opportunity to talk to them about visualizing because E. B. White writes in such a strikingly visual way.

Chapter 3, "Escape," begins with a vivid, detailed description of the barn where Charlotte, the magical spider, lives with all of the other animals in the story. The passage describing the barn is about a page and half long and is filled with specific nouns and compelling descriptions:

> The barn was very large. It was very old. It smelled of hay. . . . It smelled of the perspiration of tired horses and the wonderful sweet breath of patient cows. . . . It smelled of grain and of harness dressing and of axle grease and of rubber boots and of new rope. . . . It was full of all sorts of things that you find in barns: ladders, grindstones, pitch forks, monkey wrenches, scythes, lawn mowers, snow shovels, ax handles, milk pails, water buckets, empty grain sacks, and rusty rat traps. It was the kind of barn that swallows like to build their nests in. It was the kind of barn that children like to play in.

Steph read the passage out loud to the group and asked them to close their eyes and visualize the scene. When she finished, she asked them simply, "Tell me about your barn." Jon said that the barn was rickety and old and in need of a coat of paint. Jessica said she visualized a red barn with white trim. Jason mentioned beautiful green pastures with cows and horses grazing peacefully. Others mentioned farmers pitching hay and kids jumping from the hayloft. E. B. White had not explicitly written these details. The kids' comments reflected the movies running through their minds.

After about ten minutes of discussing their images of the barn, Steph asked them to sketch their barn. Each drawing was unique. The drawings included kids swinging on tire swings, riding the horses, and driving tractors. Some of the barn roofs were rounded; one was pointed with a rooster weathervane on top. Some pictures had farmers working and birds flying in and out of a small opening on top. Others had no people or animals. Some included wheat and corn fields. One was a detailed drawing of the interior of the barn loaded with mousetraps, milk pails, and water troughs. In some cases, none of the items drawn were mentioned in the text. As the kids shared, it became clear that many of their pictures came from their own prior knowledge of barns combined with the words of E. B. White.

This is what visualizing is all about—taking the words of the text and mixing them with the reader's background knowledge to create pictures in the mind. Good writers like E. B. White act like old-time movie projectionists who crank up the projector with their vivid words and then sit back as the reel runs unfettered for the viewer. The movie becomes the reader's own. In this case, if we were raised on a farm, we have the most detailed movie of all. If we lived around farms or have seen pictures of farms, we pick up on those. Combining the author's words with our background knowledge allows us to create mental images that bring life to reading.

Visualizing in Nonfiction Text: Making Comparisons

Purpose: Visualizing to better understand the dimensions of size, space, and time
Resources: Nonfiction trade books that use illustrations to make comparisons
Response: Drawing a comparison between one object and another

Teachers frequently tell us that they have a good handle on how to teach and use visualizing in narrative text but that they are less confident about how the strategy helps kids better understand expository text. Nonfiction text often features illustrated comparisons to help readers better understand the concepts of size and distance. Slavens Elementary first-grade teacher Michelle Meyer shows her students examples of comparisons in nonfiction text. When Michelle read that a Tyrannosaurus tooth was the size of a banana, Sean could visualize it more accurately than if he had read that a Tyrannosaurus tooth is six and a half inches long; a banana's size made more sense to Sean than the more abstract inches or feet. Michelle encourages artistic responses in her classroom, and Sean drew the image Michelle described, which further shows his understanding of the concept (see Figure 9.5).

Much nonfiction expository text relies on the concepts of size, weight, length, distance, and time to explain important information. Illustrations, graphs, charts, time lines, and diagrams provide visual support to students as they try to understand and acquire information from nonfiction text. Search for examples of nonfiction comparisons, both written and drawn. They flourish in nonfiction trade books, and they provide needed support to help readers grasp difficult concepts of time and space.

Figure 9.5 Sean's Drawing of a Comparison in Nonfiction Text

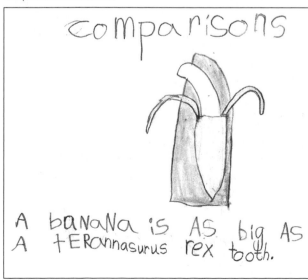

Visualizing in Reading, Showing Not Telling in Writing

Purpose: Creating images with compelling nonfiction
Resources: Baseball, the American Epic series, including *Shadow Ball: The History of the Negro Leagues* (Ward, Burns, and O'Connor 1994) and *Who Invented the Game?* (Ward, Burns, and Walker 1994)
Responses: Class discussion; charting of responses

S ome years ago, hoards of American baseball fans switched their channels from ESPN for several nights and glued themselves to their local public broadcasting system affiliate to watch documentary film maker Ken Burns's series entitled *Baseball, the American Epic*. Later, much to our delight, Knopf published a series of nonfiction trade books based on the compelling documentary programs.

The print series includes *Shadow Ball* and *Who Invented the Game?* and composes one of the most comprehensive young adult trade book accounts of baseball history. We love both books, but *Shadow Ball: The History of the Negro Leagues* stands out as one of the finest pieces of narrative nonfiction that we have ever encountered. It is striking not only for its content but also for the quality of the writing.

This book is multifaceted. We have used it to build background knowledge about the black experience in America, to develop a greater sense of the American civil rights movement, and to teach questioning and inferring. But above all, we have found it to be a terrific model for writing. *Shadow Ball* is written in such a vivid and compelling way that readers can't help but create stirring visual images in their minds when reading it. It begins this way:

> The crowd stirs with anticipation as the Indianapolis Clowns, an all-black team, take the field for their warm-ups. The second baseman's glove snaps back when he snags a quick peg from first. He hurls the ball to the third baseman, whose diving catch brings the fans to their feet. Then a batter steps to the plate. The pitcher sets, gets his signal, winds up, and throws. The batter swings. He hits it! The shortstop leaps to his right and makes a tremendous backhand stab. He jumps up, whirls, and throws to first just ahead of the sprinting runner. The low throw kicks dirt up by the first baseman's outstretched glove. The runner is out! The crowd roars.
>
> But wait! There's no ball in the first baseman's glove. The batter didn't really hit it. The Clowns were warming up in pantomime—hurling an imaginary ball so fast, making plays so convincingly, that fans could not believe it wasn't real.
>
> They called it shadow ball—and it came to stand not only for the way the black teams warmed up, but the way they were forced to play in the shadows of the all-white majors. Many black ballplayers were as good—if not better—than the big leaguers. All that kept them out was the color of their skin.

After overcoming our surprise at the pantomime warm-up and the rich shadow ball metaphor, we can't get over the compelling writing. This is a terrific piece to point out how active, visual verbs and specific nouns enhance writing quality and paint pictures in our minds. After discussing the content, we reread it and ask the kids to close their eyes, visualize the scene, and then comment on what makes this scene come alive for them. We write their comments on a large chart:

The running
The sliding

The kicked-up dirt
The outstretched glove
The tremendous back-hand stab
Snagging a quick peg from first
Hurling the ball

In this excerpt from *Shadow Ball,* all of these images and more combine to create a realistic movie in the mind. Carefully chosen nouns and verbs give writing its life. We label the nouns and verbs and ask kids to think about how these parts of speech bring such striking visual imagery to the piece. Before we finish, we encourage them to think about this vivid piece the next time they try to recount a true event in writing.

Creating Mental Images That Go Beyond Visualizing

Purpose: Using all the senses to comprehend text
Resource: A *National Geographic* article (Rudloe and Rudloe 1994), "Sea Turtles in a Race for Survival"
Responses: I see . . . , I hear . . . , I can feel . . . , I smell . . . , I can taste . . .

The term *visualizing* implies seeing pictures. Proficient readers create images from all of their senses when they read. We have all read an article about a pie baking in the oven or a steak crackling on the grill. Suddenly, our mouths water and hunger overcomes us. We can practically taste the meal. Well-written text allows us to taste, touch, hear, and smell images as well as see them when we read.

Figure 9.6 Robert's Response to "Sea Turtles in a Race for Survival"

Sea Turtles in a Race for Survive

I see turtles trying to get to the water. Thousands.

I hear the sound of thumping against there flipers.

I can feel all of the sand kicking into my eyes.

some turtles died so I can smell The rot.

I can taste other turtles backs. I can taste sand flinging in to my open mouth.

After his teacher read aloud an article in *National Geographic* called "Sea Turtles in a Race for Survival," Robert, a fifth grader, envisioned himself as one of the turtles in the piece. Over thirty thousand endangered sea turtles had come from miles around to mate on the sands of a Costa Rican beach. The article vividly describes this extraordinary scene. His teacher gave Robert the magazine and asked him to look again at the words and write what he heard, smelled, tasted, and felt as well as saw. Robert brought all of his senses to bear in his response, which clearly deepens his understanding of the text and shows his level of interaction with it (see Figure 9.6).

Inferential Thinking: Reading Between the Lines

Inferring is the bedrock of comprehension, not only in reading. We infer in many realms. Our life clicks along more smoothly if we can read the world as well as text. If our boss looks grumpy in the morning, it might not be the best day to ask for a raise. If a child's lips are quivering, it might be a sign to give him or her a hug. To help students understand the nature of inferential thinking, we might feign a terrified look and ask them what they can infer from our facial expression. If they mention scared or frightened, they've made an accurate inference. Inferring is about reading faces, reading body language, reading expressions, and reading tone as well as reading text.

Strategy Lessons: Inferring

Inferring Feelings with Kindergartners

Purpose: Helping kids to better understand their own and others' feelings; introducing inferential thinking

Resources: A feelings chart and a card with the word *sad* written on it. The card is pinned on the back of one student who doesn't know what it says.

Response: Child with card on back goes to the middle of the circle, and kids give him or her clues as to how they feel when they are sad to help the child guess the feeling word on the card.

Kindergarten teacher Sue Kempton organizes a game with a twofold purpose. She wants her students to have an opportunity to explore feelings, and she hopes to help them get a beginning handle on the notion of inferential thinking. Every few days, Sue introduces a new emotion and writes it on a card. At this point, the kids have *mad, sad, happy, disappointed*, and *frustrated* in their repertoire of cards. Sue reviews the nature of these feelings and then chooses one of the cards. She pins it on the back of a class volunteer; on this day Andrew wears the card. Andrew stands in the middle of the circle and turns around several times slowly so that everyone has an opportunity to see his card. Andrew doesn't know which card he wears on his back.

"Who has a clue for Andrew?" Sue begins. Kids raise their hands and give clues that might help Andrew figure out what word he is wearing on his back. Each student begins with "I felt that way when . . ." and completes the clue:

. . . my sister hit me with a golf club
. . . my dog died
. . . my mom said we couldn't go to the Children's Museum
. . . my dad didn't let me go to the movies
. . . my grandpa Nick died

After five or six kids have shared their clues, Sue asks, "Okay, Andrew, can you infer what the feeling is?"

"Sad," Andrew answers triumphantly.

"Good thinking, Andrew. How did you know?" Sue asks.

"Because people get sad when animals and grandparents die," Andrew answers.

And he was right, of course. The kids love this game. As they play more often, they clarify their feelings and predict which situations might lead to one feeling or another.

Inferring the Meaning of Unfamiliar Words

New

Purpose: Using context clues to crack open vocabulary
Resource: *Fly High: The Story of Bessie Coleman*, by Louise Borden and Mary Kay Kroeger
Responses: A four-column think sheet titled Word/Inferred Meaning /Clues/Sentence and a chart with the same titles

Readers are frequently frustrated when they meet unfamiliar vocabulary words as they read. Jumping up and grabbing a dictionary takes time and wrests readers out of the text. Asking the teacher can be time consuming as well. One of the quickest and most effective ways of dealing with unfamiliar vocabulary is through inferential thinking. To figure out the meaning of unfamiliar words, readers need to take what they know and gather clues in the text to crack the meaning of vocabulary. They need to consider the context to understand what they read.

James Allen, a third-grade teacher, introduced his students to a four-column think sheet headed Word/Inferred Meaning/Clues/Sentence to help them figure out the meaning of unfamiliar words. James modeled this lesson with the picture book *Fly High: The Story of Bessie Coleman*, the gripping story of an extraordinary woman who has the distinction of having been both the first woman and the first African American pilot. James created a four-column lesson chart with headings identical to the ones on the think sheet. As he read the story aloud, he asked kids to raise their hands when he came to a word that they had never heard before. Several pages into the story, he read the sentence "Bessie's brother Walter had moved to Chicago years ago when Bessie was little. Now Walter was a fine Pullman porter." Hands waved in the air. Few, if any, of the kids knew the meaning of the term *Pullman porter*.

So James wrote *Pullman porter* in the first column on the chart and then thought through how he could crack the meaning of that term. He first tried to read on, but to no avail. Then he tried rereading and that didn't help either. Luckily for him, there was a picture at the top of the page of a gentleman in a uniform carrying a suitcase and helping a young woman off the train. So James shared his thinking of how he inferred that a Pullman porter was a railroad worker who carried bags for people as they boarded and disembarked the train. He then proceeded to fill in the chart with the word, the inferred meaning, and the clue that helped him infer (which was the picture in this case). Then, together with the kids, he wrote a sentence in the final column. James explained that the purpose of writing the sentence was to demonstrate understanding of the word. As James continued reading, the kids raised their hands at different points in the text, and together with their teacher they co-constructed the following anchor chart:

Word	Inferred Meaning	Clues	Sentence
Pullman porter	Railroad worker who carries bags and helps passengers	Picture	The Pullman porter helped the woman off the train.
manicurist	Someone who trims nails	Reading on	A manicurist trims nails.
The Defender	The name of something	Capital letters	*The Defender* was a Chicago newspaper.

After James modeled this lesson for the whole class, he gave them each their own think sheet and asked them to practice this in their own reading. So they jotted down unfamiliar words and used the context to infer the meaning. This became a regular practice in James's classroom and provided ongoing support to his kids as they came across unfamiliar words and tried to discern the meaning.

Inferring from the Cover and Illustrations as Well as the Text

Purpose: Using all aspects of a book to infer meaning
Resource: *Tight Times*, by Barbara Shook Hazen
Response: Two-column note form headed Quote or Picture from Text/Inference

With picture books, readers can use the illustrations as well as the text to help them infer. Emergent readers frequently use picture clues to gain meaning, particularly when they come to a word they don't know. Older students can use pictures to enhance meaning, too.

One of our favorite picture books for teaching inferring is Barbara Shook Hazen's *Tight Times*. It tells the story of a boy, about four years old, who desperately wants a dog for a pet. Tension pervades the household as his dad loses his job and the family struggles to make ends meet and stay intact. Trina Schart Hyman's black-and-white illustrations convey moods that run the gamut from despair to hope. There's Dad with his downturned mouth, furrowed brow, and head in hands at the dining room table and Mom too busy to look up at her son as she sews a button on her blouse in the mad morning rush. These pictures say it all.

Steph joined with fifth-grade teacher Jennifer Jones to work on inferential thinking. Jennifer's students had begun learning about inferring earlier that week. On this day, Steph read *Tight Times* while the kids crowded around on the floor with clipboards and pencils at the ready. She held up the cover of the book, which shows a boy with a plate of lima beans, his fork two inches from his mouth holding one lonely lima which he refuses to even look at. Knowing that covers and titles are a good place to start with inferring, Steph asked what they could infer from the cover.

"He doesn't like those beans," Curtis answered.

"How do you know?" Steph asked.

"Look at his face and how he won't put the fork in his mouth," Curtis said.

"Yeah, and his plate is still full of beans," D. J. added as the others nodded.

"What does *Tight Times* mean?" Les asked.

This proved tougher. No one seemed to have adequate background knowledge for this term. Steph hung up a large piece of chart paper and divided it into two columns, one headed Quote or Picture from Text and the other headed Inference. "Let's read the story and find out," she suggested. "We'll record the information here as we find it." After hearing several pages, Audra burst out, "I got it! 'Tight times' is when you don't have enough money to do the stuff you want to do."

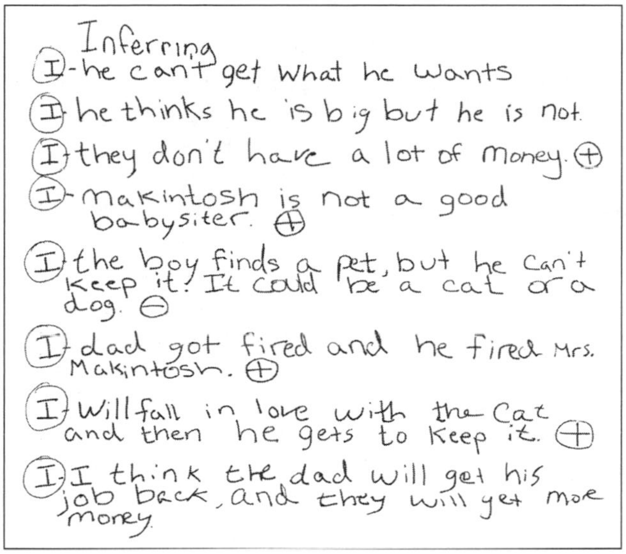
Inferring
I- he can't get What he wants
I- he thinks he is big but he is not.
I- they don't have a lot of money. (+)
I- makintosh is not a good babysiter. (+)
I- the boy finds a pet, but he can't keep it! It could be a cat or a dog. (–)
I- dad got fired and he fired Mrs. Makintosh. (+)
I- will fall in love with the Cat and then he gets to keep it. (+)
I- I think the dad will get his job back, and they will get more money.

Figure 9.7 Curtis's Inferences in Response to *Tight Times*

"Good thinking, Audra. Did the author tell you that?" Steph asked.

"No, not exactly."

"So, how did you know?" Steph asked.

"I sort of guessed it when his dad said they didn't get roast beef anymore and his mom went back to work because of tight times," Audra answered.

"She inferred it," Curtis said.

"That she did, Curtis. Let's record it on the chart," Steph suggested.

Audra came up and wrote her response on the chart.

When Curtis came upon a picture near the end of the story of the dad reading the want ads, he headed up to the chart and wrote that the dad was going to get a new job.

When Jennifer asked Curtis how he knew that, he answered, "Because he's got a smile on his face in that picture and he's a hardworking guy. I'm predicting it."

"Right on, Curtis," Jennifer told him. At that point, she and Steph released the kids to work in pairs as the teachers moved about the room, eavesdropped, and chatted with individuals who were working their way through the text and responding on an identical form on their clipboards. The kids relied on both pictures and text to predict outcomes, infer ideas, and construct meaning in the story.

Prediction or Inference?

When Curtis stated that he was making a prediction, it gave Jennifer and Steph an opportunity to discuss the relationship between prediction and inference. Predicting is related to inferring, of course, but we predict outcomes, events, or actions that are confirmed or contradicted by the end of the story. Prediction is one aspect of inferential thinking.

To help our students understand the difference, we encourage them to consider the outcome of an event or action each time they make a prediction and notice whether there has been a resolution. Curtis continued reading and found that the book ends before resolving whether the father finds a new job. But the story ends hopefully, and Curtis wasn't wrong to infer that the dad would find employment. He had good reason to believe it. Curtis made a list of inferences in his notebook as he read *Tight Times*. When he finished reading, he went back and marked those that were confirmed (+) and those that were contradicted (–). He left those that were unresolved coded with only I for inference (see Figure 9.7).

New

Inferring with Text Clues

Purpose: Teaching the inferring equation BK+TC=I (Background Knowledge + Text Clues = Inference)
Resource: *Tight Times* encore
Response: Three-column chart titled Background Knowledge/Text Clues/Inference

When we infer, we take what we know and merge it with clues in the text to draw a conclusion, to predict an outcome, to surface a theme, and so on. We can teach our students a formula of sorts for inferring: Background Knowledge plus Text Clues equals an Inference, or BK+TC=I. *Tight Times* is a wonderful book for teaching many aspects of inferential thinking, such as inferring the meaning of unfamiliar words, predicting outcomes, and surfacing themes.

Sometimes we reread books, particularly if they are exceptionally good. Certain books become what Lucy Calkins calls "touchstone books" (Calkins 2004), those books that we come back to again and again because we love them and because they are so effective at teaching something in particular. *Tight Times* has become a touchstone book for us when teaching inferring. We have to "read between the lines" throughout the book to infer meaning and make sense of it.

As we begin rereading it, we open to the first page where the boy asks the mom, who is very busy getting dressed for work in the morning, if he can please have a dog. The mom is short with him and says, "No, not now, not again," and tells him not to bother her when she's busy. As we model the inferring formula, we share with the kids how we use the equation to construct meaning. We know from personal experience that it is hard to give our children much time in the morning when we are rushing to work, and we also can tell from the mom's tone and words that she is losing patience with him. So we explain how we activate our background knowledge about times when we are rushing off to work and merge it with clues in the text that show how short the mom is with the boy. From our background knowledge and these text clues, we infer that this is not the first time the boy has asked for a dog (BK+TC=I). As a matter of fact, it is probably the umpteenth time!

As we move through the book, we come to a variety of spots where we can share how the inferring formula helps us to understand. On one page, the father comes home from work in the middle of the day and finds the little boy playing by himself in the hallway as the babysitter watches TV in the living room. The dad looks mad, has a word with the babysitter, and she leaves. We ask kids to turn and talk about why the dad looked mad. Most of them can infer that the babysitter should have been watching the little boy instead of the TV. They take their background knowledge of babysitters and what they should be doing and merge it with the clues in the text—that the babysitter was watching TV in another room instead of watching the boy. They infer that is the reason the father was mad. To hold this thinking we can co-construct an anchor chart as follows adding to it as we continue reading.

Background Knowledge	Text Clues	Inference
Moms can get cranky when they are rushing to work in the morning	She says no when he asks for a dog	He has probably asked for a dog over and over
Babysitters should be watching kids	She is watching TV and the dad looks mad	The dad is mad because she is not doing her job

This little formula BK+TC=I seems to help kids to remember to think about what they know and merge it with text clues to draw a conclusion and make an inference. When they do this, they are more likely to make a reasonable inference.

Recognizing Plot and Inferring Themes

Purpose: Differentiating between plot and theme, and inferring the big ideas or themes
Resource: *Teammates*, by Peter Golenbock
Responses: Class discussion; chart of themes; theme boards

Literature, both fiction and nonfiction, is rife with themes. Books and articles rarely promote just one main idea but rather several themes for readers to ponder and infer. When we talk to students about themes, we help them discern the difference between theme and plot. We explain that the plot is simply what happens in the narrative. The themes represent the bigger ideas of the story. The plot carries those ideas along. To demonstrate plot, we choose a simple narrative that everyone is likely to be familiar with. We might recount the plot of *Goldilocks and the Three Bears* by summarizing the events of the story as follows. A girl named Goldilocks was wandering through the forest and entered an unfamiliar, empty house. She tasted porridge that didn't belong to her, broke a chair, and slept in a bed that wasn't hers. She was caught when the bears returned, and she ran out of the house scared to death.

We explain to our students that themes are the underlying ideas, morals, and lessons that give the story its texture, depth, and meaning. The themes are rarely explicitly stated in the story. We infer themes. Themes often make us feel angry, sad, guilty, joyful, frightened. We tell kids that we are likely to feel themes in our gut. To help students more clearly understand the difference, we might ask, "What are the bigger ideas in *Goldilocks and the Three Bears*?" Kids tend to identify taking things that don't belong to you, selfishness, thoughtlessness, and so on. They have experienced these notions and they understand them.

A nonfiction picture book we have used to demonstrate inferring themes is Peter Golenbock's *Teammates*. It is the moving story of Jackie Robinson's courageous breakthrough into the all-white major leagues. It goes beyond the history and describes the personal relationship between Jackie and his white teammate Pee Wee Reese. Pee Wee was the only player on the Brooklyn Dodgers team that supported Jackie's quest.

To continue their study of inferring, Steph demonstrated a think-aloud with *Teammates* to the fifth graders in Jennifer Jones's class the day after taking them through the Goldilocks exercise. After describing the difficult, segregated life of players in the Negro leagues, Golenbock writes that life was much better for players in the major leagues. They were paid well, and many were famous all over the world. Steph coded her sticky note I for inference while noting that this kind of racial inequality might breed anger. She suggested that both racial inequality and anger might be themes in the story even though the writer hadn't written those very words. So Steph created an anchor chart headed Evidence from the Text/Themes. Under Evidence from the Text, she wrote *Words, Actions, Pictures* and explained that we can infer themes from the words in the text, the actions of characters, and the pictures and illustrations. All of these provide evidence that support the bigger ideas and themes we infer in a narrative.

When Curtis heard that Branch Rickey, the manager of the Brooklyn Dodgers, was looking for a man who "would have to possess the self-control not to fight back when opposing players tried to intimidate or hurt him," he suggested that self-control might be a theme. Steph concurred and added it to the chart and pointed out that Curtis was using evidence from the text. (See examples of two-column forms of kids' themes and evidence in the assessment section of this chapter.) When Steph finished reading the story, she facilitated a discussion about the bigger ideas in the narrative based on text evidence.

"Jackie was alone without a single friend. No one would sit near him or talk to him," Chantal mentioned.

"Good noticing, Chantal. Why didn't he get mad about that?" Steph asked.

"Because he had a lot of self-control. The manager wanted a man who wouldn't fight back, no matter how mad he got and Jackie never did."

"Chantal, that is exactly how we use evidence to infer a theme. Let's put your thinking up on the chart," Steph suggested. So she wrote *self-control* in the Theme column and then *Jackie never fought back* in the Evidence column.

"So, what might be another theme?" Steph asked.

"I know how he felt. When I moved here I didn't have one single friend. I felt really lonely," Rogers said. So Steph added *loneliness* to the theme chart and cited Rogers's evidence.

"But Pee Wee was his friend," Jaquon added.

"So, is friendship a theme?" Steph asked.

"Sort of, but most of the team would not be his friend because he was black," Jaquon continued. "That's racist," Curtis added.

"It sure is racist, Curtis. Are racism and friendship both themes in *Teammates*?" Steph asked.

The kids nodded, and Steph added both of those themes to the chart along with the evidence for them. And so the discussion went for nearly forty-five minutes, culminating in a long list of themes and evidence for them. Some of the themes that surfaced included racial inequality, segregation, anger, taking a stand, bravery, and more.

Steph reiterated that all of these themes represented the bigger ideas in the story and that most of them evoked strong feelings. We have noticed that kids are more likely to remember important themes when they derive the ideas themselves and feel them deeply. It is our role to help draw students out through engaging discussions about the bigger ideas in the story. Often, the kids used their prior knowledge to infer themes and better understand the narrative, as Rogers did when he mentioned being the new kid on the block. As students talk about the bigger ideas, it is our responsibility to help them label the ideas, articulate the themes, and cite text evidence. Inferring after all is about taking what we know, our background knowledge, and combining it with clues or evidence in the text to draw a conclusion, or in this case, surface a theme.

On the following day, Steph handed out a think sheet that matched the chart, with the headings Evidence in the Text/Themes. The kids went back and reread and reconsidered *Teammates*. They cited evidence from the text and recorded themes they discovered during the first read as well as themes that surfaced on their second reading and reviewing of the text. (See some of their think sheets in the assessment section of this chapter.)

Theme Boards: Hey, What's the Big Idea?

Jennifer continued to work on surfacing themes throughout the year. She reported that her students became quite adept at inferring themes as well as labeling them. They even began to notice when certain themes appeared over and over. To reinforce theme identification and the connections between themes in one text and those in another, Jennifer established a theme board headed Hey, What's the Big Idea? Each time the class read a book, they developed a theme list and added the list to the theme board. Themes identified from Sherry Garland's *The Lotus Seed* included

keeping traditions alive	cooperation	sharing traditions	
sadness	courage	loneliness	internal pain

It didn't take kids long to notice the overlapping themes in certain books, such as *Teammates* and *The Lotus Seed*. This was a great literary lesson. Experienced readers know that the same themes are likely to appear over and over in literature. Why not begin to teach this in elementary school?

Visualizing and Inferring to Understand Information

Purpose: Using reading comprehension strategies to better understand content area reading
Resource: *Merrill Earth Science* (1993), seventh-grade textbook
Responses: Two-column note form headed Facts/Inferences; ongoing discussion about how comprehension strategies help readers understand content reading

Throughout this book we have talked about using authentic literature and trade nonfiction to teach content. Many classrooms across the United States rely primarily on textbooks to teach content in subjects such as science and social studies. Textbooks have their advantages but also their limitations. (See Chapter 14, "Reading to Understand Textbooks.") The advantages derive primarily from the organization of the material. Each chapter usually has a number of sections, which are organized around headings and subheadings. The writing is somewhat predictable, and textbooks are chock-full of features that scaffold the reader's understanding. The disadvantages of using only textbooks to teach are many. First and foremost, kids get bored. The problem with textbooks isn't getting information out of them; the problem is staying awake while reading them! Because few books outside of school are written in the same style as a textbook, reading textbooks doesn't prepare kids for much of the authentic nonfiction reading they will do in their lifetimes. The trick is to use a multisource, multigenre, multimedia curriculum when teaching content.

Although authentic trade nonfiction—newspapers, books, videos, and magazines—is the mainstay in science teacher Margaret Bobb's classroom, she also uses a science textbook, *Merrill Earth Science*, to supplement instruction. The textbook frequently offers the information Margaret needs to share with her students. But she recognizes that all is for naught if her students can't understand what they read.

Although Margaret is a specialist in earth science, she knows that she must be a reading teacher as well. She must explicitly teach students how to read content-area textbooks to gain information rather than just tell them to read the fossil chapter and answer the questions. The unfamiliar terms and concepts in textbooks combined with the dry writing sometimes sink students. As Margaret studied strategic reading comprehension, she quickly realized how useful these strategies could be in helping her students better understand their textbooks as well as trade nonfiction. This particular lesson is one that can be a lifesaver in both textbook reading and general informational reading.

Margaret teaches her seventh graders several comprehension strategies to help them understand textbook writing. She explains that when we read, we have to be able to tell the difference between facts and opinions. "In science, we observe facts," she explains. "Your opinion is your own idea, but in science we call it a hypothesis. This is really an interpretation or inference about something." Margaret labeled a two-column overhead transparency Facts (Something We Can See and Observe)/Inferences (Interpretation).

Juan read out loud from the textbook: "The dense forest thunders as the Tyrannosaurus rex charges forward in pursuit of her evening meal. On the other side of the swamp, a herd of apatosaurs moves slowly and cautiously onward. The adults surround the young to protect them from predators. Soon night will fall on this prehistoric day, 70 million years ago" (*Merrill Earth Science* 1993). Margaret asked the class what they visualized and if they could infer anything from the text. Jana visualized a group of slow dinosaurs, peacefully hanging around, while the Tyrannosaurus raced toward them undetected in the woods. Raul commented that he thought the rex would get these plant eaters. Margaret commented that he was making two inferences—first, that the rex would eat them, and second, that the apatosaurs were plant eaters. Both were strong possibilities.

As they read on, they came to the following passage: "Usually the remains of dead plants and animals are quickly destroyed. Scavengers eat the dead organisms or bacteria cause them to decay. If you've ever left a banana on the shelf too long you've seen this process begin. Compounds in the banana cause it to become soft and moist, and bacteria move in and cause it to quickly decay." Margaret asked what the writers were doing here. "Making you visualize again," Luz called out.

"You bet they are," Margaret said. "You can just picture that black, shriveled, smelly banana. It reminds me of how the fridge smells when food is rotting in there. I can use my background knowledge to get a better picture." In reading just several paragraphs, Margaret and her students had explicitly activated background knowledge, visualized, and inferred to better understand the textbook. These strategies brought the science textbook to life. The students filled in the following chart as they read:

Facts (Something We Can See and Observe)	Inferences (Interpretation)
Apatosaurs are slow.	The *T-rex* will catch them.
Adults protect young.	The apatosaurs are plant eaters.
Took place 70 million years ago.	
Bacteria decay the banana.	Bananas get rotten when you leave them out too long.

As Margaret shows us, these comprehension strategies can improve textbook reading. By stopping and activating the strategies, her seventh graders increased their store of knowledge and actively used it.

It should be noted that Margaret looks very closely at the writing in textbooks when it is time to choose a new textbook or adopt a new series. Although content and organization are important, writing style and presentation are important, too, so that kids will stay alert, monitor their comprehension, learn, and retain information. Margaret is not seduced merely by a new copyright date. She compares the older textbook to the newer one to determine if the new one is truly better or simply newer. She looks for organizational features such as framed text and appealing photographs that scaffold the reader's understanding. For her earth science course, she chooses the best written and best organized textbook she can find and then teaches her students comprehension strategies that will enhance their understanding.

Inferring and Questioning to Understand Historical Concepts

Purpose: Inferring and questioning go hand in hand to build understanding
Resource: *Encounter*, by Jane Yolen
Responses: Discussion and sticky notes for questioning and inferring

As fourth-grade teacher Jeanette Scotti planned ways to introduce the "exploration" of the Americas in social studies, she knew that *Encounter*, by Jane Yolen, was the perfect book to launch the study. Rather than plodding through a succession of explorers in the social studies textbook, Jeanette knew that asking questions and drawing inferences about *Encounter* would immediately move the conversation beyond traditional ideas about the "discovery of the new world." The picture book focuses on important historical concepts: that the story of exploration is about the encounters between colonizers and indigenous people, whose very survival was threatened with the arrival of the Europeans.

Written from the perspective of a Taino child, this fictionalized account of Columbus's encounter with the Taino people demonstrates that history is all about understanding different perspectives. The young Taino boy, unlike his elders, is suspicious of the men's motives. He shares both his curiosity and his fears as he watches the strange "men who hid their bodies in colors, like parrots" and tries to warn his people that these visitors do not mean well.

Kids in Jeanette's classroom had experienced explicit instruction in asking questions and drawing inferences in a variety of genres, so she was curious to see how they would transfer these reading/thinking strategies to social studies content. She decided an interactive read-aloud with

Figure 9.8 Jeanette Shared Her Questions and Inferences About *Encounter* as a Model

Encounter

Background knowledge: Christopher Columbus was an explorer who was trying to reach India. He didn't get to India, but he found a new land. He was looking for gold and riches.

Questions (I wonder)	Inferences (I Think)
(Cover) Is the man on the cover Columbus? Is the boy trying to push the man away?	
	I think the little boy is telling the story.
Is the boy's dream a nightmare? Are the birds in his dream the ships?	Maybe the dream was telling him that the visitors were evil.
Do the Taino think the birds are spirits?	
Why do the men from the ships want to claim the land?	Maybe the men want gold...
	I think the chief should listen to the little boy, but he told him he was just a child.
Did other explorers just take the land for themselves?	
	We think that the explorers want the land and gold for themselves. They don't care about the people – the Tainos – who already live here.

the whole group was a good choice for instruction so that English language learners could better understand the story as they listened to it, viewed the illustrations, and talked about it.

Jeanette gathered her class together for an interactive read-aloud using a chart with two columns labeled I Wonder and I Think. First, she took a few minutes to activate the students' background knowledge by finding out what they already knew (and thought they knew) about Columbus and exploration in general. Then Jeanette modeled her own questions and inferences as she read the first few pages of the story and looked closely at the illustrations (see Figure 9.8). Although some of the English language learners found the language difficult, all the kids loved the challenge of interpreting the words and the striking pictures.

Jeanette continued reading, and the kids continued recording their questions and inferences on their own I Wonder/I Think think sheets. With *Encounter*, questioning and inferring worked in tandem to enhance the children's understanding of the story. As they read, students used the language of questioning (I wonder . . .) and inferring (I think . . ., maybe . . ., I predict . . ., I infer . . .). As a launch for the study of explorers, this book more than served its purpose, prompting further investigation into how indigenous peoples' lives changed forever.

Rereading to Clear up Misconceptions

When we come across information that surprises us, such as Nellie's blindness in *See the Ocean* or the phantom baseball game in *Shadow Ball*, we can't help but flip back through the pages and search for the clues we missed that might have led us to draw a more accurate inference earlier in our reading. Readers need to stay on their toes to make meaning, checking for misconceptions as they go. And teachers need to look closely at student work and listen intently to student comments to nip misconceptions in the bud.

As a little girl, whenever Steph heard the Christmas carol "Silent Night," an image of a large, round Friar Tuck sort of character appeared in her mind. It wasn't until later that she realized that this misconception had originated in her confusion about the words of the song. Where it actually said "round yon Virgin," Steph had always heard it as "round John. . . ." She visualized a fat, jolly monk. This misconception disrupted meaning and kept her from fully understanding the carol.

Encourage your kids to go back through the text to check their mind pictures and inferences, and remind them to check their thinking with someone else if it doesn't seem to make sense. A good reality check can go a long way toward keeping Friar Tucks at bay. Visualizing and inferring are strategies that enhance understanding, but if ill conceived, they can just as easily hinder understanding. Rereading is one of the best ways to check for meaning. It all makes so much sense the second time through.

Teaching with the End in Mind: Assessing What We've Taught

Inferring and Visualizing

Based on the lessons in this chapter, we look for evidence that

1. *Students visualize and create mental images to make sense of what they read.* As students listen to and read text, we look for evidence that they draw and write about their mental images or mind pictures to support understanding.

2. *Students infer the meaning of unfamiliar words.* We look for evidence that students are using the context to figure out the meaning of words and concepts that elude them.
3. *Students use text evidence to infer themes and bigger ideas.* We look for evidence that students are merging their background knowledge with clues in the text to surface themes and bigger ideas.
4. *Students infer and draw conclusions from informational text using features and text structures.* We look for evidence that students enhance their understanding and think beyond just the facts as they read textbooks and other nonfiction text.

Suggestions for Differentiation

Visualizing and inferring lend themselves to differentiation. We cannot overestimate the importance of drawing as a means to understanding. When kids draw to clarify understanding, they are constructing meaning. Sensory imaging is about more than just visualizing. Kids taste, touch, feel, and smell their way through books as well as through experiences. So we model using all of our senses to understand what we read, hear, and view. Many times kids can express through drawing what they may have difficulty articulating in oral or written words.

We teach inferring in many contexts outside of text. Playing charades is a wonderful way for kids to get a concrete idea of what it means to infer. Role playing and drama also encourage kids to act out their understanding of what they read. Sharing unfamiliar items and objects like kitchen utensils, old-fashioned tools, and so forth requires kids to use inferential thinking to make sense of them and infer their purposes. All of these activities give kids a more concrete idea of what it is to infer.

Visualizing and Inferring Assessment Commentary

Expanding on the lesson titled "Visualizing in Nonfiction Text: Making Comparisons" and inferring on a range of aspects in addition to comparisons

I Think ThaTa

BarN OWLS
HaVeS a Leed

As first graders learned about inferring with informational text, they drew their mental images and jotted their thoughts in invented spelling.

Figure 9.9 This student gained some information about barn owls. As she thought about the information, she inferred that groups of barn owls follow a leader. She then created an illustration to share what she was visualizing. We can see the language of inferential thinking in her words, *I think. . . .*

Figure 9.10 This student learned that woodpeckers peck holes in cactus. She combined this information with what she already knew about elf owls, inferring that they lived in holes created by the woodpeckers. In this way, she took her thinking beyond the information on the page. Then she illustrated her mental image of elf owls living in a cactus.

I infer elf owls
live in the cactus
After wood Peakers
Peck, a Hole in the

cactus.

Two-column think sheets on inferring themes using text evidence from the lesson "Recognizing Plot and Inferring Themes" with *Teammates*

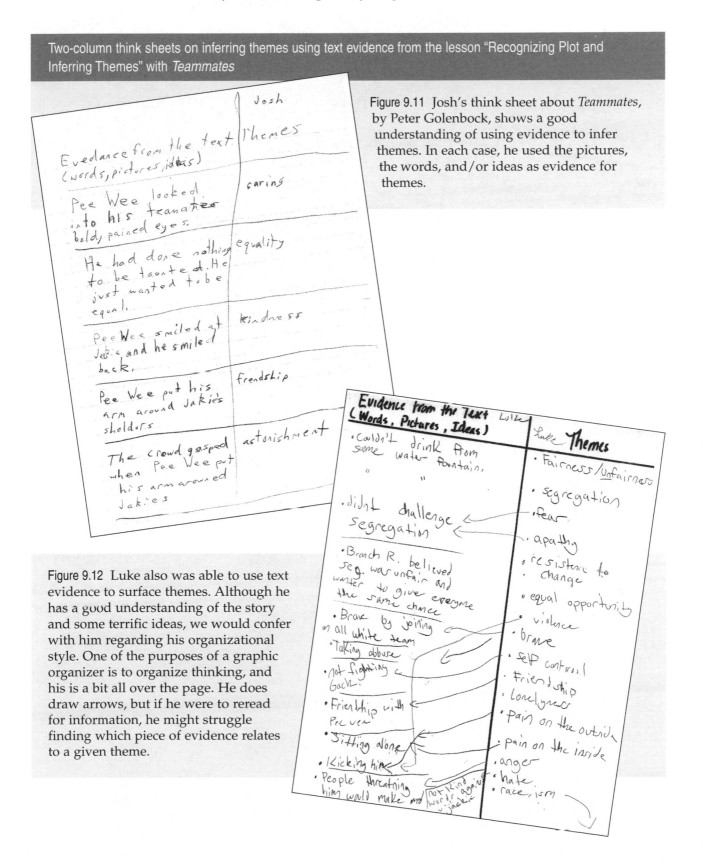

Figure 9.11 Josh's think sheet about *Teammates*, by Peter Golenbock, shows a good understanding of using evidence to infer themes. In each case, he used the pictures, the words, and/or ideas as evidence for themes.

Figure 9.12 Luke also was able to use text evidence to surface themes. Although he has a good understanding of the story and some terrific ideas, we would confer with him regarding his organizational style. One of the purposes of a graphic organizer is to organize thinking, and his is a bit all over the page. He does draw arrows, but if he were to reread for information, he might struggle finding which piece of evidence relates to a given theme.

An independent think sheet on inferring themes with text evidence from the lesson "Recognizing Plot and Inferring Themes"

Evidence from the Text (Words, pictures and ideas)	Theme
Maria	
When Papa Left To Join The Underground Marina, Mama And I Cried, Too.	This Shows Me That They Will Miss Him And Are Scared That They Wont See Him Again.
"I Gave Marina A Pitying Glance"	This Tell Me That She Tring To Tell Her That She Needs To Stop Thinking Negative
The Cold Will Be Hard On The Little One.	Caring
"It Is Getting Much To Dangerous To Stay Any Longer	Mama Wanted What Was Ever Best For Her Kids. She Is Very Caring
I Wet The Bed Three Nights In A Row.	Although The Whole Family Is Scared The Mom Is Standing Strong For Her Husband And Her Family
Mama Held Me Close. "It's All Right, Viktor. There Is No Harm Done."	Momma - Strong, Has Faith, Wont Gave Up On Finding Her Husband Or Keeping Her Kids Safe.

Figure 9.13 Maria tried using the form in her own independent reading of the book *Gleam and Glow*. She has some great ideas and shows deep thinking and understanding. However, she hasn't shaped her thinking into a big idea, but rather uses a long explanation to demonstrate her thoughts. We would help her synthesize the ideas in her theme column into a bigger idea as Luke and Josh did.

An independent two-column think sheet headed Facts/Inferences from the lesson "Visualizing and Inferring to Understand Information"

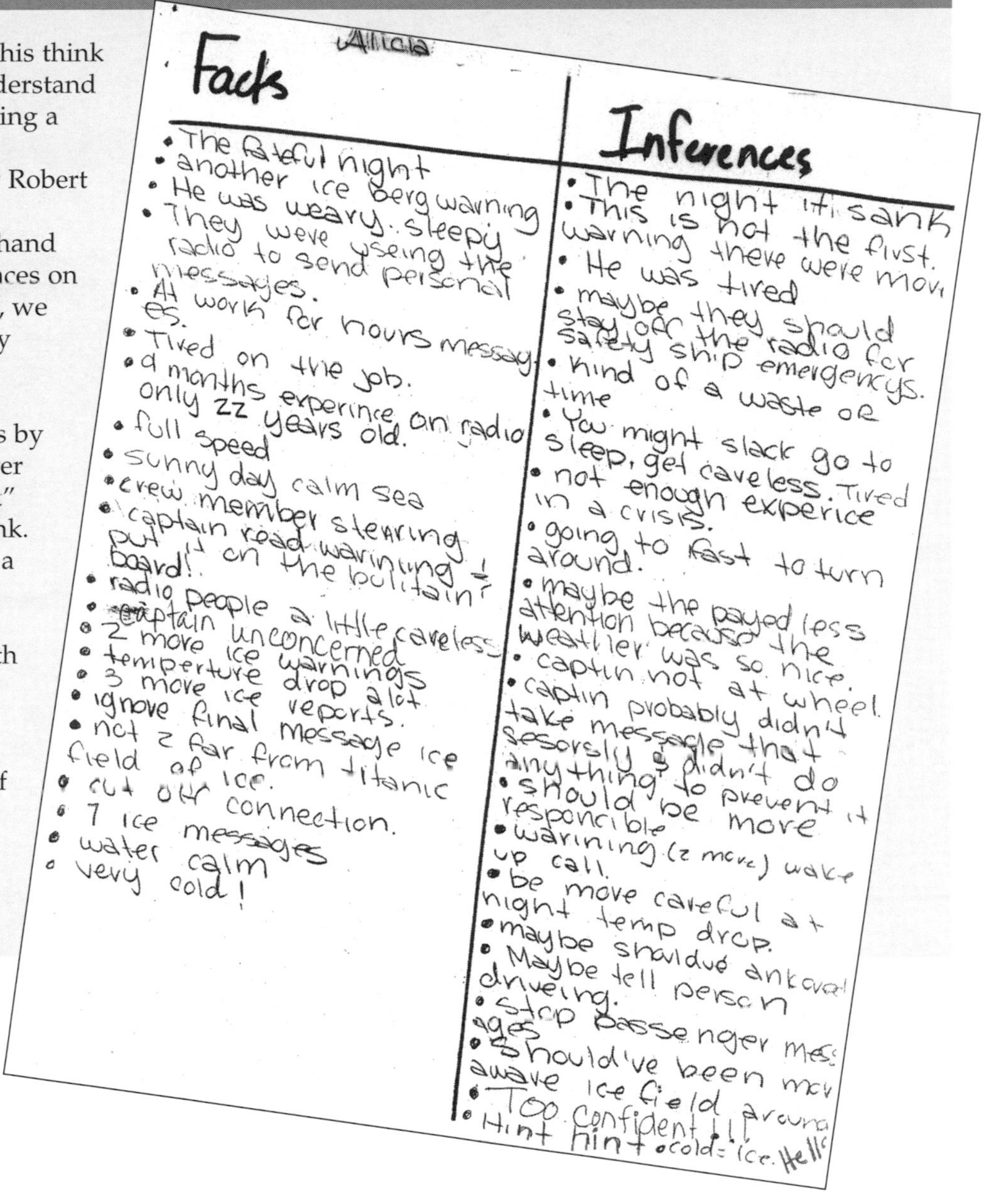

Figure 9.14 Alicia used this think sheet to record and understand information while reading a chapter from the book *Exploring the Titanic,* by Robert Ballard, putting factual information in the left-hand column and her inferences on the right. As we read it, we can see that she is really using her inferences to better understand the information. She begins by inferring that the chapter title "The Fateful Night" refers to the night it sank. Then she collects quite a bit of information and infers that the crewmembers were both careless and overly confident. And, amusingly, she is so stunned by their lack of attention that her last inference *Hint, Hint cold=ice . . . Hello!!* really seals the deal.

Alicia

Facts
- The fateful night
- another ice berg warning
- He was weary..sleepy
- They were useing the radio to send personal messages.
- At work for hours messages
- Tired on the job.
- 4 months experince on radio only 22 years old.
- full speed
- sunny day calm sea
- crew member steering
- captain read warning + put it on the bulitain board!
- radio people a little careless
- captain unconcerned
- 2 more ice warnings
- temperture drop alot
- 3 more ice reports.
- ignore final message ice
- not 2 far from titanic field of ice.
- cut off connection.
- 7 ice messages
- water calm
- very cold!

Inferences
- The night it sank
- This is not the first. warning there were more
- He was tired
- maybe they should stay off the radio for safety ship emergencys.
- kind of a waste of time
- You might slack go to sleep, get careless. Tired in a crisis.
- not enough experice
- going to fast to turn around.
- maybe they payed less attention because the weather was so nice.
- captin not at wheel.
- captin probably didn't take message that sesorsly + didn't do anything to prevent it
- should be more responcible
- warning (2 more) wake up call
- be more careful at night temp drop.
- maybe shouldve ankored driveing.
- Maybe tell person stop passenger messages
- shouldve been more aware ice field around
- Too confident !!
- Hint hint .cold=ice. Hello

Chapter 10

Determining Importance in Text: The Nonfiction Connection

A dozen or so years ago, a large footlocker arrived at Steph's door. Her parents, their kids grown, had sold the house where she had grown up and moved to another. In the move, they boxed all of her remaining possessions and sent them out to Steph in Denver. As the padlock clicked free, the top of the trunk burst open and childhood treasures of every imaginable size and shape poured out. Stuffed animals, glossy black-and-white photographs of Hollywood movie stars, her collection of Nancy Drew books, a well-loved Raggedy Andy doll, a 1954 edition of Dr. Seuss's *If I Ran the Zoo*, and even her kindergarten report card cascaded over the sides.

As Steph peeled away the layers of her life, she came upon several hulking college textbooks lining the bottom of the trunk. When she opened a tome titled *Modern European History*, a blast of yellow blinded her. Page after page of white space and black print had been shaded neon yellow, the result of Steph's bout with mad highlighting disease! Throughout her education, teachers had instructed Steph to highlight the important parts. But no one had shown her how. She assumed that if the writers of these massive textbooks had written it down, it must be important. So she highlighted just about every letter of print. Highlighting is easy; determining what to highlight is the challenge.

For years in schools, students everywhere have been asked to pick out the most important information when they read, to highlight essential ideas, to isolate supporting details, and to read for specific information. This is easier said than done. When we read nonfiction, we can't possibly remember every fact, nor should we. To expand our understanding, we need to focus on information and merge it with what we already know about a topic. We remember facts and details better when we link them to larger concepts. We separate what's important from what's interesting. Only after we sort and sift details from the important information can we arrive at a main idea.

The strategy lessons in this chapter are designed to help readers sift and sort information and make sense of the barrage of information that crosses kids' radar screens every day.

The Link Between the Strategy of Determining Importance and the Genre of Nonfiction

When we teach the strategy of determining importance, we often introduce it in nonfiction. They go together. Nonfiction reading is reading to learn. Simply put, readers of nonfiction have to decide and remember what is important in the texts they read if they are going to learn anything from them.

When readers determine importance in fiction and other narrative genre, they often infer the bigger ideas and themes in the story, as the kids in Jennifer Jones's fifth grade did when they read *Teammates* (see Chapter 9). Getting at what's important in nonfiction text is more about gaining information and acquiring knowledge than discerning themes. Nonfiction is full of features, text cues, and structures that signal importance and scaffold understanding for readers. These features, specific to nonfiction, provide explicit cues to help readers sift essential information from less important details when they read expository text. We explicitly teach readers how to use these cues to extract salient information. But first we need to ensure that they have a wide range of nonfiction at their disposal.

Steph and Anne both have wonderful memories of having been read aloud to in school. We can still hear the words of *Black Beauty* (Sewell 1941) and *The Secret Garden* (Burnett 1938) as our teachers lured us in from recess for read-aloud time. And we loved those books. But neither of us can ever recall having had a piece of nonfiction read aloud to us or even seeing it in school. It was as if the genre didn't exist—outside of textbooks, that is.

A number of years ago, we joined a group of fourth- and fifth-grade teachers in a classroom book audit to determine whether their classroom book collections included a wide variety of genres. To our surprise, we found very little trade nonfiction among the novels and textbooks. Over 80 percent of the classroom books fell into the fiction category. Considering that about 80 percent of the reading we do outside of school is nonfiction, it wasn't hard to recognize a disconnect. More nonfiction needed to be shared, explored, and taught in these classrooms and in classrooms everywhere. Classroom book audits are invaluable tools to ensure that classrooms balance their collections with respect to genres as well as other categories.

Nonfiction picture books and young adult magazines and newspapers fire kids up, especially if text quality matches the compelling photographs, charts, and illustrations. There's nothing like a photograph of the jaws of a great white shark clamping down on the front end of a surfboard to spark kids' interest in ocean life. Interesting authentic nonfiction fuels kids' curiosity, enticing them to read more, dig deeper, and search for answers to compelling questions. When kids read and understand nonfiction, they build background for the topic and acquire new knowledge. The ability to identify essential ideas and salient information is a prerequisite to developing insight.

Distilling the Essence of Nonfiction Text

In *Nonfiction Matters* (Harvey 1998), Steph wrote about overviewing and highlighting the text to help students determine important ideas and information while reading.

Overviewing

When students read nonfiction, they can be taught overviewing, a form of skimming and scanning the text before reading. Reading comprehension researcher Jan Dole suggests focus lessons on the following to help students overview the text:

- Activating prior knowledge
- Noting characteristics of text length and structure
- Noting important headings and subheadings
- Determining what to read and in what order
- Determining what to pay careful attention to
- Determining what to ignore
- Deciding to quit because the text contains no relevant information
- Deciding if the text is worth a close reading or just skimming

A careful overview saves precious time for students when reading difficult nonfiction text. The ability to overview eliminates the need for kids to read everything when searching for specific information. Overviewing represents an early entry in the effort to determine importance. Teachers can model these aspects of overviewing in their own reading and research process.

Highlighting

To effectively highlight text, readers need to read the text, think about it, and make conscious decisions about what they need to remember and learn. They can't possibly remember everything. They need to sort important information from less important details. They need to pick out the main ideas and notice supporting details, and they need to let go of ancillary information. But it's not enough to simply run that yellow highlighter over the text. In order to remember why we highlighted something, we teach kids to jot their thoughts in the margin or on a sticky note right next to where they highlighted information they deemed important. This prevents them from ending up with a sea of yellow and very little understanding. We encourage students to consider the following guidelines when they highlight, and we provide explicit instruction in each of these points:

- Look carefully at the first and last line of each paragraph. Important information is often contained there.
- Highlight only necessary words and phrases, not entire sentences.
- Jot notes in the margin or on a sticky note to paraphrase the information, merge your thinking with it, and better remember it.

- Don't get thrown off by interesting details. Although they are fascinating, they often obscure important information.
- Make notes in the margin to emphasize a pertinent highlighted word or phrase.
- Note signal words (see Chapter 15). They are almost always followed by important information.
- Pay attention to the vast array of nonfiction features that signal importance.
- Pay attention to surprising information. It might mean you are learning something new.
- When finished, check to see that no more than half the paragraph is highlighted. As readers become more adept, one-third of the paragraph is a good measure for highlighting.

Nonfiction Features That Signal Importance

When a word is italicized, a paragraph begins with a boldface heading, or the text says "Most important, . . ." readers need to stop and take notice. This may sound obvious, but it's not. No one ever taught us to pay attention to these nonfiction elements. Steph was so textbound as a young reader that to this day she still skips over the title to get to the text. This is a shame. Titles, headings, framed text, and captions help focus readers as they sort important information from less important details. Nonfiction is one of the most accessible genres for reluctant and less experienced readers because the features scaffold the reader's understanding. A photograph and a caption sometimes synthesize the most important information on the page, rendering a complete reading of the text unnecessary. Nonfiction features are user-friendly. Some that we teach follow.

Fonts and effects. Teachers can note examples of different fonts and effects, such as titles, headings, boldface print, color print, italics, bullets, captions, and labels, that signal importance in text. We can remind kids that font and effect differences should be viewed as red flags that wave "This is important. Read carefully."

Signal words and phrases. Nonfiction writing often includes text cues that signal importance. Signal words (sometimes referred to as cue words), like stop signs, warn readers to halt and pay attention. Proficient adult readers automatically attend to these text cues. Less experienced readers don't. We need to remember to point these signal words out to readers. Writers choose phrases such as *for example, for instance, in fact, in conclusion, most important, but, therefore, on the other hand,* and *such as* so that readers will take note. As students come across signal words, they can add them to a classroom chart headed Signal Word/Purpose, with the signal word on the left and the purpose of that word on the right. Kids and teachers co-construct these charts to help readers navigate difficult expository text. Standardized tests as well are full of signal words, and familiarity with these cues may boost scores.

Illustrations and photographs. Illustrations play a prominent role in nonfiction to enhance reading comprehension. Nonfiction trade books and magazines brim with colorful photographs that capture young readers and carry them deeper into meaning.

Graphics. Diagrams, cut-aways, cross-sections, overlays, distribution maps, word bubbles, tables, graphs, and charts graphically inform nonfiction readers of important information.

Text organizers. Teachers cannot assume that kids know concepts such as index, preface, table of contents, glossary, and appendix. When kids are surveying different texts for information, knowledge of these text organizers is crucial for further research.

Text structures. Expository text is framed around several structures that crop up in both trade and textbook publications and standardized test forms. Understanding different expository text structures gives readers a better shot at determining important information. These structures include cause and effect, problem and solution, question and answer, comparison and contrast, and description and sequence. If students know what to look for in terms of text structure, meaning comes more easily.

Strategy Lessons: Determining Importance

In the classrooms portrayed here, teachers at various grade levels surround their students with nonfiction trade books and other materials to help them build background knowledge of the genre, to see how certain features signal importance, and to model interesting as well as accurate writing. The first three lessons that follow illustrate these goals.

Nonfiction writing does not have to be boring. All we have to do is pick up a newspaper, look through a *National Geographic,* or read a nonfiction bestseller to see that nonfiction writing can be rich in voice. Sometimes, indeed, it is so compelling that sifting important information from the overall text can be challenging. Readers are likely to become so engrossed in authentic trade nonfiction that they may get carried away by the rich details and miss the essence of the text. But the first purpose of real-world nonfiction is to convey factual information, important ideas, and key concepts. The strategy lessons in this chapter show how teachers help students read to extract important information and essential ideas from nonfiction text.

Building Background Knowledge of Nonfiction Features

Purpose: Building background knowledge of nonfiction features by creating books that illustrate these

Resources: *Hungry, Hungry Sharks,* by Joanna Cole, photographs from home or school, 8" x 11" booklets containing six blank pages folded in half and stapled

Responses: A different nonfiction feature on each page; a two-column class chart headed Feature/Purpose, which serves as a record for all of the kids

To help her first graders become aware of the features of nonfiction, Michelle Meyer had them create nonfiction feature books. These little booklets were made up of six sheets of 8" x 11" paper folded over and stapled together with a construction paper cover. The kids wrote the title "Nonfiction Features" on their books and decorated them (see Figure 10.1). To help build their background knowledge for nonfiction features, Michelle filled her room to capacity with nonfiction books and read them aloud each day, pointing out various nonfiction features as they came up.

The first feature Michelle presented for these nonfiction feature books was captions. She pasted a photograph of her and her cat, Madison, on the first page and wrote the following caption under the picture: "Here I am with Madison wearing her princess look as she drapes herself over the pillow while lounging on my bed." Then Michelle labeled the page "Caption." Later, the kids each brought in a photograph, pasted it on the first page, wrote a caption under the picture, and labeled the page "Caption." (Michelle had a digital camera for those kids who were unable to come up with a photograph from home.) The photograph and the caption made for a very appealing page to begin the nonfiction feature books.

Each day as she read a nonfiction book out loud, Michelle added a new feature to her own book. The kids joined in the search, and when they came across an unfamiliar nonfiction feature, they shared it with the class and added it to their booklets as well as to a large two-column class chart headed Feature /Purpose. Along with Michelle, the kids recorded the new nonfiction features in the first column and indicated their purposes in the second column.

One day, while flipping through Joanna Cole's *Hungry, Hungry Sharks*, Catie found an illustration of a whale shark stretched across the roof of a bus, a visual marker of its great size. Michelle suggested that Catie teach the other kids about this new feature, called a comparison. Catie drew the whale shark on top of a school bus and labeled her new page with the heading "Comparisons" (see Figure 10.2). The next day she taught the class about the notion of comparisons by sharing her illustration. Michelle reinforced this by reading a written example of a size comparison between a Tyrannosaurus tooth and a banana. Sean's drawing in Chapter 9 (see Figure 9.5) illustrates his rendition of those words.

Figure 10.1 Cover of a Nonfiction Features Book

Figure 10.2 Catie's Illustration of a Comparison in Nonfiction Text

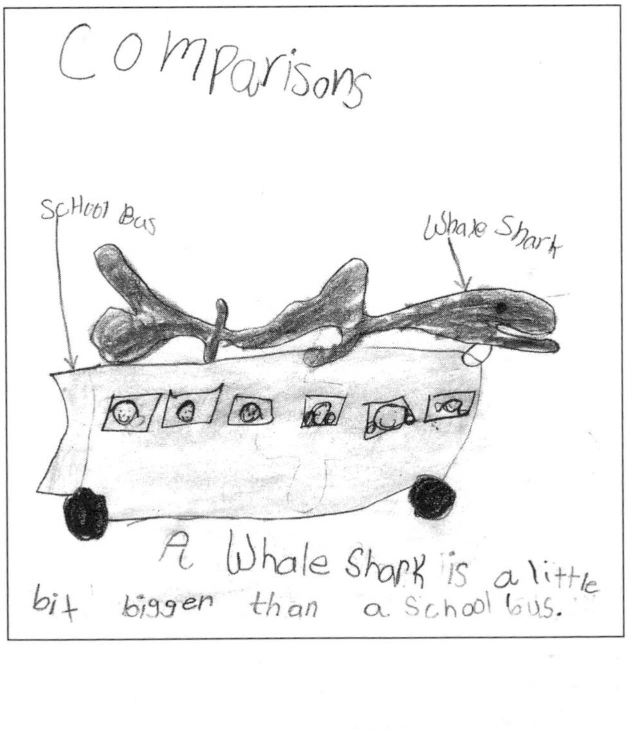

Michelle pointed out to the class that Catie and Sean used different words to compare these items. Catie wrote *a little bit bigger than* and Sean wrote *as big as*. The class discussed the difference in these phrases and their meanings because Michelle wanted them to begin to notice the language of comparison. Just telling kids about the special features and language of nonfiction is not enough. But having them search for their own examples and talk about nonfiction characteristics scaffolds their nonfiction reading and enhances their understanding of the genre.

Becoming Familiar with the Characteristics of Nonfiction Trade Books

Purpose: Acquiring information about an interesting topic, asking some questions, and designing pages based on authentic pages in nonfiction trade books

Resources: Nonfiction trade books, students' own nonfiction feature books, paper, and markers

Responses: Prior knowledge form; question form; 11" x 17" paper for page design

Slavens Elementary teacher Barb Smith led her second graders through a nonfiction study. After surrounding them with nonfiction material, teaching them about nonfiction features, encouraging them to choose a topic for exploration, and having them read for information and write down what she called WOW facts (striking information that makes one say Wow!), Barb helped her students design nonfiction pages that looked very much like the pages we find in nonfiction trade books.

Barb thought about having her students write nonfiction picture books, but wisely decided to have them create single pages instead as a first effort. These pages included both factual content about a chosen topic and the nonfiction features that kids had noticed in trade books. These topics ran the gamut from Sherman tanks to the life of Elvis Presley.

Barb asked her students to begin their research by recording what they already knew about their topic. Turner listed five things he already knew:

Research Topic: Elvis Presley
Prior Knowledge: Write down facts that you already know about your topic
1. Elvis was the king of Rock and Roll.
2. He was very famous.
3. He sang many great songs.
4. He was very tall.
5. He died of drugs.

Next, Barb asked her students to record their questions on a Questions form. After thinking through what he already knew about his topic, Turner made a list of questions:

Research Topic: Elvis Presley
Questions I have before I begin my research are . . .
1. Did Elvis have any other jobs?
2. Did he have children?
3. Did he have brothers and sisters?
4. What were his parents' names?
5. What instruments did he play?

Figure 10.3 Turner's Nonfiction Page

An additional sheet asked the kids to list five new facts they learned as they conducted their research. In their final form, these nonfiction pages included interesting factual information, answered questions, resembled published nonfiction, and were visually striking (see, for example, Figure 10.3).

This was a terrific project that helped build background knowledge about the genre of nonfiction as well as demanding that kids sift through interesting information and choose what they deemed most important to include on their page. This would serve as an important step in creating nonfiction picture books at a later date.

Determining What's Important When Writing Information

Purpose: Becoming a specialist on a favorite topic, choosing what is important to include in a piece of writing, and writing informational teaching books

Resources: Nonfiction trade books, magazines, and former students' work; 8" x 11" construction paper booklets containing about twelve pages folded and stapled

Responses: Teaching books that replicate authentic nonfiction trade books, features and all. The writers write about their specialties, something they know about, care about, and would like to teach someone.

On a visit to Jacqueline Heibert's third-grade classroom at Crofton House School in Vancouver, British Columbia, Steph worked with the students on writing important informa-

Equiptment for Downhill Skiing

boots

poles

skis

hooks

binding

goggles

Skis are usualy made out of plastic and metal. The bottom should always be waxed so you can slide easely. The poles are made out of metal. If you hold it upsidown it should be arm length, that is the right size for you. They also help you turn. The goggles are made out of plastic. They are to keep the snow and the sun out of your eyes. The boots are specialy designed to keep your feet warm. The boots also have little hooks to clip on to your binding.

Figure 10.4 Hillary C.'s Teaching Book Page on Skiing

tion about a topic of choice in the form of a "teaching book." Jacqueline had surrounded her third graders with nonfiction trade books, and they were becoming increasingly knowledgeable about the characteristics of the genre. When Steph arrived, she encouraged them to flip through nonfiction books, magazines, and examples of former students' teaching books and note the features and the writing. After they perused the resources for twenty minutes or so, Steph talked to the kids about writing books whose purpose is to teach something. "Everyone is a specialist in something," she told them as she wrote the following on a large chart:

A specialist is someone who
• Cares a lot about a topic, is passionate about it
• Knows a lot about the topic
• Wants to teach someone about the topic

She then made a list of several topics she knew and loved. Her list of specialties included

• Teaching and learning
• Reading and writing
• Her family
• Snorkeling
• Snow skiing
• The country of Tibet
• Hiking in the Colorado mountains

After sharing the topics she specialized in and choosing snorkeling for further exploration, she asked the kids to think of at least three specialties of their own. She asked for at least three in the belief that one will almost always emerge, even from more reticent kids, and that three or more would be a welcome bonus. The kids jotted down their specialties and shared them in pairs.

Next, Steph modeled writing her own teaching book. She wrote different information on each page of a construction paper booklet containing about twelve pages of paper, lined on the bottom half and unlined on the top for illustrations. She explained that since the purpose of nonfiction writing is to teach something, writers need to choose the most important information to include in the writing. To do this, writers ask themselves, "What information will best help my reader understand the topic?"

Steph began with snorkeling equipment on the first page, wrote about getting into the water on the next page, and followed with safety, coral, fish, and hazards on subsequent pages. Writing these parts on a page served as a preamble to later paragraphing. Steph explained that she chose these particular components of snorkeling because she felt they represented the most important information she could teach on the topic. She illustrated each page and included some nonfiction features, such as labeling her illustrations and marking each page with a heading.

The kids leaped at the chance to share their considerable information in the teaching-book format. They filled their teaching books with interesting content as well as an array of nonfiction features, including illustrations. Creating these nonfiction books gave kids opportunities to draw as well as write. Hillary C. used labeling to enhance her informational book about skiing (see Figure 10.4), and Hilary W. headed each section in her manatee book with a pertinent question,

Figure 10.5 Hillary W.'s Teaching Book Page on Manatees

which she answered on the page (see Figure 10.5). Making these teaching books provided a terrific follow-up to the earlier nonfiction convention books and page designs.

Later that week, after they had completed the teaching books, Jacqueline gave the kids plenty of time to share their information with each other. Sharing their specialties built community. The kids came to see each other as specialists in a particular area. Some specialties were expected. Some were a complete surprise. Everyone learned new information on fresh topics as well as building background for nonfiction features. Because the kids included information they deemed important, their classmates learned essential content. When kids do the teaching, their peers take note.

A thought occurs to us here. To model outcomes, share student work as well as trade publications. One of the most effective ways to give our students an idea of what a project looks like in the end is to share completed examples of other students' work. Copy and save kids' work. Ask their permission to share it with future students. Flattery will get you everywhere! Student work is more authentic and powerful than any model we can think of. Kids love to read the work of other students, and they learn from it, too.

Making Students Aware of Primary Sources

New

Purpose: To notice and learn from primary sources
Resources: *The Journey That Saved Curious George: The True Wartime Escape of Margret and H. A. Rey,* by Louise Borden
Responses: Sticky notes

We were thrilled when we came across *The Journey That Saved Curious George*. This book chronicles the remarkable story of the Rey's 1940 escape from Paris on bicycles with the *Curious George* manuscript in tow just before the Nazis marched into the city. The narrative is fascinating. Who doesn't love *Curious George*? But we also love the illustrations, photos, and particularly the primary sources. The book explodes with original primary source documents—letters to editors, photographs, diary entries, original manuscript pages, telegrams, passports, and identity cards. They lend an air of authenticity that makes the reader feel as if she or he is smack in the middle of the City of Lights just before the Nazi occupation.

We have searched long and hard for engaging text to introduce kids to reading primary sources. Just as we teach about nonfiction features and their purposes, we also teach them to notice, think about, and read primary sources. We point them out, talk about them, and discuss how they relate to and enhance the narrative. We explain the purpose of primary source documents is to give the reader a sense of history, make that historic time period come alive, and inform them about content. After introducing kids to primary source documents with this book, we have them search their classroom and school libraries to find other examples of primary sources, make interpretations, and share them with each other. Another terrific resource for teaching primary source reading is Joy Hakim's series *A History of US*, which is chock full of documents of every imaginable type.

Coding Important Information on Unfamiliar as Well as Familiar Topics

Purpose: Noticing and selecting new information on familiar and unfamiliar topics
Resources: The picture book *The Unhuggables*, published by the National Wildlife Federation, and a variety of animal books for independent practice
Responses: Sticky notes coded L for learned something new about a familiar topic, or * for important information about an unfamiliar topic

Our background knowledge plays a major role when we read informational text. As an avid lover of the country of Tibet and a passionate reader about the plight of Tibetans, Steph has extensive background knowledge on the topic. Each time she picks up an article about Tibet, she focuses on new information to add to her store of knowledge and develop further insight into this wonderful country. Much of what she reads about Tibet she knows already. On the other hand, if she were to pick up an article about Colorado water conservation, she would likely be overwhelmed with a mass of new, unfamiliar information, since she knows so little about the topic to begin with.

Kids are no different. Every teacher has met a kid who knows practically everything there is to know about dinosaurs, black holes, or the Civil War. The amount of background knowledge we have on a topic has a lot to do with what we deem important about it. If we already know the information, we are less likely to consider it important when we read it again.

When kids are reading about topics they know a great deal about, we encourage them to notice when they've learned something new and code the text L for learned. That new information means a lot to students with considerable background knowledge about a topic. When kids read about a little-known topic, however, coding the text L for learned is useless because the text would likely disappear under a sea of Ls. We encourage these readers, instead, to code parts they deem important with *, a kind of a universal code for importance. We suggest that they use the same criterion for coding with * as they use to highlight important text.

Nick, a sixth-grade spider specialist, was reading *The Unhuggables*, a collection of short text pieces about animals you wouldn't want to cuddle up to. The compelling content, the rich writing style, and the engaging short text combine to make *The Unhuggables* one of our favorite books. In the section on spiders, he coded the text and wrote the following comments:

L   Tarantulas protect jewelry stores at night. Burglars are scared just by the look of them.
L   Spiders are a sign of good luck in some countries.
L   Of 30,000 spiders, only a dozen are dangerous.

Nick was delighted to have this additional information. No topic intrigued him more than these eight-legged creatures. For someone who knew little about spiders, the ratio of poisonous to harmless might not be so important, but for Nick this was essential new information to add to his arachnid arsenal.

After reading about spiders, he turned to the section titled "Octopus," a sea creature he knew next to nothing about. His teacher encouraged him to read the text and code information he thought was important with *. She suggested that information that surprised him might be important. The response on several of his sticky notes included surprising information:

•   Octopuses are one of the shyest sea creatures.
•   Octopuses do not grab swimmers and suck them in with their arms.
•   Most of their bodies are the size of a grown man's fist and none are bigger than a football.

Nick's reading exploded octopus myths right and left. He knew so little about them that this new information was very important to him. In *The Unhuggables*, Nick experienced reading both as a spider specialist and as an octopus novice. These were two different experiences, and determining what was important in the text was related primarily to his background knowledge and interest in the topic.

Finding Important Information Rather Than Just One Main Idea

Purpose: Understanding that there are often several important ideas in a piece of text rather than a single main idea

Resource: A piece of like kind text for each student

Responses: Three sticky notes, each one coded * to mark three important ideas in the text

When we are trying to wean kids from the one and only main idea mentality, we give them three sticky notes and ask them to draw a big asterisk on each one. Sound a little hokey? We thought so, too, until we saw how well it worked, particularly when students are reading the same text.

Our point is to show students that there is more than one important idea in anything they read. So we ask them to place the sticky notes at three different points in the text that they deem important. We model this, too, and when we come back together to discuss the reading, each child and the teacher shares what he or she has determined to be important in the text. Naturally, we aren't all in agreement, and that is the point. We ask kids to defend their stance, cite evidence, and explain the thinking behind their decision. This contributes to our students' capacity to speak out about what they think, and it reminds them that text includes many important concepts and issues, not just a single main idea.

Important to Whom?

New

Purpose: Understanding that there may be a difference between what the reader thinks is most important and the writer's big ideas

Resources: Articles from magazines like *Time for Kids, Scholastic News, National Geographic Explorer* or writing from nonfiction trade books.

Responses: Response notebooks

Teachers often report that their kids have trouble picking out the most important information when they read. And test scores are frequently depressed in the "find the main idea" category. One of the primary reasons that kids have trouble picking out the most important information is that in a sense they are asking themselves, "Important to whom?" In other words, what the reader thinks is most important is not necessarily the author's main idea.

Readers frequently find a detail to be more important than the big idea in the article. For instance, let's say a reader reads an article that focuses primarily on antismoking programs that are effective at stemming the tide against teen smoking. As the student reads, she comes across a factual detail that states that over 400,000 people die of smoking each year. If that student's mom is a smoker, that detail surfaces as more important to her than the main idea of the success of antismoking programs. The main idea often depends on who the main reader is!

We teach our kids to make a distinction between what they think is most important to remember and what the writer most wants them to take away from the article. So whenever we ask kids to pick out the main idea, we ask them first to write down something they learned that they think is important to remember. Then we ask them to draw a line under that response and write down what they think the author most wanted them to learn and remember. Sometimes they jot down the same response. Other times, their responses are quite different. We have found that kids are much better at picking out the main idea if they first consider what they think is most important and then think about what the author most wanted them to learn from the article.

We want our kids to know that nothing matters more than their thinking when they read, and giving them an opportunity to consider what they think is most important serves that goal. But we also want them to recognize that nonfiction writers have something in mind that they are trying to convey to the reader and that it is the reader's responsibility to pick up on that as well.

One caveat: we can't forget to let kids know that when they are taking a standardized test, the only answer that counts is the one that reflects the author's main idea. So we remind them to choose the answer that expresses what they think the author most wants them to take away from the reading. And the good news is that we have found that our kids do even better on these tests once they understand how to distinguish between their notion of what's most important and the writer's big ideas.

Sifting the Topic from the Details

Purpose: Discriminating between key topics and supporting details

Resource: "Howling Again" from *Wild Outdoor World*

Responses: Two-column note form headed Topic/Details; three-column note form headed Topic/Details/Response

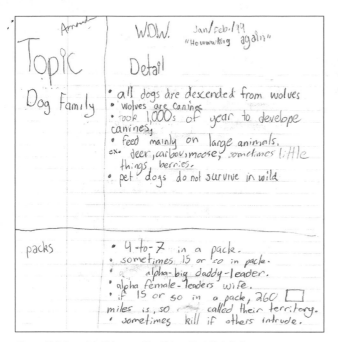

Figure 10.6 Amanda's Notes on a Two-Column Topic/Details Form

Figure 10.7 Rebecca's Response in the Added Third Column of a Topic/Details Form

Mary Buerger generally uses a young adult magazine to introduce two-column note taking to her fourth-grade class. We have found the Topic/Details note form to be particularly effective at helping students organize their thinking as they read for information. The most difficult part of this form is figuring out the primary topics. Mary introduces this two-column note taking with nonfiction text that is structured around sections with separate headings. She explains that the headings represent the topics and that the text is full of details that give information about the topic. Much nonfiction text is structured this way.

To introduce two-column note taking, Mary found an article in *Wild Outdoor World*, "Howling Again." This article was structured around a series of six headings followed by two or three paragraphs of details under each heading. The headings were

Fifi, Is That You?
They Run in Packs
They Have Babysitters
They Howl to Communicate
They Use Body Language
They Stay Out All Winter

Mary began by reading the first section. "Fifi, Is That You?" didn't provide much in the way of clues for a topic. The first few sentences read, "Wolves belong to the canine family. All dogs are descended from wolves. That means that your pet poodle, basset hound, retriever, or mutt developed from wolves." The section went on to discuss canine behavior and some basic wolf information. Mary mentioned that when you can't infer the topic from the heading, you should take a look at the first sentence or two to help ascertain what the section is primarily about. She decided that her first topic could be "Dog Family." As she wrote that on an overhead transparency, kids wrote it in their Wonder Books on a page headed Topic/Details.

The next topic she explored was "Packs," taken directly from the second heading. As kids read through the paragraphs that followed, they included details supporting the topic. After reasoning through the first few sections, the kids continued on their own with a partner, using each section heading as a topic on their Topic/Details form (see Figure 10.6).

These headings support students as they practice two-column note taking. Not every nonfiction article is written in this user-friendly way, although many are. When introducing a new concept or strategy, we choose the most accessible material so that grasping the concept will be relatively easy.

As Mary continued teaching two-column note taking, she sought out articles in which it was harder to sort the topics from the details, because, for instance, the text was not broken up into sections by headings. We move to more challenging material after students have had practice with more accessible material.

This reflects our ongoing commitment to the gradual release of responsibility approach to instruction. Eventually, students use the two-column Topic/Details note form independently.

Adding a Third Column for Personal Response

As her students gain facility with two-column note taking, Mary introduces a third column for personal response. Her kids let her know that the Topic/Details form was effective for listing essential information but lacked a place for their responses. A third column for response allows kids to interact with text personally and ensures that they have a place to record their thoughts, feelings, and questions. Since it is impractical to place three columns on one page of notebook paper, Mary's students divide one page of their Wonder Books into two columns headed Topic and Details, and use the entire opposite page as a third column for Response. We have found that the more space we allow for responding in writing, the longer and more in-depth the responses are likely to be. Rebecca listed the following topics and details for her research on Spain on the first page:

Topic	Details
Employment	Work hours—9 A.M.–1 P.M. and 3 P.M.–6 P.M.
	Go home for lunch
	Spanish sometimes eat dinner at 10:30 P.M.
Education	In 1900, sixty out of one hundred people could not read
	1987—Only 3% could not read.
	1st—Pre-Primary
	2nd—Primary
	3rd—Secondary
	4th—Bachillerato (optional)
Art	Great tradition in art, architecture, and music

Clearly, Rebecca was much impressed by the late dining hour favored by Spaniards because she started her third-column response on this theme (see Figure 10.7).

Reading Opposing Perspectives to Form an Opinion

Purpose: Reading persuasive material carefully to make an informed judgment
Resource: "Should Cities Sue Gunmakers?" an article from *Junior Scholastic*
Responses: Group discussion; a three-column note form headed Evidence For/Evidence Against/Personal Opinion

Junior Scholastic magazine includes a regular feature called "News Debate," which presents an issue in the news and gives two opposing perspectives (see, for example, Figure 10.8). *Junior Scholastic* is one of our favorite magazines. We remember it fondly from when it floated around our own junior high classrooms, and it has only improved with age. It covers a spectrum of issues and does not steer clear of controversy.

Helen Wickham, an eighth-grade teacher in Atlanta, explained to her social studies class that essays and editorials are written to promote a certain perspective and persuade the reader of that view: "It is the job of readers to read carefully and weigh the evidence to make a thoughtful decision regarding their own opinion." She provided her students with a three-column note form headed Evidence For/Evidence Against/Personal Opinion. She passed out the magazine

Figure 10.8 "News Debate" Article from *Junior Scholastic*

Should Cities Sue Gunmakers?

New Orleans is suing gun manufacturers. Mayor Marc Morial wants them to pay for police and health-care costs resulting from gun violence. The city's lawsuit claims that gunmakers manufacture "unreasonably dangerous" guns that lack effective safety devices.

Although gun sales are banned in Chicago, gun violence remains a big problem. The city has filed a $433 million lawsuit accusing the gun industry of "negligent marketing." The lawsuit argues that gunmakers deliberately flood nearby suburbs with more guns than law-abiding citizens can buy. The guns end up in the hands of Chicago's criminals.

A similar lawsuit, known as the "Hamilton Case," has been filed in Brooklyn, New York. The suit claims that gun manufacturers "negligently market" too many guns to states that have weak gun-control laws. Gun traffickers then sell the guns in states that have strong gun-control laws, such as New York and Massachusetts.

Other cities planning to sue the gun industry are closely watching the Hamilton Case. They hope the threat of expensive lawsuits will force the gun industry to better regulate itself.

What do you think? Should gun manufacturers be held legally and financially responsible for gun violence in cities? Read both arguments below, then decide.

We **Should** Sue Gunmakers	We **Should Not** Sue Gunmakers
The time is right to make gun manufacturers responsible for the financial cost of gun violence. States across the country recently sued tobacco companies and recovered billions of dollars to cover the health-care costs of treating smokers. Like tobacco companies, gun manufacturers have disregarded the health and safety of Americans. They have failed to develop basic safety devices on guns that could spare hundreds of lives each year. According to the Center to Prevent Handgun Violence, more than 33,000 people were killed by gun violence in 1996 alone. Despite these statistics, gun manufacturers refuse to regulate how their products are bought or sold. In fact, they market their products in ways that make guns even more unsafe. Says Kristen Rand, director of the Violence Policy Center, "These lawsuits will force us to take a closer look at an industry that is killing people. And the public won't like what it sees."	Guns are legal to manufacture and safe when used properly. It isn't the fault of the manufacturer if criminals use their products to shoot people. People don't sue a liquor company or a car company when a drunk driver kills someone. "The most important [safety] device with any gun is the brain of the person using it," says Richard Feldman, executive director of the American Shooting Sports Council. Using lawsuits to force gun companies to regulate the buying and selling of guns is a misuse of the court system. It is the responsibility of state and local governments to control crime and violence. "These things are supposed to be decided in the legislature," Feldman says, "not the courts." More important, the public does not support lawsuits aimed at gun manufacturers. A recent survey by DecisionQuest, a legal research company, found that 66.2 percent of those surveyed were against suing gun manufacturers.
YES	**NO**

with an article on gun safety and violence to each class member and asked the kids to read the piece silently and record their thinking about the issue. Helen read along with the students silently and completed the task, also.

When they had finished reading, the students had a lively discussion, which bordered on a raucous debate. Callie's form shows the factual information she acquired as well as her personal opinion:

Evidence For

Tobacco companies can be sued.
No safety devices on guns.
33,000 people dead in a year.

Evidence Against

Liquor companies can't.
The best safety device is the person using the gun.
The public doesn't agree with suing gun manufacturers; 66.2% against.

Personal Opinion

Guns kill way too many people. Guns should have safety locks and checks, but I'm not sure we should sue the gun companies. There are too many lawsuits already. Hot coffee and all that stuff. But if suing would make a difference in people dying, maybe we should do it.

This form and the ensuing discussion helped kids sort out their thinking and informed their opinions. Some wrote more in the Personal Opinion column after participating in the discussion. Much of the short text adults encounter is written with a slant. Readers must be trained to recognize persuasive writing and exercise judgment as they read it. Elementary school is not too soon to start.

Using FQR Think Sheets to Understand Information

New

Purpose: Determining importance, asking questions, and responding to historical fiction
Resources: Picture books relating to the Civil War
Aunt Harriet's Underground Railroad in the Sky, by Faith Ringgold
Follow the Drinking Gourd, by Jeanette Winter
Nettie's Trip South, by Ann Turner
Sweet Clara and the Freedom Quilt, by Deborah Hopkinson
Response: Three-column note form headed Facts/Questions/Response (FQR)

Fifth-grade teachers Susan Prentiss and Dave Shinkle were ready to try something new as they planned their yearly Civil War study with the school librarian, Nell Box. They were concerned that students spent so much time learning about the facts and details of this period that they seldom had time to focus on history as the experiences and narratives of individual people. Although the social studies textbook and other materials provided the students with interesting information, Susan, Dave, and Nell wondered if reading historical fiction picture books might present issues, dilemmas, and perspectives missing from the sources the students typically read. Understanding the stories of people living long ago, they hoped, would bring historical facts from this time period to life.

Guided by Nell's expertise in linking literature with the curriculum, the trio met one day to plan lessons using historical fiction picture books sophisticated enough to challenge fifth graders. Nell suggested they launch the study with Faith Ringgold's *Aunt Harriet's Underground Railroad in the Sky*, a complicated narrative of two modern-day kids who find themselves on a journey on the Underground Railroad with Harriet Tubman. The book was full of interesting information about slavery, and Nell anticipated its puzzling narrative would hold the children's attention and prompt lots of questions. Susan recommended Ann Turner's *Nettie's Trip South*, having read this picture book to students in prior years. She remembered how the deceptively simple text jolted students with the story of a Northern girl, Nettie, traveling in the South, who came upon a slave auction and was outraged by it.

Nell, Susan, and Dave were confident that these and other picture books would provoke their students to think about historical issues and ideas. If their students really were to grapple with these issues, however, they would have to do more than simply read through the books. The teachers knew that these fifth graders would think more carefully about the information they encountered in the books if asked to record significant facts and ideas. A two-column note form headed Facts/Questions would elicit important information and provide opportunities for questions. A third column, labeled Response, was added to encourage the students to think about their reactions, opinions, and feelings about the books. Susan, for her part, was thrilled that she wouldn't have journal responses in one place and facts, usually collected in the kids' social studies notebooks, in another. For once, all the information they were learning, as well as their questions and responses, would be in one place!

To launch the study, Nell, Dave, and Susan began reading *Aunt Harriet* aloud. After reading a few pages, they modeled the kind of thinking they expected from the students, discussing what they had just read and jotting down important facts. Dave chimed in with several questions, which they wrote right next to the facts, and Nell added a response, so that kids could observe how the teachers worked across the page to record the information and their thinking. As Susan continued reading, the students chimed in with their own facts, questions, and responses. Nell recorded their comments for all to see, and the kids recorded their thinking on their own FQR think sheet. Once students understood how to gather facts, ask questions, and respond with their own opinions, they finished reading *Aunt Harriet* in pairs and continued to fill out the three-column FQR forms on their own. At the end of the session, students were eager to share their own personal responses based on facts they gathered and the questions they asked. The following three-column FQR form illustrates their in-depth reading of the text.

Title: *Aunt Harriet's Underground Railroad in the Sky*
Author: Faith Ringgold

Facts	Questions	Response
Harriet Tubman escaped and started the Underground Railroad.	How did she escape?	I would be afraid of getting caught.
Black people were taken as slaves from Africa.		I think slaves' spirits died on those ships.
More slaves died on those ships than reached the shore.		If they made it alive, they had probably given up hope.
Slaves weren't allowed to learn to read.	Why were they stopped from learning?	Reading was a power that white owners did not want slaves to have.
People would jump brooms to get married.	What is "jumping the broom?" Why couldn't they go to a church?	
The Underground Railroad was a way for slaves to get to the free land.	Were they dreaming in this story?	

Nicole's three-column FQR form illustrates her in-depth reading of the text (see Figure 10.9).

The next day, eight children crowded around a table, sharing multiple copies of Ann Turner's *Nettie's Trip South*. After deciding they would read the book out loud together, Nell watched as her group of students zipped through the pages, seldom stopping to record facts or questions. To slow them down, Nell suggested that they stop after each page or so to discuss their ideas and note information and questions. As a result, they thought more carefully about their reading. This sample of one student's Facts/Questions/Response form illustrates how students focused on the important ideas in each book and shared their opinions.

Title: *Nettie's Trip South*
Author: Ann Turner

Facts	Questions	Response
Slaves weren't allowed to learn.	Who is Addie?	I think Nettie is writing to her friend Addie.
I can't believe the Constitution could say that slaves were 3/5 of a person.* (*How could I check this?)	Who is writing the letter? Why were slaves considered to be only 3/5 of a person? Were the husband and wife split apart?	She didn't expect to see what she saw. It makes me angry that slaves were sold away from families who were in tears because they were split apart and sold. You can tell Nettie had a mind of her own.

Title: Aunt Harriet's Underground RR.   **Name:** Nicole

Author: Faith Ringgold

Facts	Questions	Response
(I Know) the underground RR was a path the slaves took to get away. Slaves lived + worked in the South not in the North. Slaves would go North to be free. Harriet Tubman carried hundreds of people to freedom on the underground RR. Never lost a passenger. Slaves traveled on cramped boats. They were sold in auctions. They were seperated from families. They couldn't get married or learn.	Are BeBe + Cassie dreaming? What's the train in the sky? How can a train be in the sky? Can the conductor be Aunt Harriet? What does "Go North or die" mean? Why North? When does the story take place? Why are they flying? Is the whole story a memory? Could this be heaven? Why were people so mean to black people? Why didn't they pay the slaves? How cramped were they? In one boat, about how many slaves were in them?	I think the whole book is just half fantasy and half true. I think it's just a book that puts facts in a fantasy book. It could mean most of the people died on the ships than on the slave grounds. I think that it is just horrible to have a slave to do your work for you or your family. I think that they were mean.

Figure 10.9 Fifth-Grade Student's Facts/ Questions/Response Sheet on *Aunt Harriet's Underground Railroad in the Sky*

Some of the students were able to connect information learned during a study of the Constitution to the information they encountered in the picture books. Joanne said, "I thought the Constitution was written to protect people. Didn't the Bill of Rights give people rights like freedom of religion and freedom of speech?" Her background information, accurate to a point, did not include the knowledge that slaves were not protected by the constitution. Like Nettie, Joanne was outraged at the slave auction and subsequently investigated why slaves were counted as "3/5 of a person." Rather than merely summarizing the events of each story, the FQR form encouraged students like Joanne to investigate and find answers to her lingering questions.

 For more information on creating FQRs with history topics, see our video series *Strategic Thinking: Reading and Responding, Grades 4–8* (2004).

Reasoning Through a Piece of Historical Fiction to Determine Importance

Purpose: Using a guided discussion to understand important information
Resource: *Bull Run*, by Paul Fleischman
Response: A guided discussion between the teacher and five members of a book club

Historical fiction creates a clear context for different times, places, and people. Historians Levstik and Barton (2001) argue there is no better way to learn about other times and places than through carefully researched, well-written historical fiction. They suggest that portraying human experiences from the past in realistic, engaging narratives enables students to understand perspectives and ideas that would be difficult if they were first encountered in summary form in a history textbook.

We've noticed that nothing helps kids think through information more than talking about it. When students read and discuss historical fiction, they construct interpretations based on the words and ideas in the text. More challenging historical fiction requires students to proceed slowly and carefully, taking time to reason through new ideas and information to build their knowledge about a particular period of time.

Seventh-grade students were studying the Civil War by reading Paul Fleischman's *Bull Run* in small groups. *Bull Run*, a fictionalized account of the first battle of the Civil War, introduces students to ordinary people, all of whom experienced or were connected to this moment in history. The vignettes explore how war profoundly affects these individuals. Fleischman's characters include a doctor, a woman slave who has gone to war with her Confederate officer master, a twelve-year-old Southern boy "desperate to kill a Yankee," and a number of other "eyewitnesses."

Each character tells his or her story through a first-person narrative that encourages questions and inferences, allowing students to then draw conclusions about these individuals and their perspectives. Students' reading was guided by questions such as Who was this person? How was he or she connected to this battle and this war? What was he or she doing, thinking, and feeling about it all? Figuring out each person's point of view and connection to the battle encouraged several levels of questioning and thoughtful discussion. This excerpt from a discussion captures how students sorted and sifted the details in each vignette to come to an understanding of the important ideas about how war changes peoples' lives.

Anne conducts a guided discussion of a vignette about Carlotta King, the story of a young slave who was forced to journey to Virginia with her Confederate soldier master. Carlotta's words are represented in italics.

Anne: Right now, let's read Carlotta King's first-person narrative. Think about who she was, where she was, what was happening to her, and why. Let's read the first few sentences and jot down any questions we have. It's not really clear what's happening to her, so we have to determine what's important based on her words.

> *I come up from Mississippi with the master. He was a lieutenant or some such thing. I heard him bragging to another man that he had five thousand acres and loads of slaves, which was a bare-headed lie. And that his slaves would sooner die than run off and leave him, which was a bigger lie yet. Lots of the soldiers brought their slaves with 'em. We washed and cooked and mended same as back home. Except we weren't back home.*

Carla: What?! Why did the officers bring their slaves to war with them?
Lynda: She said they cooked and did the laundry just like on the plantation, but it doesn't sound like she liked her master.
John: So she was in the North now, or close to the North? So they were at Bull Run or not yet?
Anne: Remember, Bull Run was a stream in northern Virginia, where the Union and Confederate troops first met on the battlefield.

> *The Union men weren't more than a few hills away. I'd look at them hills. They did call to me powerful. I was a young woman and fast as a fox. I knew I'd surely never get another chance and made up my mind and picked the night I'd go. My heart beat hard all that day. I didn't tell nobody.*

Mike: It sounds like she's going to try to escape.
Anne: Which words made you think that?

Mike: She said, "Them hills, they did call to me powerful," and she also said she could run fast with the words, "I was a young woman and fast as a fox."

Amber: Won't that be dangerous if there's fighting? Won't somebody notice her?

Lynda: But she says it's her only chance.

Then at supper another slave told how those that crossed over were handed back to their owners by the Yankees! My bowl slipped right out of my hands. I thought the Yankees had come to save us.

Anne: What does it mean . . . "those that crossed over were handed back to their owners by the Yankees"?

John: So they return slaves who escape. Couldn't she have used the Underground Railroad and gotten away?

Carla: I bet not every Yankee did that; maybe some of them helped the slaves.

Mike: Remember in the Aunt Harriet book there were those people—the bounty hunters—who would try to spy on runaway slaves and catch them and return them?

Lynda: And at the end it said something about a law which made people in the North do that.

Anne: Do you mean the Fugitive Slave Act?

John: Well, maybe that's why they have to return the slaves that escape, maybe that's why Northerners couldn't just help them escape.

Carla: Or that's why they have to go all the way to Canada to be free.

Amber: So why didn't they just hide until the battle was over?

Mike: I wonder if she'll try to escape at all, she might have just given up.

Anne: So what do you think happened to her? What do you think she decided to do?

Lynda: I think she might have escaped, at least for a while, but I wonder if she ever made it to freedom.

As it turns out, Carlotta did try to escape during the heat of the Battle of Bull Run, but Fleischman left us hanging with Carlotta's last words: "If Union soldiers sent slaves back, I'd just have to keep clear of 'em. When I came to Bull Run, I just waded across and kept movin' North."

In order to understand the dilemmas Carlotta faced at Bull Run, the students needed information about many aspects of the Civil War, such as the Fugitive Slave Act and the Underground Railroad, which they were able to gain through this guided discussion. Reasoning through the text meant that students used a guided conversation to come to an understanding of important issues, events, and information.

Reading for Details

Throughout this chapter we emphasize reading to answer questions and reading for important information. We tend to downplay reading for details, perhaps because we spent so much time doing it in school ourselves. But authentic reading experiences remind us that there are many reasons to read, often for the big ideas and also for the details. Close reading of text of any sort is frequently central to understanding, as Steph discovered one day at the dog kennel.

Upon heading out of town, she left written directions to bathe and groom her beloved ball of fur, a keeshond named Indiana Jones. Upon her return, the kennel keeper retrieved a dog Steph was convinced was not in any way hers.

The dog he presented to her was shaved down almost to the skin. As the dog leapt at her in great glee, it dawned on her that this bald-as-a-ping-pong-ball dog was in fact hers. We ignore details at our peril!

Seriously, we see the value in all kinds of reading. Reading is about purpose, and there is a time and place for every type of reading, reading for details as well as reading for the big picture.

Teaching with the End in Mind: Assessing What We've Taught

Determining Importance

Based on the lessons in this chapter, we look for evidence that

1. *Students gain important information from text and visual features.* We look for evidence that students are paying attention to text and visual features when they read and incorporating them when they write nonfiction.
2. *Students sift and sort the important information from the details and merge their thinking with it.* We look for evidence that students acquire information and decide what's important to remember. They also think more deeply about the information by asking questions and responding.
3. *Students learn to make a distinction between what they think is most important and what the author most wants them to take away from the reading.* We look for evidence that students can sort out their own thinking from the important ideas in the text and the author's perspective.
4. *Students use text evidence to form opinions and understand big ideas and issues.* We look for evidence that students tie their opinions and ideas to the text.

Suggestions for Differentiation

Text coding offers many opportunities for differentiation. Kids leave tracks of their thinking with a variety of codes that will remind them of what they want to remember. Question marks, exclamation points, asterisks, and stars can all be indications of what's important and what kids think about it. Highlighting and underlining alone are not enough. We need to see our kids' thinking, and they need to express it to remember why they highlighted in the first place. So we teach kids to jot a quick note or sketch a picture next to important information to better learn, understand, and remember it. We also teach kids to bracket paragraphs and sections and paraphrase what they learned. When all of us, and especially English language learners, put information into our own words, we are much more likely to understand what we are reading. So we focus on supporting kids to put information into their words and to shape it into their own thought.

Determining Importance Assessment Commentary

Facts/Questions/Response (FQR) think sheets from the lesson on "Using FQR Think Sheets to Understand Information"

Kids read informational text and applied the FQR strategy to science topics independently.

Figure 10.10 Kyle records facts that represent the important information in an article on saving the Everglades. You can see how he asks authentic questions, such as, *Are we really the smartest mammals on earth?* He keeps trying to think of solutions to the problem posed by the article in the response column. This is a terrific example of using an FQR to work out thinking and better understand the information.

Facts — Kyle
- Settlers thought the Everglades was a worthless swamp.
- Everglades is not worthless but unique.
- Many species in everglades all need eachother and a steady supply of water.
- Humans messed up because they took away animals homes to make homes for themself.
- Everglades were now only half their former size, ove
* 68 endangered or threatened species.
- 1 of top ten most endangered places.
- Bush has a plan to restore everglades w/ 8 billion dollars.
- biggest environmental plan ever.

Questions
- why is it called a river of grass?
* Is the number of species going down after this.
- what was the size of the Everglades?
- Are we really the smartest mammals on earth?
- how can they fix it?
- why does it matter?
- where will he get the money?
- when will this start?
- How long has the water been gone from the everglades?
- How many species lived there?

Response
- Maybe the everglades are this river of grass.
- Probably settlers saw everglades as an obstacle.
- There's some type of problem with the water supply.
- There are many more endangered species which is a real drag.
- We need more water
- We should help the animals.
- Maybe taxes.
- named the river of grass because it is a river flowing into a grassy field.
* Make a zoo for the animals.
- In stead of blowing everything away just reconstruct.

Facts — Rebecca
- Walruses spend most time in water
- they rest and give birth on the ice
- ~30 below in Arctic
- North Polar reg. is Arctic Ocean and surrounding land
- a treeless plain where soil remains frozen all year
- spends all spring, summer, and fall eating and storing up fat. Then it hibernates and lives off the fat
- it grows longer front claws to dig tunnels to hibernate in.
* Walruses have 6 in. of body fat to keep out the

Questions
- why don't the babies freeze?
- how could animals live in such a harsh place
- warm blooded or cold blooded?
- what's tundra?
- What does the temperature drop down too
* how does their fur change from grayish brown to white?
- how do they get all of this information if it's way too cold

Response 4th grade
- this is so cold I can't even imagine it being this cold
- probably warm because cold blooded would freeze
- their body fat helps them keep warm

Figure 10.11 Rebecca did a nice job recording factual information. Her questions are focused on details and help to clarify unfamiliar vocabulary. She hasn't used the response column as effectively. We would want to help her get the idea that exploring her thinking in this column will make a difference in her understanding.

Students learn to make a distinction between what they think is most important and what the author most wants them to understand after the lesson "Important to Whom?"

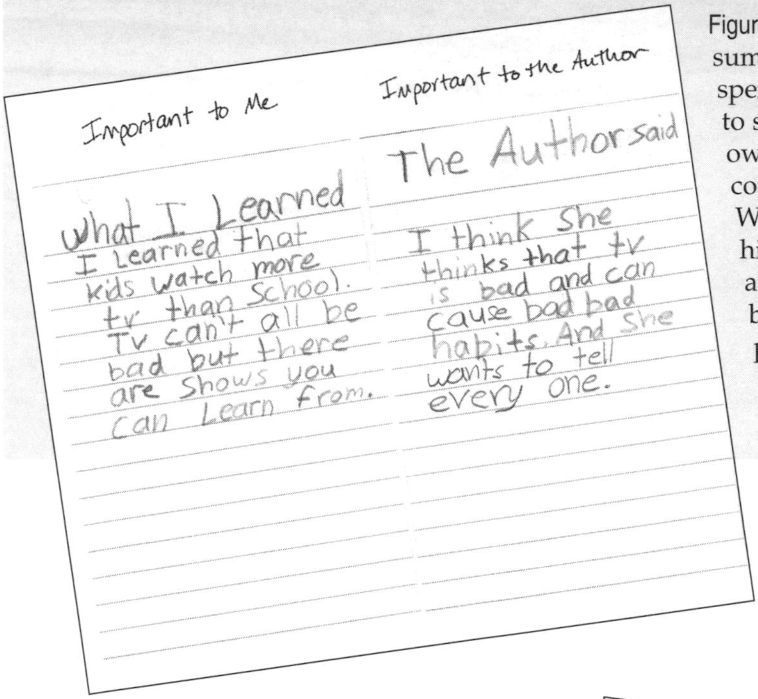

Important to Me | Important to the Author

What I Learned
I Learned that kids watch more tv than school. Tv can't all be bad but there are shows you can Learn from.

The Author said
I think She thinks that tv is bad and can cause bad bad habits. And she wants to tell every one.

Figure 10.12 This child was able to summarize important information—kids spend more time watching TV than going to school. He couldn't resist adding his own thought—TV wasn't all bad and you could learn from it—and we applaud that. With respect to what the author said, he hit the nail on the head saying that the author's perspective was that TV causes bad habits. And, picking up on the persuasive slant of the article, he noted that the author "wants to tell everyone" what she is thinking.

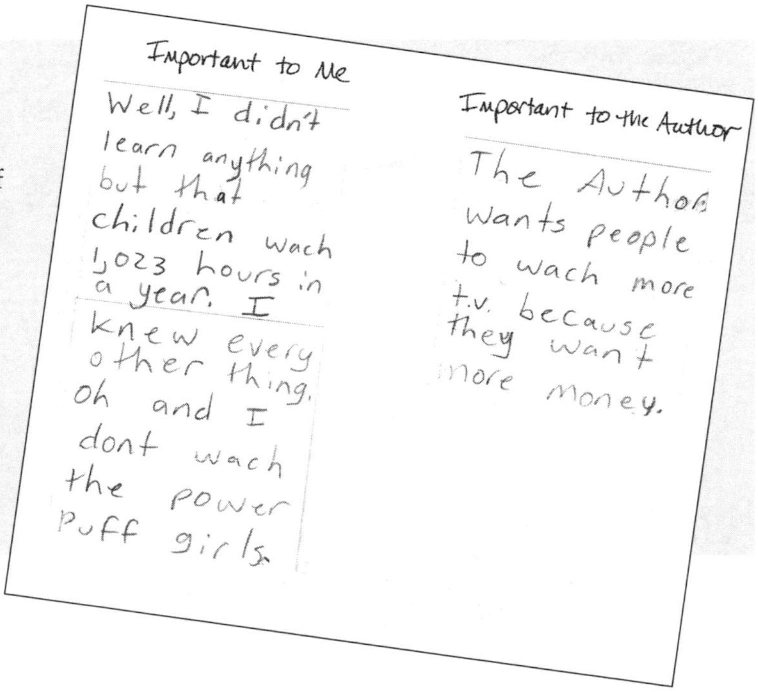

Figure 10.13 We work hard to encourage students to be open to and interested in learning new information. This child is overly confident of her understanding of the article, especially since her summary of what the author thought was important has no basis in fact. She demonstrates why it is so important to teach distinguishing your thinking from the author's. Over time, we would work with this student to be more open to new ideas and to make a clear distinction between what the text says and what she brings to it.

Important to Me
Well, I didn't learn anything but that children wach 1,023 hours in a year. I knew every other thing. Oh and I dont wach the power puff girls.

Important to the Author
The Author wants people to wach more t.v. because they want more money.

Chapter 11

Summarizing and Synthesizing Information: The Evolution of Thought

Among Steph's fondest childhood memories are the summer afternoons spent in the great room of her grandparents' log house on a lake in northern Wisconsin. The musty smell of worn Oriental carpets, the shiny pretzel log walls, the Scott Joplin tunes on the player piano, and the continuous whir of the ceiling fan filled her senses as she whiled away those lazy days, in tandem with her grandmother, working jigsaw puzzles of every size and shape. A card table in the far corner of the room housed all the action. One week a Bavarian castle, the next a nineteenth-century painting of the Grand Canyon. As the years went by, a portrait of Captain Hook, a can of Coca-Cola, and a pepperoni pizza materialized on that card table. A battalion of two, grandmother and granddaughter attacked the puzzles together and were delighted as entire pictures slowly emerged from the hundreds of scattered cardboard pieces.

When we summarize information during reading, we pull out the most important information and put it in our own words to remember it. Each bit of information we encounter adds a piece to the construction of meaning. Our thinking evolves as we add information from the text. Synthesizing is a process akin to working a jigsaw puzzle. In the same way that we manipulate hundreds of puzzle pieces to form a new picture, students must arrange multiple fragments of information until they see a new pattern emerge (McKenzie 1996). Sometimes when we synthesize, we add to our store of knowledge and reinforce what we already know. Other times, we merge new information with existing knowledge to understand a new perspective, a new line of thinking, or even an original idea. Our thinking may evolve slowly over time, as Steph's jigsaw puzzles did, or we may have a flash of insight based on startling, new information.

How Background Knowledge Impacts Synthesizing

We begin by teaching our students to take stock of meaning while they read, summarizing the information to add to their store of knowledge. To do this we encourage readers to stop every so often and think about what they have read. Steph and Alverro, the incredulous giraffe reader who we met in the second chapter, agreed that Alverro would view the end of each page as a red light to stop and think about what he had read. In this way, he would construct meaning before powering through the text. There may not be an original thought in it, but stopping and actively thinking about the information helps readers stay on track with the text and monitor their understanding. Sometimes the goal of reading is to sift and pare down meaning to get the gist. Other times we pull the details together to draw conclusions, consider implications, or even take action.

Background knowledge makes a difference. Steph recently had an experience that led her to understand how much prior knowledge is a determining factor as we synthesize information. She read an article in *The Washington Post* called "More Questions than Answers" that focused on the effectiveness of polygraph testing (Eggen and Vedantam 2006). Although she had known that polygraphs were by no means perfect, she did believe that they were reasonably reliable and had even thought a person was likely guilty if they failed a polygraph test. The *Post* article reported a study that found if polygraphs were administered to 10,000 people, ten of whom were spies, 1600 innocent people would fail the test and two of the spies would pass. The article concluded that one of the main reasons law enforcement continues to use polygraphs is that so many perpetrators actually confess while undergoing a polygraph test. This was stunning new information for Steph which led her to change her thinking and come to an entirely new understanding of polygraph testing. She recounted the article and her astonishment to her friend Lydia at lunch. Lydia was terribly interested in the article, but not at all surprised by the information. Her husband was in law enforcement, and she had known the limitations of polygraph testing for years. As she read the article, her thinking did not change, but the article confirmed, reinforced, and enhanced what she already knew.

Both Steph and Lydia synthesized the information. Steph's lack of background about polygraph testing led her to a whole new perspective on the topic. Lydia added to her accurate and substantial knowledge base. If we know a lot about something and we read more about that topic, we add that information to our store of knowledge and come to understand the topic more completely. If we know little about a topic and then read further on that topic, our thinking is likely to evolve and change because of all the new information we have gained. And we may have a flash of insight as Steph did.

So how does this type of insight come about in reading? When readers synthesize, they use a variety of strategies to build and enhance understanding. They summarize the information, listen to their inner voice, and merge their thinking so that the information makes sense and is meaningful to them. They connect the new to the known, they ask questions, they pick out the most important information—all of these strategies intersect to allow us to synthesize information and actively use it.

Genre makes a difference too. In fiction, we might gain insight into the characters by observing their actions and piecing together their motives. In a mystery, we gather clues, ask questions, and draw inferences to solve it. Nonfiction text often conveys information that leads readers to a particular point of view. Readers' thinking may change as they ingest new information gleaned from the text. An article on rain forest deforestation might point a finger at governmental forestry policies. A synthesis could involve forming an opinion about the shortsightedness of the government in question. The new information combined with readers' thinking can lead to new insight.

The following strategy lessons support an evolving notion of synthesizing. We realize that "Summarizing and Synthesizing" is the last chapter in Part II. But in truth, we have been asking kids to summarize and synthesize throughout this book. We teach summarizing—getting the facts, ordering events, paraphrasing, and picking out what's important—as one aspect of synthesizing information. When kids are able to understand information on the page and can organize their thinking around it, they are more prepared to synthesize the information. So as we teach kids a repertoire of reading and thinking strategies, there is no reason to wait until the end of the year to bring up summarizing and synthesizing. In this chapter, we share lessons that we have found help our kids to do both. But we wager you'll find, as we did, that kids have been summarizing and synthesizing all along.

Strategy Lessons: Summarizing and Synthesizing Information

Retelling to Summarize Information

Purpose: Providing a basic framework to help students begin to summarize information through a brief retelling of a story

Resources: Assorted picture books, including *For Every Child a Better World*, by L. Gikow

Responses: Recording brief summaries on sticky notes or charts, or through discussion; one-word lists of a synthesis

When teacher Debbie Miller introduces summarizing to first graders, she provides them with a basic framework for thinking and talking about summarizing. She tells her students that when readers summarize, they

- Remember to tell what is important
- Tell it in a way that makes sense
- Try not to tell too much

Debbie models this with a variety of well-loved picture books. After she finishes reading a story, she shows students how she restates the story in her own words, following the above guidelines. Sometimes she records her thinking on a chart, sometimes on a sticky note. At other times she merely talks about her summary. But she always keeps it brief, salient, and to the point.

Young kids in particular have trouble with brevity when they attempt summarizing. We've all heard a retelling of *Star Wars* that lasted longer than the movie itself. But as Debbie models extensively, kids begin to get the hang of it.

Several weeks into the teaching of this strategy, Kent shared his summary of the book *For Every Child a Better World*. During sharing time, he took out a piece of paper and began to read: "Every child needs food, but sometimes there isn't any. Every child needs clean water, but sometimes they can't find it. Every child needs a home, but some don't have one." When he finished reading, Debbie commented on his good thinking and asked him about his writing. Kent explained that after he read, he thought about what was important and how it would make sense and then he made some notes to help him remember. His notes, translated from his temporary spelling, follow:

food
clean water
home
clean air
medicine
school

Kent went on to explain that when he finished reading, he went back through the book and thought about the most important information and then wrote only a word to help him remember. "Then when you tell somebody, you can just look at your paper and put in all the rest of the words that are in your head." Kent's note taking helped all of the kids in the class who tried to summarize information the next day. In fact, what Kent was really doing by merging his thinking with the information was moving towards a synthesis of the piece. He discerned what was important, and he kept his notes short enough to help him remember the information, a valuable skill for kids as they move on through school and life (Harvey et al. 1996).

Paraphrasing to Summarize Expository Text

Purpose: Making margin notes in your own words to summarize sections of the text
Resource: "In Sickness and in Health," an article in *Kids Discover Magazine*
Responses: Brackets in the margins for summarizing information; sticky notes coded S for summarize; two-column note form headed What's Interesting/What's Important

One of our absolute favorite magazines for students, *Kids Discover,* addresses a specific science or social studies topic each month. We couldn't keep the April 1999 issue, titled *Blood,* out of kids' hands. Along with articles on how to make fake blood and blood typing was a longer article, "In Sickness and in Health," which discussed the importance of blood in the battle to stay healthy. (Go to www.kidsdiscover.com to get a copy of this issue as well as other past issues of *Kids Discover* magazine.)

Gloria Mundel lifted a section of the article on blood and health to teach sixth graders to summarize information and then gave them some time to practice. She explained that she would read a paragraph or two and then write about the essence of the text in her own words. Gloria knew that if kids could use their own words to describe what they read and the words made sense, then they understood the text. She said that to summarize what she was reading, she would try to write the most important information and keep it brief.

She also told her students that there was no need to write full sentences, as long as what they wrote made sense. As she read out loud, Gloria explained the concept of bracketing to the

Figure 11.1 Bracketed Part of an Article and Brief Summaries

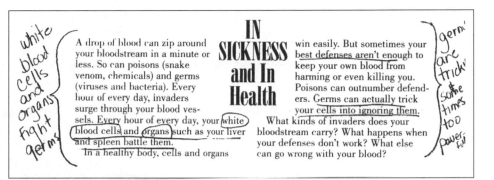

Figure 11.2 Ashley's Paraphrasing on Sticky Notes

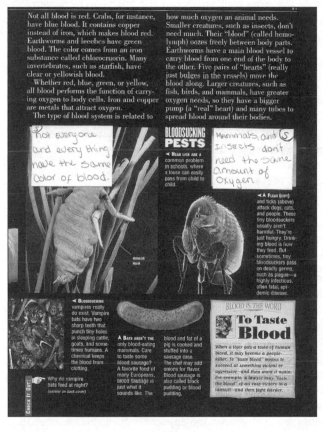

kids. On an overhead transparency, she bracketed off a section of the article and then wrote in her own words what that section meant (see Figure 11.1).

After Gloria showed her students her thinking, she encouraged them to do the same on the following page of the article. The kids attached sticky notes to summarize the sections. They coded the sticky notes S for summarize and then wrote down the gist of the passage in their own words.

Ashley's notes hit the nail on the head (see Figure 11.2). Ryan, on the other hand, coded the same text with two sticky notes, one that said, "People eat blood sausage" and another that said, "It's also called blood pudding." Ryan had picked out the most interesting rather than the most important information on the page. The trouble was that this response captured rich details rather than key ideas. To accurately summarize when reading, readers need to get at the essence of the text. When readers respond in their own words, teachers can quickly tell if they are getting the key ideas.

A two-column form that helps kids focus on the difference between what's important (the essence) and what's interesting (the rich details) is headed What's Interesting/What's Important (Harvey 1998). Sometimes they are one and the same, sometimes not. Gloria shared this response form with Ryan so that he would have a place to record the compelling details while also recording the important information and capturing the essence of the piece as he read.

Synthesizing: How Reading Changes Thinking

New

Purpose: To notice how our thinking evolves and changes as we read
Resource: "Freedom Readers," an article by Fran Downey in *National Geographic Explorer*
Response: Keeping track of changed thinking in reading logs

To make synthesizing understandable for our kids, we talk with them about how reading changes and adds to thinking. The main purpose of reading is to add to our knowledge base, think about new information, and integrate it. Sometimes the new information reinforces and gives us a more thorough understanding of what we already know. Other times, new information changes us in certain ways—gives us a different perspective, a new angle on our thinking, or some further insight. Whichever the case, we are synthesizing the information as we go. We need to ask kids every day to think about how their reading and learning is adding to and/or revising their thinking.

One of the simplest yet most important considerations we can suggest to our kids is simply to notice their thinking before and after they have read or heard something. Mary Buerger found an article in *National Geographic Explorer* titled "Freedom Readers," which reported that, by law, slaves were not allowed to read, discussed the reasons why, and provided portraits of slaves who learned to read despite this law. This article led with the question, "What does reading mean to you?" So before thinking through the article together, Mary asked her fourth graders to consider this question and jot down a response in their notebooks. The kids wrote down some terrific responses regarding what reading meant to them including:

- Reading teaches you new information
- Reading lets you picture stuff in your minds
- The movie gets going and you can't stop
- Reading is a pastime that cures boredom
- You play someone else's voice in your mind
- Reading takes you on an adventure
- Excitement—Reading puts you on the edge of your seat
- Reading takes you places you have never been
- The truth is there are a lot of things I'd rather do than read, but then I get interested and I can't stop

After the class shared their responses, Mary read and thought through the article with the class. As she read about the struggle certain slaves endured just to learn to read, the kids' thinking began to evolve. Before reading the article, no one had mentioned that reading was power or that reading meant freedom. Their own personal experience hadn't prepared them to think in this way. But as Mary read and guided a turn-and-talk discussion about the article, the powerful role that reading played in the lives of slaves began to impact the kids' thinking about the role of reading in everyday life. By the time they finished, they had a new take on reading and a new insight on the power of reading to inspire freedom and independence in a democratic society.

When she finished the interactive read-aloud, Mary simply asked the kids to open their notebooks again, draw a line under their first answer, and answer the question Now what does reading mean to you? Most of their answers reflected some additions to or changes in thinking after having read about the topic. We ask kids to reflect on how their thinking changes after they have read something. Additionally, we try to remember to ask them to consider this before and after a unit of study. What does immigration mean to you? Then after they investigate the topic of immigration we ask, Now what does immigration mean to you? This gives us information about what students have learned and how their thinking has changed, but even more importantly, it gives our kids a clear understanding of the power of learning to influence and change thinking. Nothing gives us a better idea of how our kids' thinking changes as they learn. Lessons such as this one encourage them to regularly reflect on how new information impacts thinking. (See the assessment section of this chapter for examples of kids' work related to this lesson.)

Comparing and Contrasting in Science and Social Studies

Purpose: Comparing and contrasting properties to better understand their essence
Resources: Science trade books or science textbooks on marine biology
Response: Three-column note form headed Compare and Contrast

Seventh-grade science teacher Margaret Bobb has developed an interesting form that supports synthesizing in the content areas. She uses a three-column Compare and Contrast note form. The first and third columns are headed with the content to be compared, in this case Kelp in the first column and Coral in the third column as Margaret explores marine biology with her students. The middle column is headed Alike. As Margaret and her students read, they record the properties of kelp in the first column and the properties of coral in the third. When they encounter similarities between the two, they record that information in the middle column. The middle column is a synthesis of the similarities between coral and kelp. Margaret explains to the kids that this three-column form is similar to a Venn diagram, since they both report similarities in the middle.

Teachers have used this form with social studies as well. For example, in a Revolutionary War study, the first column could be labeled The British and the third column could be headed The Colonists. The middle column would once again be reserved for the similarities between the two. Middle school content area teachers have found this form to be invaluable when trying to help their students make sense of two different properties or concepts.

Summarizing the Content and Adding Personal Response

Purpose: Summarizing the content of a piece of text and responding personally
Resources: Young adult magazines, including *Kids Discover, National Geographic Explorer,* and *Time for Kids*
Response: A page of notebook paper divided horizontally with the top half marked Summary and the bottom half marked Response

Fourth-grade teacher Mary Buerger models summarizing and responding in her own Wonder Book. First, she divides a notebook page in half horizontally and labels the top half Summary and the bottom half Response. She summarizes a piece of text in the summary portion and then gives her personal response below. When she demonstrates summarizing, she tries to pick out the most important ideas in the text and keep the writing to a minimum. Brevity is a virtue when summarizing, and Mary wants her fourth graders to learn this. She explains to them, however, that synthesizing is about more than summarizing. It's also about integrating thinking with the content and getting the reader's personal take on a piece of text. In the response portion, she mentions her use of comprehension strategies and the process by which she constructs meaning along with her personal reflections on the text itself.

Jonathan picked up on this in the most delightful way. He describes the content of an article on muskies in his summary and then explains how he visulizes with a "picture in your mind" in the response portion (see Figure 11.3). Jonathan's response shows how he summarizes the content, responds personally to reading, and reflects on his process as a reader. The kids in Mary's room use this form to acquire content as well as to respond to their own reading process. It is also a scaffold for a later kind of writing that we have come to call a Summary Response, which merges the summary with the response into one complete piece. If kids have used this form first,

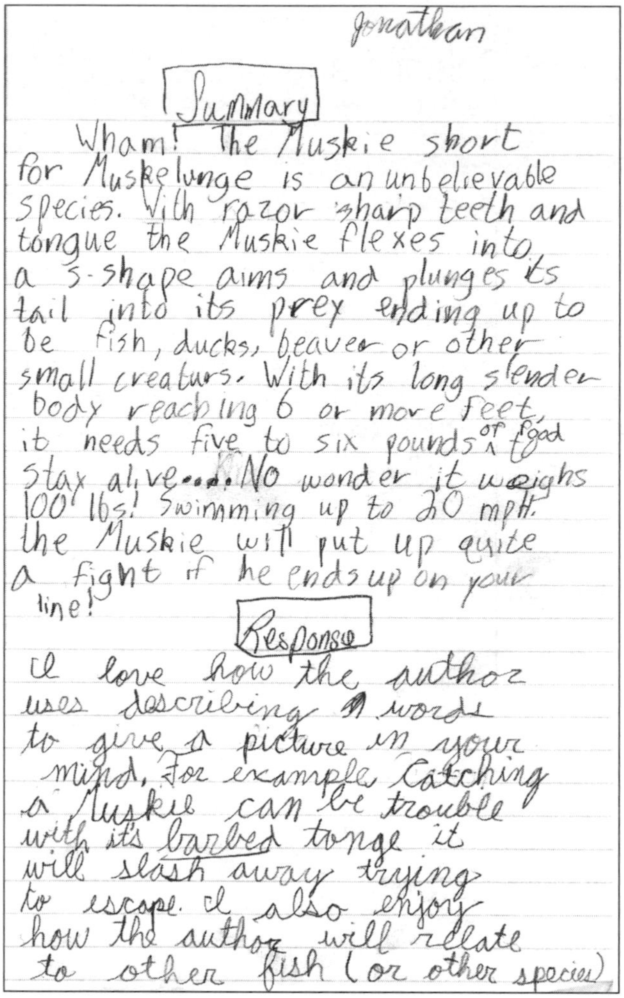

Jonathan

Summary

Wham! The Muskie short for Muskelunge is an unbelievable species. With razor sharp teeth and tongue the Muskie flexes into a s-shape aims and plunges its tail into its prey ending up to be fish, ducks, beaver or other small creatures. With its long slender body reaching 6 or more feet, it needs five to six pounds of food stay alive... No wonder it weighs 100 lbs! Swimming up to 20 mph. the Muskie will put up quite a fight if he ends up on your line!

Response

I love how the author uses describing words to give a picture in your mind. For example Catching a Muskie can be trouble with its barbed tonge it will slash away trying to escape. I also enjoy how the author will relate to other fish (or other species)

Figure 11.3 Jonathan's Summary/Response of Muckies Article

they can more easily adapt to combining these components into one integrated Summary Response.

Summary Responses

After kids had a good deal of time to practice using the Summary/Response form, Mary moved on and taught them how to combine the two elements. A Summary Response includes a summary of the most important content, along with the writer's personal response throughout the piece rather than simply as an addendum to the summary. To teach Summary Response writing, Mary modeled her own on the overhead projector. She chose an article from *National Geographic for Kids* on humpback whales titled "Humpbacks Make a Comeback" (2001). After she read the article and kids had time to talk about it, Mary explained that she was going to try to incorporate her thinking directly into the summary, rather than separate the content (summary) and her thinking (response). As she modeled, she occasionally stopped and pointed out where she did this, so the children would get an idea of how this new Summary Response looked and how it differed from the scaffold they had been using. Her completed Summary Response contained both important content from the reading as well as her own thinking.

Humpback whales are making a comeback. Thirty years ago, humpback whales were in such short supply that they were on the brink of extinction. It's hard to believe but their numbers had dwindled from years of relentless hunting down to about 1,000 individuals. In recent years, however, laws have been passed that ban hunting humpback whales. And now there are nearly 30,000 humpback whales roaming our oceans. That is 30 times more than in 1965. This is really good news for whale lovers around the world, including me!

Humpback whales are amazing animals. One interesting behavior they exhibit is called breaching. When humpback whales breach, they catapult their enormous bodies out of the water. Scientists are not exactly sure why they breach, but they suspect it could be to frighten predators or even perhaps to communicate, very different reasons for sure. Full-grown humpbacks weigh nearly forty tons. Now that is heavy!! I wonder how long it takes them to grow to full size? More good news is that with their increasing numbers, it should be easier for scientists to study them and solve their many mysteries, such as why they breach. I look forward to reading and learning more about these remarkable creatures as scientists continue to learn more and more about them.

When she finished, she had her kids turn and talk about spots where she summarized the content and places where she added her own thinking. She reminded her kids that Summary Responses are higher-level thinking than "just plain" summaries, because the reader's thinking is integrated with the information. But she also let them know that in most standardized writing tests, the people who score the tests are interested only in standard summaries not in the reader's personal responses. So she reminded her kids that they would get a chance to practice standard summaries when they practiced the genre of test writing. (For more of this lesson see Mary and her class on Program 3, *Reading and Understanding Nonfiction*, in our video series *Strategy Instruction in Action* [2001].) For examples of Summary Responses, see the assessment section of this chapter.

Reading for the Gist

Purpose: Taking notes and using a variety of strategies to synthesize
Resource: The picture book *An Angel for Solomon Singer*, by Cynthia Rylant
Responses: Lists of notes and strategies; one-page written responses

Near the end of a two-year loop through fourth and fifth grade, the kids in Glenda Clearwater's class had become increasingly adept at reading strategically, having practiced strategies over the course of two years. They understood that reading was about constructing meaning, and they read for that purpose. Glenda knew that writing while reading can show the reader's evolution of thought. Although her students had been coding the text and writing in margins while they read independently, they hadn't done much note taking while she read aloud. This was more of a challenge.

Glenda decided to up the ante and have them take notes as she read. She chose to read them Cynthia Rylant's picture book *An Angel for Solomon Singer*, the story of a sad, lonely old man who lives in a New York boarding house and laments his station in life. Things change when he wanders into a twenty-four-hour café and sees a friendly waiter with a smiling face.

Glenda began by having her students list the comprehension strategies they'd studied, and reiterated that these strategies could help them make sense of the text. She asked them to write down their thinking as well as story events as they took notes. She believed that notes of their questions, predictions, important ideas, and visual images would be of more use to them than mere content notes as they tried to synthesize the material. She knew that this book was difficult to understand and required questioning, visualizing, and inferential thinking to gain meaning.

As Glenda read *Solomon Singer* out loud, she stopped and took notes in her own journal periodically and then shared her writing with the kids. Some of the students wrote practically nonstop throughout the read-aloud. Others needed a few moments to collect their thoughts and record their thinking. So Glenda paused intermittently to allow them to jot down some notes and complete their thoughts. When they finished, their notes revealed that they had visualized, asked questions, made connections, inferred, and synthesized while Glenda read.

Jessica's notes, which follow here, include examples of her flexible use of multiple strategies, a requirement when readers synthesize:

He doesn't like where he lives.
I think all of his wishes will come true.
His life isn't that great.
The café has made him happy.
He is poor.
I think the waiter is an angel.
He is lonely/I've been lonely before.
He wants to go back home.
He likes to dream.
He really likes to go to the Westway Café.
He's starting to like New York better now.

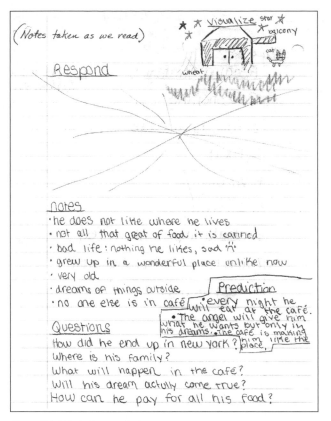

Figure 11.4 Claire's Response to *An Angel for Solomon Singer*

The Westway Café brightened up his life and made him feel like New York was his home.

Why is he in New York City if he loves Indiana so much?

How come he is so poor?

When Jessica wrote that she thought the waiter was an angel, she was inferring. When she mentioned that she'd been lonely before, she was making a connection. When she commented that the Westway Café made New York feel like home, she was synthesizing.

Claire drew a barn on her notes, which showed she was visualizing. She labeled the barn, and wrote notes, predictions, and questions (see Figure 11.4).

When Glenda's students finished their note taking, they wrote responses in their journals based on their notes, their memories of the story, and their thinking. These notes and responses show how thinking evolves as kids read. As they derive more information from the text, they begin to synthesize it into the bigger picture. Claire's response follows:

> I think Mr. Singer has a horrible place to live. He hates everything in New York until he wanders into the Westway Café, "where dreams come true." This is a wonderful book about feelings, dreams, and angels. When our teacher was reading, it made me visualize. I had a picture of a perfect home for Solomon, in Illinois where I used to live. It had a balcony, bouncy grass, everlasting fields of corn and wheat. At night, he could lie down and stare at the stars in the sky. He would have three cats, two dogs, five fish, ten hamsters, etc. They would be free to run all over and Mr. Singer wouldn't be lonely. The sun would shine all day long. But New York isn't that bad, now that he found the Westway Café, especially when the angel watches over him.

In her response, Claire shows how she activates multiple strategies to understand the story. Ultimately, she reads for the gist of the story, how the Westway Café changes Solomon Singer's life. When readers synthesize, they get the gist.

Writing a Short Summary

Purpose: Distinguishing between a summary of the text and the reader's thinking

Resource: *The Librarian of Basra: A True Story from Iraq*, by Jeanette Winter

Response: Two-column think sheet headed What the Piece Is About/What It Makes Me Think About

For this lesson, Steph chose to read *The Librarian of Basra* and use one of her favorite think sheets, a two-column form titled What the Piece Is About/What It Makes Me Think About. With the kids gathered in front of her, Steph read the book aloud. After she finished reading, she handed out the think sheet folded on the center line so that only the right column titled What It Makes Me Think About was showing and asked kids to write what the story made them think about. (See Chapter 6, "Monitoring Comprehension.") She reminded them that nothing is more important than the reader's thinking. She always emphasizes this by having her students record their thoughts first and then do the task at hand. While the kids wrote their thoughts, she wrote hers on the same think sheet.

After kids finished writing down their thinking, they read what they wrote to a partner. After sharing with a partner, Steph invited them to share their thinking with the class, and she shared her own. The right side of Steph's think sheet follows:

> This story reminds me that one person can truly make a difference. Alia, elderly and relatively powerless, risked her life to preserve the history and culture of Iraq by saving the books from the ravages of a war. It makes me think about Oscar Schindler, who saved so many Jews from the Nazis. What is it that makes some people risk their lives for others or for a cause? Passion maybe? I wonder for what I would risk my life other than my family.

Steph then asked the kids to unfold their two-column form and focus on the first column, What the Piece Is About. She explained that this is the summary part, not so much the reader's thinking about it. After they had a chance to turn and talk about what the story was about, she asked them to consider three things when trying to write a summary, things very similar to the ones Debbie Miller, in an earlier lesson, asked kids to consider when retelling orally.

1. Pick out the most important ideas
2. Keep it brief
3. Say it in your own words in a way that makes sense

Steph than asked the kids to turn and talk about what they thought were some of the most important ideas in the story and then share them with the class. As they shared, she recorded their ideas on a chart.

Important Ideas
Librarian saved the books
She was passionate
She loved books
War
Teamwork—her friends helped
Loyalty
Risked her life
30,000 books
Iraq

After completing the chart, they talked about each one and decided whether it was important enough to include in the summary with an eye toward keeping it brief. They agreed that most of the ideas were important but some details could be combined into one idea, such as the fact that she was passionate and loved books, or that they really didn't have to include the specific number 30,000 but needed to include that she saved most of the books in the library. Finally, together they wrote the following in the first column of the think sheet.

> At the beginning of the war in Iraq, a brave, passionate librarian risked her life to save many books with the help of loyal friends.

Strategies That Work

Figure 11.5 A Student's Think Sheet
Distinguishing Between a Summary and
a Personal Response

What the piece is about...	What it makes me think about...
An amazing libarian who loved books saved alot of them so they wouldn't be destroyed by the War in Iraq.	Would I risk my life for some books proably not IS she going to build a new library? She has alot of guts to stay there with her books. I would proably be on my way to Egypt or Turkey. Why would she go out in a middk of a war to ask someone to help her move her books? I would feel like crying IF I didn't not leave I would be in my house trying to calm my self down and saying it's okay not worried about some books. How did she feel after the war? She should definatly be honored and she should have her name like mohmad

Figure 11.5 A Student's Think Sheet Distinguishing Between a Summary and a Personal Response

Summaries don't have to be only one sentence. Two or three work. At the conclusion of the lesson, Steph thanked them and reminded them that although it is important to be able to summarize the story as they did, the most important thinking is always the reader's thinking!

A thoughtful example of a completed think sheet is shown in Figure 11.5.

Writing as Synthesis: Personalities from the Past

Purpose: Writing from a first-person perspective to better understand the contributions of historical figures
Resources: Picture book biographies
Responses: Note-taking forms that support writing

When we're studying famous people, we try to gain insight into their lives. It makes sense to ask, What's important to remember about them? What lessons can we learn from their lives? Teacher Barbara Munizza wanted to take a thoughtful approach to the study of biography,

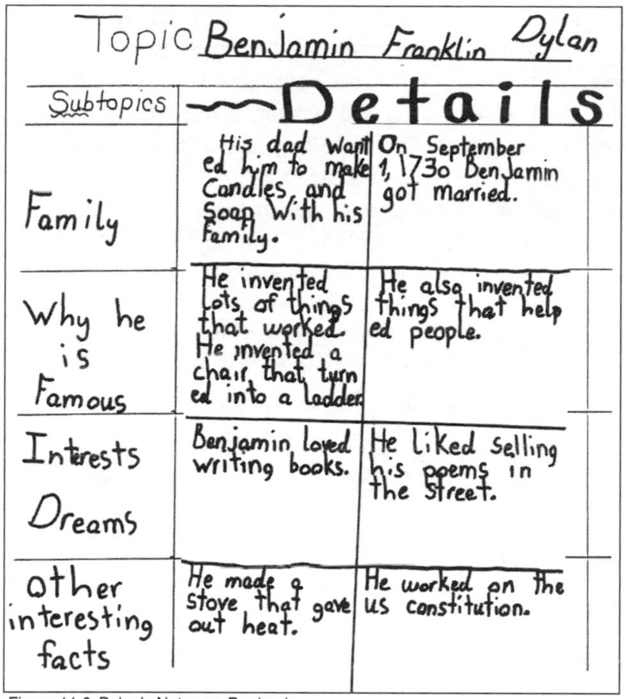

Figure 11.6 Dylan's Notes on Benjamin Franklin

so she asked her students to read and think about famous people who had made a difference in the world or who had overcome adversity or obstacles in their lives.

Barbara's goal was for each child to read about and research a person of their own choosing, using their responses and notes to eventually write a thoughtful "first-person" sketch. Knowing that she would need to support her students as they explored a new genre, took notes, and developed their written pieces, Barbara planned out a series of lessons. These included modeling thoughtful responses to reading, taking notes on important ideas rather than trivial details, and organizing notes to support writing. Making sure that children's voices weren't lost in the midst of all this information was important, and a tall order for these third graders.

Barbara chose Joseph Bruchac's *A Boy Called Slow*, the story of Sitting Bull's transition from childhood to adulthood. As she modeled her own reading, thinking, and responding with the book, it dawned on her that she was teaching her students about synthesis. As the class read Sitting Bull's story of learning to be brave, Barbara pointed out that thinking can change during reading. After completing their own responses, the children discussed how their thinking about the "boy called Slow" had changed over the course of the story. Dylan's response illustrates that although he originally was incredulous that Slow had the courage to scare his tribe's enemies away, by the end of the story he realized that Slow deserved his new name. He states, "I can't believe that Slow scared the Crow warriors away. I think Slow was very brave. If I were there, I would give him a big reward and I would give him a new name."

When the children began to read their biographies independently, they responded to important events and details, often with honesty, amazement, or outrage. Kevin's response to David Adler's *A Picture Book of Anne Frank* noted his personal reactions to important events in Anne Frank's life. He recorded them on the following two-column form:

Facts from the Text	Response
Six million Jews were murdered.	I wish there were no Nazis because it's not fair that others couldn't have food and homes.
They were cold and suffering.	I wonder how it felt to hide and to be tortured by the Nazis.
Margot died.	I felt bad for them when she died because I wouldn't like to be killed or get sick and die.
Anne hid for more than two years.	I can't believe that she hid for more than two years because some of them got caught right away.
Anne died.	I wouldn't want to be Anne Frank because she died in a death camp and hid for most of her life.

Dylan's note-taking sheet on Ben Franklin illustrates the next step in this process. The Details form (see Figure 11.6) illustrates how the children sorted their notes, ensuring that categories such as "Why He Is Famous" and "Interests and Dreams" are covered.

Donald Graves has said that "writing is the ultimate act of synthesis." Dylan collected a lot of fascinating information that captured his imagination, including the surprising fact that Ben Franklin liked to sell his poems in the street. His genuine interest in and engagement with Ben Franklin, as well as his thoughtful and clearly organized notes, helped him internalize the information over time. This excerpt from Dylan's "first-person" biography illustrates how Dylan synthesized interesting details about Ben Franklin's life, making it possible for him to write convincingly from Ben's point of view:

In the 1700s your father could pick what you learned in school and what your job was. When I was little, my dad told me to be a preacher. Later, he told me that they are poor. At school I learned to write well, but I failed arithmetic. Two years later, my dad told me you will work for me and your family making soap and candles. It was hard smelly work, but I did it for two years. Then one day I said, "I want to go to sea." But my father said "No, your brother drowned at sea. You will stay in Boston!"

When I was seventeen, I decided to run away. I ran away to Philadelphia, Pennsylvania. There I worked for a printer. Then I started my own print shop. Later I owned a newspaper and a store. I was a busy man. But I wanted to do more, so I started a library and a fire department. I did experiments and wrote about science and I sold my poems in the streets. Later, I invented a chair that turned into a ladder and a stove that gave heat away. I called it the Franklin stove. Everyone wanted one! Then I wrote a book about farming and weather and holidays. For twenty-five years, each year I would write a new one.

Synthesizing to Access Content

Purpose: Noticing the thinking we do to access content and acquire knowledge
Resource: "Moonstruck Scientists Count 63 and Rising" (Boyd 1999), an article in the *Denver Post*
Responses: Two-column note form headed Content/Process; class discussion

Content-area reading demands that readers pick up factual information as they read. One of the things we hope for our students is that the reading strategies described in this book will help in their quest for information. We want our students to become aware of their thinking process as well so that they can call up a strategy to access content, particularly in difficult, more challenging text.

In Kim Worsham's fifth grade class, Steph and Kim decided to test a form they thought might help students articulate their thinking as they read for information. The form was simple enough—two columns, with the first column headed Content (Facts) and the second column headed Process (Thinking). They added the terms *facts* and *thinking* in parentheses to provide more explicit language.

Knowing that this might not be the mini-lesson to end all others, from the kids' perspective at least, Steph chose the most compelling piece of expository text she could find. A rule of thumb we have tried to adhere to for many years is that the more boring the task, the more compelling the text must be. So Steph was delighted when she happened upon the article "Moonstruck Scientists Count 63 and Rising" (Boyd 1999), the majority of which is reprinted here from the *Denver Post* (as written before Pluto's demotion as a planet):

Moonstruck Scientists Count 63 and Rising

Here's a trivia question sure to stump your friends: How many moons are there in our solar system?

It's a rare person who knows the answer—63 moons and climbing.

Just last year, two more satellites were discovered circling counterclockwise around Uranus, the seventh planet from the sun.

"It's almost inconceivable there aren't more moons out there," said Brett Gladman, an astronomer at Cornell University in Ithaca, NY, who detected the new Uranian moons in October 1997. "Almost every time there is an advance in detector efficiency, we find more satellites."

The search for new moons—as well as planets, comets, asteroids, rocks, and dust littering the starry skies—is part of humankind's age-old quest to understand the universe we live in. By studying them, scientists have learned much about how the solar system, including our own Earth, formed and what its fate may be.

Moons Everywhere

Besides, as poets, lovers, and mystics know, moons are cool.

Earth and Pluto are the only members of our sun's family to have just one moon each. Mercury and Venus have none. But Mars has two, Jupiter 16, Saturn 18, Uranus 17, and Neptune eight.

Even a little asteroid, Ida, floating between Mars and Jupiter, has its own pet moonlet, named Dactyl, only 1 mile wide.

The giant planets—Jupiter, Saturn, and Neptune—have so many moons that they resemble miniature solar systems. Astronomers have assigned them romantic names culled from Greek mythology and the plays of Shakespeare: Atlas, Pandora, Ophelia, Ariel, Juliet, and the like.

This burgeoning horde of satellites indicates that moons may be common around other planets in the universe, offering more potential habitats for life.

The moons in our solar system come in a rich variety of sizes, temperatures, atmospheres, and behaviors.

Mighty Jupiter boasts the biggest and the smallest satellites detected so far. Little Leda is only 6 miles across, while Ganymede, 3,266 miles in diameter, is half again as big as Earth's moon, which measures 2,155 miles. Saturn's Titan, 3,193 miles wide, is the next biggest. Ganymede and Titan are actually bigger than two planets, Mercury and Pluto. . . .

Unlike our own dead moon, some satellites lead active lives.

Io, a moon of Jupiter, is so volcanic that it "glows in the dark," said Paul Geissler, an astronomer at the University of Arizona in Tucson. A NASA photo caught one volcano in mid-eruption, shooting a plume of hot gas hundreds of miles into space.

"Io glows green, blue, and red," said Geissler. "It looks like a Christmas tree, colorful and mysterious."

Moons also perform useful tasks, such as helping to preserve the shiny rings, composed of small rocks, dust, or ice, that surround some planets. A ring around Uranus is shepherded by two moons, one on either side. Four of Jupiter's moons cling to the edge of that planet's faint rings. Saturn's gorgeous rings also may have shepherded moons, but they have not been detected yet.

Our own moon probably deflected a number of asteroids that might have smashed into Earth, causing enormous damage. The huge craters on the moon bear witness to its service as a shield for our planet. ■

As Steph lifted the text for overhead display, the kids followed along with the Content/Process form on their clipboards. They began by reviewing some of the thinking readers do when they read. The class had spent time on several strategies, including questioning, connecting, and inferring. This form required readers to keep track of their evolving thinking, commenting on their process of synthesizing information by noting information on the content side of the form and noticing what they did to access that information on the process side of the form.

When Steph read the title of the article, James immediately asked, "What does *moonstruck* mean?" Steph recorded his question in the Process column, coding it Q for question, and then tossed it out to the crowd. The kids looked puzzled. Steph asked them to stop and turn to another student and try to construct meaning together. After a few moments, Ryan and Jessica raised

Figure 11.7 Allison's Content/Process Notes on "Moonstruck Scientists"

Content (Facts) *Allison*	Process (Thinking)
• There are 63 moons and will be more.	• What does moonstruck mean? (question)
• They discovered 2 new moons circling counterclockwise.	• Maybe 'its' scientists who like moons. (inference)
• Uranus is the 7th from sun.	• What did they mean 63 and rising? (question)
• Each time they get a new more advanced better piece of equipment they find more moons because they can see more.	• Why didn't they know if they launched those satellites? (q)
• Detector efficiency means we can pick up better images + see them more clearly.	• Maybe satellite are moons. (I)
	• It could be a natural satellite. (I)
	• An astronomer looks through giant telescopes. (I)
• They are searching for other things besides moons.	• What do they mean by its fate? (q)
• Earth + Pluto-1, Mercury + Venus-0, Mars-2, Jupiter-16, Saturn-18, Uranus-17, Neptune-8.	• Maybe it means future or destiny. (I)
	• What is a pet moonlet? (q)
	• What does "burgeoning horde" mean? (q)
• Genymede is 3,266 miles in diameter.	• Maybe 'it' means a group or a bunch. (I) (context clues)
	• What do they mean by "chemical reactions on Titan like those that preceded the formation of living molecules on Earth?" (q)
	• Does that mean that life could form on it? (q)

their hands and said, "Maybe it's scientists who like moons a lot." Steph acknowledged their good thinking, coded their inference I, and wrote it down on the transparency in the Process column as the kids recorded it on their forms. She read the first few sentences and paused after, "It's a rare person who knows the answer—63 moons and climbing."

She asked if anyone noticed any factual information here. "There are sixty-three moons in our solar system," Julie called out. Astonishing information, to say the least. Steph quickly showed her amazement. She wanted to fire the kids up about the content so that they would stay engaged in the task. She wrote the information down on the Content column as the kids followed her lead. Soon the form looked as follows:

Content (Facts)	Process (Thinking)
There are 63 moons and more to come.	What does moonstruck mean? (Q)
	Maybe it's scientists who like moons. (I)
	Wow! 63 moons! No kidding!
Uranus is seventh from the sun.	Why didn't they know if they launched those satellites? (Q)
	Maybe when they say satellites, they mean moons. (I)
	A moon could be a natural satellite. (I)
	What is detector efficiency? (Q)

As we reasoned through the text, the kids' conversation helped them build answers to questions, clear up misconceptions, and immerse themselves in the content. Misconceptions arose, such as confusion surrounding the term *satellite*. The kids' background knowledge for that term had more to do with telecommunications. Most had no idea that the term could be used interchangeably with the word *moon*. They talked it through and came to understand. Not surprisingly, the notion of detector efficiency was difficult, but as they thought it through, they made sense of it from the context. After about twenty minutes of discussion, Steph and Kim released the kids to work in groups of two or three around the room. The kids loved working through this article. It completely captivated them.

Allison's form is typical of many of the responses (see Figure 11.7). Reading and understanding requires a great deal of ongoing thinking. This form gave us a window into that evolution of thought.

Reading Like a Writer

Purpose: Noticing the craft of a piece as well as the content and the reading process
Resources: "Moonstruck Scientists Count 63 and Rising"(Boyd 1999) and "Rhino Dehorned by Rangers" (Edlin 1992), articles in the *Denver Post*
Response: Three-column note form headed Content/Process/Craft (CPC)

When Steph told fourth-grade teacher Mary Buerger about the Content/Process form and about the "Moonstruck" article. Mary wanted to try it as soon as she heard about it. As Mary read the lead at the overhead, Ryan blurted out, "The writer just hooks you when he says 'Here's a trivia question sure to stump your friends. How many moons are there in our solar system?' What a great way to start the article!" The kids nodded in agreement as Mary commented that Ryan was "reading like a writer," noticing the words and the structure of the language in the piece as well as the content. Mary proceeded to model the Content/Process form, but as the kids continued to comment on the writing quality, Mary wondered how she and Steph might improve upon the two-column form, which was concerned solely with reading. Upon reflection, Steph and Mary decided that maybe they needed a third column that would allow responses to the writing style as well.

The next day Mary presented a new form, the first two columns as before but with a third column headed Craft (Writing). She explained that kids could comment on the writing quality in this third column. She modeled it first, noting her observations about the writing as well as about content and process. They thought through several paragraphs together and then Mary released them in pairs to practice. Mary and Steph were astounded by their attention to the third column. The kids were immediately drawn to the engaging writing style, and they commented on it at length, as Kaitlin's three-column CPC form shows (see Figure 11.8).

Mary continued to let kids practice with this form. The CPC form required them to read as writers. Later, as they read a *Denver Post* article independently about the devastating problem of rhino poaching in Zimbabwe (Edlin 1992), their comments in the Craft column included the following:

I like how the writer used the word *slaughtered* instead of *killed*; it's stronger.
The beginning paragraph pulls you in when it says "In a desperate attempt to save the rhino."
I like how he put the numbers of all the rhinos in the world and then used the word *dwindling* instead of something boring.

Name Kaitlin

Content (Facts)	Process (Thinking)	Craft (Writing)
• 63 moons and climbing - (Prediction confirmed !)	• Moonstruck means obsessed (inferring)	• WoW! when it said littering the starry skys. They were very strong words that painted a picture in my mind.
• Two new moons are circleing Uranus	• 63 means number of moons maybe there are more. (inferring)	• When the lead asks a question it pulls you into the article.
• Uranus is the seventh planet from the sun.	• Just a question to clarify. Are satalites and moons the same thing?	• We can try to do the same thing.
• Every time they get a better teloscope they find more moons.	• Why diddn't they tell us about the moons they discovered in 1997?	• Fate may be. Moons and fate
• Scientists study the moons to find out more about the solar system and our earth.	• I think I know that other people had to confirm it.	• Fate makes me want to read on
• Earth and Pluto are the only members of our suns family to have just one moon.	• What does advanced in declor efficiancy mean?	• Give you the purpouse.
• Mercury and Venus are the only planets with no moons.	• It's kind of like a radar detector. Connection.	• Moons are cool! The writer says this to get your attention. It does too!
	• Wow! every time it gets better there will be more! (Inferring)	• Members of our suns family! The writer says this to get your attention.
	• What is an age old quest?	• "Pet moonlet" the writer uses an unusual word to surprise you.

Figure 11.8 Kaitlin's Content/Process/ Craft Notes on "Moonstruck Scientists"

The author jumps right into what is happening.
It is creative when the writer says "under cover of darkness."
The words really grab you, like *dugout canoe* instead of just plain *canoe*.

    Mary's kids read and wrote every day and studied writing, which is why they noticed the writer's words. They were writers themselves. This form gave them an opportunity to reflect on the writing, which could only help them as they continued with their own nonfiction writing. In subsequent work with this form, we have found that most kids need extensive practice with the two-column Content/Process form before exploring a third column for Craft. But after practicing the Content/Process form with three or four articles, we launch and begin to explore the Craft column, or the kids lead us there, as Ryan did.

    The three-column CPC form is the ultimate synthesizing response form. The three columns cover the major bases. If readers can record factual content, explain their thinking process while reading, and reflect on writing, they are well on their way to becoming truly literate thinkers.

Trying to Understand: Seeking Answers to Questions That Have None

Purpose: Synthesizing information by attempting to answer difficult questions
Resource: *The Triumphant Spirit: Portraits and Stories of Holocaust Survivors, Their Messages of Hope and Compassion,* by Nick Del Calzo
Responses: Sticky notes with questions

The genre of narrative nonfiction personalizes the human experience for readers in ways other genres simply can't. Personal tales of triumph and tragedy become indelibly etched in our brains when we read it. Sometimes these experiences are horrific and unthinkable. The Holocaust, above all else, reflects the worst, most grotesque aspects of human nature. Teachers understandably shy away from topics that are almost beyond comprehension. We feel ill-equipped to deal with such horrendous information, and we are at a loss to explain reasons for this behavior when children ask how such a thing could happen. Anne and Steph believe, however, that children deserve to know about what has really happened in the past. Furthermore, there are clear connections between historical events such as the Holocaust and situations of intolerance and genocide in many parts of the world today. In some ways, not to deal with these tragic events is to prevent children from learning about the strength of the human spirit and the triumph of survival.

Seventh-grade teacher Carla Mosher understands that it is easier not to think about unthinkable acts. And she knows that if we don't think about them, we will forget them. Carla wants her students to leave her class with an understanding of, and a personal commitment to, the warning "Never Again." To do this, she and her students build background knowledge about these times by reading a wide range of literature, including novels, picture books, poetry, editorials, essays, and feature articles. Their inquiry culminates with each student entering a local writing contest named in honor of Anne Frank. Carla's commitment to the vow of "Never Again," along with a message of compassion and hope, is central to their exploration.

Carla subscribes to the *Denver Post*'s Newspaper in Education Multicultural Program. As a subscriber, she receives occasional special student supplements published by the *Post.* One such supplement included multiple copies of a student edition of *The Triumphant Spirit: Portraits and Stories of Holocaust Survivors, Their Messages of Hope and Compassion.* This excerpt is from a book by the same name written by Nick Del Calzo. The *Denver Post* excerpt includes fourteen inspirational portraits of Holocaust survivors. To preserve this treasure, Carla cut up each copy and laminated every page. In that way, there were more than enough to go around.

Carla asked her students to think about the title as they read these portraits. She recognized that the text would be shocking and disturbing, and she wanted her students to keep the notion of the triumphant spirit of survival in mind. She gave them sticky notes and encouraged them to record their thinking as they read, reminding them to use the strategies they had practiced to help comprehend text.

Carla was not surprised that most of her students were recording questions as they read. Marcus was reading the story of Harry Glazer, who at age 22 arrived at Auschwitz from his native Romania. His tragic story tells the horrors of becoming separated from his family and never seeing them again, of being forced to drag dead bodies to mass graves at Auschwitz and Bergen-Belsen, and of triumphant survival and eventual liberation by the British in 1945. A photograph taken by the British liberators accompanies the written portrait and shows Mr. Glaser holding a newspaper photograph of mass graves and dead bodies.

MARCUS

I wonder how he survived the Holocaust It's Amazing how he survived that camp It would be hard to tell the story. I would cry to see people die.

I wonder how Harry Glaser can go three days without food or water. I know in 3 hours I'm hungry right away and I'm a little guy.

I wonder how Harry Glaser would feel Not ever to see your family. I would cry every single Night I can't imagine how he would feel just thinking about it. It's Sad

I wonder how hard that gas chamber would affect His Life. I bet he has alot of nightmares about the Holocaust And his parents dieing.

I wonder how Harry Glaser would feel about Collecting dead bodies and seing them dead. I'd throw up And then he was ordeard to do that, they would have to shoot me I would not Do it

I wonder how you Can shoot Some one with a machine gun and Killed 25,000 Prisoners I cant Imagine Seeing bodies Scatterd all over the place.

Figure 11.9 Marcus's Questions About *The Triumphant Spirit*

When Carla stopped to confer with Marcus, his sticky notes were jammed with written questions, beginning with What is in that photograph he's holding? As Carla began to help him look at the horrifying photo and work through it with him, he told her that he had thought those might have been bodies, but he couldn't believe it. Each sticky note he wrote began with "I wonder" and included his own reaction (see Figure 11.9). Most of what he read was inconceivable to him. Carla realized that his questions were so prolific because he was trying desperately to make sense of this tragedy. He just couldn't comprehend it. These questions seemed to have no answers.

As the students shared their disbeliefs, most were overwhelmed with questions. It soon became clear to Carla that the discussion spawned by these questions helped the class construct meaning. Their questions led them to synthesize their thoughts and feelings. These questions nudged their thinking and gave them insight into personal feelings that they had not explored before. The more the students shared their questions and talked about these portraits, the more they knew about the Holocaust, and the more they came to realize that some things can't be explained and some questions can never be answered.

What they did come to understand, however, was the spirit of triumph that tied these survivors to one another and the sense of hope and compassion that is still with them today. Their stories live on. They bravely speak out about the unspeakable horror they endured to ensure that people will not forget. Carla's students read the survivors' personal stories, and remember never to forget. This was their synthesis.

Teaching with the End in Mind: Assessing What We've Taught

Summarizing and Synthesizing

Based on the lessons in this chapter, we look for evidence that

1. *Students summarize information by retelling.* We look for evidence that students can summarize by picking out the most important information, keeping it brief, and saying it in their own words.
2. *Students become aware of when they add to their knowledge base and revise their thinking as they read.* We look for evidence that students are learning new information, adding to their background knowledge, and changing their thinking.
3. *Students synthesize information through writing.* We look for evidence that students pick out the most important information and merge their thinking with it to come up with responses that are both personal and factual.

4. *Students use a variety of ways to synthesize information and share their learning.* We look for evidence that students use authentic questions, inferences, and interpretations to synthesize information and teach it to others through a variety of projects and products.

Suggestions for Differentiation

When kids actively use their knowledge, they create many different ways to synthesize and share it. When we go beyond book reports, all of our kids—English language learners, developing readers, students with special needs—have a much better chance at exploring and sharing their learning and teaching others about it. Giving them choices about how to organize and present their new learning to others insures that they are interested and engaged in the process. Kids love to create a variety of posters, projects, books, models, mobiles, murals, and so on to demonstrate learning and understanding. See Chapter 13, "Topic Studies," for more examples of differentiated work products.

Summarizing and Synthesizing Assessment Commentary

Sticky notes from independent reading done after the lesson on "Retelling to Summarize Information"

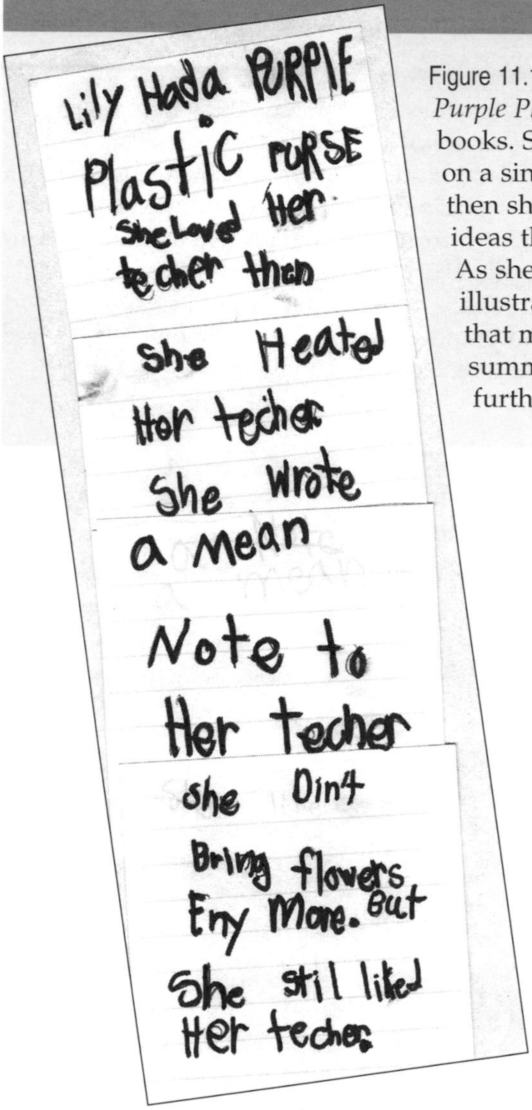

Lily Hada PURPIE
PlastIC PURSE
She Loved Her
techer than

She Heated
Her techer
She Wrote
a Mean

Note to
Her techer
she Oint

Bring flowers
Eny More. But

She stil liked
Her techer

Figure 11.10 First graders, like this child who responded to *Lilly's Purple Plastic Purse*, by Kevin Henkes, often have a lot to say about books. She starts her response with a simple fact about the story on a single sticky note—Lilly had a purple plastic purse—and then shares her thoughts about Lilly's feelings about her teacher, ideas that are central to the story and among the most important. As she describes Lilly's actions on additional notes, she illustrates her line of thinking and remembers to say it in a way that makes sense. We applaud and build on these attempts at summarizing, and we see an opportunity here to work with her further to keep her summaries brief.

Responses from the lesson "Synthesizing: How Reading Changes Thinking," where the teacher asks what the reader thinks about a topic both before and after reading an article

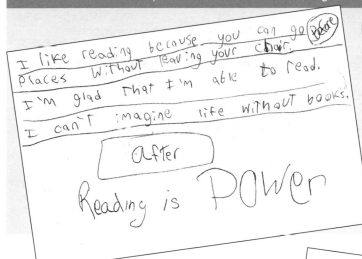

I like reading because you can go **Before** places without leaving your chair. I'm glad that I'm able to read. I can't imagine life without books.

After

Reading is POWER

Figure 11.11 This student had some good thoughts about the meaning of reading before reading "Freedom Readers," an article by Fran Downey about slaves not being able to read. She even said she couldn't imagine life without books. However, after reading the article, she realized that reading also meant power, something she hadn't thought of before. She understands something about reading that she didn't know before, which is what education is all about.

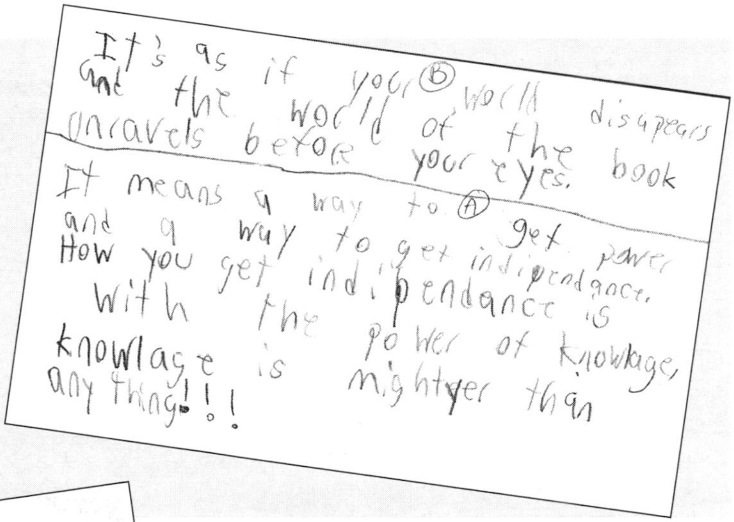

Figure 11.12 This student has a marvelous way of expressing what reading means to him. But his brain comes alive with the entire new world of thinking after reading the article. He recognizes that reading also gives us power and independence and that there is nothing more important than the power of knowledge. He now seems to understand that reading is one way to achieve that knowledge. Again, we see how reading the article added to and enriched his already terrific notions about reading.

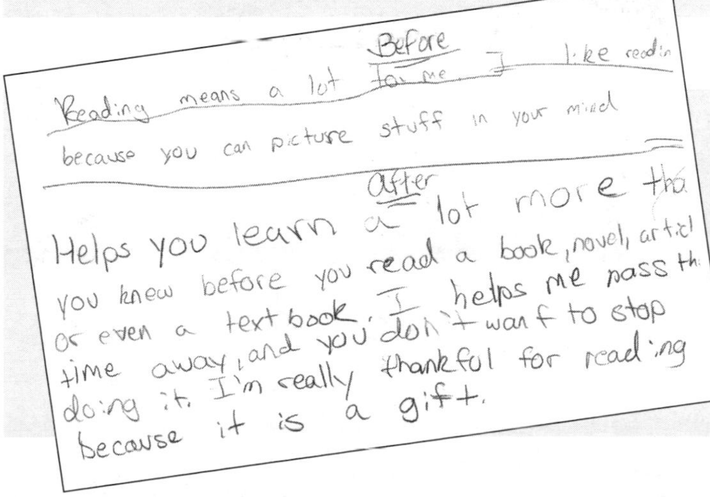

It's as if your ⓑ world disapears and the world of the book unravels before your eyes. It means a way to ⓐ get and a way to get indipendance, power How you get indipendance is with the power of knowlage, knowlage is mightyer than any thing!!!

Before Reading means a lot to me I like readin because you can picture stuff in your mind

After Helps you learn a lot more tha you knew before you read a book, novel, articl or even a text book. I helps me pass th time away, and you don't want to stop doing it. I'm really thankful for reading because it is a gift.

Figure 11.13 In this response, we don't see much change in thinking after reading the article. As a matter of fact, there is little evidence that the student thought much about the article or understood the assignment. We would meet with this student and reread the article with her to help her understand how reading can add to and change thinking.

Examples of Summary Responses done after the lesson "Summarizing the Content and Adding Personal Response"

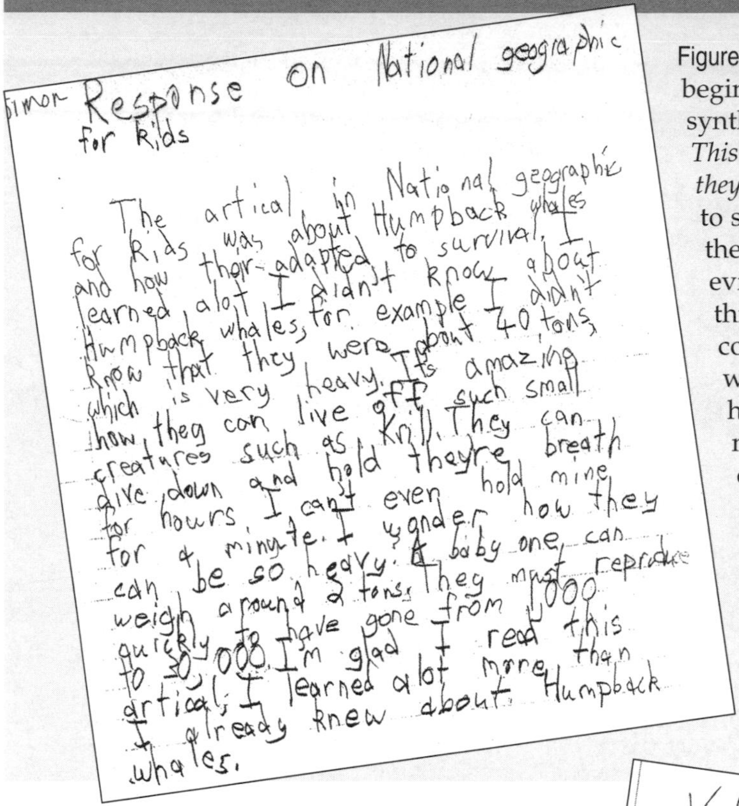

Simon Response on National geographic for Kids

The artical in National geographic for Kids was about Humpback whales and how their-adapted to survival. I learned alot I didn't know about Humpback whales, for example I didn't know that they were about 40 tons which is very heavy. It's amazing how they can live off such small creatures such as krill. They can dive down and hold theyre breath for hours. I can't even hold mine for 4 minute. I wonder how they can be so heavy. A baby one can weigh around 2 tons. They must reprduce quickly. Its have gone from 1,000 to 20,000. I'm glad I read this artical, I learned alot more than I already knew about Humpback whales.

Figure 11.14 Simon's Summary Response begins with a statement that basically synthesizes the article on humpback whales, *This article was about humpback whales and how they are adapted to survival*. We are delighted to see him pull together the information in the article into a leading statement. We see evidence of his merged thinking throughout the piece—new learning, connections, and questions. His use of the words *I didn't know* shows us how much he learned from reading the article. He noticed some interesting details and demonstrated explicit understanding when he inserted himself into the discussion of how long humpback whales can hold their breath in comparison to his own experience. Ultimately, he used the details in the piece to support his big idea about adaptation, which is exactly what we want kids to do.

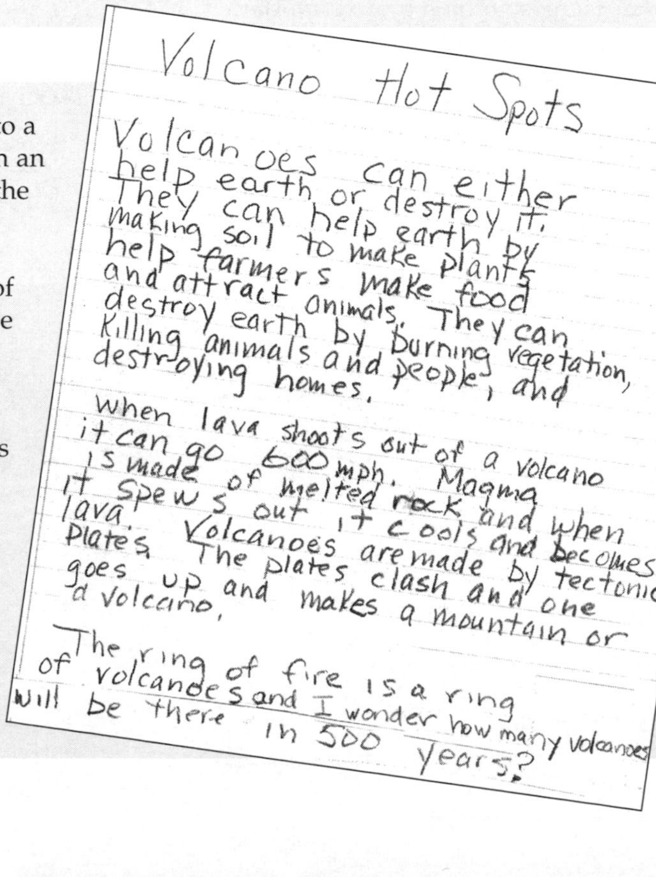

Figure 11.15 Jimmy's Summary Response to a magazine article on volcanoes begins with an original idea, one not explicitly stated in the text. This idea—that volcanoes are earth forces that are both helpful and destructive—demonstrates his synthesis of the information in the article, just what we are looking for in summary responses. In the second paragraph he summarizes information he learned about volcanoes, putting the information in the text into his own words. He wraps up his summary response with a question, wondering how many volcanoes there will be in 500 years. Jimmy's piece demonstrates how kids can take an information-packed article and synthesize their learning as they write about information they are interested in and want to remember.

Volcano Hot Spots

Volcanoes can either help earth or destroy it. They can help earth by making soil to make plants help farmers make food and attract animals. They can destroy earth by burning vegetation, killing animals and people, and destroying homes.

When lava shoots out of a volcano it can go 600 mph. Magma is made of melted rock and when it spews out it cools and becomes lava. Volcanoes are made by tectonic plates. The plates clash and one goes up and makes a mountain or a volcano.

The ring of fire is a ring of volcanoes and I wonder how many volcanoes will be there in 500 years?

Part III

Comprehension Across the Curriculum

Chapter 12

Content Literacy: Reading for Understanding in Social Studies and Science

We're worried. Front-page headlines trumpet: "Schools Cut Back Subjects to Push Reading and Math: Responding to No Child Left Behind, Thousands Narrow the Curriculum" (*The New York Times*, March 26, 2006). Teachers and principals interviewed for this article noted that many children, particularly those who weren't scoring so well on high-stakes tests, now received double or triple doses of math and reading every day and had few opportunities to study history or science. In a democracy, we don't think history, civics, or science should be optional.

Teachers we know report that their crowded schedules leave them merely twenty-five minutes for social studies or science two or three times a week. A recent survey tallied the average number of minutes per week spent on literacy, math, and science (Pearson 2006). Literacy clocked in at 750 minutes per week, math at 300 minutes per week, and science at sixty-five minutes per week. That's about thirteen minutes a day for science, and social studies isn't even on the radar screen. So it's no secret that the national emphasis on reading, math, and writing tests have squeezed social studies and science into an ever smaller corner of the school day.

Oddly enough, this is happening at the very moment that calls for more rigorous standards and higher expectations for our kids reverberate from one coast to the other. Curricular demands and mandates are at an all-time high; the list of what we're asked to teach gets longer and more complicated every year. However, trying to "cover" mandated curriculum topics by rushing students through a textbook to prepare for the state test makes no sense. Worse, it sends the message that a cursory look or quick overview is all kids need to know about history or science. But on a more hopeful note, we believe that teaching content is the perfect opportunity to design curriculum that kids can really sink their teeth into. We're happy to pick up the pace and keep things lively, creating a thoughtful, challenging curriculum that immerses students in rich content area topics, gets them to think, and fosters the active use of knowledge. Maxine Greene views the promise of literacy as extending across many subject areas and disciplines:

We owe young people the open doors and expanded possibilities that only literacy can provide. Teaching for literacy conceives of learning not as behavior but as action—of process, of restlessness of quest. To encounter the arts and other subjects in a mood of discovery and mindfulness and rational passion is to have experiences that exclude inertness. Literacy empowers people, it is a beginning, a becoming—not an end in itself. (1982)

Active Literacy in the Content Areas

Content classrooms that make a difference spur curiosity and spark exploration. Magazines, big books, globes, aquariums, maps, and charts fill the room. One child sketches a molting crayfish in the classroom terrarium. A small group works on a giant map of Alaska complete with animals in their respective habitats and a key to guide the observer. Whether it's literacy block, science, or social studies, kids are reading, writing, drawing, talking, listening, and investigating. They observe, discuss, debate, inquire, and generate new questions about their learning. Active literacy in all content areas is the means to deeper understanding and diverse, flexible thinking.

In this chapter we share some suggestions for ways to tackle the overcrowded curriculum and make it fun, interesting, and active. We teach comprehension throughout the day in every discipline and often integrate science and social studies topics with literacy instruction. Content area specialists, whether they teach history, science, or geography, are all teachers of reading. No one knows better how to teach kids to read and think about science than a scientist. History teachers are the best prepared to teach kids the ins and outs of reading primary sources. Reading, writing, and thinking across disciplines promote literacy in the broadest sense of the term. For more information on best practices for teaching content literacy see *Subjects Matter* by Harvey Daniels and Steven Zemelman (2004) and *Do I Really Have To Teach Reading?* by Cris Tovani (2004). And for building a democratic community in the classroom (and beyond) by weaving together teaching, learning, and the curriculum, there is no better resource than *A Reason to Teach: Creating Classrooms of Dignity and Hope* by James Beane (2005).

Lately we've spent a lot of time working with teachers and librarians to develop practices and lessons that integrate content and comprehension instruction in science, social studies, health, geography, you name it. Where content literacy is concerned, kids are our most enthusiastic fans. Who wouldn't want to read about women spies during the American Revolution? No kid we know would yawn through an article on violent storms happening right now around the world. And we have yet to encounter a single child (or adult, for that matter) who wasn't stunned to read that Pluto was demoted to an ice chunk. Moreover, this scientific decision has the potential for integrating subject areas: we were amazed to hear that scientists actually took a vote to decide Pluto's fate! What a perfect opportunity to integrate science with civics. We've noticed that the more kids explore and delve into a topic, the more excited and enthusiastic they become, seeking out more information as well as answers to their authentic questions.

Thinking About Content

Harvard professor David Perkins suggests that genuine learning requires thinking.

> *Learning is a consequence of thinking. . . . This sentence turns topsy-turvy the conventional pattern of schooling. The conventional pattern says that first students acquire knowledge. Only then do they think with and about the knowledge they have absorbed. But it's really just the opposite: Far from thinking coming after knowledge, knowledge comes on the coattails of thinking. As we think about and with the content we are learning, we truly learn it. (Perkins 1992)*

A number of years ago, Perkins introduced the idea of creating a culture of thinking and learning in schools (1992). He and Ron Ritchhart (2002) suggest that we cultivate student thinking by encouraging attitudes of curiosity, mindfulness, and inquiry. These ideas resonate with our goals for content literacy. Perkins, Ritchhart, and their colleagues at Harvard's Project Zero suggest that teachers look for signs that thinking is happening in classrooms. They ask, Are students explaining things to one another? Are students offering creative ideas? Are students (and teachers) using the language of thinking? Are students debating interpretations? We agree and add some of our own questions to the mix: Are kids wondering and asking questions? Are they synthesizing as they read informational text? Are they connecting the new to the known? Are they using text evidence to draw conclusions and infer themes?

We keep these questions in mind as we work with our students, and we use the following hallmarks as guidelines for sustaining a culture of thinking across the curriculum. When we design instruction in the content areas, we focus on comprehension and understanding. As teachers, we take stock of what happens in our classrooms, considering the following hallmarks that support content literacy (adapted from Ritchhart 2002):

Hallmarks for Creating an Environment for Thoughtful Content Literacy Instruction

The learning opportunities we create

- focus on comprehension and understanding rather than memorization.
- connect us with real-world, real-life issues.
- center around content-related big ideas, essential questions, and key concepts.
- engage students' interest and enthusiasm.
- encourage student choice and independent thinking.
- provide time for thinking to take place.
- set expectations that push students towards higher levels of thinking.

When we demonstrate our thinking, we

- illustrate what good thinking looks like.
- focus on topics and ideas worth thinking about.
- reveal our curiosity, interests, and passions.
- explicitly show how we understand what we read through questioning, drawing inferences, synthesizing information and ideas, and so forth.

We support attitudes and interactions that

- emphasize a common language for talking about thinking and learning.
- encourage and respect different viewpoints and perspectives.
- ensure that students experience positive ways of thinking about and engaging with content.
- spark thoughtful discussion and debate.
- support students' enthusiasm for discovery and their readiness to investigate what's new or unusual.

Student artifacts and work products

- are the result of thoughtful work and send the message that thinking matters.
- make thinking visible.
- involve sharing knowledge and teaching others.
- illustrate the process of thinking and learning.

Materials/texts/literature that students read

- encourage a variety of perspectives, opinions, and interpretations.
- require students to solve or discover problems.
- provoke discussion and raise significant issues.
- focus on content-related themes, issues, and/or essential questions.

To learn more about classroom environments that teach for understanding, we suggest you pick up a copy of Ron Ritchhart's *Intellectual Character: What It Is, Why It Matters, and How to Get It* (2002). We know of no better book for educator study groups.

Practices for Reading to Learn in Social Studies and Science

We teach kids to think about and actively use the knowledge they are learning as they read. To merge comprehension and content instruction, we engage kids in real-world reading and focused content reading. Real-world reading is the kind of reading we usually do outside of school, such as newspapers, magazines, nonfiction books, and historical fiction. Focused content reading is the reading we do in school that is directly related to our content areas. But we believe in bringing the real world into the classroom in social studies, history, and science instruction, so these practices work with a wide variety of texts and sources.

To do this, we work with our school librarian to search and scrounge for all kinds of resources: realia, picture books, trade nonfiction books, videos, maps, magazine articles, websites, documents, and even textbooks. We make sure kids have as many hands-on experiences as we can find and the field trip budget will allow. Allington and Johnston (2002) have many more suggestions for the multiresource, multigenre curriculum than those suggested here. But most important of all is that kids have ongoing opportunities to express their thoughts, questions, and ideas about what they are reading and experiencing.

Many of the practices suggested here are described in detail in the previous pages of this book. We use the lessons in the strategy chapters again and again to teach science and social studies. We show how interactive read-alouds with picture books can launch a study of the civil rights era, dangerous avalanches, or quirky animals. In Chapter 10, we describe a variety of note-taking strategies that are useful for a range of informational text in any discipline, and in Chapter 11, we share ways to pull together larger concepts and themes so that kids come away with important ideas rather than disconnected facts. In the following section, we suggest practices that you might easily adapt to your own content areas.

Literacy Practices for Social Studies and History

These literacy practices link reading comprehension instruction with what we view as best practices in history and social studies teaching. We have listed specific lessons in Part II that incorporate these practices. When we design history and social studies instruction, we teach students to

- ask and investigate authentic questions about other people, places, and times.
- learn to read and understand a variety of sources—primary and secondary sources, historical fiction, first-person accounts, and so on.
- understand multiple perspectives and interpretations.
- actively use reading, writing, discussion, and artistic expression to acquire knowledge.
- merge thinking with information and ideas to glimpse "ways of thinking" in the discipline.
- speak, write, and advocate to express opinions and take a stand.

Interactive Read-Alouds with Picture Books

When we share a great picture book through an interactive read-aloud, we immerse kids in narratives about historic people and events. Listening to picture books creates a common experience for the whole class and provides an imaginative entry point into times and places that are far away and long ago. Through narratives, kids are introduced to big ideas and themes or thought-provoking questions. With young children especially, we often use props and artifacts to make story events and characters come alive. Kids of all ages are eager to act out important events or take on the roles of historic characters. As kids engage in all manner of responses, they talk, write, and sketch their way to understanding. (See a variety of lessons in Chapter 9 and Chapter 10.)

Read, View, and React to Primary Sources

To read and think like historians, kids react and respond to photographs, pictures, journals, diaries, and other documents. Constructing meaning from historical sources requires students to combine their background knowledge with text clues to draw inferences about historical people and times. They leave tracks of their thinking, showing how the evidence they gather from sources leads to conclusions or to further exploration of questions about the significance of the documents. Kids learn firsthand what it means to be a historian and practice historical interpretation. (See "Making Students Aware of Primary Sources" in Chapter 10.)

Book Club Discussions with Historical Fiction Picture Books or Nonfiction Trade Books

There's no better way to build kids' background knowledge than to read historical fiction picture books that zero in on authentic information and engage their interest. Historical fiction gives kids a sense of the drama, emotions, and excitement of history. Well-written nonfiction trade books, such as biographies, also work well with book club discussions. Historical fiction and nonfiction trade books provide opportunities for kids to learn about dilemmas, issues, and ideas that are missing from most textbooks.

To get started with the book clubs, students meet in small groups and read and talk about a variety of picture books that present different perspectives on a topic. They can use the Facts/Questions/Response think sheet (one of many possible forms for holding thinking) to ask questions about and merge their thinking with the historical information they glean from the text. After kids read and talk about several books in their small groups, the class comes together to discuss important themes and lingering questions. As the topic study continues, kids often investigate those lingering questions arising from book club discussions. (See "Using FQR Think Sheets to Understand Information" in Chapter 10.)

Create Concept Maps: Visual Representations of Events, People, and Ideas

In social studies and history, it's tempting to try to "fill kids up" with information—dates, events, people, and more. We know these details are important, and so we ask kids to do this work themselves by teaching them to organize and share all the important information they are learning on concept maps. Kids organize and visually represent concepts and information in a way that makes sense to them. For instance, concept maps show how historic details support a larger idea or demonstrate the causes and effects of historical events. A biographical map of a famous person illustrates many facets of that person's life and accomplishments. Illustrations, diagrams, and other features provide ways for kids to blend artistic and written expression as they share important information with others.

Create Maps of Stories and Folktales to Understand Cultural Themes and Traditions

Folktales and stories provide a window into people from other cultures and places, allowing kids an understanding of people very different from themselves. Through interactive read-alouds, kids listen to stories that introduce traditions and cultural practices, and then together we construct large story

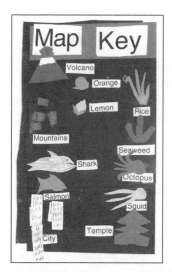

Figure 12.1 Key for Map of Japan

maps that focus on characters, problems, conflicts, and messages to record important story elements. As students learn to create these maps on their own, the class collection of anchor charts grows—visually representing a variety of story elements and themes.

Stop, Think, and React to Videos

Historical reenactments of events get kids engaged in a topic by showing the drama and dilemmas of history. Videos from cultures far and wide provide a sense of being there that books can't match. To discourage kids from watching videos on autopilot, we frequently pause the video and ask them to stop, think, and react to what they see and observe. We provide a variety of scaffolds to guide kids' thinking—forms headed Observations/Questions and Comments or Notes/My Thinking—and ask kids to turn and talk about their reactions to the video before recording their thoughts. Kids learn more when they talk and write about what they are viewing.

Figure 12.2 Map for a Study of Japan

Create Maps of Countries or Cultures: Merge Thinking with New Information

Kids create large wall maps of a region, country, or continent so they can share their new learning in ways that are visible and concrete. They gather information, paraphrase it in a sentence or short paragraph, and then illustrate what they have learned about people, places, physical features, natural resources, and cultural traditions. Kids love using their imaginations to create three-dimensional forests, pop-up mountains, or pebble-spewing volcanoes in appropriate places on the map. They incorporate a variety of nonfiction features such as close-ups, captions, labels, and diagrams and create a key to help viewers navigate and learn from the map. As a giant visual, the map captures children's thinking and learning over time. (See Figures 12.1 and 12.2.)

Co-construct a Time Line of Historical Events, People, and Places to Support Historical Thinking

Providing children with a context for understanding events in history is a challenge. To make the journey back in time as concrete as possible, we create time lines that serve as reference points. We examine pictures and text about cultural aspects of the time period we're studying: for instance, what people, homes, farms, and towns looked like in the colonial era. As kids learn more information about specific events and people, they add to the time line with their own illustrations and descriptions of events. Then they teach their classmates about their individual contributions.

According to Levstik and Barton, children's learning is enhanced when they "associate visual images of history with time periods and dates" (2001). To construct the time line, we teach kids different ways to read for the gist, summarize information, and illustrate their learning through drawing and sketching. Since kids gravitate to interesting, unusual, or quirky details about people

In 1607, settlers in Jamestown built a fort to protect their houses.

Figure 12.3 Time Line Entry for the Jamestown Settlement Project

Figure 12.4 Colonial Journal Entry from the Perspective of a Young Woman on the *Mayflower*

October, 1620

    I got this journal from my own dear great, great grandmother in England. She wanted to come on this voyage, but we lost her before we left. Her heart was strong, but her body was not strong enough to deal with all the sickness and filth of this voyage of the Mayflower. I miss her.

    But I live on for all the blessings in life. I had an extremely beautiful baby boy today. I named him Oceanus because he was born aboard this ship sailing in the ocean.

    This is not what I would call a luxurious or a healthy place to have a baby, but at least God has provided me a place out of the cold gale. There are cracks and leaks on this ship. The sailors laugh at us and say that we were stupid to come on this voyage and expect to survive.

    As I look down at my tattered and filthy clothing, I long to wash and mend and be ladylike again.

                  I bid you a worried but hopeful goodbye,
                              M. Hopkins

and events, we teach them to incorporate what's interesting without losing sight of what's important. Kids use their note-taking skills to illustrate, paraphrase, and summarize the information. When we move on to another period of history, the time line is there to build on and refer back to—an ongoing representation of how our learning grows and changes. (See Figure 12.3.)

Create Journals and Personal Narratives to Understand Historical Perspective

Historical fiction diaries and journals contain riveting information about the lives of people and events of the times. When we focus on a time period, we teach students that people living in those times had many different perspectives—and that those different points of view are important to understanding history. Kids gather into literature circles that focus on narratives and journals of people living in the time period under study. After reading and gathering information about historical events and personal perspectives, kids write a journal entry from the point of view of a historical person—real or fictional. They weave information and personal reactions into their writing, as this child did—writing from the perspective of a young woman on the *Mayflower*. (See Figure 12.4.)

Explore Current Events and Issues

As news fanatics, it's a no-brainer for us to share with kids our passion for reading the newspaper, keeping up on current events via magazines or the Internet, and thinking about issues that affect our lives. We are just trying to do our part to create a nation of skeptics and informed citizens! As we read a variety of news stories, essays, and editorials with our students, we show them how we distinguish the authors' ideas and perspectives from our own. We demonstrate how we weigh arguments and evidence, helping kids articulate how to merge their thinking with the information to form an opinion. Kids learn how to discern writing that tugs at their emotions and to identify ways that writers use information to persuade us. They learn to read closely and with a critical eye, becoming aware of how language and writing can influence thinking.

Literacy Practices for Science

The real world is rich, fascinating, and compelling. Science, more than many areas, requires a careful, thoughtful approach to reading. Science literacy practices include:

- Learning through observation; recording and reflecting on these experiences
- Gaining accurate information from a variety of texts, visuals, and realia
- Constructing meaning with vocabulary, concepts, and information by drawing and writing to make learning visible
- Investigating questions that invite discovery and add to learning
- Investigating how natural phenomena impact society—environmental, medical, health issues, and so forth, to develop informed opinions.

Science Journals and Teaching Books

Kids keep track of their own learning via science journals, Wonder Books, and self-authored books that teach others what they have learned. (See the lessons in Chapter 10, "Determining What's Important When Writing Information.") If there's one thing we want kids to do in science, it's keep those questions coming! Wonder Books provide a way for them to capture, wonder about, and reflect on experiences and observations. They are a record of new learning and evolving thinking. We view science writing as more than "just the facts," and encourage kids' natural curiosity and personal reactions. Careful observation and descriptive writing introduce children to scientific habits and ways of thinking.

Anchor Charts That Document Thinking and How It Evolves

When we begin a science topic study, we often begin with a conversation and chart the kids' thinking about the subject. Often we begin an anchor chart of kids' questions which we add to over time. Anchor charts that capture kids' prior knowledge about, experiences with, and "theories" about the natural

Figure 12.5 Anchor Chart of Children's Questions About Insects

Figure 12.6 Science Poster on the Life
Cycle of the Butterfly Incorporating
Nonfiction Features

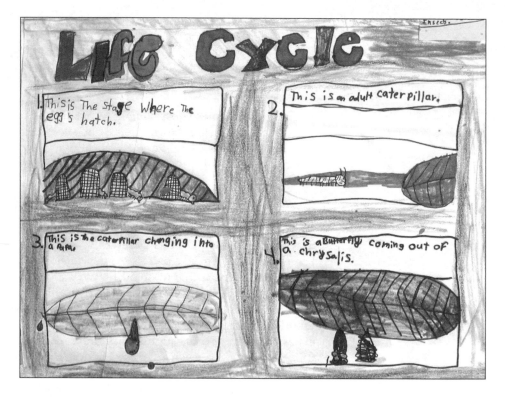

Figure 12.6 Science Poster on the Life Cycle of the Butterfly Incorporating Nonfiction Features

world are a great way to launch kids into a study of a new topic. As they explore a topic through observation, experiences, or photographs, we often ask them, "What do you notice or see?" or "What's going on here?" so that they begin to describe what they are observing and experiencing (Housen, Yenawine, and Arenas 1991; Perkins 2006). When kids record and reflect on information, they think more deeply about what they are learning. The anchor charts keep track of what kids learn over time. (See Figure 12.5.)

Learning and Teaching Information from a Variety of Features

We encourage kids to pay close attention to all manner of features found in informational text—photographs, diagrams, close-ups, cut-aways, maps, charts, tables, graphs, and so forth. As kids learn from these visual representations of information, we pose questions that encourage them to think more deeply about what they are seeing and learning. We create a Feature/Purpose chart so kids can review the features and keep track of new ones in their reading. When it comes time to write up and share information, kids add these features to their own written and illustrated books and posters to convey information visually. (See Figure 12.6.)

Learning Vocabulary and Concepts Through Picture Dictionaries and Content Word Walls

When introducing kids to new vocabulary and building background, we make sure they understand the language and concepts essential to an understanding of the topic. Kids love illustrating and writing up short definitions of words. (See Figures 12.7a and 12.7b.) They write definitions of the vocabulary and

Figure 12.7a and b Content Word Wall Examples from the Weather Topic Study

illustrate the concepts they are learning, posting them to create a concept word wall for a particular topic. When kids illustrate and write about concepts in their own words, they are much more likely to remember the information.

Noticing New Learning
When kids encounter new concepts or information in science, we ask them to read and notice their new learning—by using an L on a sticky note when they learn something new, or by using language that signals new learning, such as, "Wow, I never knew that before" or "Now I think. . . ." Very young children can do this without reading the text; they respond to a photograph or illustration by drawing a picture on a sticky note that illustrates what they learned. Kids often keep a two-column chart in their notebooks for collecting "old thinking" and "new thinking." Or we create anchor charts headed What I Used to Think and Now I Know That. Keeping track of how our thinking changes and evolves sends the message to kids that learning is all about revising and deepening our understanding. (See the lessons in Chapter 7: "Noticing and Thinking About New Learning" and "Rethinking Misconceptions: New Information Changes Thinking.")

Note-taking Strategies for Merging Thinking with New Information
Sorting out details, relationships, and important ideas in information-laden science texts can be a challenge. Note-taking scaffolds such as the Facts/ Questions/Responses or Topic/Details/Response forms support students to organize the facts they are learning in the face of TMI—Too Much Information. Information and ideas in science articles are often organized around cause-and-effect relationships or a problem-solution format. Giving kids a heads up about these different text structures and designing note-taking scaffolds that reflect these structures make it easier for them to paraphrase, take notes on, and remember the information. Adapting note-taking to the ways information is organized in science textbooks, especially, can be particularly helpful, as these are famous repositories of TMI! See Chapter 10 for ideas on determining importance.

Figure 12.8 Insect Poster Incorporating
Nonfiction Features

Creating Posters, Projects, Murals, and Mobiles

Kids love working big! As they learn information, there's nothing like sharing what they've learned on large paper. This mural (Figure 12.8) demonstrates this child's careful observation and attention to detail as she summarizes her learning about butterflies, qualities of a budding scientist. Young children can create murals of all their learning about a topic—often kids work together to illustrate their thinking and learning and write captions to share it. Other kids write comments on sticky notes about what they've learned from the work, so that everyone's a learner and everyone's a teacher. See Chapter 11, "Summarizing and Synthesizing Information," for lesson ideas.

Summarizing and Synthesizing Learning on a Mind Map

Mind maps of all sorts give kids opportunities to share their learning in visually interesting ways. As kids create mind maps, they synthesize their learning—imagining new possibilities for thinking about and organizing it. Mind maps are a genre unto themselves (Buzan 2005). One way to start a mind map is to put the topic in the center of a big piece of paper. Kids draw giant arms branching off in different directions, with each branch containing illustrations and information about different aspects of the topic. Mind maps are ultimately collaborative efforts, as kids work together to represent their learning and thinking. Buhrow and Garcia (2006) describe how kids represented information about insects with accuracy and precision—each arm of the mind map contained illustrations and descriptions of insect body parts, food, movement, whether an insect was harmful or useful, and so forth. When the mind map was complete, the children shared how and why they organized their thinking

---

Websites and Resources for Content Teaching

Seeds of Science/Roots of Reading: www.scienceandliteracy.org. A website supported by the National Science Foundation and the Lawrence Hall of Science at the University of California, Berkeley, that investigates the convergence of science and literacy—a great source for learning about the work of P. David Pearson, Jacqueline Barber, and their colleagues.

National Science Teachers Association: www.nsta.org. Publishes the magazine *Science and Children*, along with many excellent resources on best practices.

Harvard's Project Zero: www.pz.harvard.edu. Updates on current research projects and home to Ron Ritchhart, David Perkins, and others whose research focuses on "teaching for understanding."

National Council for the Social Studies: www.ncss.org. Curricular resources, publications, papers, and national conferences for all areas of social studies.

The National Council for History Education: www.nche.net. Their motto is History Matters! They have lots of resources for teaching history, such as the booklets *Building a K–4 History Curriculum* and *Building a World History Curriculum.*

Union of Concerned Scientists: www.ucsusa.org. Scientific information on world and national issues that impact our environment and our lives.

Teaching for Change: www.teachingforchange.org. Curriculum ideas, videos, and other resources for teaching and learning about social justice.

International Reading Association: www.reading.org. This website includes a huge span of resources for literacy, including publications, journals, conference schedules, and curriculum programs.

National Council of Teachers of English: www.ncte.org. This organization focuses on language arts, reading, and writing for kindergarten through college. Publications, papers, curriculum materials, conference schedules, and more are available.

Rethinking Schools: www.rethinkingschools.org. This group offers a wide variety of teaching resources on current events, social issues, and school reform.

Teaching Tolerance: www.tolerance.org. A project of the Southern Poverty Law Center that provides free resources and curriculum materials to educators on issues of civil rights and social justice.

---

this way, a thoughtful synthesis of their learning (see Chapter 13, page 225, for a photo of a mind map about the weather.)

Delving Deeper into Content

One big caveat—these practices are shared for the purpose of integrating reading comprehension instruction with content topics. Although we are big enthusiasts of content instruction, we are not content specialists ourselves. Therefore, we've included resources and websites, where knowledgeable experts in the fields of science, history, geography, and so forth offer best practices for teaching in the various disciplines.

We know many teachers who have used reading and thinking strategies in literacy for many years who have inquired about ways to teach these same strategies in mathematics. Art Hyde, a professor at National-Louis University, has finally come to the rescue with *Comprehending Math: Adapting Reading Strategies to Teach Mathematics, K–6* (2006). We have all been waiting a long time for this book, and Art's book is well worth the wait.

Content literacy gives kids the tools to learn information, ideas, and ways of thinking in a variety of disciplines. When kids ask important and thoughtful questions, evaluate information and evidence, observe and wonder about nature, and read, write, and talk about current events and issues, they eagerly explore their world. In the next chapter, we show how to use these content practices in a primary science study and an intermediate history study, enabling kids to build their knowledge in these disciplines and use comprehension strategies to design and carry out research and investigations.

Chapter 13

Topic Studies: A Framework for Research and Exploration

Teaching reading and thinking strategies as tools for acquiring and actively using knowledge in history, science, and other curriculum topics is paramount. Any topic can be engaging if we organize the learning in interesting, thoughtful ways. To make sure kids are engaged with the topic, we seek out ways they can connect their own lives and experiences to what we study. We provide as much choice as possible, so we encourage students to do research projects that interest them and that are an extension of the classroom topic study. Other times, they do their own independent research on topics they choose. When we teach these same reading, writing, and research strategies over time and across the curriculum, children become independent thinkers who know how to conduct investigations and apply their knowledge insightfully.

"Topic study" is simply our term for a curriculum unit, although there are some important differences. Gone are the activities for activities' sake. Kids explore, investigate, and do research as an important part of every topic study. And, frequently, the librarian is right there with us as we work together doing research and investigations. What matters most is that we take advantage of children's natural curiosity about the real world.

A Topic-Study Framework for Content Instruction

We design topic studies using a four-part framework that merges comprehension and content instruction to build knowledge over time. (See Figure 13.1.) Kids read, write, draw, talk, listen, and investigate across the curriculum. We have found that this framework works well with content literacy in many topics: science, social studies, history, geography, the arts, health, and so forth. Kids then go on to use this same process as they pursue their own independent research projects with topics of their own choosing. The following framework describes what teachers and children do during each phase.

Activate, Explore, and Build Background Knowledge

Teachers	*Kids*
Plan instruction and teach with central concepts and focus questions in mind.	Connect new information to their background knowledge and experiences.
Connect curriculum topics to kids' interests, lives, and experiences.	Explore essential questions they are interested in and care about.
Gather and organize resources and materials related to the topic—picture books, nonfiction trade books, articles, videos, realia, and so forth.	Acquire vocabulary and concepts central to the topic.
	Explore and read extensively about the topic.
Engage kids in experiences that encourage their questions and build background knowledge.	Respond with authentic questions, connections, and reactions.
Immerse kids in short text and picture-book clubs and lit circles to add to their knowledge base and prompt questions.	Experience the topic through simulations, field trips, drama, and role play.

Read to Gather Information and Develop Questions

Teachers	*Kids*
Wonder out loud, showing kids how to ask thoughtful and searching questions.	Articulate questions and connections that stem from their interests and experiences.
Demonstrate ways to read and respond to information, code the text, jot notes in margins, and paraphrase information.	Read, write, talk, and think about the information.
	Develop questions and read to answer them.
Demonstrate how to ask and search for answers to questions.	Use evidence to distinguish between their thinking and the author's.
Demonstrate how to read and determine what's important.	Use text features to gain information.
Show kids how to distinguish the reader's ideas from the author's.	Target key ideas and information.

Summarize and Synthesize Information and Ideas

Teachers	*Kids*
Show how to infer answers to questions and draw conclusions.	Seek out and review a variety of sources.
	Use text evidence to answer questions and draw conclusions.
Demonstrate reading to get the gist.	Use details and evidence in the text to infer big ideas and themes.
Demonstrate how to write summary responses.	
Engage kids in guided discussions and debates.	Sort out fact and opinion—cite evidence to support an opinion.
Encourage authentic writing through essays, letters, and other ways to express opinions and take action.	Discuss information and gain new insight.
	Consider ways to express their ideas about what they have learned through artistic expression, written responses, and discussion.

Demonstrate Understanding and Share Learning

Teachers	*Kids*
Establish expectations for final projects.	Demonstrate understanding and learning in a variety of ways—posters, models, essays, picture books, poetry.
Model a variety of possibilities for final projects.	
Respond to and evaluate student work and projects.	Become teachers as they share their knowledge with others.
Encourage kids to share their learning through community service and advocacy work.	Articulate their learning process and how learning changes.
	Investigate new questions that come from discussions.
	Take action through writing, community work, or advocating for a cause.

Figure 13.1 Teacher and Student Roles in Framework for Content Instruction

Topic Studies in Science and History

From our experience, kids are curious, enthusiastic learners who can get excited about almost any topic under the sun. Come with us into a primary classroom in Boulder, Colorado, to experience a topic study on weather, demonstrating kids' learning during each phase. The anchor lessons shared here are practices that we use again and again, varying the resources we use as the topic study unfolds. We also share lessons from a Civil War topic study in an upper elementary classroom. In this example, we map out lessons in each phase of the framework to show how kids explore a topic, gather information and seek answers to their questions, summarize and synthesize their learning, and take their learning public. Both of the topic studies described here are required district curriculum.

We understand that these topics may not be relevant to your curriculum. As you read through them, think about how the practices and lessons might apply to your own curricular topics and grade levels and how the topic-study framework can guide your content instruction.

Science Topic Study—Weather

Extreme weather is a source of endless curiosity to young kids, not to mention all the rest of us. During a bout of extreme weather in the southeastern United States, second graders grabbed the local paper every day on their way to the classroom. They scanned the headlines and poured over photographs of the most recent storm and its aftermath. Hurricanes and tornadoes attracted most of the attention, as the Katrina landfall coincided with the opening days of school, making it the perfect time to learn about extreme weather. Later on, the class investigated thunderstorms and blizzards—weather events with which these Colorado kids were familiar.

Teachers Anne Upczak Garcia, Brad Buhrow, Lynn Albert, and Marisol Payet integrated district science standards and key concepts to create several focus questions to guide their study of extreme weather.

- How do storms and extreme weather affect people?
- What happens during a hurricane? Tornado? Thunderstorm? Blizzard?
- What causes tornadoes? Hurricanes? Thunderstorms? Blizzards?
- How can we stay safe during these kinds of storms?

Activate, Explore, and Build Background Knowledge
Anchor lesson: Read, talk, write, and draw in response to newspaper articles, photographs, interviews, and other resources. Teachers and kids posted newspaper articles on large pieces of chart paper and began writing their thoughts, comments, and questions next to the photographs and text. Teachers modeled a language of thinking for learning new information, asking questions, and making connections. Kids incorporated this language into their responses as they read, talked about, and reacted to the mesmerizing yet sobering news of the hurricanes' power and devastation. The photographs and personal stories

Figure 13.2 Children's Responses to Newspaper Articles About Extreme Weather

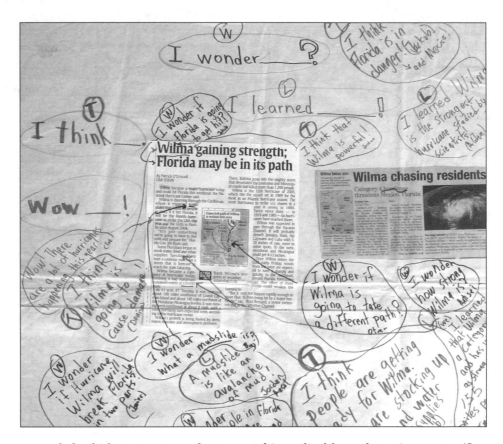

moved the kids to try to make sense of inexplicable and tragic events. (See Figure 13.2.)

Figure 13.3 Poetry Incorporating Children's Learning About Extreme Weather

Anchor lesson: Make vocabulary and concepts visible via word walls and poetry. To support all the informational reading kids were tackling, the classes also created a large picture dictionary and a content word wall to share important vocabulary words and concepts. When unfamiliar vocabulary and concepts are concerned, we can't to be too explicit. Kids chose words to illustrate and wrote definitions in clear, simple language. This was particularly helpful for English language learners because the words and concepts were visible and accessible. The children's illustrations reflected and often included examples of features they had seen in the newspapers—especially cutaways, cross sections, diagrams, and maps.

One day, the group brainstormed descriptive language to put up on the word wall: *roaring winds, swirling dust cloud, it's a twister.* Listening carefully, Ansel exclaimed, "Wow, that sounds just like a poem!" With that, the kids were off and running with weather poetry. Using the descriptive language, information, and ideas they had culled from newspapers, books, and visuals, they created poems together and then on their own. Poetry generated new interest in describing the weather events they were studying—providing a way for them to express their learning in vivid and colorful language and illustrations. (See Figure 13.3.)

Read to Gather Information and Develop Questions
Anchor lesson: Read and wonder about information. As much as kids were curious about and engaged with the stories, articles, and photographs of the storms, they had difficulty fathoming the enormity of the situation and had many, many questions. As kids talked about, wondered about, and responded to the information and photographs, the list of questions posted on the wall got longer and longer.

- Why did the Hurricane Katrina hit New Orleans?
- How did it start?
- Were there other hurricanes that were this big?
- What was the strongest hurricane?
- Where will the people go?
- Why isn't anyone helping them get food and water?
- Why couldn't they stop the floods?
- Will the people get a new house? Do the kids have a school?
- What can we do about this?

To make weather matters worse, tornadoes began to crisscross the central United States, so now these powerful storms garnered the kids' attention.

- How does a tornado begin?
- How fast does a tornado go?
- How do tornadoes hurt people?
- Why do tornadoes hit some houses and not others?
- What's a twister?

As kids kept reading and learning more information, they began to notice that they were finding answers to some of their questions. They began to record these answers and their thinking on sticky notes and add them to the questions on the charts. They also noticed that questions had more than one answer, or that there were differences of opinion with respect to the information that answered the question.

Summarize and Synthesize Information and Ideas
Anchor lesson: Read with a question in mind and answer it in your own words. With so many questions, the teachers taught kids ways to answer different kinds of questions: more specific, information-seeking questions as well as questions that might be difficult or even impossible to answer. To take advantage of all the new information the kids had learned, teachers initially emphasized questions that could be answered with specific information. They began with

- What is a tornado? How can we describe a tornado?
- What is a hurricane? How can we describe a hurricane?

Teachers modeled how to keep a question in mind while reading and showed kids how to put the information they found in their own words. Kids worked with partners or in small groups to find, read, and talk about the information before summarizing it themselves.

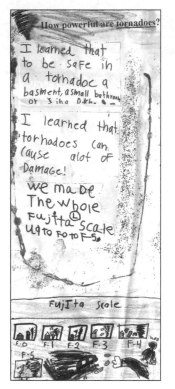

Figure 13.4 Children's Answers to the Question "How Powerful Are Tornadoes?"

The class created a chart.

What Do We Do When We Read to Find Answers to Our Questions?
- Check the Table of Contents for information that might answer our question
- Check the index for information about our question
- Look through the book for photographs or illustrations that answer our questions
- Check to see if we can match our question to information we find
- Read the information and *think* about it
- Try to say the information in our own words
- Summarize the information by drawing and sketching what we're learning

To share their learning, children created posters to display their questions with the appropriate answers. As one question led to another, their posters grew to amazing proportions and even included a discussion of the Fujita tornado intensity scale. Once kids figured out strategies for answering their questions, there was no stopping them! (See Figure 13.4.)

Demonstrate Understanding and Share Learning
Anchor lesson: Creating ways to actively use learning and take action. Kids' lingering questions remained a source of discussion. The children continued to wonder about and respond to the sheer enormity of the devastation and difficulties they saw people experiencing. Their questions reflected their concern for what was happening to people in New Orleans and other areas, and the kids yearned to take action. They asked, "How can we help the victims of the Hurricane Katrina?"

As they discussed this last question, the kids remembered a list of charities assisting Hurricane Katrina victims that they had noticed in the newspaper. Oliver suggested they hold a bake sale. Several kids mentioned that the Red Cross was raising money for the victims of the storm, so the children decided to ask for donations and advertise their bake sale. They shared the fruits of their efforts on posters and through letters. The second graders' letter to the Red Cross follows:

> *Dear Red Cross,*
> *We wanted to help people. We made posters about hurricane Katrina so we could teach our friends about what happened. Then we made presentations to every class in our school and asked for money. In our studies we learned a lot. Please share this money with the people who need it.*
> *From the second grade students of Columbine Elementary*

Anchor lesson: Creating a mind map to summarize and synthesize learning. At the end of the weather study, the classes came together to create mind maps of their learning. They shared information about tornadoes, hurricanes, and blizzards. They wrote about the effects of the storms on peoples' lives. Illustrations, 3-D visuals, photographs, diagrams, cutaways, and all manner of features made for an eye-popping synthesis of all their learning and hard work. (See Figure 13.5.)

History Topic Study—The Civil War

A study of the Civil War is a mainstay of the history curriculum in intermediate classrooms in many districts. Not surprisingly, few fifth graders walk in with

Figure 13.5 Section of a Mind Map Synthesizing Information About Extreme Weather

extensive background knowledge on the topic, so teachers build their understanding from the ground up. When a subject is less familiar like this one, more time is spent exploring the topic and building kids' background knowledge in it. Then kids can move more quickly into other phases of the topic study. But no matter where we begin, students' own research projects are an important wrap-up to any topic study, so it makes sense to devote plenty of time to investigations.

Columbine Elementary teachers Steve Ollanik, Melanie Pappageorge, and librarian Nell Box worked together to design and teach the Civil War study. They began by formulating questions that merged the district history standards with issues and information that would engage kids. The classes launched into the study with the following questions as a guide, and students added their questions to the list throughout the study. Teaching with these questions focuses the study on important ideas and issues, not just learning the facts about this time in our history:

Essential Questions/Focus Questions

- What is a Civil War? Why did it happen in the United States?
- What were some differing perspectives of Americans engaged in/touched by the Civil War?
- What was life in the Northern and Southern states like during this time period?
- What was slavery? How did it impact the Civil War?
- Does slavery still exist today?

Activate, Explore, and Build Background Knowledge

Build background about slavery. Kids viewed the powerful drawings from the large format picture book *The Middle Passage* by Tom Feelings. They considered the question, Can we imagine what it would be like to be a slave? They also listened to the story of Ibrahim, an African prince who was captured, taken to the African coast, and put on a slave ship to the west, from Walter Dean Myers' "Now Is Your Time." Their written responses to the searing words and stunning visuals were full of empathy, outrage, and other emotions at this glimpse of the slaves' tragic and almost unfathomable experiences. (See Figures 13.6a and 13.6b.)

Use classroom book clubs to read and respond to picture books about the Civil War. Kids read four or five historical fiction picture books in book clubs. The focus on different perspectives, the journey on the Underground Railroad, and so forth, prompted engaged discussions of compelling issues such as slavery and the tragedy of war. The Facts/Questions/Response note-taking sheet held kids' thinking and enabled them to return to their notes throughout the topic

Figure 13.6a and b Responses to *The Middle Passage,* by Tom Feelings

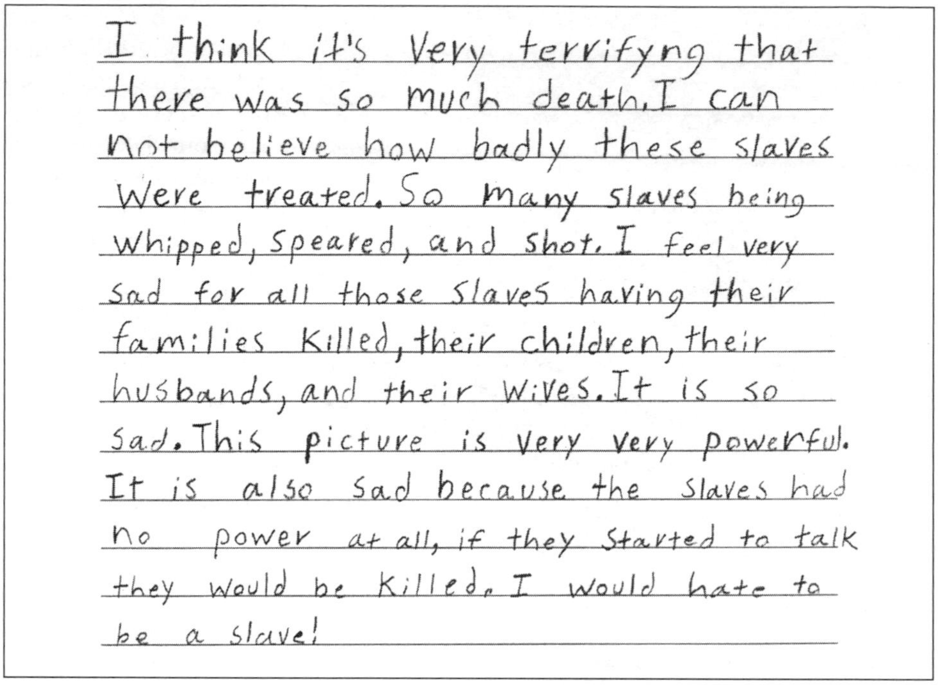

> I think it's very terrifyng that there was so much death. I can not believe how badly these slaves were treated. So many slaves being whipped, speared, and shot. I feel very sad for all those slaves having their families killed, their children, their husbands, and their wives. It is so sad. This picture is very very powerful. It is also sad because the slaves had no power at all, if they started to talk they would be killed. I would hate to be a slave!

> I felt sad that people betrayed their people just to have power and riches. White people bribed Africans to capture their own people. It was tragic. I think the slaves lost the ability. I wonder if the slaves died of frost bite when they were on the boat? I also wonder if some rich people bought slaves to let them free? I learned that slavery was a lot more serios than I thought. I knew it was painful, but not that painful.

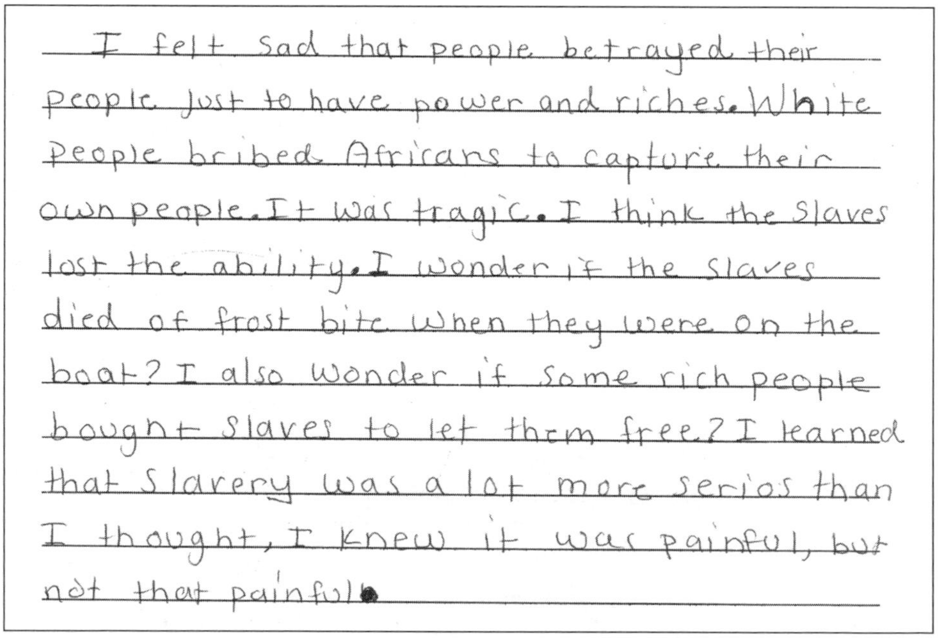

study. Extended discussion and debate drew kids into these narratives and stories of people in these times. (See Chapter 10 for the lesson "Using FQR Think Sheets to Understand Information.")

Read a variety of information sources to build background and construct a class time line. As kids encountered specific information about people, events, and places, they read and paraphrased important information and put it on a time line. Illustrations accompanied the text they wrote and as the students added to the time line, their fuller understanding of this time period unfolded on the wall. (See Chapter 12 for an example of a time line entry and illustration.)

Read to Gather Information and Develop Questions
Mini-research on authentic questions from the book clubs. Students reviewed their FQRs from the picture book discussions and realized that they still had many lingering questions. The kids were full of questions, as evidenced by the question column on their FQR think sheets. Melanie, Steve, and Nell were surprised one day when one of the kids piped up, asking, "Aren't we ever going to answer any of these questions we've been asking?" Children are our best teachers, and this one query propelled the class into a mini-research project: researching a lingering question. The teachers facilitated a conversation about finding a "researchable question" and the kids pursued questions that were particularly interesting to them. Some questions that kids researched follow:

- Why if a slave escaped would he or she go back to help someone else to freedom?
- Once slaves got to Canada and were free, what happened to them?
- Could slaves live in the Northern states, or were they always sent back to their masters?
- Why did some young boys become soldiers? Why were they so eager to fight?
- Who were some Civil War spies? Were they men? Women? What happened to them if they were caught?

Write a summary/response to answer the mini-research question. Students summarized what they learned about their respective questions and merged their thinking with the information to create a summary response. Kids sought out information that answered their questions by investigating different resources, searching online, and then paraphrasing the information in a summary that also incorporated their voice and thinking. (See Figure 13.7.)

Figure 13.7 A Mini-Research Summary to Answer a Lingering Question

Why go back + risk your life for someone else?

"When I crossed the line to be free I will help others." Said Harriet. Some of the runaway slaves wanted to go back to help the other slaves get away because they knew how bad it was to be a slave. Some also thought it was good to be free but it was better with their familys.
Free Slaves weren't the only ones to risk their lives. Some abolitionists risked their lives helping the slaves get free. Harriet Tubman knew she wasn't free until all her people were free. Only some helped others get free because the others were too scared to go back to help others.

Read and respond to a primary source. Librarian Nell Box brought in primary sources from the historical society from her native Tupelo, Mississippi, including a gripping account of an imprisoned Northern sympathizer named John who made several daring attempts to escape from an underground prison. After digging a tunnel with his bare hands and tricking his guards, John was a free man. This first person account wowed the kids to the point where, hungry for more information, they couldn't wait to go online to investigate further.

Summarize and Synthesize Information and Ideas
Compare and contrast life in the Northern states with life in the Southern states. To sort and sift information about the differences between life in the

North and life in the South, the teachers posted a giant chart with these headings. As kids learned additional information about daily life and historical events in the North and South, they added their information to the chart. Conversations abounded as kids discussed and compared their findings.

Read historical fiction to understand different points of view and synthesize the information. Getting up close and personal with historical fiction brings historical characters to life. Kids gained an understanding of the power of historical events in people's lives. Using Paul Fleischman's *Bull Run*, kids coded different selections from the book, keeping the following questions in mind: What happened to these people? How did their experiences change their feelings about the war? (See Figure 13.8.) Children were so engrossed with these

Figure 13.8 Student's Coded Text from *Bull Run*, by Paul Fleischman

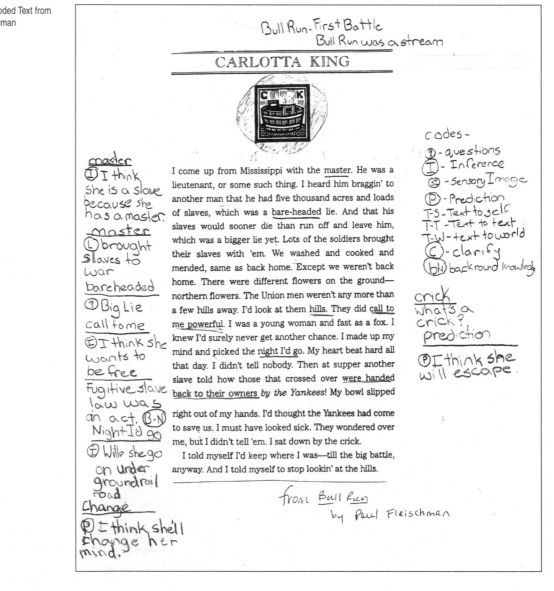

Figure 13.9 Student's Journal Entry from the Perspective of Toby Boyce, a Character from Bull Run Who Enlisted to Fight for the Confederacy

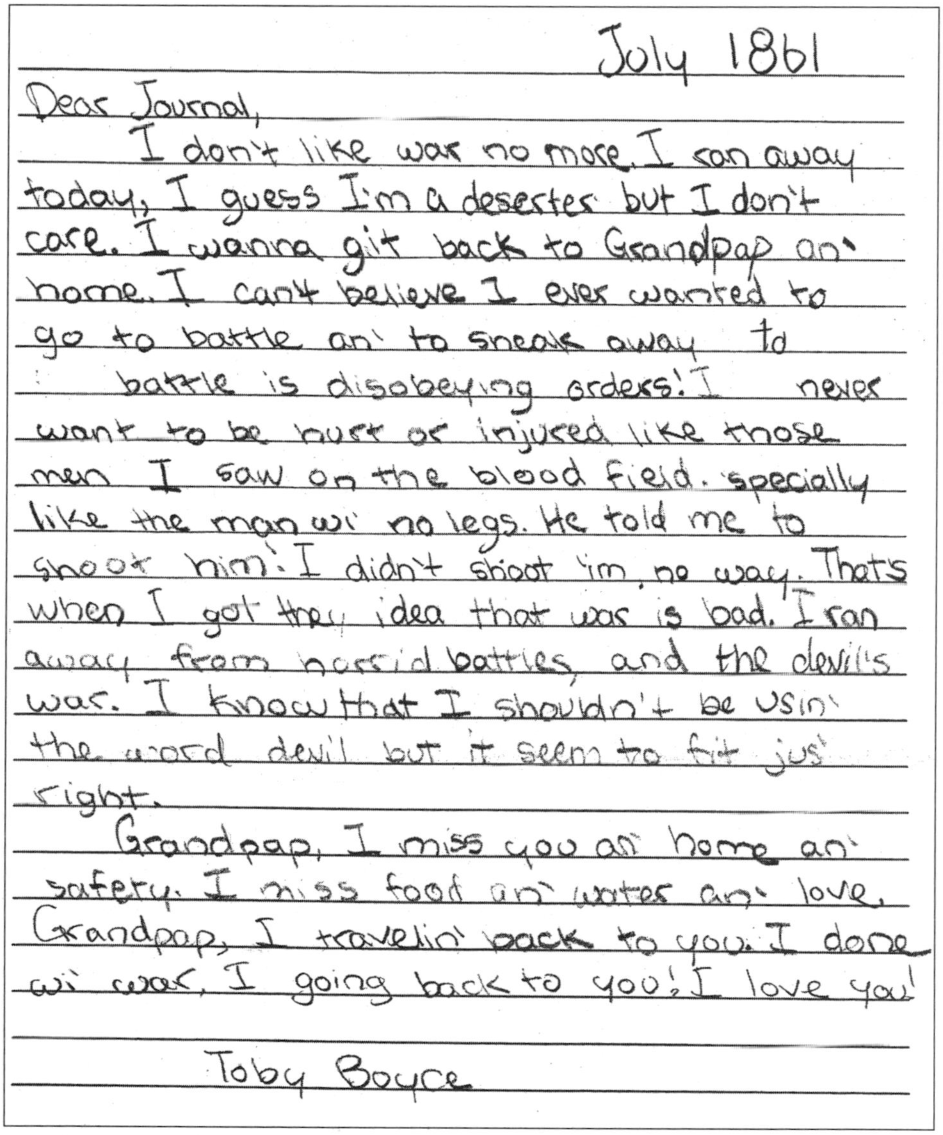

July 1861

Dear Journal,
        I don't like war no more. I ran away today. I guess I'm a deserter but I don't care. I wanna git back to Grandpap an' home. I can't believe I ever wanted to go to battle an' to sneak away to battle is disobeying orders! I never want to be hurt or injured like those men I saw on the blood field. specially like the man wi' no legs. He told me to shoot him. I didn't shoot 'im, no way. That's when I got the idea that war is bad. I ran away from horrid battles, and the devil's war. I know that I shouldn't be usin' the word devil but it seem to fit jus' right.
        Grandpap, I miss you an' home an' safety. I miss food an' water an' love. Grandpap, I travelin' back to you. I done wi' war. I going back to you! I love you!

                Toby Boyce

characters' stories that they were able to write journal entries from the characters' perspectives. (See Figure 13.9.)

Demonstrate Understanding and Share Learning
When it came time to choose research projects, these fifth graders had a wealth of topics and questions to investigate. Together, Melanie, Steve, and Nell reviewed the research process—asking questions, reading with a question in mind, taking notes, and merging thinking with the information. Students combined factual information with their voice and thinking and designed a variety of ways to share information: posters, picture books, first-person journals, newspaper articles, murals, and poems.

Researcher's Workshop

Just like these second-grade meteorologists and the fifth-grade Civil War buffs, the kids we know are dying to do research. We just need to give them time to do it. Voila! Researcher's workshop. When kids in our classrooms are engaged in research, we give them long blocks of time to read about a topic, find information, write about it, and actively use their knowledge as they teach others. Just as in reader's and writer's workshop, teachers and librarians do mini-lessons and confer with kids as they practice using a variety of resources to answer questions and find information. Our mini-lessons come from the framework that we have shared here as well as from lessons throughout this book. Kids really come to life when given a chance to do their own research on topics they choose.

A word about the role of librarians here. As with the Civil War study, it makes sense to integrally involve the librarian in topic studies from beginning to end. Librarians are coteachers, who not only provide resources and teach library skills, but also work with teachers and students in both the classroom and the library. Team teaching with the librarian ensures that research skills are merged with reading and thinking strategies so that kids read to learn. We think of librarians as the information learners-in-chief if you will, who can teach kids to find the information they need, sort and sift through it, and think critically about it. In schools where librarians and teachers collaborate, the library functions with a flexible schedule. No more dropping kids off once a week for book checkout. Teaching is the priority with teachers and librarians working together throughout the day based on children's needs.

Third graders in Carole Suderman's class were thrilled to do research projects on self-selected topics as part of researcher's workshop. Most of the kids had some experience in finding information because Carole and librarian Nell Box had been teaching reading and thinking strategies from the get-go. Nell and Carole reviewed lessons on asking questions, noticing new learning, and on note-taking to support the kids to work independently. Once kids had found just the right books and online sources on sharks, dinosaurs, geysers, or whatever, they grabbed their sticky notes and note-taking sheets and headed to a spot on the floor to have at it. Since Nell and Carole were coteaching, there were two teachers to model, guide, and confer with students, effectively cutting the class size in half.

As Carole looked up from her small-group lesson one day, she noticed kids reading and writing independently, talking and taking notes together, and sketching out designs for their posters. The room was awash in chart paper, markers, sticky notes, and books, but Carole and Nell were thrilled to see such concentrated activity. Kids are different, and not every one finished a picture-perfect poster in a matter of days. Those who needed a bit more time kept working the next week during researcher's workshop—they persevered because they were motivated to finish. And everyone shared their learning with the class and then displayed the posters in the hallway for all to see.

For an in-depth look at researcher's workshop, grab a copy of *Ladybugs, Tornadoes, and Swirling Galaxies* (2006) by Brad Buhrow and Anne Upczak Garcia. Our colleagues Brad and Anne show how kids move from personal narratives at the beginning of the year to studying curriculum topics as a class and finally to research on topics they choose. Steph's *Nonfiction Matters: Reading, Writing and Research in Grades 3–8* (1998) describes an in-depth process for independent inquiry and is loaded with practical ideas for reading and especially writing nonfiction as part of kids' own investigations. *Reading the World* (2005) also shows primary and intermediate classroom teachers collaborating with the librarian and kids who are immersed in science and social studies projects and research. Several of these resources stress how teaching and learning occur in classrooms with English language learners where differentiation is the cornerstone of instruction.

DVD

If we want classrooms brimming full of kids who are engaged, enthusiastic, and independent learners, they must have ownership in what they study and investigate. Look at Figure 13.10. Wouldn't you want to pat yourself on the back if on the last day of school you got a letter like this?

Figure 13.10 Anna's Letter to Her Teacher

Dear Mr. Buhrow,
    I need a big paper, a good gluestick, (if there's any, because I always break them,) some of this tape: with tape
and a pen. I bring it back in Fall I need to use this for my research.
                        Sincerly,
                        Anna
P.S. I will do it on 3. fish. They are in my book. I will get more books at the Boulder Public Library I will miss you!
this was for picture ──────>

FlashLight Fish

Tripod Fish

Sea Cumber

Chapter 14

Reading to Understand Textbooks

Nobody has ever come up to us clutching their textbook and raving about how much they love it. Not a single teacher has ever told us how easy their textbooks are to read and how much their kids enjoy them. Come to think of it, neither of us has ever taken a textbook off to read on summer vacation. Quite the opposite! What we frequently hear are the many obstacles that kids encounter when using textbooks and the difficulties teachers have in helping students get information from them. Why is it that so often when we assign textbook reading, we ask kids to read the chapter and answer the questions, leaving them to their own devices? Of all the text that children meet in school, textbooks are the most challenging.

We have learned that the more difficult the text, the more interactive the read must be and the more need there is to talk about it. The denser the text, the greater the need for kids to interact with it and leave tracks of their thinking. So we design instruction that is at its core interactive when teaching textbook reading. We teach kids to slow down, really think about the information, connect the new to the known, ask questions, jot thoughts and work together to summarize the information.

The American Association for the Advancement of Science recently issued a report critical of science textbooks (Nelson 1999). A study examined nine science texts and found that not one was rated "satisfactory." Middle school teachers, curriculum specialists, and professors of science education found that the textbooks "cover too many topics, fail to develop any of the topics well and offer classroom activities that are nearly useless in helping teachers and students understand important concepts." George Nelson, the former director of Project 2061, summarizes the problem: "Our students are lugging home heavy texts full of disconnected facts that neither educate nor motivate them" (1999). We don't disagree, but the reality is that kids have to read and learn from them.

Issues with Textbooks

As teachers we have many hats, and when it comes to text, materials, and resources, we need to be critical consumers. We realize that sometimes we may have no choice in this matter, because we are required to use the mandated textbook. So the suggestions here are intended to help kids navigate whatever textbook ends up in their desk. However, some are definitely better than others. If we have a voice in choosing ours, we search for "considerate text," where terms are fully explained, the content is well organized, and the relationships between the ideas are clear. When kids read text like this, learning goes smoothly. "Inconsiderate text" makes unwarranted assumptions about the reader's background knowledge, often has an overload of unfamiliar vocabulary and concepts, and contains ideas that are not fully explained. In addition, the information is often poorly organized (Armbruster 1984). It is a fact of life that we will encounter "inconsiderate text," particularly in textbooks.

And to that end, we have encountered two problems over and over again as we read and review textbooks: TMI and NEI—that's right, Too Much Information and Not Enough Information. Textbooks seem to be rife with both problems. When reading about Eleanor Roosevelt, you might find only a paragraph, but the Archduke Ferdinand of Austria gets an entire page. TMI and NEI can really make the going tough. So when there is too much information, we help kids to sort and sift it. When the text doesn't fully explain an event or an issue, we encourage them to ask why and seek out more information. And we always remind them, whatever problem they encounter when reading textbooks, talking to someone else can be a lifesaver. The truth is we are eternally on the search for JEI—just enough information—but rarely find it!

As you plan lessons with the textbook, think about the book itself as well as your kids' needs so you can anticipate and troubleshoot some of the obstacles they may encounter. We consider the following:

- Quality and accuracy of information
- Clarity of the writing and explanations
- Amount and accessibility of the information
- Logical organization on the page and within and across chapters
- Reasonable use of features, fonts, and call-outs and how they explain information
- Headings, subheadings, and other signposts that guide the reader through the text

Throughout this book we have advocated the use of a multisource, multigenre curriculum to teach content. The texts we use in the lessons include an enormous selection of magazines, picture books, trade books, primary sources, and so forth. Just take a look at the length of the appendices lest you doubt us! We view these many resources as the core of content area instruction. The problem occurs when textbooks are the single source, the fount of all information on a topic. Unfortunately, school districts and state legislatures too often have reinforced this notion by requiring a single textbook and not supporting the purchase of supplemental resources. So keep in mind textbooks are most effective when surrounded by a variety of other resources. If we want to teach kids to be serious scientists or thoughtful historians, we can't rely solely on textbooks. We need to think of the needs of our learners first and then choose resources with them in mind.

In most of our classrooms, we have textbooks for every student, and if used appropriately they can be a good reference tool. Harvey Daniels and Steven Zemelman remind us that textbooks really fall into the genre of reference-variety nonfiction (2004). Rather than reading them from stem to stern, we dip in and out of them to get specific information quickly. If we need to check a fact or a date, where else can we find that information in a matter of minutes? If we want a quick summary of the Battle of Bull Run, we consult the index of a history text. Textbooks are chock full of important and even interesting information. But kids are frequently overwhelmed just by the sheer size of their textbooks, not to mention the extent of the information between the covers.

Active Reading with Textbooks

When our goal is to "cover" the textbook, kids don't learn much. And plodding through a textbook page by page leaves everyone bored and overwhelmed with information. The challenge is to teach kids how to read textbooks and learn from them. If there were ever a need for readers to use comprehension strategies, this is it! When we teach kids to read textbooks, we share many of the active literacy practices we've described in this book: text lifting, thinking aloud, interactive reading aloud, strategic note taking, leaving tracks of thinking on sticky notes, and more. These practices incorporate all of the comprehension strategies: activating background knowledge, asking questions, inferring meaning, sorting and sifting important information, and summarizing and synthesizing the big ideas and concepts.

When text is peppered with new vocabulary, difficult concepts, and unfamiliar ideas as textbooks often are, teachers need to scaffold instruction and do what they can to support readers in constructing meaning. Unfortunately, when text is this tough, teachers often have little choice but to tell kids what's in the chapter and simply abandon any effort to have them read it. But that won't improve their reading! If students never have a chance to work through difficult, dense textbook material, they're unlikely to get better at reading it.

Kids need to merge their thinking with textbook information in the same way we have them merge their thinking in other text. It is not about just memorizing the facts. We all know that when we do that, we forget them as quickly as we "learn" them. Readers cannot just move their eyes across the page to understand. They need to think their way through the text.

We have a responsibility to provide kids with an arsenal of strategies to help them deal with and get the most out of the textbook (see Figure 14.1). As we design instruction for reading and learning from the textbook, we always consider our purpose for reading first. Is it to answer a central question? Is it to gather information about a topic? Is it to compare and contrast issues, ideas, or events? Is it to understand a process or concept? We design instruction with a clear focus, rather than asking kids to try to read and remember every detail.

Active Reading with Textbooks

- Be selective. Read smaller sections more carefully.

- Read selections in class so the teacher can guide.

- Preview the chapter—notice the features, visuals, headings, subheads, and so forth.

- Preteach new vocabulary and unfamiliar concepts.

- Slow down the rate of reading.

- Use a variety of comprehension strategies to construct meaning, including activating background knowledge, questioning, determining importance, and synthesizing information.

- Merge thinking with the information by stopping, thinking, and reacting to the section.

- Code the text with sticky notes to hold thinking.

- Take notes on think sheets—two- or three-column forms and graphic organizers to demonstrate thinking.

- Paraphrase the information.

- Become familiar with and use the index to get information quickly.

- Turn and talk about the information.

- Read and respond to the textbook with a partner.

- Discuss sections of a chapter in small groups.

- Use the jigsaw strategy to read and share sections, reporting information.

- Take on different roles and perspectives and share with the group.

We know there is a better reason to read a textbook than to simply answer the questions at the end and we want our kids to understand the concepts and topics as much as possible.

Teaching Kids to Read Textbooks

Before we delve into reading for information, we teach kids to navigate the dense text they frequently encounter in a textbook. We spend time at the beginning of the year pouring over our textbooks and talking about how we can best learn from them. We explicitly teach text format, text and visual features, and text organization. This may seem time intensive, but we have learned the hard way. If we send kids off to read textbooks without teaching them how, they don't get much out of them. We agree with kids when they say the textbook is too hard. It *is* too hard if we haven't explicitly taught them ways to read it.

Navigating the format. The way a textbook is organized has an impact on what kids learn from it. We look at the progression of ideas both in and across chapters. Textbooks include a variety of signposts that signal information. It makes sense to consider the general format of the book—how chapters are organized: the titles, the headings, the summaries. We teach kids to use indexes, glossaries, and other text organizers that help them find their way through the textbook.

Learning from text and visual features. Textbooks are chock full of call-outs and features that give information. We teach kids to notice and gain information from text features, which include bold print, italics, subheads, titles, captions, framed text, tables, and so forth. We also teach ways to notice and learn from visual features such as maps, diagrams, graphs, photographs, illustrations, and flow charts. We need to teach the purpose of these text and visual features to clarify, elaborate, and extend students' knowledge of a topic.

Previewing the chapter. We show kids how the information in a textbook is organized by previewing the chapters. We page through the entire chapter quickly. We think aloud about what we notice as we skim and scan material. If a section begins with a question in bold print, we encourage kids to read with that question in mind. We notice the writing structure. Textbook paragraphs often begin with a topic sentence and conclude with a summation, not always the case but often. We encourage students to look closely at the features. As they preview the text, they get a sense of what they'll be reading about and what they can anticipate.

Once we have taught ways to navigate the textbook and have given kids some time to get acquainted with it, our instruction shifts to teaching kids to learn, understand, and remember the content. We design lessons that incorporate reading comprehension strategies as well as some of the active literacy practices listed in the previous section. Many of these lessons are described in Part II of this book and can be easily adapted to textbook reading. Here are a few basic lessons out of many possibilities that we use over and over again when teaching kids to read textbooks.

Vocabulary and Concept Lessons
- Front-load the content by activating background knowledge about the concepts. Have kids turn and talk about some of these concepts and record their understanding to share with the class.
- Preteach a very few unfamiliar concepts that are essential to understanding the chapter. *Few* is the operative word here. Don't overload kids with unfamiliar vocabulary. Focus on a few important concepts.
- Infer the meaning of unfamiliar words. Teach kids to use context clues to sort out meaning. (See "Inferring the Meaning of Unfamiliar Words" in Chapter 9.)
- Talk to a partner about what a word means. When kids meet unfamiliar words or concepts, we ask them to turn and talk to construct meaning.
- Create picture dictionaries of important words or concepts. Kids write a short definition of a word and illustrate the meaning to better remember it.
- Create word walls of important concepts. Put picture dictionary entries on a content word wall so the kids can refer to them when needed.

Note-taking Lessons
- Stop, think, and react on sticky notes to notice and wonder about new information. (See Chapter 6 for lessons on monitoring comprehension.)

- Copy small sections of the text to practice note taking. Underline important information on the copy and write about it in the margins. (See the lesson in Chapter 11, "Paraphrase to Summarize Expository Text.")
- Use a two-column think sheet labeled Notes or Facts/My Thinking. Kids write information from the text on the left and their merged thinking on the right. (See "Reading with a Question in Mind" in Chapter 8.)
- Use FQR think sheets to merge thinking with the information. Kids notice and record the factual information, but also ask questions about it and respond. (See "Using FQR Think Sheets" in Chapter 10.)
- Use Topic/Details/Response charts to show how details support a bigger idea. (See the lesson in Chapter 10, "Sifting the Topic from the Details.")

Summarizing and Synthesizing Lessons

- Read to get the gist. Kids read a section and paraphrase it in their own words on sticky notes.
- Target key information. After kids have read a section and taken notes, they look back at their notes and pull out the most important information.
- Read with a question in mind. When we read with a question in mind, we sort and sift information related to that question. This is reading with a specific purpose in mind. (See "Reading with a Question in Mind" in Chapter 8.)
- Distinguishing between what the reader thinks is important and the author's big idea. Kids need to consider what most strikes them about the information and then think about what the writer most wants them to take away from the text. (See "Important to Whom?" in Chapter 10.)
- TMI—Too Much Information. When kids meet a text that is packed with information, they need to sort and sift to pick out what is most important. We teach them to read the first and last sentences of a paragraph or the first and last paragraphs of a section to discern what to remember since important information is often revealed here. We have them turn and talk about this because two heads are always better than one.
- NEI—Not Enough Information. When the text has insufficient information, kids work together to talk about ways to fill in the gaps in their understanding. They may ask questions, draw inferences, or seek out other resources to find additional information.

The best resource we know on reading and effectively using textbooks is Harvey Daniels and Steve Zemelman's *Subjects Matter: Every Teacher's Guide to Content-Area Reading.* They suggest five ways to use textbooks more effectively. These suggestions sum up in a few words what we all need to remember as we teach with textbooks. We have captured the gist here but encourage you to pick up a copy of the book yourself.

1. *Have empathy.* You know the information in the textbook but kids don't.
2 *Help kids get started.* Front-load our teaching so kids can understand the text.
3. *Don't leave kids alone with their textbooks.* Make sure kids work in pairs, groups, and teams to discuss and sort out the ideas.
4. *Choose wisely.* Assignments should be selective and strategic.
5. *Supplement richly.* Textbooks are no longer the sole source for content learning. Kids need a wide range of text for content area reading. (2004)

Chapter 15

The Genre of Test Reading

Test reading is a genre unto itself. Think about it. Did you ever pick up a copy of the newspaper and have to answer ten fill-in-the-blank questions about the lead article or take a quiz on a Thanksgiving dinner recipe? Unlikely. The last time you probably had to answer a list of questions was to renew your driver's license, take the SATs, or take a final for a graduate college course. The only time adults have to answer a list of questions at the end of a section is when we take a test of some sort. For kids, however, test reading has taken on greater importance than ever before. "No Child Left *Untested*," as we have come to call the federal law, requires tests every year in grades three through eight, with many more on the way.

Frankly, we are concerned about the ever-increasing amount of time and energy spent on testing and test preparation. An article in *Bloomberg Markets*, "How Test Companies Fail Your Kids," which analyzes the effects of the eye-popping $2.8 billion testing and test prep industry reports, "The US is in a testing frenzy. Students in the 92,816 American public schools will take at least 45 million standardized reading and math exams this year. That will jump to 56 million in the 2007/08 school year, when states begin testing science as part of the 2002 federal No Child Left Behind Law" (Glovin and Evans 2006). One conclusion the article reaches is that "With the stakes for making the grade so high for so many, errors by test companies have dramatic consequences" (2006). From 2003 to 2006 scoring errors affected literally hundreds of thousands of students in the United States. Even Tester-in-Chief Roderick Paige, former U.S. education secretary, expressed concern that testing may not be done accurately and competently (Glovin and Evans 2006). These are staggering statistics, and they don't even begin to describe what concerns us most: the monumental effects on instruction as a result of NCLB and its focus on testing and test preparation.

David Pearson's prescient warning "Never send a test out to do a curriculum's job" (2005) is more important than ever. When the primary purpose of education is scoring high on tests, it is easy for the test and test prep to become the default curriculum. Now more than ever we are convinced that the best way to develop proficiency in reading, including test reading, is by reading widely and extensively every day, responding to reading by talking and writing and receiving explicit instruction in reading strategies. We continue to advocate engaged active literacy every day in classrooms around the country.

But we are realists; we know these tests are not going anywhere fast. And we understand that proficient readers have a better shot at scoring well on standardized tests than less developed readers. We also know that being a good reader does not a great test taker make. Anyone who is reluctant to shout their SAT scores from the rafters knows what we are talking about. Taking a test requires some skills and strategies that are quite distinct from the ongoing reading we do every day. Since reading is about purpose and once a year the purpose of reading is to pass the test, we teach the genre of test reading right before the annual test. We do not teach test prep all year. We begin to prepare kids to take the test about two to three weeks ahead of the test date (Zemelman, Daniels, and Hyde 2005).

During this time, our mini-lessons focus on modeling and thinking about how we approach test reading. We model our thinking as we read and consider a test item, and we engage kids in guided practice for a variety of test-taking strategies that will help them feel more comfortable and prepared. We teach test format, pacing, key words for recognizing a variety of test questions, signal words to anticipate what's to come, and general guidelines for reading through the test and choosing the correct answers. This chapter will focus on some hints and suggestions we have adapted and developed for helping kids take the test. But first let's look at some of the most effective things we can do all year long to build terrific readers as well as better test takers.

Building Good Readers and Test Takers All Year Long

Our work is all about helping kids become better readers and thinkers in every context across the school day and throughout the year. For instance, we know that a great deal of prior knowledge and exposure to a wide range of topics gives the reader as well as the test taker a leg up. So we focus a good deal of our instruction on activating and building background knowledge when reading. (See Chapter 7.)

Additionally, we know that taking these tests requires stamina. So we build in time for kids to read daily in a range of text—fiction and nonfiction, short and long, accessible and more challenging—to help them build stamina and perseverance. We also know that all types of reading require thinking, so teaching comprehension strategies all year will give kids an advantage not only in reading but on the test as well. And there is ample research to back this up. As Trabasso and Bouchard (2002) argue, there is strong scientific evidence that teaching comprehension strategies in a classroom context improves student performance on standardized comprehension tests. See our section titled "Research That Supports Comprehension" in Chapter 2.

The ongoing practices that follow help our kids to read and think, preparing them first to be better readers, but also better test takers.

Build in Lots of Time Every Day for Kids to Read, Just Read

"Reading volume—the amount that students read in and out of school—significantly affects the development of reading rate and fluency, general knowledge of the world, overall verbal ability and last, but not least, academic achievement" (Shefelbine 1999). Simply put, we get better at reading by reading, and the more we read, the better we get. So we build in lots of time for kids to read in school every day. There is no better way to build background knowledge in school than to read broadly. Reading extensively also builds stamina, which readers really need when they meet challenging text, as well as when they sit for the standardized tests. And in terms of acquiring vocabulary, *you don't need a good vocabulary to read, you get a good vocabulary by reading.* Extensive reading builds vocabulary, which is critical in life as well as on the test!

Teach Comprehension Strategies

We teach our kids to think and apply comprehension strategies in every reading context—real-world reading, focused content reading, textbook reading, and test reading. When readers flexibly apply comprehension strategies, they are more likely to bridge the background knowledge gap that so often derails meaning. For instance, if they are able to infer the meaning of an unfamiliar word, they can construct meaning and move on. If they are able to think about what they know to make sense of new information, they can better grasp the content. Reading strategically is imperative to becoming a good reader as well as a decent test taker.

Flood the Room with Nonfiction

No genre gives us a better window into the world and everything in it than nonfiction. It is simply the most accessible genre. Even if readers can't read the words, they can usually get some meaning from the text and visual features. No genre is more effective at building knowledge than nonfiction, since it covers such a span of topics and ideas. We flood the room with an array of compelling nonfiction that captures kids with stunning photographs, vivid illustrations, colorful diagrams, and so forth. As they read nonfiction, they build background about a plethora of content and topics. We also know that the reading on many standardized tests is predominantly nonfiction. Who knows, our kids might get lucky and end up with a thunderstorm test passage after having just read Steven Kramer's *Lightning!* Flood the room with nonfiction to build background, gain knowledge, and have some fun along the way.

Teach the Elements and Features of a Particular Genre

We teach the elements and features of a particular genre so kids become more familiar with the genre, better understand it, and can anticipate what is to come. In fiction, we teach about such things as character development, inferring themes, and noticing conflict so that readers have a better underlying understanding of the genre and of what is going on in the narrative. We teach readers to notice the white space in poetry as well as to infer the meaning of metaphoric language. We teach that nonfiction reading is reading to learn, that it comes packed with text and visual features that aid understanding if we pay attention and think about them. Text features such as titles and subheads give us an idea of what the piece is about and what is most important. When we read daily as well as when we read for the test, we can get a lot of information about the passage by scanning the features. We teach the elements and features of a genre so kids will have a better understanding when they meet them in novels, trade books, articles, as well as on the test.

Teach Signal Words

Teaching signal words that help readers navigate the text is essential in both real reading and test reading. Signal words cue readers to pay attention to what's coming up. These words signal a change in thinking, a contrast, or a similar relationship between ideas. As kids read text, they will encounter a wide variety of signal words. Point out signal words you come across while reading, share them with the kids, and co-construct an anchor chart titled Signal Words/Purpose for display in the classroom. Encourage kids to be on the lookout for signal words in their own reading. As they notice some, they can add the new signal words to the anchor chart. Soon they will become quite adept at paying attention to a signal word and reading more thoughtfully because of it. This is an important real-reading strategy with a test-reading bonus!

Signal Words	Purpose
Surprisingly	Be prepared to expect the unexpected
Importantly	Signals importance; stop and pay attention
On the other hand	Signals a change
Before	
After	
Next	
Finally	
Then	All show sequence
But	Signals a change to come
However	Prepare to change your thinking
As opposed to	Signals a contrast
Likewise	Signals a similarity
Consequently	Signals a result/cause and effect
In conclusion	Synthesizes the information
In sum	Sums up the information

Test-Reading Tips

There are a number of suggestions that can be helpful when preparing kids to take standardized tests. When we came to write the following sections on test reading, we looked back at what we had written on the topic in *The Comprehension Toolkit: Language and Lessons for Active Literacy* (2005a) and realized there was very little we would want to change or add. So here you have it, our tips for test reading, some categories of questions, and a sample test item. You may see small revisions here and there, but we have left much of what follows intact from *The Comprehension Toolkit*.

Building strong readers is still the best test preparation. Our reading workshops and literacy blocks do not come to a halt right before test day. We continue our focus on explicit comprehension instruction and practice in the weeks before high-stakes tests. We recognize, however, that in addition to thoughtful reading instruction and building in time for kids to read, it makes sense to practice test reading and responding with short passages that are similar to those kids will encounter on the test. As you have seen, we do not advocate the use of fill-in-the-blank worksheets in this book. Instead we use think sheets—sticky notes on a page, two- and three-column forms, margin writing on text, graphic organizers, and so forth—to encourage responses and hold thinking. However, when we teach test reading, we use worksheets that resemble the form of the state test and we model how we approach them, read them, and make decisions about them. Then we give kids some time to practice themselves.

But our test reading lessons are truly *mini*-lessons, a few minutes of modeling and several more minutes of practicing. We spend no more than fifteen to twenty minutes a few days a week, two to three weeks before the test, teaching and learning about test reading and test format. When we finish with our modeling and their guided practice around test reading, kids continue reading in a wide range of texts and genres as they do every day in the reading workshop.

So here are some practical test-taking strategies that will help our kids navigate standardized tests and build some confidence as they face them. A confident student is one who goes into a test knowing they will be familiar with whatever awaits them on the test. It's our job to ensure there are no nasty surprises!

To be sure, this section does not address short constructed responses, writing tests, and so on, but rather offers general advice regarding multiple-choice standardized reading tests. With that in mind, we urge you to get up close and personal with your particular test. Seek out and study released items and follow the format explicitly or these test-reading tips could be a waste of time. We share a number of suggestions here, many more than you could reasonably introduce in the recommended time frame. Some of these tips are general and have the goal of promoting a positive attitude when it comes to test taking. Others are more specific. Based on what you know about your state test, we suggest you pick and choose the tips that are best suited to your purpose.

Build Confidence

Build students' confidence through thoughtful practice. Seize every opportunity during regular instruction to point out that the thinking kids are doing is exactly what they'll need on the upcoming tests. Provide additional opportunities for kids to practice under authentic test conditions. Thoughtful practice builds confidence. If they feel prepared on test day, they will feel more relaxed and are likely to score higher.

Justify answers. During test practice, teach kids to explain and justify their answers. Encourage them to talk to a partner to think about and articulate why they answered a question a certain way. Invite them to share strategies they used to get to the right answer. This will build their confidence for when they actually take the test. Confident test takers are more successful test takers

"Beat the Test." Turn the test-reading and test-taking experience into a challenge, a competition of sorts to "beat the test." We want kids to have a "can-do" attitude. Get kids fired up about the prospect of psyching out the test.

Know the Test Format

Know test rules. Know every detail about your test. Know in advance whether kids can write on the test and show their work. If so, encourage them to practice this way. Know the time constraints, if any. State tests all vary. So make sure you familiarize your kids with any other quirky test rules that you know about your particular test.

Review the design and layout of the test. Share sample tests on the overhead projector. Discuss the layout and design and share anything you notice. Have kids practice with similar materials. Being comfortable with format is half the battle.

Learn the test-question vocabulary. Model and share the different types of questions that are found in test items, and make sure that kids understand the difference and what each one is asking them to do. (See the section "Test-Question Categories" further on in this chapter.)

Become familiar with the answer-sheet format. Practice reviewing and filling out the answer sheet before kids take the test. If they need to work on a separate bubble sheet, show them how to match the question number with a bubble number. Most published tests, however, have kids fill in the bubble right on the test. If that's the case with your test, make sure you show them how to do that.

Work within time constraints. If your test is timed, have kids practice test items in a timed situation. Model how you approach and work on a test passage that is timed. Point out how you read the questions first and don't work on one question for too long. Then give kids a chance to practice this. You might have them work through some timed passages three or four times before they take the actual test to help them get a sense of time management.

Get the Big Picture Quickly

Look for and carefully read directions. When practicing, have kids restate the directions in their own words to make sure they understand them and will be familiar with them on test day.

Read the title of the passage. It may give the test taker a sense of the big idea. If it doesn't seem to help , encourage kids not to dwell on it and move on.

Skim and scan. Teach kids how to skim and scan quickly to get an idea of what the passage is about, noticing the genre, the topic, the length, and so forth.

Check out the features quickly. Teach kids to scan the text and visual features to get information. Remind them that some questions may be answered by information from the text and visual features. Have them check out the sub-heads to get an idea of where information can be found.

Identify the genre. Have kids consider whether the passage is nonfiction, fiction, poetry, and so on. Teach important aspects of each genre and how the reading requirements differ. For example, if the passage is nonfiction, they will likely be asked to pick out the most important information; if it's a poem, they may have to infer.

Review the Questions

Read the questions first. Teach your kids to keep the questions in mind as they read. When they are able to answer one, remind them to fill in the bubble right away, rather than finishing the entire passage before answering.

Underline key words or phrases in the questions. If it is allowed, encourage students to underline key words or phrases in the questions. It is easier to notice those words when they come across them in a passage if they have coded them earlier. And students just might find that phrase or word will answer a question.

Read the Passage and Answer the Questions

Think about what you know on the topic but concentrate primarily on what's in the text. We walk a fine line when it comes to using our background knowledge as we take standardized tests. It is always useful to bring some background knowledge to the text. However, we teach kids not to rely too heavily on what they already know, because they need to draw on the text for their answers. In some states, the answers actually must be contained within the text. So know your state test. But remind kids that thinking about what they know and connecting it to new information will generally make a difference in reading and understanding.

Pay close attention to the first paragraph. Important information is often included in the first paragraph of a passage. We may find some hints of the big idea of the passage here, so encourage your kids to pay close attention to it.

Read the end of the passage carefully. Teach kids that the last paragraph often contains a big idea or a conclusion. Remind them to slow down their reading and think carefully about the end of the passage.

Reread to clarify understanding. Teach your kids to reread when they have lost meaning or to find an answer. Rereading is a particularly useful strategy if your test is untimed. In a timed test, kids need to be careful about too much rereading.

Don't overinfer. Have kids practice answering questions with inferences that are supported with evidence from the text. Let them know that they need to find clues in the text to support their answer, rather than merely guess, which is, of course, not the same as inferring.

Attend to signal words. Teach the kids that some words signal us to pay attention to the text at that point, words like *surprisingly, sometimes, most importantly, in conclusion,* and so forth. (See the signal word list previously in this chapter.)

Watch for tricky "distractor" answers. Test publishers include answers to questions that seem reasonable but are actually placed there to distract kids from a better answer. These distractors often appeal to kids, because they make sense and even sound correct. Distractor answers may feature details that capture children's attention, luring them away from the correct answers. Distractor answers are often the ones that the test taker may think seems most important, even though the test writer has a bigger idea in mind for the answers. Practice picking out these distractors and discuss how and why they are tricky.

Eliminate answers you know to be incorrect. Teach kids to use the process of elimination and cross out unreasonable answers. Have your students practice eliminating answers they know to be incorrect, but remind them to be certain of these before they eliminate them. Explain to them that if they eliminate incorrect answers right away, there will be fewer to choose from and therefore the question will be easier to answer correctly.

Recognize the difference between literal and inferential questions. Teach kids to differentiate between literal questions that are answered directly in the text and those questions that require inferential thinking. (See the section "Test-Question Categories" in this chapter.) Encourage them to keep the distinction in mind as they read.

Keep track of answers in relation to bubbles. If your test requires a separate bubble sheet, teach kids to check their bubbled answers every so often to make sure the numbers match.

Stay calm. Share with your kids that it is normal to feel a little nervous before the test but that these tests are not the end of the world. Tomorrow will still come, and life will still go on once the test is over. For those kids that you suspect may really freak out, show them how to take in deep breaths and let them out slowly to relax. Teach some yoga exercises, a great idea even if they never had to take a test!

Keep Moving

Watch the time. In timed tests, pacing is particularly important. Teach kids to remember to think about the time constraint so they don't lose track of time. Remind them to check the clock occasionally to notice how much time remains. If your test is untimed, this is something you don't have to worry about. Lucky you!

Don't stop. It's easy for kids to lose focus, particularly if the test is difficult for them. Remind them to keep at it. This is where your work on stamina—having kids read daily for a good amount of time all year—will really pay off.

Avoid spending too much time on one question. Teach kids to skip questions that confuse them and come back later if time remains.

Focus thinking, and don't let attention wander. Remind your students to stay focused even in difficult circumstances. Tell them that taking a test is about persistence and talk about what that word means. Also help them to remember that the test won't go on forever even though sometimes it seems that way. Staying focused is central to performing well on these tests.

The two-pass system. Teach your kids to try to go through the test two times, that is, take two passes at the test. On the first pass, encourage them to answer all of the easy questions. Let them know that if they come to a tough question they can't answer, they shouldn't waste a lot of time worrying about it but should just skip it and go on. Then take a closer look at it on the second pass (Scholastic News 2006).

Review the Answers

Use extra time to check over the test. If your test is timed and time remains after students have finished, teach them to go back and check their answers. If your test is untimed, still encourage them to go back and check their answers before they turn in their test.

Check bubble sheets. If your test has separate bubble answer sheets, remind kids to look them over to make sure they have matched each question to the correct bubbled answer. It is easy to get off track on these forms. And for those of you whose test has the answers right on the page, encourage kids to go back and review answers to make sure have filled them all in and marked them clearly. And make sure you know the rules about going back and changing answers, erasing, crossing out, whatever the test parameters are.

Review confusing questions. Teach kids to go back when they have finished and review any answers that confused them. They may have a better idea at this point in time.

Test-Question Categories

Reading tests have predictable kinds of questions, and each type requires a unique approach. Here are some of the most common question types and some ideas for helping kids deal with them.

Vocabulary Questions

Questions About Specific Words

- Which is the best meaning for the word _____?
- The word _____ in the story means . . .
- What is a synonym for _____?
- Which word means the same as _____?

Teaching Suggestions

- Teach kids to read the entire sentence to figure out the meaning of the word in context. Have them use the context to infer a general meaning of the word. Remind them to look back to previous sentences or read ahead for clues in the text that help infer the meaning of the word.

- What is an antonym for _____?
- Which word means the opposite of _____?
- The word _____ in this story means about the same as . . .
- What does the word _____ in the (_____) paragraph mean?

- Have students match parts of speech—nouns to nouns, verbs to verbs.
- Teach words like *synonym, antonym, opposite,* and *similar,* so kids will be prepared when they meet them on the test.
- Sometimes the definition of a word appears right in the sentence along with the test word. Teach kids to look and see if the definition is nearby.
- Teach suffixes and prefixes, and teach kids to look at the parts of the word. For example, if the word *reignite* comes up and kids know that *re* means to do something again and they know that *ignite* means to light, they can deduce that *reignite* means to relight.
- Remind them to eliminate definitions that they know do not fit the meaning of the unfamiliar word and choose the closest match.

Literal Questions

Questions Whose Answers May Be Found in the Text
- What . . .
- When . . .
- Which . . .
- Where . . .
- How . . .
- Questions about sequence: for example, Which of these events happened first?
- Items that ask for objective information from the passage: for example, Glaciers form when . . .

Teaching Suggestions
- Teach kids to skim and scan the text, matching the words of the question to specific words in the text.
- Have them find the section of text that refers specifically to the words in the question and scan that part.
- Teach them to overview several paragraphs to notice events or steps in a sequence.
- Teach kids to visualize the passage in their mind. Their mental images can help the reader remember details that may answer literal questions in the piece.
- Remind kids to eliminate answers they know to be untrue.

Summarizing and Synthesizing Questions

Questions That Require Identifying Important Ideas and Pulling Information Together
- Which statement best summarizes . . .
- What is the main idea?
- What is the main reason . . .
- What is the most important idea in this article?
- What is the article/story mostly about?
- What is the article/story mainly about?
- This article (section) mainly describes . . .
- The story/article was written mainly in order to . . .
- What is another title for this story/article?
- What is another good name for this story/article?

Teaching Suggestions
- Teach kids to use the determining importance strategy to think about a big idea or theme that is central to the story or article. (See Chapter 10.)
- Remind kids that the "mostly about, mainly about" questions require them to read for the gist.
- Teach kids that when they are asked to identify the main idea, they need to ask themselves what the passage is mostly about. They should look through the passage to see how many times a word is repeated as a clue to what it is mostly about.
- Explain that distractor answers often answer questions that are the most interesting to kids but not the most important to the test writer. Remind them that when they are taking a test, the author's big idea is what is most important whether it matters to the reader or not. Have them carefully consider distractor answers and eliminate any that don't relate to the big idea. (See the lesson in Chapter 10, "Important to Whom?")

- Teach kids to screen out their own personal opinions and stick to the information in the passage.
- Teach kids that the most important information is often revealed in the first or last paragraph of the passage and that the most important information in a paragraph is often revealed in the first or last sentence of the paragraph.
- Kaplan suggests that the wrong answers are often actual facts or details from the passage. They can be appealing options, so kids need to know the difference between a main idea and a supporting detail. "Remind kids that just because a piece of information appears in the passage doesn't make it the main idea" (Johnson and Johnson 2000). Kids who have practiced sorting and sifting details from big ideas as discussed in the Determining Importance chapter should be able to eliminate ancillary information.
- As always, encourage them to use the process of elimination.

Inferential Questions

Questions That Require Deduction or Drawing Conclusions from Text Information

- Why . . .
- What can you conclude . . .
- What can you generalize . . .
- What lesson does this teach?
- What is the problem?
- What lesson did the characters learn?
- Which of these is most likely true about . . .
- From this story/article you can probably guess . . .
- What is probably true . . .
- How does the author feel about . . .
- Which of these is also an appropriate title for . . .
- After reading this, what will probably happen next?
- Questions about characters actions, motives, feelings.

Teaching Suggestions

- Inferential questions require readers to come up with answers that are not explicitly found in the text. Teach kids to merge their thinking with text clues to infer an answer. (See Chapter 9, "Visualizing and Inferring," for more lessons on how to teach kids to infer.)
- Have them search for evidence in the text to support an answer they think might be correct and underline the clues, assuming they can write on the test.
- Teach them to use information in the text to support inferences about the characters, their feelings, their behaviors, and so forth, but don't overly rely on background knowledge.
- Teach kids to merge their thinking with clues in the text to determine the author's message or purpose in writing the piece.

For further information, we suggest you pick up a copy of *A Teacher's Guide to Standardized Reading Tests: Knowledge Is Power*, by Lucy Calkins, Kate Montgomery, Beverly Falk, and Donna Santman (1998), which describes a thoughtful approach to test reading. And to keep ourselves abreast of what is going on in the testing world, we frequently go online to www.fairtest.org, the website of The National Center for Fair & Open Testing (FairTest), whose mission is to advance "quality education and equal opportunity by promoting fair, open, valid, and educationally beneficial evaluations of students, teachers, and schools." They publish and share thought-provoking articles in the monthly *FairTest Examiner*, a free online email newsletter. Check it out.

Thinking Through a Test

In this section, we have a sample test that we have marked up and annotated with our thinking. We could model with this sample test in one of our test-reading mini-lessons. We would place it on an overhead and read and reason through it, showing our kids the kinds of thinking we do as we read the test. Our point here is to give our kids an idea of how we approach standardized tests and how we think through them (Harvey and Goudvis 2005a).

We hope that some of these test-reading tips and practices will give your kids a few helpful strategies and a dose of confidence when they sit down to take a test. But let's not forget what really matters. As Ruth Simmons, the president of Brown University, reminds us, "The purpose of education is to nourish your soul and transform your life" (2001), not merely to score high. And we mustn't ever lose sight of that.

Figure 15.1 Sample of How to Think Through a Test

Thinking Through a Test: "Natural Disasters"
Sample Test

Our Thinking

Get the big picture quickly.

- We review the title and subheads to get a general idea of what the article is about.

Review the questions.

- We read through all of the questions so that as we read the article, we can read with questions in mind.
- We underline key words and phrases in the questions that we think we might find in the article.
- We notice that three of the questions, **Questions 3, 4, and 6,** are about big ideas and conclusions, so the answers might not be right there in the passage. We'll probably answer those after we finish reading the whole article.

Read the text and answer the questions.

- We quickly read the first two paragraphs of the article, remembering that we noticed a question about a specific word, *devastation*, in **Question 1.** We circle the word and attempt to answer the question. If we can't answer it, we move on.
- We put the number of the tornado question, **Question 2,** next to the tornado section of the text. We recognize this is a literal question. We skim this section to see if we can match the words "Most tornado deaths are caused by . . ." We try to find those exact words and answer the question.
- We keep on reading, moving through each section fairly quickly. When we come to the phrase "deadliest of storms in the United States," we slow down,

Natural Disasters

Humans seem to have an instinct to control things but nature keeps some things out of our reach. Natural disasters make no distinction between the types of people or the areas of the world they affect—rich, poor, seaside, mountains, congested Asian cities, or the wide open American "bread basket" are all subject to a possible natural disaster.

What are "natural disasters"? They are natural events that cause destruction often of enormous proportions. The most dramatic ones include tornadoes, hurricanes, earthquakes, volcanoes, and tsunamis but wildfires, blizzards, droughts, mudslides, and landslides can also cause devastation to humans and the environment.

Tornadoes
Approximately 1000 tornadoes form each year in the United States. The least-damaging tornado packs winds of 70-plus miles per hour. A "killer tornado" is defined as one that has winds in excess of 205mph lasting over an hour. Luckily, only 2% of all tornadoes fall into the "killer" category, but they account for 70% of all tornado-related deaths. Most tornado deaths are caused by flying debris. A tornado "watch" means the conditions are right for a tornado to pop up in your area; a tornado "warning" means an actual tornado has been sighted by radar.

Hurricanes
Even though hurricanes can usually be tracked better than tornadoes, they rank as the deadliest of storms in the United States and cause widespread damage. Hurricanes are tropical storms that form in a counterclockwise direction around an "eye" and have winds of over 75mph. The strongest hurricane is called a "category 5" with winds in excess of 155mph and an ocean storm surge of as much as 18 feet. An average of six hurricanes form in the Atlantic each year but not all reach land.

Volcanoes
Volcanoes give us one distinct advantage over other natural disasters: We know where they are located—with a few exceptions! There are four main kinds of volcanoes: cinder cones, composite, shield, and lava domes. Some of our most beautiful mountains, like Mount Rainer in Washington and Mount Fuji in Japan are volcanoes. In 1963, a volcano erupted off the southwest coast of Iceland and created the newest land mass on Earth, the one-square-mile island called Surtsey Island.

Earthquakes
When the earth's crust moves, it causes vibrations we call earthquakes. Earthquakes often happen along a "fault lines," which is a place in the earth's crust where two pieces of crust have slipped past each other. Like many natural disasters, the earthquake itself is often not as vastly damaging as the other events that earthquakes trigger, such as tsunamis and landslides.

Tsunamis
The giant waves called tsunamis are caused by a few different natural events such as crashing meteorites and pieces of glaciers falling into the sea. But tsunamis most commonly tend to be the offspring of earthquakes.

However, in 1883, a tsunami was caused by the eruption of a volcano, Krakatoa, and killed at least 34,000 people.

The 2004 Asian tsunami that killed over 150,000 people in several Asian countries was caused by an earthquake resulting from a natural process known as "subduction." Deep below the ocean, separations in the earth's crust, called "plates," shifted. This resulted in a deep ocean wave that, by the time it reached shore, had picked up height and speed and became a tsunami.

remembering the same phrase in a question. We recognize a literal question and match the words in the text to **Question 5** to try to answer it.

- We continue reading and slow down when we get to the last paragraph. We know the information in the last section can be important because it often contains a synthesis of the bigger ideas in the article.

- Now that we've read the whole article, we review the three questions we haven't answered. We tackle **Question 3** first. We recognize this as a summarizing/synthesizing question. So we eliminate the first answer, (a) tornadoes, hurricanes, and earthquakes, because we know the article is about much more than those three types of extreme weather. We know that (b) is a strong possibility because it is what the article is about, but we consider the other alternatives to make sure it is the best answer. We eliminate (d) because there is no evidence at all that human beings can control the weather. This leaves (c), which is true, but the article really isn't about this topic and the question asks, "What is the article mainly about?" We decide that (b) is indeed the best answer.

- Reading **Question 4,** an inferential question, we see that each of the answer choices suggests a reason behind the inference. We eliminate (a) and (b) because the reasons aren't logical: most weather doesn't happen at weather stations, and the article says nothing about altitude increasing danger. We keep (c) as a possibility because Washington state does have volcanic mountains, but so do a lot of other places. When we read (d) we quickly check the text; the hurricane, volcano, and tsunami sections all mention ocean origins, so (d) seems to have the most text evidence behind it.

- To make sure we understand **Question 6,** an inferential question that asks us to draw a conclusion, we read the answer options carefully. We eliminate (b) because natural disasters occur

all over the world. We have learned (d) is not correct and we eliminate (c) because we can't always predict earthquakes and tornadoes. So (a) is the strongest answer.

Review the answers.

- If we have time, we go back and check to make sure we've answered all our questions, recheck each answer, and make our answers match up with the appropriate items.

Early Warning

We haven't managed to control our weather. But what humans have managed to do is create devices to monitor things like volcanoes and tornadoes. This allows people to be able to get as much warning as possible so they have time to protect their property and themselves.

Some impending disasters allow for more warning than others—hurricanes and blizzards, for instance, usually take a long enough time to form that people in the path can get several days of warning. These storms can unexpectedly change course or build into much more or less of a storm than predicted, but for the most part people can be forewarned.

Events like tornadoes and tsunamis can form in a matter of minutes, providing little chance for warning. However, even these events are being better predicted by scientists who are constantly monitoring the atmosphere and the ocean floor looking for hints of a coming tornado or tsunami.

---

1. In paragraph 2, the word <u>devastation</u> means_____.
   - Ⓐ large proportion
   - Ⓑ dramatic forest fires
   - Ⓒ human failure
   - ● enormous destruction

2. Most <u>tornado deaths</u> are caused by_____.
   - Ⓐ lightning
   - Ⓑ the funnel cloud
   - ● flying debris
   - Ⓓ hail

3. What is the article mainly about?
   - Ⓐ Tornadoes, hurricanes, and earthquakes
   - ● Natural disasters that cause enormous destruction all over the world
   - Ⓒ Scientists' ability to predict natural disasters
   - Ⓓ Human beings controlling the weather to avoid loss of life and property

4. Based on the article, where would you be most likely to find extreme and dangerous weather?
   - Ⓐ at a weather station because that's where the most weather happens
   - Ⓑ on a mountain because altitude increases danger
   - Ⓒ in Washington State because there is evidence of volcanic activity
   - ● near the ocean because many natural disasters seem to start there

5. Which type of natural disaster ranks as the <u>deadliest</u> in the United States?
   - Ⓐ Volcanoes
   - Ⓑ Tornadoes
   - ● Hurricanes
   - Ⓓ Earthquakes

6. What can you conclude from the article?
   - ● Even though we are better able to predict natural disasters and storms, we still can't control the weather.
   - Ⓑ Natural disasters occur most frequently in the United States.
   - Ⓒ We can predict when tornadoes and earthquakes are going to happen.
   - Ⓓ Natural disasters hurt people but not the environment.

Afterword

Michael Lynton (2000), the CEO of Sony Pictures, has said, "The book is the greatest interactive medium of all time. You can underline it, write in the margins, fold down a page, skip ahead. And you can take it anywhere." And this from the guy who makes more joysticks than anyone on the planet. We are not sure our kids know this. We are not even sure their parents understand this. Given our increasingly plugged-in world of computers, IPods, video games and YouTube, reading is at risk. We're half expecting to see books appear on the endangered species list.

The truth is books are nothing without readers. When readers interact with text, a good read is as active as a fast-moving video game. Books and reading are every bit as enticing as roller coasters and sporting events. Teachers know this. They come up to us with dog-eared copies of novels brimming with sticky notes, tabs, and margin scrawls, recounting stories of how their own participation in book clubs has transformed them as readers and as teachers of reading. They tell us that reading great books with their kids has spawned a community of learners and how reading professional books has changed their teaching. Now *that's* active literacy for you!

Reading is about so much more than grades, quizzes, and test scores. Distinguished author and Newbery Award winner Katherine Paterson says, "It is not enough to simply teach children to read; we have to give them something worth reading. Something that will stretch their imaginations—something that will help them make sense of their own lives and encourage them to reach out toward people whose lives are quite different from their own" (1995). When teachers flood their rooms with great text, teach kids to read for understanding, and give kids plenty of time, their classrooms explode with thinking. Kids can't wait to share their excitement, talk about burning questions, express opinions, and even take action based on their reading and learning.

This is why we educators must care so passionately about helping children become real readers who eat, drink, breathe, and live books. Reading changes everything from the way we view our world to the way we view ourselves. We read not because we are teachers or students but because we are human beings.

Part IV

Resources That Support Strategy Instruction

Great Books for Teaching Content in History, Social Studies, Science, Music, Art, and Literacy

World Exploration

Historical Fiction

Encounter by Jane Yolen

A Taino Indian child watches Columbus's ships arrive. Although the little boy is suspicious of the men and their motives, his elders do not listen until it is too late. Presents issues of discovery from the perspective of indigenous peoples; puzzling narrative and language encourage questioning and inferring.

Nonfiction

The Adventures of Marco Polo by Russell Freedman

Was Marco Polo the world's greatest explorer? Or was he the world's biggest liar? This book will be a great addition to explorer collections. Narrative text, though lengthy, is well written. Book could be used as a read-aloud, as a good model for writing reports, and certainly to provoke questions about historical facts vs. fiction. Evidence, according to the author, is inconclusive as to whether Marco Polo ever went to China. Illustrations are accompanied by archival, period artwork.

The History News: Explorers by Michael Johnstone

Written in newspaper format with a bit of glib humor, the book begins with the Polynesians and the Phoenicians. Includes maps, interesting information, and even "letters to the editor" from the likes of Columbus.

Land Ho! Fifty Glorious Years in the Age of Exploration by Nancy Winslow Parker

This book reports on twelve Europeans who explored the American continents—and the mistakes, accidents, and cruel treatment of native peoples. Layout (with illustrations and diagrams) and text are reader friendly.

Lewis and Clark: Explorers of the New American West by Steven Kroll

> Excellent for questioning, focusing on important ideas, and developing research questions based on the events of the journey. Introduces Native American tribes along the way, and famous personalities including Sacajawea. The afterword contains additional information about what happened to the members of the expedition in later years.

Lost Treasure of the Inca by Peter Lourie

> The author/adventurer takes the reader along on an edge-of-your-seat hunt for Inca treasure in Peru.

Spirit of Endurance: The True Story of the Shackleton Expedition to the Antarctic by Jennifer Armstrong

> Fabulous paintings and photographs will attract readers to this over-sized book about the remarkable Antarctic explorer, Ernest Shackleton.

U.S. History

Colonial Times

Historical Fiction

Molly Bannaky by Alice McGill

> An exiled English dairy maid is sent to America as an indentured servant. Molly stakes her own land and, although she deplores the institution of slavery, buys a slave to help start her farm. She eventually marries this former African prince, and they become successful landowners, despite the unusual circumstances of their marriage. Their grandson, Benjamin Banneker, a self-taught scientist and astronomer, was the first black man to publish an almanac. A wonderful piece of historical fiction, full of fascinating historical details about a real family, the Bannekers.

Samuel Eaton's Day: A Day in the Life of a Pilgrim Boy by Kate Waters
Sarah Morton's Day: A Day in the Life of a Pilgrim Girl by Kate Waters
Tapenum's Day: A Wampanoag Indian Boy in Pilgrim Times by Kate Waters

> Photographs from Massachusetts' Plimoth Plantation portray many aspects of colonial and Native American life. Children's work, clothing, school, and play are illustrated with simple, easy-to-read text. Great for research on the people of the times.

Stranded at Plimoth Plantation: 1626 by Gary Bowen

> The fictional journal of one Christopher Sears, who, indentured by his unscrupulous uncle on a ship journeying west, finds himself stranded in Plimoth when his ship founders on the rocks.

Christopher's journal includes information about other famous pilgrims, hardships and daily life, diseases, and encounters with the Native Americans.

Nonfiction

The New Americans: Colonial Times 1620–1689 by Betsy Maestro and Giulio Maestro

> Begins with the Native Americans who first peopled the North American continent, putting the arrival of the Pilgrims in perspective. The history of Native American tribes and individuals is woven throughout colonial history, with helpful maps and illustrations detailing home life as well as historical events.

Roanoke: The Lost Colony—An Unsolved Mystery from History by Jane Yolen and Heidi Elisabet Yolen Stemple

> A group of English people who travel to the American continent in the 1500s to begin a new settlement disappear. Setup of the book is just like *Mary Celeste* and other unsolved mysteries in the series. Format contains text of story, notebook entries about clues, definitions of important words, and numerous theories to consider. This series also includes *The Salem Witch Trials: An Unsolved Mystery from History*.

Poetry

Hand in Hand: An American History Through Poetry collected by Lee Bennett Hopkins

> Beginning with the Pilgrims and continuing through Neil Armstrong's moon walk, this collection shares American history through poetry.

American Independence

Historical Fiction

Charlotte by Janet Lunn

> This picture book, based on Charlotte Haines Peters's life, tells the story of a family torn apart by the Revolution. Charlotte, the daughter of a determined patriot, pays a high price for going to say good-bye to her loyalist cousins as they are about to leave for Canada and a new life.

Emma's Journal: The Story of a Colonial Girl by Marissa Moss

> Written by ten-year-old Emma in journal form with entries spanning a two-year period from May 1774 until July 1776, this clever book describes life and times in this period. Emma overhears enemy battle plans and sneaks information out to the Colonial Army. She is a terrific role model for girls everywhere.

John, Paul, George and Ben by Lane Smith

> This 2006 "Quills" nominee highlights personality traits of young John Hancock, Paul Revere, George Washington, Ben Franklin, and "also Independent Tom (Jefferson)—always off

doing his *own* thing." Illustrations are hand drawn with pen and ink and will be familiar-looking to readers, as the author also illustrated *The True Story of 3 Little Pigs*. True/false section at the end of the book establishes historical correctness of text.

Katie's Trunk by Ann Turner

As Tories, Katie's family runs away to the woods when the rebels come to their house looking for valuables. When she returns and hides, one of the patriots searching the house, a friend of her family's, keeps her secret and calls off his companions, illustrating compassion in the midst of war. Children's questions and inferences stimulate a thoughtful discussion of the meaning of themes such as loyalty and allegiance.

Redcoats and Petticoats by Katherine Kirkpatrick

A story of a boy who lives near a Redcoat encampment on Long Island who, without knowing it, becomes part of a Setauket spy ring. Thomas's mother seems to act peculiarly as she washes laundry, when she is in fact signaling the patriots about the comings and goings of the Redcoats. Excellent background information about patriots, loyalists, how the British kept prisoners on prison ships, and other aspects of the Revolutionary War.

Sleds on Boston Common: A Story from the American Revolution by Louise Borden

A nine-year-old colonial boy convinces British General Thomas Gage to allow him and his friends to go sledding on Boston Common even though it is occupied by British troops.

Nonfiction

The Boston Tea Party by Steven Kroll

A blow-by-blow account of events leading up to the Boston Tea Party, in particular, the meetings of the Long Room Club, which included luminaries such as Sam Adams, John Hancock, and Paul Revere. The Tea Party itself is described in detail with striking illustrations.

Can't You Make Them Behave, King George? by Jean Fritz

A hilarious description of King George and his difficulties with the rebellious colonies tells the story of America moving toward independence. The author's remarkable sense of interesting detail and humorous style make this and the following titles a great set for introducing Revolutionary War themes and ideas.

Dangerous Crossing: The Revolutionary Voyage of John Quincy Adams by Stephen Krensky

John Adams, the second president of the United States, sails to France in midwinter 1778 to seek support for the American side in the War with the British. Ten-year-old John Quincy sails with his father and endures bad conditions, a lightning strike, and encounters with British ships. A different angle on the Revolutionary War.

Dear Benjamin Banneker by Andrea Davis Pinkney

Unlike many black people of his time Benjamin Banneker grew up free. A brilliant student, he never forgot how his brothers suffered under slavery, and he spoke out about it throughout his life. A great book for questioning, since Benjamin Banneker asked many questions himself.

George vs. George: The American Revolution as Seen from Both Sides by Rosalyn Schanzer

George Washington, who freed the colonies from the British, and King George III, who lost them, are given equal time in this text. Speech balloons with real quotes from real people (with sources) add to the authenticity. Great background about the main characters' families, lives, governments, and times.

George Washington, Spymaster: How the Americans Outspied the British and Won the Revolutionary War by Thomas B. Allen

This narrative describes how Washington outwitted the British using spies to gather intelligence during the Revolutionary War. Great opportunity for young readers to learn about codes, double agents, and so forth.

In Defense of Liberty: The Story of America's Bill of Rights by Russell Freedman

This award-winning book combines a clear, readable history of both the Bill of Rights and the Constitution with real-life examples of how the amendments and challenges to them affect our lives today. Freedman's examples are relevant to intermediate and teenage readers and encourage kids to engage in critical thinking and reading, so important to the life of a democracy.

Sybil's Night Ride by Karen B. Winnick

True story of young Sybil Ludington's ride (April 26, 1777) to warn of British invasion in Putnam County, New York. An unfamiliar and surprising story to many kids who are more familiar with Paul Revere. Could be partnered with a Paul Revere ride story to provide depth to that historical time.

And Then What Happened, Paul Revere? by Jean Fritz

This book about Paul Revere's adventurous life includes information about colonial Boston and the beginning of the American Revolution.

A Voice of Her Own—The Story of Phillis Wheatley, Slave Poet by Kathryn Lasky

The amazing story of a young African girl, kidnapped into slavery and then educated by the Boston family who bought her at the age of seven. Phillis's talent, determination, and voice, along with her new family's support, gradually overcome the prejudice surrounding her to make her America's first black woman poet.

Will You Sign Here, John Hancock? by Jean Fritz
The story of the writing and signing of the Declaration of Independence and the interesting personalities who played a part.

Native Americans: Past and Present

Historical Fiction

A Boy Called Slow by Joseph Bruchac
A Lakota Sioux boy, named Slow at birth because of his careful and deliberate actions, became a hero in battle when he was fourteen. The boy earned the name Sitting Bull, and because of his bravery and determination became one of the greatest Lakota warriors.

The Ledgerbook of Thomas Blue Eagle by Jewel Grutman and Gay Matthai
Written as a facsimile of a ledgerbook by the fictional boy Thomas Blue Eagle, the story recounts his early years with his family on the plains. Sent to an Indian school in Carlisle, Pennsylvania, he recalls life among white people and his eventual return to his people. The illustrations are similar to those in the real ledgerbooks of the late nineteenth century. Reading this beautiful volume, written in longhand, is like studying an authentic historical document.

Squanto's Journey by Joseph Bruchac
The fascinating story of the famous Native American. This narrative reveals many surprising twists and turns in his life which make his contribution all the more remarkable.

Nonfiction

Buffalo Hunt by Russell Freedman
Told through the story of the buffalo, "a gift from the great spirit," this history of the Plains Indians describes the importance of the buffalo in all aspects of life, especially buffalo magic, the hunt, and its eventual disappearance. Paintings by George Catlin, Karl Bodmer, and others who documented the life of the Plains Indians add to the book's authenticity.

Clambake: A Wampanoag Tradition by Russell M. Peters
A present-day story of young Steven Peters, a Wampanoag Indian who lives in Plymouth, Massachusetts, illustrates the contemporary world of this tribe. One of an award-winning series called We Are Still Here: Native Americans of Today.

The Long March by Marie-Louise Fitzpatrick
The story of a group of Choctaw Indians who aided the victims of the Irish potato famine by donating $170 to this cause in the 1840s. Choona, a young Choctaw, speaks out against helping the Nahullo, or Europeans, but gradually changes his mind as he listens to his grandmother's story of his tribe's long and tragic march west. Encourages students to infer important ideas, including overcoming bitterness and resentment.

The Lost World of the Anasazi: Exploring the Mysteries of Chaco Canyon by Peter Lourie
The book details the author's personal journey to the sacred ruins of the early Anasazi in Chaco Canyon. Stunning photographs help to explain the beauty of the Anasazi people and their way of life. The author conveys what is known about the Anasazi but is careful to point out that much remains a mystery.

In a Sacred Manner I Live: Native American Wisdom edited by Neil Philip
Native Americans write about historical and twentieth-century themes, past and present. Poems, essays, and speeches include Chief Joseph's speech "I Will Fight No More Forever" and Tecumseh's words at a treaty signing: "My heart is a stone, heavy with sadness for my people." Traditions and beliefs about the power of Native American cultures come through in these original writings.

Sacagawea by Liselotte Erdrich
Beautifully illustrated, this is the story of the young Shoshone girl who was kidnapped by the Hidatsu Indians, married off to a Canadian fur trader, and traveled with Lewis and Clark and the Corps of Discovery. Her ability to interpret and negotiate with the Shoshone was invaluable to the success of the expedition. Useful timeline and map give additional information.

Sequoyah by James Rumford
Circa 1820, this is the story of a determined Cherokee Indian man who invented a writing system for the Cherokee—quite an accomplishment! The system contains a syllabary of eighty-four signs, one for each symbol of the Cherokee language, and is still used today. Code-lovers will be thrilled with the Cherokee writing below the English text on each page.

Shadow Catcher: The Life and Work of Edward S. Curtis by Laurie Lawlor
Edward Curtis, a famous photographer, traveled the country and worked tirelessly to capture Native American life in the late 1800s and early 1900s. Curtis endured a lifetime of personal and financial problems to complete *The North American Indian,* an exhaustive portfolio of Indian life.

Poetry

Between Earth and Sky: Legends of Native American Sacred Places by Joseph Bruchac
Paintings by Thomas Locker illustrate nature poems by Seneca, Wampanoag, Navajo, and other Native Americans.

Creation poems by Cherokee, Cheyenne, and Hopi people describe how the sacred permeates all aspects of life.

The Circle of Thanks: North American Poems and Songs of Thanksgiving by Joseph Bruchac
Excellent short poems illustrating different ways of life among tribes in different regions of North America. The poems and songs depict ceremonies, beliefs, hunting practices, and other aspects of daily life. Excellent for introducing important themes in different tribal cultures.

Dancing Teepees selected by Virginia Driving Hawk Sneve
Short poems include songs to the blue elk, the stars in the sky, poems and prayers about children, and the importance of the natural world. This easily read collection stimulates discussion of Native American values, traditions, and beliefs.

Series

The Cherokee, The Iroquois, The Navajo, and other books by Virginia Driving Hawk Sneve
Her books present thoughtful information about traditional and present-day Native American life. Beginning with creation myths from each tribe, short chapters include the traditional roles of men, women, and children, the difficulties tribes faced as they lost their lands, and other aspects of the tribes' rich history and culture, including ceremonies and the arts.

The American West—Pioneers and Cowboys

Historical Fiction

Dandelions by Eve Bunting
A story of a family's journey west from the perspective of a pioneer mother and her daughter who experience loneliness and isolation. Great for inferring and visualizing. Several beautifully descriptive scenes of nature as well as of people's feelings provide an in-depth understanding of how difficult life was for pioneers.

Exiled: Memoirs of a Camel by Kathleen Karr
Ali was a camel exported from Egypt to Texas in 1856, who helped build roads from Texas to California. A different take on the history of the old west, as told through the eyes of Ali, the camel!

Going West by Jean Van Leeuwen
Told from the point of view of seven-year-old Hannah, the simple but descriptive text tells the story of hardships and building a new life on the plains. Harsh weather and loneliness challenge the family, but springtime brings hope.

Klondike Gold by Alice Provensen
Detailed, colorful drawings and a triptych format help drive home the hardships faced by gold-seekers heading to Alaska in 1897. Little-known topic will become a topic of interest for readers.

Rachel's Journal: The Story of a Pioneer Girl by Marissa Moss
Written in journal form over a seven-month span in 1850, this book traces the family's covered wagon crossing from Illinois to California. The journal form is great for modeling writing.

Sunsets of the West by Tony Johnston
Watercolor illustrations make this a beautiful, though simple, story of the six-month westward trip that a young family shares from the Northeast to the Sierras in their covered wagon.

Nonfiction

Bill Pickett: Rodeo-Ridin' Cowboy by Andrea Pinkney
The true story of an extraordinary young man who grew up to become a famous black rodeo performer. The author's note gives extensive information on the black American cowboy.

Black Women of the Old West by William Katz
The author features black women who played central roles in the settling of the West. The chapters describe women who were members of the Seminole tribes, nurses for Buffalo soldiers, mail-order brides, homesteaders, and agitators who fought for social justice. Authentic photographs and vignettes of individual women add to the book's interest and provide opportunities for students to infer from photographs and historical journals.

Children of the Gold Rush by Claire Murphy and Jane Haigh
Historical photos, memorabilia, and narratives of life in Alaska during the Gold Rush portray the lives of children in mining camps and boomtowns. Journal entries and photographs complement the stories of the children's lives.

Children of the Wild West by Russell Freedman
The lives of pioneer and Native American children are portrayed as families journey west and settle down. Pioneer schools, celebrations, and games are described in detail with numerous photographs. A separate chapter describes the life of children in several different Indian tribes and how it changed as they were forced to give up their lands.

Shooting for the Moon—The Amazing Life and Times of Annie Oakley by Stephen Krensky
This account includes quotes from Annie, based on her own writings. She broke barriers in the field of sports for women as the legendary sharpshooter. Narrative traces her early love of hunting and trapping through her work as a circus performer and then as star of Buffalo Bill's Wild West Show. Oil paintings are an added highlight.

The Civil War

Historical Fiction

A. Lincoln and Me by Louise Borden
A young, gawky boy who shares a birthday with the sixteenth president learns that Lincoln too was teased in childhood. A great story about a boy who studies Lincoln and learns of the many possibilities for his own future.

An Apple for Harriet Tubman by Glennette Tilley Turner
Harriet's favorite outdoor job, in her early childhood as a slave, was picking apples. She takes a beating one day for tasting one. Story continues with her escape and "conducting" on the Underground Railroad. Eventually, she plants her own orchard to enjoy and share with her neighbors.

Aunt Harriet's Underground Railroad in the Sky by Faith Ringgold
Harriet Tubman meets up with two modern-day children, and the story flashes back to the time of the Underground Railroad. Filled with information about slavery and the Underground Railroad. The puzzling narrative invites questions; the factual information about slavery is helpful for building background knowledge.

Bull Run by Paul Fleischman
Vignettes from the perspective of people who experience or are related to those at the Battle of Bull Run. Each person's story unfolds as the battle begins. Of particular interest is how each person's feelings about the war change once they experience it. The vignettes prompt lots of questions and inferences; written in the language of the 1860s.

Cassie's Sweet Berry Pie, A Civil War Story by Karen B. Winnick
Cassie takes charge of her younger siblings when Yankee soldiers arrive at their Mississippi home. Her quick and clever thinking scares the Yankees into thinking that the children are infected with measles, and so they exit the house immediately. Interaction between Cassie and a young soldier (who catches on to the deceit) is touching.

Follow the Drinking Gourd by Jeanette Winter
The story, including the words to the song, of how the slaves journeyed North, following the Big Dipper.

Freedom Ship by Doreen Rappaport
A slave crew, led by Robert Smalls, kidnaps a ship and delivers it to the Union Army. Smalls also persuaded Lincoln to allow African Americans to join the Union Army. Based on a true story.

Friend on Freedom River by Gloria Whelan
Enchanting artwork and well-written text describe a night-time journey across the chilly Detroit River. Twelve-year-old Louis escorts a slave and her two children to their freedom in Canada. His father is gone, but Louis responds "by doing what his father would do" even though it is 1850 and a new "Fugitive Slave Law" could have him jailed for helping slaves escape.

Journey to Freedom: A Story of the Underground Railroad by Courtni Wright
The story of one family's escape north, and the hardships they endured on the way. Told from the perspective of a young slave girl who travels with Harriet Tubman.

Minty: A Story of Young Harriet Tubman by Alan Schroeder
A revealing account of the early life of this heroic figure. She was spunky and individualistic even as a young slave girl.

Moon Over Tennessee: A Boy's Civil War Journal by Craig Crist-Evans
A thirteen-year-old boy and his father, a Confederate soldier, journey to war together. The boy helps take care of the horses and does other chores but, most important, he keeps a journal. The journal entries are a series of poems capturing the sights, smells, sounds, and feelings of war. Poetic descriptions of the countryside, snapshots of camp life, and the horrors of the Battle of Gettysburg.

Nettie's Trip South by Ann Turner
A little girl journeys south and sees a slave auction, which outrages her. Told in the form of letters to a friend, Nettie's experiences strongly affect her sense of decency and justice.

Night Boat to Freedom by Margo Theis Raven
Story is based on a combination of ex-slave interviews from the *Slave Narrative Collection*. This beautifully illustrated book tells the story of a young male slave who spent four years rowing others across the river between the slave state of Kentucky and the free state of Ohio. He did not free himself (and his grandmother) until the risk of being caught grew too strong.

The Patchwork Path—A Quilt Map to Freedom by Bettye Stroud
Winning illustrations add to this moving, fictionalized account of historically accurate events. Story is based on oral accounts of how slaves used quilts to communicate on the Underground Railroad. As they undertake their journey, ten-year-old Hannah's father reminds her, "You've always been free on the inside. Soon you'll be free on the outside, too."

Pink and Say by Patricia Polacco
A poignant book about two boys, one black and one white, bravely fighting for the Union. The tragic story, told through the eyes of one of Patricia Polacco's ancestors, is eloquent testimony to the humanity that exists in the midst of the horrors of war. Questions and inferences abound as this story unfolds. Lest anyone have romantic ideas about bravery, courage, and sacrifice, this book dispels them.

Runaway Jack by Stewart Lees
Set in the 1840s, as told to a great-great-great-grandson, this is the story of a young slave's escape on a Mississippi steamboat and through the Underground Railroad.

Secret Signs by Anita Riggio
A deaf child helps pass information along the Underground Railroad using his paintbrush and a panoramic egg. Kids brim with questions about the outcomes of this compelling story.

Sweet Clara and the Freedom Quilt by Deborah Hopkinson
Clara is a quilter and realizes how much she can help escaping slaves once she begins sewing a quilt that is a map to guide their escape.

Nonfiction

Abraham Lincoln: Great Speeches edited by John Grafton
A compilation of Lincoln's sixteen greatest speeches with historical notes that explain the context for each. A terrific book for looking at primary source documents and reading authentic writing from the time.

Bound for America: The Forced Migration of Africans to the New World by James Haskins and Kathleen Benson
Between 1500 and 1850, millions of Africans were captured and sent across the Atlantic in one of the greatest tragedies in history. The authors examine every aspect of the Middle Passage and share historical details about this crime against humanity.

The Boys' War by Jim Murphy
The story of boys who fought, often lying about their youth, in the Civil War. Sad stories of young boys eager to enlist who find out all too soon about the horrors of war.

Frederick Douglass: The Last Day of Slavery by William Miller
When a white overseer tries to break Frederick's spirit, he fights back, "an act of courage that frees his spirit forever." This vividly sad story of the early life of Frederick Douglass illustrates his determination to fight against overwhelming cruelty and injustice.

From Slave Ship to Freedom Road by Julius Lester
Lester's hard-hitting prose and no-nonsense style complement Rod Brown's graphic, contemporary paintings of escape, punishment, and life as a slave. Lester challenges readers to imagine themselves as slaves by including pointed, thoughtful questions throughout the text. The nature of the pictures and words make this most appropriate for middle school and up.

Hold the Flag High by Catherine Clinton
Sargent William H. Carney becomes the first African American to earn a Congressional Medal of Honor for preserving the flag during a Civil War battle. Illustrations are a strong point of the book.

Lincoln: A Photobiography by Russell Freedman
The Newbery Award–winning story of the sixteenth president. Superb for lifting short excerpts and reasoning through them together to determine important information and ideas.

Mr. Lincoln's Whiskers by Karen Winnick
The true story of the young girl Grace Bedell, who wrote Abraham Lincoln to suggest that he grow a beard. Readers can't help but infer how Mr. Lincoln will react to this suggestion. Will he take her advice?

A Separate Battle: Women and the Civil War by Ina Chang
Women's experiences during the Civil War include portraits of Harriet Beecher Stowe, nurse Clara Barton, and Dorothea Dix. One of the most interesting chapters describes women who successfully posed as male soldiers and spies.

The Silent Witness—A True Story of the Civil War by Robin Friedman
In July of 1861, General Beauregard uproots Lula's family and uses their Manassas, Virginia, home as his headquarters. Eventually, Lee surrenders to Grant in the parlor of their home. Soldiers on that day dubbed Lula's doll (left on the couch) "the silent witness," and Lieutenant Colonel Thomas WC Moore took it as a souvenir. The doll is now housed in Appomattox Court House, Virginia.

Poetry

Under the Quilt of Night by Deborah Hopkinson and James E. Ransome
Poems about the Underground Railroad incorporate important themes (running, waiting, hiding), beautiful language, and stunning illustrations to engage kids in the narratives of slaves and their difficult journeys.

The First Great War, the 1920s, and the Depression

Historical Fiction

The Babe and I by David Adler
Babe Ruth's hitting streak comes just in time for a needy family in the midst of the Great Depression. A young boy has no trouble selling papers thanks to the great baseball player.

Hannah and the Perfect Picture Pony—A Story of the Great Depression by Sara Goodman Zimet
This sweet Depression-era story is illustrated in sepia tones. At bargain prices, children could be photographed on ponies by photographers who "work the streets."

The House in the Mail by Rosemary and Tom Wells
Interesting topic and fun format! This is written as a letter from a twelve-year-old girl to readers in the future. The year is 1928, and this is the story of a family in Kentucky who chooses, orders, and puts together a house from the Sears catalog. Scrapbook format includes sketches, original catalog entries, and clippings.

Leah's Pony by Elizabeth Friedrich
During the 1930s Depression and in the midst of the Dust Bowl era, young Leah saves her family's farm. The book centers on Leah's love for her pony and describes her family's dilemmas as they almost lose their farm in a penny auction. Their neighbors refused to bid seriously when their friends were forced to auction off land and belongings.

Nora's Ark by Natalie Kinsey-Warnock
Twenty-three people, three horses, a cow, five pigs, a duck, four cats, and one hundred chickens find shelter in a newly constructed house which sits on higher ground. It is 1927 and a flood in Vermont washes away the houses of the majority of these people. As they face starting over, they realize what is important in life. Readers will recognize Emily Arnold McCully's illustrations, similar to her award-winning ones in *Mirette on the High Wire*.

The Rag Coat by Lauren Mills
Minna is desperate to go to school, but first she needs a coat. The quilting mothers make one for her, but she is quite unprepared for the reaction of the kids at school. The author leaves many clues along the way, and readers can practice inferring.

Saving Strawberry Farm by Deborah Hopkinson
"The sun was so mean that summer, it seemed to chase all the clouds away." Thus begins a beautifully written and illustrated story of a child who learns about and promotes the practice of saving money. He eventually influences the auctioning off of a neighbor's farm. Provides a clear, understandable glimpse of hard times.

True Heart by Marissa Moss
The story of a sixteen-year-old girl who dreams of becoming an engineer. A good example of a story that places a girl in an unusual role. A thoughtful book about someone who had the determination to live out her dream.

Nonfiction

Children of the Dust Bowl by Jerry Stanley
Okie children who have moved to California are treated with disdain until one courageous soul from the town school board encourages the community to create its own wonderful school. A heartwarming story about how innovative educational experiences can transform lives. Superb photographs of life in the Depression era provide documentation of a truly remarkable project.

Children of the Great Depression by Russell Freedman
This is the 2006 Orbis Pictus Award Winner from the National Council of Teachers of English. Freedman's trademark documentation of children's lives during these times also shows that "kids will be kids" despite all the difficulties and struggles to survive. Photos of kids at work, on the move, at school are paired with many first-hand accounts. Photographs from the Library of Congress collection add to the authenticity and provide real insight into these kids' experiences.

Dust to Eat: Drought and Depression in the 1930s by Michael L. Cooper
Personal stories of people who survived the Great Depression and the Dust Bowl times. Many photographs add to the personal vignettes of hardships and survival.

Good Girl Work: Factories, Sweatshops and How Women Changed Their Role in the American Workforce by Catherine Gourley
This complete history of working women in the nineteenth and early twentieth centuries, from the early mill girls to "rebels" who fought for better working conditions, incorporates letters, journal entries, and photographs. The moving stories of famous events such as the Triangle Shirtwaist Factory Fire and of the people who changed working women's lives make for inspiring reading.

Pig on the Titanic: A True Story by Gary Crew
Though seemingly far-fetched, this is based on a true story. Miss Edith Rosenbaum, a famous fashion buyer en route from Paris to New York City takes onboard "Maxixe"—a music box pig—as a good luck charm. Maxixe is carried everywhere and on the night of the Titanic's sinking is mistaken for a baby and thus hurried into a lifeboat. Today, Maxixe is preserved in a special glass case in a private collection.

Restless Spirit: The Life and Work of Dorothea Lange by Elizabeth Partridge
Dorothea Lange was famous for photographing migrant workers during the Depression and Japanese Americans interned during World War II. This biography recounts her life and work. Once again, the photographs offer great opportunities for inferential thinking.

Something Permanent by Cynthia Rylant
Walker Evans's Depression-era photographs tell the stories of everyday Americans during those very tough times. Cynthia Rylant's text takes off from these photographs and brings them to life. It encourages kids to look at photographs and imagine

the stories behind them.

World War II

Historical Fiction

Boxes for Katje by Candace Fleming

Based on a true story about war-ravaged Holland in the aftermath of World War II, this book describes the joy a young girl and her family experience with the arrival of boxes from Mayfield, Indiana, containing necessities. As the boxes continue coming, the supplies help the family and their neighbors survive a terrible winter. In the spring, the grateful Dutch reciprocate, sending a box full of "surprises"—tulip bulbs, of course—which grace the generous town of Mayfield for years to come.

The Bracelet by Yoshiko Uchida

When a Japanese American family leaves San Francisco for an internment camp, two little girls learn a great deal about the meaning of friendship. When seven-year-old Emi loses her best friend's bracelet, she learns that it is the memory of her friend that matters most.

The Butterfly by Patricia Polacco

This is a beautifully moving story of a child whose mother hides a Jewish family in her basement and tries to help them escape. Set in Nazi-occupied Paris during World War II, it is a true story from a relative of Polacco's and includes actual events during the French Resistance.

The Cats in Krasinski Square by Karen Hesse

A young girl and her sister risk their lives to help those still trapped behind Warsaw's Ghetto walls. Cats literally outfox the Gestapo. Historical note concludes this simple and beautiful story.

The Greatest Skating Race by Louise Borden

This suspenseful picture book is told from the point of view of a ten-year-old Dutch boy who leads two young neighbors to safety in Belgium. An amazing story of how these brave, resourceful children skate for hours along frozen canals and hide from German soldiers to escape from occupied Holland.

The Lily Cupboard by Shulamith Oppenheim

When the Nazis invaded Holland during World War II, many Dutch families living in the country hid Jewish children. In this story, the Dutch family who keeps and hides a little Jewish girl on their farm takes a considerable risk, especially when soldiers come to search the house.

The Little Ships: The Heroic Rescue at Dunkirk in World War II by Louise Borden

In 1940 half a million British and French soldiers were trapped by Germans in a corner of northern France. The only way out was the sea. This book describes a heroic rescue effort by British civilians as well as military personnel.

Mercedes and the Chocolate Pilot by Margot Theis Raven

This is based on the true story of the Berlin airlift (1948–1949) and the candy that dropped from the sky. Airplanes flew 24 hours a day, three minutes apart, to feed 2.2 million people for fifteen months. Content focuses on a seven-year-old girl and an American pilot who befriends her. The introduction and epilogue are reader-friendly and explain the historical context.

Rebekkah's Journey—A World War II Refugee Story by Ann E. Burg

An eight-year old girl (the narrator) and her mother escape from the Nazis and end up in a refugee camp. Author's note at the beginning of the book explains how 1,000 displaced individuals were housed on a vacant army base in Oswego, New York, during 1944. This tear-jerker emphasizes the importance of tolerance and the impact of kindness.

Rose Blanche by Roberto Innocenti

This book recounts the story of a young German girl who passes a concentration camp on the way to school each day. Her daily journey leads her down the path from curiosity to sympathy to action. An extraordinary book that prompts many questions, particularly because the ending remains unresolved.

The Unbreakable Code by Sara Hoagland Hunter

Navajos encoding secret messages during World War II. See description in the preceding section "Native Americans: Past and Present."

Nonfiction

Anne Frank by Josephine Poole

This story begins with an ordinary little girl, and is told for younger readers to understand. Focus is on her life before her family's incarceration. Illustrations are somewhat haunting.

Anne Frank: Beyond the Diary by Ruud van der Rol and Rian Verhoeven

Pictures from Anne Frank's family photo albums illustrate what her life was like before and during the war, providing mesmerizing reading for anyone interested in Anne's diary and her fate as a Jewish child during World War II. Photographs and cut-away drawings of the secret annex explain the Franks' life in hiding.

Baseball Saved Us by Ken Mochizuki

Based on the author's own experience, the story describes how Japanese Americans interned during World War II organized a baseball team and built a baseball diamond, which provided a diversion during this sad period in their lives.

The Children of Topaz: The Story of a Japanese-American Internment Camp by Michael O. Tunnell and George W. Chilcoat

The diary kept by a third-grade class taught by Anne Yamauchi in 1943 at the Topaz internment camp. The book describes, from a child's point of view, how Miss Yamauchi and her students tried to continue with normal school life despite difficult conditions. Archival photographs provide a detailed look at life in Topaz.

Faithful Elephants by Yukio Tsuchiya

The true story of the elephants at the Ueno Zoo in Tokyo at the height of World War II and their zookeepers, who were torn about whether to kill them or save them. The text sparks deep discussion about how war takes a toll on the innocent.

The Harmonica by Tony Johnston

A true, powerful account of a young boy in Nazi Germany who is ripped from his family and placed in a concentration camp where he survives by playing his harmonica. The story makes a case for the power of music to give us strength and sustenance in times of great tragedy. An afterward provides additional information about Henry Rosmaryn, the man who was that young boy.

The Journey That Saved Curious George: The True Wartime Escape of Margret and H. A. Rey by Louise Borden

Louise Borden was "curious" about the story of the Rey's flight from Paris on bicycles in June 1940 to escape from the Nazi invasion. She has pulled together old photos, paintings, illustrations by H. A. Rey, and many anecdotal stories to narrate this biography. Text is lengthy but worth reading in segments. Adults who love Curious George will want to store this background knowledge on his conception (he was originally called Fifi!) to share with young readers.

Luba: The Angel of Bergen-Belsen by Michelle R. McCann and Luba Tryszynska-Frederick

As told to Michelle McCann, this is a truly amazing story of a nurse at the Bergen-Belsen concentration camp who worked secretly and tirelessly to save the children there. When the camp was liberated, soldiers were stunned to find so many children who had survived solely because of her efforts. A story of how one person can make a difference.

Passage to Freedom: The Sugihara Story by Ken Mochizuki

Told from the point of view of Hiroki Sugihara, the son of the Japanese consul to Lithuania during World War II. Hiroki describes how his father disobeyed orders from his government and granted visas to as many as ten thousand Jewish refugees from Poland, enabling them to escape the Nazis threatening Lithuania.

Remember D-Day: Both Sides Tell Their Stories by Ronald J. Drez

The best book we know to give intermediate-grade readers an in-depth look at the turning point in World War II. With a foreword by David Eisenhower about the human side of his famous grandfather, *Remember D-Day* explores the invasion with survivor stories from both sides. Similar format to Thomas Allen's *Remember Pearl Harbor* (also on this list).

Remember Pearl Harbor by Thomas B. Allen

The notorious attack on Pearl Harbor is reconstructed here through the stories of Japanese and American survivors. The phrase "Remember Pearl Harbor" united Americans to fight against the Japanese. Today it is a reminder to choose peace.

Rosie the Riveter by Penny Colman

The women who filled the civilian and defense jobs during World War II deserve to have their stories told. Their determination and hard work resulted in a phenomenal rate of production of necessary goods that helped to win the war. Builds background for what life was like on the home front during World War II.

Sadako by Eleanor Coerr

A picture book version of the famous short chapter book *Sadako and the Thousand Paper Cranes.* This quiet story tells how Sadako bravely fought leukemia, the "atom bomb disease." Working to fold one thousand paper cranes so that the gods would grant her wish to get well, Sadako never gave up hope for a peaceful world.

V Is for Victory: The American Home Front During World War II by Sylvia Whitman

Recounts what happened in the United States as women found new roles in the workforce, shouldered family responsibilities, and joined other citizens of all ages to support the war effort. Important themes include strife between races and ethnic groups, and hardships such as rationing. War posters, photographs, and excerpts from personal letters and memoirs are useful to study as historical documents.

Poetry

I Never Saw Another Butterfly: Children's Drawings and Poems from Terezin Concentration Camp, 1942–44 edited by Hana Volavkova

Poetry written in Terezin concentration camp is both tragic and hopeful. The children's generous and thoughtful spirits come through despite their horrendous situations.

Post–World War II to the Present

Historical Fiction

America's White Table by Margot Theis Raven

"It was just a little white table" but it honors men and women missing in action and held as prisoners of war, including the story of a POW during the Vietnam War. The author, who wrote *Mercedes and the Chocolate Pilot,* again brings an abstract concept to a young child's level of understanding. A must-read on Veteran's Day.

Nonfiction

The CIA by Brendan January
This book about a high-interest topic (there's also one about the FBI) covers the history, organization, and mission of the CIA. It also cites stories and cases. Great nonfiction features with contents, timeline, index, glossary, words in boldface throughout the text, and captioned photos.

Escape from Saigon: How a Vietnam War Orphan Became an American Boy by Andrea Warren
An Amerasian orphan boy lives through dangerous times during the fall of Saigon, eventually coming to the United States.

Thura's Diary by Thura al-Windawi
In 2003, Thura is a teenager in Iraq during the invasion of the Coalition Forces. She describes life in this war-torn country. A postscript and afterword provide additional information for readers.

Witness to History: September 11, 2001 by Brendan January
An exploration of the tragic event that forever changed our world with personal accounts from many of those on the scene including firefighters, Trade Tower workers, reporters, flight attendants, medical personnel, and more. Powerful and memorable.

General History Series

A History of U.S.: The Story of America by Joy Hakim
This series of ten volumes of U.S. history begins with *The First Americans* and concludes with *All the People*, covering over two hundred years of American history. Great photographs and primary source documents along with compelling writing make this series a must for upper elementary and middle school kids.

Social Studies

Civil Rights and the African American Experience

Historical or Realistic Fiction

Dear Willie Rudd by Libba Moore Gray
A woman late in life thinks back to the things she would have liked to have done with her beloved black housekeeper: go to the movies, have dinner, and ride the bus. Segregation prevented all of this.

Freedom School, Yes! by Amy Littlesugar
During the summer of 1964, many courageous people worked together to launch freedom schools in Mississippi. This story tells about the experiences of one young girl who, with community members and a committed young teacher, fought for the right to build schools and learn.

Jackie's Bat by Marybeth Lorbiecki
This is the fictionalized story of Jackie Robinson's first season with the Dodgers as told by the team's batboy. His father's racism troubles the young batboy as he watches Jackie deal with it on and off the field. He learns "what a man is." Brian Pinkney illustrates this thought-provoking, sometimes uncomfortable-feeling text.

More Than Anything Else by Marie Bradby
Written in the first person, the story concerns nine-year-old Booker T. Washington, who is determined to learn to read. Because he wanted to read "more than anything else," Booker won't rest until he finds an adult to help him.

The Other Side by Jacqueline Woodson
The powerful story of two neighbor girls, one white and one black, and how in spite of the "fence" of segregation that separates them, their friendship grows and flourishes. A great story to begin an in-depth discussion of racism, prejudice, and the Civil Rights movement.

Remember—The Journey to School Integration by Toni Morrison
"This book is about you. Even though the main event took place many years ago. . . . It is now a part of all of our lives. Because remembering is the mind's first step towards understanding." And so begins Toni Morrison's moving narrative about school integration in the American south. An excellent window into the beginnings of the Civil Rights movement with telling black-and-white photographs and an informative time line.

Nonfiction

The Day Martin Luther King, Jr. Was Shot: A Photo History of the Civil Rights Movement by James Haskins
This account begins on the day Dr. King was assassinated and looks back over the history of the American Civil Rights movement through realistic illustrations, photographs, and primary sources.

Free at Last by Sara Bullard
A history of the civil rights movement, including the Little Rock Nine, freedom riders, and individual portraits of people who gave their lives for the cause. A time line from 1954 to 1968 and archive photographs bring this era to life.

Freedom Rides: Journey for Justice by James Haskins
"My family and I could not try on shoes in the white-owned stores downtown. We had to select what we wanted and hope they fit. We were served in the back of the store." Jim Haskins's childhood experiences strengthened his determination to tell

the truth about school segregation, the Montgomery bus boycott, and the freedom riders' nonviolent protests.

The Great Migration by Jacob Lawrence
Paintings by the artist of African Americans who forsook the South for what they hoped would be a better life in the northern industrial cities.

I Have a Dream by Dr. Martin Luther King, Jr.; illustrated by fifteen Coretta Scott King Award Winners
Stunning pictures by award-winning artists illustrate Dr. King's most famous speech. This book deserves an honored place in every classroom and library in America.

I've Seen the Promised Land: The Life of Dr. Martin Luther King, Jr. by Walter Dean Myers
Key moments in the civil rights movement stress King's belief in nonviolence overcoming racial discrimination and his dream that people be judged by their character. Good model for nonfiction writing (interesting lead, then back to facts).

Let Them Play by Margot Theis Raven
The setting is 1955, South Carolina. An all-black Little League team is the only black team in the league, and the rest of the teams boycott the Little League program rather than play them. By default this team gains a spot in the Little League Baseball World Series, but is only allowed to warm up, not compete. Spectators' chants on that day give the book its title. This is a heart-wrenching, hard one to read—children will "get" it.

Let's Talk About Race by Julius Lester
"I am a story. So are you. So is everyone. Those who say 'my race is better than your race' are telling a story that is not true." This text is elementary in writing, but contains a strong and clear message—that race is just one detail in an individual's story and identity.

Maritcha: A Remarkable Nineteenth-Century American Girl by Tonya Bolden
Based on a 1928 memoir by long-time teacher Maritcha Lyons, this pictorial biography tells the story of a girl who was determined to become educated. Excellent drawings, excerpts from Maritcha's memoir, and other documents provide the reader with information about New York in the mid-1800s. A 2006 Orbus Pictus recommended book.

The Power of One: Daisy Bates and the Little Rock Nine by Dennis and Judith Fradin
Daisy Bates was determined to change what was going on in segregated Arkansas, eventually leading the Little Rock Nine to integrate the public schools.

Powerful Words: More Than 200 Years of Extraordinary Writing by African Americans by Wade Hudson
The black experience in America is chronicled in this book of powerful speeches and writings from figures such as Rosa Parks, Paul Robeson, Thurgood Marshall, and many more. Each piece of writing culminates with a short author biography and a description of the response engendered by the piece. A truly remarkable book about the power of words!

Richard Wright and the Library Card by William Miller
This story is based on a scene from Wright's book *Black Boy*. In the South, Richard could only use the library by saying the books he checked out were for a white coworker. Determined to learn, Richard experienced derision and insult to borrow and read books, learning about people and places that would change his life.

Shadow Ball: The History of the Negro Leagues by Geoffrey Ward, Ken Burns, with Jim O'Connor
A richly written account of the baseball leagues for black Americans in the 1930s, 1940s, and 1950s. Kids will be amazed at this part of our history when black baseball players, no matter how talented, could not play in the major leagues.

The Story of Ruby Bridges by Robert Coles
Ruby Bridges bravely went to school in New Orleans each day, one of the first children to attend an all-white school. But Ruby ended up being the only child in her class, because the white children stayed home to protest. Ruby stood her ground, her teacher supported her, and gradually the other children returned to school.

Through My Eyes by Ruby Bridges
An autobiographical account of one of the first children to attend all-white schools in New Orleans. The photographs and supporting information about the civil rights movement, the events that touched Ruby's life, and what happened as the community gradually accepted integration are an excellent first-person account of the struggle for integration and social justice.

When Marian Sang: The True Recital of Marian Anderson by Pam Ryan Munoz
Marian Anderson is best known for her historic concert at the Lincoln Memorial in 1939, which drew an integrated crowd of 75,000 people in pre–civil rights America. Before that, Anderson was little known in her own country because of her race. This narrative fills us in on her remarkable story.

Poetry

Honey I Love by Eloise Greenfield
A collection of rhythmic poems from around a city neighborhood. Great for snapping fingers, dancing, and choral reading.

Soul Looks Back in Wonder compiled by Tom Feelings
A collection of poems by famous African American poets,

including Maya Angelou, Langston Hughes, and Lucille Clifton.

This Is the Dream by Diane Z. Shore and Jessica Alexander
Powerful rhyming verses highlight experiences before, during, and after the civil rights movement. Fabulous illustrations! Be sure to study the collages on the end pages.

Women's Rights and Other Social Justice Issues

Historical Fiction

Ballot Box Battle by Emily Arnold McCully
Poor Elizabeth Cady Stanton. Every time she was successful as a child, her father couldn't resist saying how she should have been born a boy. Eventually the story finds Stanton's young neighbor Cordelia at the voting booth with Ms. Stanton, who points out to those present (all men, of course) that someday Cordelia will vote. Excellent short biography of Elizabeth Cady Stanton in the afterword.

The Bobbin Girl by Emily Arnold McCully
A story of the heroic mill girls working in Lowell, Massachusetts, who, in the 1830s, worked hard to become independent wage earners. When the mill owners try to lower their wages, the girls protest, and although they were replaced by new workers, they set a precedent for workers' strikes and encouraged other women to rebel when treated unfairly. Excellent afterword provides additional information.

Mama Went to Jail for the Vote by Kathleen Karr
Father believes that women "were meant to be an ornament to man and to comfort him after his labors." Mama fights for the right of women to vote. She and her friends picket President Wilson's White House, are arrested, and serve six months in jail. A historical note at the end includes the wording of the Nineteenth Amendment and details about the arrests of women. (All 168 picketers were pardoned by Wilson, who supported their cause in Congress.)

Nonfiction

I Could Do That! Esther Morris Gets Women the Vote by Linda Arms White
On December 10, 1869, Wyoming women vote, thanks to Esther Morris and her "I could do that!" attitude. Her determination also leads her to become the first woman in the country to hold public office.

Let Me Play: The Story of Title IX by Karen Blumenthal
This 2006 recommended Orbus Pictus book tells the story of efforts to make sure that girls enjoy the same opportunities in sports and related careers that men do. Includes many political cartoons, photographs, and personal profiles that add to this history of breaking down cultural barriers.

A Woman for President: The Story of Victoria Woodhull by Kathleen Krull
As Woodhull (1838–1927) herself said, "The truth is I am too many years ahead of this age." In 1872, she ran for president—even though she was not allowed to vote. She is a forgotten figure, one who opened doors for women. She took on the male-dominated worlds of business, publishing, religion, and politics. Born into extreme poverty, her goal was to help women reduce the hardship in their lives.

You Forgot Your Skirt, Amelia Bloomer by Shana Corey
The heartening story of Amelia Bloomer, the first editor of the Lady's Temperance Society newspaper. She took to writing editorials about women's rights along with temperance editorials. The issue that made her most famous was that of women's clothing reform. And soon the first pants came to be known as "bloomers"!

Biographies

The Amazing Mr. Franklin: Or the Boy Who Read Everything by Ruth Ashby
Ben's insatiable curiosity and determination to read everything he could get his hands on is woven through the narrative of his life, including many of his sayings, quotes, and poems.

Amelia to Zora—Twenty-Six Women Who Changed the World by Cynthia Chin-Lee
Interesting cross-section of women, from the familiar to the unfamiliar. Includes childhood anecdotes, brief biographies, quotes, and detailed collages to portray stories of women who "have made a difference in people's lives."

Confucius: The Golden Rule by Russell Freedman
"More than 2500 years have passed since Confucius walked the dusty country roads of China . . . yet his voice rings clear and true down through the centuries." So begins Russell Freedman's fascinating biography of the Chinese scholar.

The Daring Nellie Bly—America's Star Reporter by Bonnie Christensen
Elizabeth Cochran, always daring to defy convention, became the first female stunt reporter. In 1889, she traveled around the world in seventy-two days (beating her goal of eighty days). Her writing "beats" focused on the rights of women and the working class. A chronology of her life and accomplishments is included.

Eleanor by Barbara Cooney
"From the beginning the baby was a disappointment to her mother." So begins this account of Eleanor Roosevelt's childhood. Inspires much discussion about how this lonely child went on to become such an impressive woman in light of her early years.

Fly High: The Story of Bessie Coleman by Louise Borden
The inspiring story of Bessie Coleman, the first woman pilot and the first African American pilot. Written in a poetic, lyrical style, this gripping narrative gives us a peek into the life of the brave woman from Chicago who broke two major barriers.

Franklin and Eleanor by Cheryl Harness
This "dual" biography includes Franklin's four terms as president and the couple's personal struggles as well as wartime- and Depression-era struggles. A family tree lists the relatives of these two cousins.

Good Queen Bess by Diane Stanley
The story of Elizabeth I of England, whose strong will and love of her people won their favor. The text and finely detailed paintings build background for life in Elizabethan times.

Harvesting Hope: The Story of Cesar Chavez by Kathleen Krull
The moving biography of a towering figure in Mexican American history. Beautifully written and illustrated, this book includes a two-page author's note that provides additional background on the life and times of Cesar Chavez. Also available in Spanish.

Heroes: Great Men Through the Ages by Rebecca Hazell
Rather than fighting battles or ruling kingdoms, these men changed the world by their good deeds and vision (Gandhi and Sequoyah), their brilliance and talent (Ben Franklin, Mozart, and Shakespeare), or their courage and wisdom (Socrates). Appealing paintings bring the men and their accomplishments to life.

Heroines: Great Women Through the Ages by Rebecca Hazell
Women who were queens (Elizabeth I), saints (Joan of Arc), and explorers (Sacajawea) fit Hazell's definition of a heroine. Women who fought for justice as well as artists and scientists are included in this lively volume. Maps with accompanying time lines provide excellent information on the women's lives and times.

If the Walls Could Talk: Family Life at the White House by Jane O'Connor
Fun stories and a fun format about the White House and the families who have occupied it over the years. Lots of condensed information included in the text, as well as in labels and bubbles. It is arranged chronologically but can be read in any order. Interesting "Ask the Presidents" question-and-answer page ends the book.

In the Promised Land: Lives of Jewish Americans by Doreen Rappaport
Introduces thirteen extraordinary Jewish Americans—including Harry Houdini, Jonas Salk, Ruth Ginsburg, and Steven Spielberg—and focuses on one key scene from each of their lives.

The Librarian Who Measured the Earth by Kathryn Lasky
Eratosthenes, who lived two thousand years ago, asked lots of questions. All those questions led to his figuring out how to measure the earth, something no one had ever done before. A great story for encouraging us all to keep thinking and wondering.

Lou Gehrig: The Luckiest Man by David Adler
Courageous and self-effacing, Lou Gehrig met challenges throughout his life. But he faced his greatest challenge with a positive attitude and a quiet dignity that is his legacy today.

The Man Who Made Time Travel by Kathryn Lasky
The award-winning story of John Harrison, a self-taught mathematician, who figured out how to measure longitude, is beautifully written and illustrated. Harrison's amazing work in finding the solution to this problem is juxtaposed with the injustice of being denied the prize for doing so.

Mother to Tigers by George Ella Lyon
Sweet story about the Bronx Zoo's first woman keeper. In the 1940s, she and her husband raised tiger cubs in their apartment. Animal lovers will adore this!

Outrageous Women of Ancient Times by Vicki Leon
Fifteen stories of ancient women from about 1500 B.C. to the second century A.D. who had an impact on the world in which they lived. They are called outrageous because powerful women were such a rarity in those days. A great book as a role model for girls.

Paths to Peace—People Who Changed the World by Jane Breskin Zalben
"The sixteen people profiled in this book come from different times, different countries, and different walks of life, but all of them were brave enough to try to make the world a better place." The impressive list includes JFK, Ghandi, Einstein, and the Dalai Lama.

Saint Valentine by Ann Tompert
This book begins and ends with "Saint Valentine's life is a mystery." Legends about this third-century Roman are explored in this narrative text.

Wilma Unlimited by Kathleen Krull
Wilma Rudolph overcame childhood polio to become the first woman to win three gold medals in a single Olympics. Her childhood struggles and determination are described in clear language that enables young readers to understand and applaud Wilma's courage and persistence. Excellent model for blending interesting facts with vivid language if students write their own biographies.

Zora Hurston and the Chinaberry Tree by William Miller
   The childhood story of the great writer Zora Neale Hurston, whose mother died when she was young and whose father couldn't understand her daydreaming and adventurous spirit. She promises her mother that she will always reach high.

Poetry

Cesar Si, Se Puede! Yes, We Can! by Carmen T. Bernier-Grand
   These poems pay tribute to Chavez's legacy of "helping migrant workers improve their lives by doing things by themselves for themselves."

Immigration: Past and Present

Historical or Realistic Fiction

Grandfather's Journey by Allen Say
   Like his grandfather, Allen Say feels that "the moment I am in one country, I am homesick for the other." The story moves between two cultures, describing his grandfather's life in Japan and adventures in the United States.

How Many Days to America? by Eve Bunting
   A compelling story of leaving what appears to be a Caribbean land full of soldiers to find safety in the United States. The story invites comparisons to more recent situations in Cuba and Haiti.

The Lotus Seed by Sherry Garland
   The story of a young woman who flees Vietnam, taking a lotus seed as a remembrance of her country. Her dangerous journey and life in a new land with her family illustrate the importance of family strength and traditions.

Maggie's Amerikay by Barbara Timberlake Russell
   Set in New Orleans, 1898, an Irish family deals creatively and positively with poverty, sickness, and education. Young girl learns that she can choose who she will be. A beautiful story.

Marianthe's Story: Painted Words/Spoken Memories by Aliki
   A little girl from Greece first tells her story in paintings before she knows enough English to talk with her classmates. As she learns English, she begins to tell her story in words. The book is two books in one. Begin by reading *Painted Words,* then flip it over and read *Spoken Memories.*

One Green Apple by Eve Bunting
   This is the story of a young Muslim immigrant, written from her perspective. Farah is the new girl at school and does not speak or know the language of her classmates. The class travels to an apple orchard where she discovers familiar sounds. Another real-world, thought-provoker from Eve Bunting.

A Picnic in October by Eve Bunting
   Tony doesn't understand why the whole family is taking the ferry out to the Statue of Liberty for a picnic until he sees how much it means to his grandmother. Kids have no idea why the grandmother is so insistent on going out on this blustery October day. The author drops gentle clues along the way.

When Jessie Came Across the Sea by Amy Hest
   The rabbi in Jessie's village chooses her to travel to America to start a new life. Jessie's letters back to her beloved grandmother tell about her new life on New York's Lower East Side. Letters from Jessie are interspersed throughout the text.

The Whispering Cloth by Pegi Deitz Shea
   A little girl and her grandmother who remain in a Hmong refugee camp tell their memories in a beautifully embroidered p'andau. Children ask lots of questions to find out what's really happening in the story and what is part of the character's imagination.

Nonfiction

Dia's Story Cloth by Dia Cha
   The story of Dia Cha's family and their journey from Laos to a refugee camp in Thailand and finally to the United States. This family story is told in a large, exquisite story cloth sewn by Dia's aunt and uncle. It preserves important memories and the history of the Hmong people's journey.

Everyone Counts—A Citizen's Number Book by Elissa Grodin
   An easy way to gain information, each page contains a rhyming verse as well as factual information. Text can be skimmed or read cover to cover. Illustrations are appealing.

I Was Dreaming to Come to America by Veronica Lawlor
   Memories from the oral history project at Ellis Island capture the recollections of people who arrived in America during the heyday of immigration. In their own words, people remember coming over on ships, their days living at Ellis Island, and the excitement of coming to a new land to start a new life.

Immigrant Kids by Russell Freedman
   Photographs of children coming to this country and then at home, school, and work in the early decades of the twentieth century illustrate hardships they experienced when they left their countries and cultures. Using the photographs of kids working, playing, and going to school provides kids an opportunity to think like historians—gleaning information from historical documents.

Journey to Ellis Island by Carol Bierman
   Because of Yehuda Weinstein's injured hand, he and his mother and sister are almost sent back to Europe. Yehuda proves himself able to run around Ellis Island and shows the immigration inspectors that his hand is healing. Actual photos

of the family, documents, and journal recollections add to the authenticity of the story.

My Freedom Trip by Frances Park and Ginger Park

The story of a little girl, Soo, who has to brave crossing the border alone to escape during the Korean War. Soo's mother, who promises to follow her to South Korea, encourages her to be brave. Themes like waiting, courage, and the price of freedom are woven into the story.

One More Border by William Kaplan with Shelley Tanaka

The story of the Kaplan family's journey across Russia, through Japan, and finally to Canada during World War II. Photographs of people, places, and original documents fill the text.

Poetry

America, My New Home by Monica Gunning

Jamaican-born poet voices her own immigrant story with such poems as "No One Knows My Name," "Skyscrapers," "Why Such a Hurry," and concludes with "My America."

Global Cultures and Geography

Realistic and Historical Fiction

The Best Winds by Laura E. Williams

Jinho, a young boy, and his grandfather engage in the age-old art of kite flying in Korea. When Jinho finds himself unable to wait for the "best winds" to fly the kite with his grandfather, he learns some important lessons about keeping family traditions.

Brothers by Yin

Two young boys overlook their differences to become friends and teach their families and neighbors to do the same. Setting is Chinatown, San Franciso; characters are Chinese and Irish. With detailed paintings, the book is by the author of *Coolies*.

Coolies by Yin

Told through the experiences of two brothers, this is the story of Chinese laborers in 1865 who were hired by the Central Pacific Railroad Company to build railroad tracks east from California to Utah. "Coolies" are the lowly workers who endured prejudice and low pay while working in extremely dangerous situations. Vivid, bold illustrations add to the sense of achievement of these workers.

The Day Gogo Went to Vote by Elinor Sisulu

In South Africa in 1994 great-grandmother Gogo, who is one hundred years old, takes her great-granddaughter Thembi with her to vote. Gogo's relatives say she is too old to go, but she insists. This story is about the South African election that elected Nelson Mandela as president.

Erandi's Braids by Antonio Hernandez Madrigal

A moving story about a seven-year-old Mexican girl's willingness to sell her hair to help her financially strapped mother. The story is based on the hair-selling practice of the 1940s and 1950s. This practice will spur questions from many kids who have never heard of it.

Sammy and the Time of Troubles by Florence Parry Heide and J. D. Gilliland

Sammy lives in war-torn twentieth-century Beirut, a life riddled with fear, uncertainty, and violence. The story describes how his family attempts to have a future amid civil chaos.

The Shaman's Apprentice by Lynne Cherry and Mark J. Plotkin

In the Amazon rain forest, the Indian way of life is endangered by outside influences. As the native Indian people look for solutions to these problems, a young boy comes to understand the healing power of the shaman and his use of native plants. And readers learn how important it is to protect the ways of traditional cultures.

Tea with Milk by Allen Say

May, raised in San Francisco, struggles upon her family's return to Japan with Japanese customs and expectations much different from what she was used to in America. This is the story of how the author's parents met and what home means to them. Young readers may have further questions about the Japanese culture and will infer well beyond the point of the story.

When Africa Was Home by Karen Lynn Williams

When a young child has to return to the United States, he misses the warm African village where he spent his early years. A wonderful book that evokes the experience of belonging to and feeling at home in a different culture.

Where Are You Going, Manyoni? by Catherine Stock

Join Manyoni on her morning walk to school through the African veld. Beautiful watercolor pictures and descriptions of all Manyoni sees and hears present a charming peek into the life of a young child who lives in Zimbabwe.

Nonfiction

Barrio—Jose's Neighborhood by George Ancona

Jose lives in San Francisco's mission district, El Barrio. The homes, food, daily life, celebrations such as fiesta and the Day of the Dead, and family activities in this culturally rich neighborhood are depicted. Excellent photos and definition of Spanish terms.

The Birdman by Veronika Martenova Charles

The author obsessed over a newspaper article about The

Birdman of Calcutta, and so traveled there to meet and interview him. A lonely tailor finds solace in nursing sick birds. He continues to set aside a quarter of his earnings in order to rescue, heal, and free thousands of illegally captured birds. Photos add to the story.

Building Liberty—A Statue Is Born by Serge Hochain
This book offers brief stories of four boys who play a role in the building of the Statue of Liberty—a French apprentice metal worker, a boy on a French navy ship, a NYC newsboy, and a young American iron worker. Detailed illustrations add to its allure.

Day of the Dead by Kathryn Lasky
Photographs and an information-filled text explain this important day in Latino cultures. The customs and traditions honoring family members in Mexico are vividly portrayed.

Going to School in India by Lisa Heydlauff
In India a school can be a tent in the desert, a bus that travels the city streets, or a classroom in the shade of a mango tree. Street children attend school in the railway station where they live. Girls determined to get an education come to school in the darkness after helping their families at home during the day. The amazing photographs tell the story of children learning in many interesting and unusual ways—all determined to get an education.

Hottest, Coldest, Highest, Deepest by Steve Jenkins
Filled with all sorts of nonfiction features, this picture book describes extreme places, illustrated by Jenkins's collages. Text and visual features abound, making this a great book for introducing how visuals and pictures enhance learning.

Looking Down by Steve Jenkins
Another creative and original offering from artist and writer Steve Jenkins, who begins this wordless picture book with a satellite view of earth from outer space. As the reader gradually falls toward earth, the bird's-eye view changes, offering opportunities for observation and discussion.

One Day We Had to Run by Sybella Wilkes
Refugee children tell their stories in words and paintings, explaining war in Africa and other cultures where children and their families are the victims of political disputes and economic problems. Paintings and drawings by the children themselves bring their stories to life.

Talking Walls by Margy Burns Knight
Walls around the world, the Lascaux caves in France, the granite walls in Zimbabwe, Nelson Mandela's prison walls, and Diego Rivera's murals, among others, introduce children to the art, sculpture, and architecture of different cultures. Contains a map locating all of the sites. Great for visualizing.

Tibet: Through the Red Box by Peter Sis
Peter Sis recounts the story of his father, who spent much time away from home when Peter was a child in the far-off country of Tibet. His father kept a diary of his time there, and when Peter grew up, he read it and recounts his father's tale here.

Poetry

Beyond the Great Mountains—A Visual Poem About China by Ed Young
Beautifully done, unique format will attract and inspire poets of all ages. The author juxtaposes seal-style characters (circa 500 B.C.) against more modern symbols.

Got Geography! selected by Lee Bennett Hopkins
"If you've got geography, you're ready for adventure. . . ." Fun selection of topics to be enjoyed by all ages.

Contemporary Social Issues

Realistic Fiction

Amelia's Road by Linda Altman
The story of a migrant child who wishes for one thing—a home. Amelia's aversion to roads stems from her family's constant moving around. Teachers may want to encourage kids to discuss Amelia's hope about "someday."

Coming On Home Soon by Jacqueline Woodson
It is wartime and Ada Ruth's mother must go to work. She heads to Chicago, leaving Ada Ruth with her grandmother. This beautifully illustrated, timeless piece captures the feelings of missing and waiting, sadness, emptiness, and finally hope that permeates a separated family's daily life.

A Day's Work by Eve Bunting
A grandfather teaches his grandson about honesty when things go awry with their landscaping work. Understanding the characters and inferring from their actions encourage students to draw conclusions about integrity and the importance of hard work.

Fly Away Home by Eve Bunting
Tough times have forced a boy and his father to take up residence in the airport to stay off the street while the father tries to get work. Kids can't stop wondering why they are in the airport, will they get a home, how does one become homeless, and more.

Gleam and Glow by Eve Bunting
The moving story of a family caught in the war in Bosnia. With

father off at war, the mother and two children head to a refugee camp where they are reunited with their father. But when they return home, little is as it was except for their pet fish! Based on a true story, a powerful book about hope, resilience, and survival. Great as an interactive read-aloud.

Good Luck, Mrs. K by Louise Borden

Everyone's favorite third-grade teacher, Mrs. Kempczinski, gets cancer and must leave school for treatment. This touching story from the perspective of one of her students delves into how kids deal with this. Hopeful in the end, Mrs. K comes back for a visit.

Just Add One Chinese Sister—An Adoption Story by Patricia McMahon and Conor Clarke McCarthy

Mother and young son team up to write this story of their family's trip to China to "get" their daughter/sister. Perspectives from each make this insightful, moving story one that children will understand. Another discussion provoker and also a good model for writing from different points of view.

La Mariposa by Francisco Jimenez

A picture book adaptation of a chapter from Jimenez's *The Circuit,* illustrating a migrant boy's struggle to learn English and survive in school. Issues of acceptance and determination to succeed are central to the story.

Little Mama Forgets by Robin Cruise

The poignant story of a little girl and her beloved grandmother who suffers age-related memory loss. The author explores the tender relationship between these two characters "criscrossing in the universe" with the girl growing stronger and the grandmother forgetting more each day. And yet, the reader experiences the joy of their love and affection.

A Name on the Quilt by Jeannine Atkins

Lauren and her family make a panel for the NAMES Project AIDS Memorial Quilt in memory of her uncle, who died of AIDS. As they sew, they reminisce and celebrate experiences with Uncle Ron. This book will provoke questions regarding the disease as well as death. Readers who have experienced death will identify closely with Lauren's feelings.

Our Gracie Aunt by Jacqueline Woodson

This is the thoughtful story of two kids whose mother can no longer take care of them. When the social worker comes to take them to live with their aunt Gracie, they are understandably wary. As the story unfolds, the kids and their family learn all about forgiveness and trust.

Smoky Night by Eve Bunting

A story set during the Los Angeles riots in the 1980s. Two lost cats go a long way toward bringing people together who couldn't get along. Kids brim with literal questions as well as deeper, more thoughtful questions.

Some Frog! by Eve Bunting

An all too familiar story of twelve-year-old Billy, who waits patiently week after week for his dad to come. The frog-jumping contest is just around the corner. Once again dad doesn't show up, but Billy's got one special mom!

Sunshine Home by Eve Bunting

A family goes to visit their grandmother after putting her in a nursing home. Many kids who have experienced the angst in their family around this issue can relate to this difficult decision.

The Wall by Eve Bunting

A boy visits the Vietnam Veterans Memorial with his father and finds the name of his grandfather. Observing other people as they remember loved ones brings home both the tragedy of the war and this remarkable way of remembering those who died.

Your Move by Eve Bunting

Ten-year-old James thinks that the K-Bones are the cool group to hang with until he, along with his six-year-old brother, begins his initiation and realizes the reality and danger of gang life. Readers may identify with being dared, trying to be cool, and the adult life many young kids live. Those without background for this will learn about the harsh reality of gangs and will realize the importance of taking a stand.

Nonfiction

In Your Face: The Culture of Beauty and You by Shari Graydon

Messages about beauty bombard our culture and have a huge effect on kids' views of themselves. This book suggests ways to examine and question the media messages we receive on a daily basis. A 2005 Notable Social Studies Tradebook.

The Storm: Students of Biloxi, Mississippi, Remember Hurricane Katrina by Barbara Barbieri McGrath

A collection of writing and artwork created by kids in grades K–12 stemming from their personal experience with the devastating hurricane. In the end, the book stresses the resilience of children and the healing power of art.

Voices from the Fields by S. Beth Atkin

Vignettes of migrant children and young adults who tell about their experiences living and moving around as the children of farm workers. The ties and values of Hispanic families come through in poems and interviews, as does the strain of moving constantly to new places and being poor in an affluent culture.

Science

Space

Fiction

Dogs in Space by Nancy Coffelt
Dogs visit the different planets, deciding it's too hot on one or too cold on another, but sharing what they learn with young readers. An afterword, "The Great Solar System Tour," provides interesting information and statistics on each planet.

Messages from Mars by Loreen Leedy and Andrew Schuerger
From the author of *Postcards from Pluto,* the format is the same; the year is 2106; fun facts abound; letters are sent back and forth; some photographs are included. The author says the book is "mostly factual, with a little fiction and a lot of looking ahead to a possible future."

The Night Rainbow by Barbara Juster Esbensen
Poetically written words and beautiful illustrations about the aurora borealis that are based on legends. At the end the book includes scientific notes and more information about related legends.

Postcards from Pluto by Loreen Leedy
Postcards from the planets provide interesting information when a class visits the solar system and writes home to their families. Great as a model for writing a class book of postcards from the planets.

Zodiac: Celestial Circle of the Sun by Jacqueline Mitton
Readable, short stories of the Zodiac constellations. Lots of facts and dazzling (some stars seem to shine) illustrations. The book proposes to share the reality behind the myths.

Nonfiction

Galaxies, Galaxies by Gail Gibbons
The author guides readers through the Milky Way and beyond, describing some of the billions of galaxies recognized by astronomers today as well as the equipment they use to explore the universe. Fun fact page concludes the book.

Godspeed, John Glenn by Richard Hilliard
A good read-aloud. Narrative is accompanied by sidebars which explain further facts and details about John Glenn and his space travel. Illustrations by the author are realistic and bold.

Kingdom of the Sun: A Book of Planets by Jacqueline Mitton and Christina Balit
Short, first-person (that is, "I am Jupiter") essays about each planet. Good model for writing shorter pieces.

The Moon by Seymour Simon
Great photographs from the Apollo journeys blend with Simon's clear explanations of what the astronauts found on the moon and all we have learned from their explorations.

Next Stop Neptune: Experiencing the Solar System by Alvin and Steve Jenkins
And experience the solar system we do. Illustrator Steve Jenkins and his astronomer father take us to all the planets as well as to far reaches of the solar system, sharing fascinating statistics, maps, and diagrams. The "you are there" descriptions help junior astronomers feel what it's like to be there, as do the beautiful cut paper illustrations.

One Giant Leap by Don Brown
The story of Neil Armstrong, who as a child dreamed of floating in space, flying, and exploring. He was the first person to set foot on the moon, on July 20, 1969. Armstrong's life is portrayed in simple language and illustrations appropriate for primary-age space fans.

The Space Shuttle by Peter Murray
"Imagine that you are on the flight deck of the space shuttle, waiting for lift-off." So begins this first-person perspective as the space shuttle blasts off and you hurl into space. A brief history of the space program follows, with amazing photographs and simple, well-written text. An index makes this book useful for researchers.

Ten Worlds: Everything That Orbits the Sun by Ken Croswell
Real images from outer space and well-written text will appeal to readers. Updated with information about the "tenth planet," spotted in 2005, the book offers lots of nonfiction features from an extensive index to informative charts to a page of "extreme" facts.

Poetry

Comets, Stars, the Moon, and Mars: Space Poems and Paintings by Doug Florian
A charming collection of space poems that range from a galaxy poem to a minor planet poem and everything in between. The paintings and the poetry are great for teaching inferring. An added bonus is the "Galactic Glossary" at the end that provides factual information about many things celestial.

The Moon by Robert Louis Stevenson
An illustrated version of a familiar poem (from 1885 *A Child's Garden of Verses*) about a father and young son's nighttime boat trip around a small cove. Will appeal to younger children.

Weather

Nonfiction

Lightning! by Stephen Kramer
The book is organized around questions such as, What is lightning? What happens during a lightning strike? and What is

thunder? A superb writer, Kramer includes a "fascinating facts" section full of amazing information.

The Reasons for Seasons by Gail Gibbons
Gail Gibbons, famous for her well-written and clearly illustrated nonfiction for younger children, explains everything one would want to know about the seasons. Diagrams of the Sun and Earth, explanations of equinoxes and each season, all with the author's careful wording and thoughtful pictures, provide an excellent introduction to this topic.

Tornado by Stephen Kramer
Once again the author does not disappoint. As much information as one could ever desire about tornadoes coupled with compelling nonfiction writing makes this a must-have for classroom libraries.

Poetry

Our Seasons by Grace Lin and Ranida T. McKneally
Why do I sneeze? Why is there frost on the window? What makes wind? These and other questions are presented "seasonally." Haiku and illustrations will appeal to younger readers.

Environmental Issues and Nature

Fiction

And Still the Turtle Watched by Sheila MacGill-Callahan
Kids with spray paint deface a Native American rock carving of an ancient turtle. Community members come together to restore the turtle and move it to a safe place. Sparks discussion of community responsibility and respect for traditions and beliefs.

Antarctica by Helen Cowcher
A visually stunning story about the relationship between the animals of Antarctica and their endangered continent.

The Great Kapok Tree by Lynne Cherry
When a man comes to the rainforest to cut down a huge kapok tree, all the animals living there come together to persuade him to save their home.

A River Dream by Allen Say
A boy's imaginary fishing trip leads to the realization of beauty of all living things. Proud of catching a fish, Mark decides it's better to release the fish than to kill it in order to "keep" it.

She's Wearing a Dead Bird on Her Head by Kathryn Lasky
Based on the turn-of-the-century founding of the Audubon Society, this book mixes fact and fiction as two sisters begin the crusade to end the use of birds and their feathers for decorating ladies' hats.

Stellaluna by Janell Cannon
Gorgeous authentic illustrations complement the story of a fruit bat who gets separated from her mother. Great for inferring themes.

Nonfiction

Actual Size by Steve Jenkins
Illustrations seem geared toward younger readers, though all ages will enjoy this "perspective" on selected animals. Jenkins illustrates animals/parts of animals at their actual size. Statistics and further information on each animal are included. Steve Jenkins's *Prehistoric Actual Size* with animals who have lived on earth for millions of years is also available.

Animal Faces by Darlyne A. Murawski
Photographs will capture animal-lovers' attention. Text is simple, yet factual.

Animals Eat the Weirdest Things by Diane Swanson
The author gives us a sampling of the strange dinners that animals consume. She throws in some rather bizarre meals for humans, too!

Animals in Flight by Steve Jenkins and Robin Page
Gorgeous collage illustrations and fascinating information introduce readers to flight as an adaptation that works in many different ways for many different animals. Jenkins also explores starting animal statistics in his book *Biggest, Strongest, Fastest*.

The Best Book of Nighttime Animals by Belinda Weber
Table of contents is "clued" with pictures. Text is limited, pictures are labeled, lots of good information is included.

Cats by Seymour Simon
Cat lovers will delight in the color photographs. Narrative text begins in Egypt 5000 years ago and ends with points to consider for would-be cat owners. Many interesting facts are included; text is to be read cover to cover.

Challenger—America's Favorite Eagle by Margot Theis Raven (in cooperation with the American Eagle Foundation)
True story about an orphaned eagle who is reared by humans and eventually is used to educate people about the plight of the endangered American Bald Eagle. Includes his flight around the stadium at the 1996 Para-Olympic games in Atlanta.

A Desert Scrapbook by Virginia Wright-Frierson
This book, the scrapbook of painter-author Wright-Frierson, allows us a peek into her observations, sketches, and paintings of all that goes on in the Sonoran Desert. A superb model for notebook writing with kids, especially young observers who love to study and write about the natural world. Wright-Frierson also wrote *An Island Scrapbook* about nature on a barrier island.

An Egg Is Quiet by Dianna Aston
Poetic text and elegant illustrations will force readers to think differently about eggs. From quiet eggs to noisy eggs, from colorful eggs to clever eggs, this is a celebration of their variety. Egg facts are interspersed throughout the text.

I See a Kookaburra! Discovering Animal Habitats Around the World by Steve Jenkins and Robin Page
Husband and wife team up to explore how a number of animals grow and thrive in very different environments. Bold, vivid illustrations will attract younger readers. The setup is "In the desert [tide pool, forest] I see. . . ." A map and more extensive information is included at the end of the book. This could be a good way for younger readers to learn animal names and to place them/picture them by habitat. Good format to use as writing model, too.

Ice Bear—In the Steps of the Polar Bear by Nicola Davies
Polar bears are protected but global warming may be melting the sea ice they depend on. This well-written narrative ends with a plea and ideas for readers to help preserve the polar bears' Arctic home. Facts are threaded beneath and along the exquisite illustrations. Readers will be heartened.

The Island That Moved: How Shifting Forces Shape Our Earth by Meredith Hooper and Lucia deLeiris
This well-written text introduces readers to the science of plate tectonics through the story of a single island. A terrific nonfiction read-aloud.

The Journey: Stories of Migration by Cynthia Rylant
A favorite author teaches readers about six migratory animals. Language use provides strong model for nonfiction writing.

Leaf Man by Lois Ehlert
"A leaf man's got to go where the wind blows," and he provides an imaginative journey for young readers. Shapes of leaves become birds, ducks, fish, and other objects in this signature Lois Ehlert piece. Familiar leaves are identified on endpapers, pages are leaf- shaped, illustrations are bold, text is limited, print is large.

Letting Swift River Go by Jane Yolen
The all too common story of wild rivers being dammed to create reservoirs across America, particularly during the 1920s, 1930s, and 1940s. Rooted in the author's own experience, this book laments the loss of these vital rivers.

Mammoths on the Move by Lisa Wheeler
Written in rhyming verse, this book follows the mammoths' trek south for the winter. Fun read-aloud for younger students.

Monarchs by Kathryn Lasky
The story of the monarch butterfly's migration from Canada to Michoacán, Mexico, each winter. The monarchs roost in trees that the locals had been clear-cutting for years. But the advent of the monarchs brought tourists, and now both the trees and the monarchs are out of harm's way. A great win-win story!

Owen and Mzee—The True Story of a Remarkable Friendship by Isabella and Craig Hatkoff
"Our most important friends are sometimes those we least expected. . . ." This is an amazing account of a 600-pound baby hippo and a 130-year-old giant tortoise, brought together as a result of the disastrous tsunami of December 26, 2004. Craig Hatkoff and his daughter Isabella were captivated by the story that appeared in the news early in 2005 and joined forces with the general manager of Haller Park in Mombasa to share the adventure with readers. Fabulous photos will captivate all ages.

Owls by Gail Gibbons
Attractive, well-written text by a favorite nonfiction author offers many features including definitions and pronunciations within context, fact-filled and labeled illustrations, and section headings. Can be used as a read-aloud.

Rattlesnake Dance by Jennifer Owings Dewey
At age nine, the author was bitten by a rattler, and she has been fascinated with them ever since. She weaves her own personal accounts with factual information about the legends and truth of rattlesnakes.

Rio Grande: From the Rocky Mountains to the Gulf of Mexico by Peter Lourie
Peter Lourie explores the Rio Grande to find out what makes the great river great. As with his other books on rivers, the author/adventurer follows the river by canoe and learns the history of the surrounding areas. Other river titles by Peter Lourie include *Amazon: A Young Reader's Look at the Last Frontier; Hudson River: An Adventure from the Mountains to the Sea; Yukon River: An Adventure to the Gold Fields of the Klondike; Erie Canal: Canoeing America's Great Waterway;* and *Everglades: Buffalo Tiger and the River of Grass.*

A River Ran Wild by Lynne Cherry
The history of the Nashua River in Massachusetts and New Hampshire is a long and stormy one. First inhabited by Indians, the river was spoiled by years of development. In the 1960s environmentalists, led by activist Marion Stoddart, fought to restore the river to its former pristine state. Today it remains a refuge for birds, fish, and people.

Snakes—Biggest! Littlest! by Sandra Markle
Snake lovers will be thrilled by the photographs in this book. Nonfiction features include diagrams, labels, map, and glossary.

Spots: Counting Creatures from Sky to Sea by Carolyn Lesser
A great book for primary kids for learning about animals and counting. Award-winning illustrations complement the poetic text.

Survivors in the Shadows by Gary Turbak
Beautifully crafted short pieces about animals who are not easy to find. Great for text-lifting mini-lessons on synthesizing.

The Tale of Pale Male: A True Story by Jeanette Winter
A compelling narrative with fun illustrations that tells the true story of two red-tailed hawks, Pale Male and his mate, who nest atop a fancy apartment building in New York City directly across from Central Park. The author recounts the controversy that ensued between the "apartment people" who have the nest removed and the protestors in Cental Park who rally in support of the hawks and ultimately prevail in allowing the hawks to rebuild their nest.

The Top of the World by Steve Jenkins
Imagine you're headed to the world's highest mountain, Mt Everest. What dangers will you encounter? What equipment will you take? What's likely to happen when you get there? All these questions, and many more, are answered as Steve Jenkins's signature collages and essential information tell us all we need to know about this mighty mountain and those who try to conquer it.

The Tree of Life by Peter Sis
Drawing on the writings of Charles Darwin, Peter Sis creates a fascinating picture of the naturalist whose ideas about the origins of life and natural selection challenged seventeenth-century thinking and continue to impact modern life and science to this day.

Why? by Lila Prap
Why do hyenas laugh? Why are zebras striped? Why do crocodiles cry? And why don't snakes have legs? These and more questions about animals are answered both laughably and factually. A fun read for child/adult partners or as a read-aloud. Great for encouraging the strategy of questioning.

Wild Dogs Past and Present by Kelly Milner-Halls
These are not your everyday house pets. Kids will be fascinated as the author takes the reader to every continent in the world, save Anarctica, to learn about wild dogs, how they survive or fail to thrive, and how they play a role in the balance of nature.

Wild Fibonacci—Nature's Secret Code Revealed by Joy Hulme
The Fibonacci sequence, noted in 1202, is a vital element in nature's grand design. The code determines the curve of tusks, beaks, teeth, tails, and much more "to help creatures to survive." Rhyming text supports sophisticated theory.

Will We Miss Them? by Alexandra Wright
This book, written by a middle school student, describes the plight of disappearing and endangered animals and asks the title question.

Wings of Light—The Migration of the Yellow Butterfly by Stephen R. Swinburne
Beautifully written and illustrated, the book follows a butterfly's journey from the Yucatan rain forest to southern Vermont. That's right—an insect weighing half a gram travels 2000 miles!

Series

Earthworks series includes:

Mountains—The Tops of the World by David Harrison
Begins with and traces how a fish from the sea could reach the top of a mountain. Well-written text includes definitions of relevant terms within context; diagrams and illustrations clarify meaning. Good for reading aloud, especially to kick off a study of the earth. Other titles in this series by the same author are also good for reading aloud and include *Earthquakes, Caves, Rivers, Volcanoes, Oceans, Glaciers.* All of the book are accurately and beautifully illustrated.

Poetry

Butterfly Eyes and Other Secrets of the Meadow and *Song of the Water Boatman and Other Pond Poems* by Joyce Sidman
Each featured poem is flanked by a factual write-up in these two poetry collections. What a great writing model! Scientists can try their hand at poetry after a study and/or poets can learn to research facts about their subjects.

Count Me a Rhyme—Animal Poems by the Numbers by Jane Yolen
This is the latest work of author Jane Yolen and her son, photographer Jason Stemple. Readers will enjoy a variety of poems and vivid photographs. They've collaborated on other titles with the same format, including *Fine Feathered Friends, Horizons, Least Things* (poems about things small in nature), *Color Me a Rhyme* (nature poems), and *Snow, Snow.*

Creatures of the Earth, Sea, and Sky by Georgia Heard
Poems about endangered animals and the importance of nature in our lives. Heard's carefully crafted yet accessible poems are wonderful models for children as they learn to write poetry themselves.

Feathers—Poems About Birds by Eileen Spinelli
For bird lovers or a classroom bird study, this collection highlights bird antics and behavior. "Some feathery facts" are included at the end. Another great example of poetry and nonfiction writing featured back to back.

Mites to Mastadons—A Book of Animal Poems by Maxine Kumin
Maxine Kumin, a favorite poet, shares her fascination with animals in this engaging and lively illustrated book.

Safe, Warm, and Snug by Stephen Swinburn
Lovely poems about how each animal species protects its babies from predators. Accurate information presented in a compelling way.

Scientists, Inventors, and a Collection of Quirky Topics

Fiction

Building with Dad by Carol Nevius
Younger readers will be drawn to the design of this simple story. The shape of the book is familiar but needs to be held differently as pictures and text run top to bottom. Lots of machines are named and simply explained in rhyme as the son watches his father help build his new school.

The Greatest Potatoes by Penelope Stowell
A prominent businessman/world traveler (maybe Cornelius Vanderbilt) is on a mission to find the best potatoes. At a particular restaurant, he sends french fries back and angers the chef who, in turn, decides to make the "worst" potatoes he can. The traveler loves them—and potato chips are born! Includes recipe for potato chips.

Squirrel and John Muir by Emily Arnold McCully
The year is 1868, the setting, the Yosemite Valley, and John Muir, the naturalist, is looking for evidence to support his theory of glacial formation. Based on historic events, the author creates this story between Muir and "Squirrel," a young girl of the Yosemite Valley. Although this is a fictionalized account, the afterword details the actual relationship and reveals a great deal about the fascinating founder of the Sierra Club.

Twenty-One Elephants and Still Standing by April Jones Prince
In May of 1884, P.T. Barnum proves that the newly constructed Brooklyn Bridge can be trusted by lining up twenty-one of his circus elephants across it. (One elephant = 10,000 pounds!) Paintings are striking; this story is a memorable one.

Nonfiction

The Boy Who Drew Birds—A Story of John James Audubon by Jacqueline Davies and Melissa Sweet
Audubon (in 1804) was the first person in North America to band a bird. He proved the theory of homing—birds *do* return to the same nest each year and their offspring nest nearby. Emphasis is on his love of birds as a young boy and his obsession with them throughout his life.

The Buffalo Nickel by Taylor Morrison
This book takes place between 1880 and 1913 and tells the story of the creator of the coin, American sculptor James Earle Fraser. It also describes the process by which coins are designed and minted. An interesting man and an unusual topic.

Built to Last—Building America's Amazing Bridges, Dams, Tunnels, and Skyscrapers by George Sullivan
A beautiful resource, this coffee-table-sized book covers big projects from 1790 to the present and includes the history of the people involved, anecdotal stories, and fabulous photographs.

Bread Comes to Life—A Garden of Wheat and a Loaf to Eat by George Levenson
Rhyming verse traces how bread is made. Close-up, vivid photos. *Very* simple, yet scientific!

Climbing Everest: Tales of Triumph and Tragedy on the World's Highest Mountain by Audrey Salkeld
This book explores six of the most famous Everest climbing stories in history, some tragic, some triumphant, all compelling. Great photographs, maps, time lines, and even an Everest Hall of Fame that describes the most famous climbers of the mountain the Himalayans call Chomolungma, Mother Goddess of the Land

A Drop of Water: A Book of Science and Water by Walter Wick
A creative way of looking at the physics of water. Close-up photographs of water drops and water in all forms. The text explains the physics of water by suggesting some experiments you can do at home.

Gargoyles, Girders and Glass Houses: Magnificent Master Builders by Bo Zaunders
Describing the builders who built the world's "most stunning structures" tells us a lot about both the buildings and the brains behind them.

Gregor Mendel—The Friar Who Grew Peas by Cheryl Bardoe
This story begins, "All his life, Gregor Mendel hungered for knowledge . . . he yearned to unlock nature's secrets and to share them with everyone." Although he received no glory during his lifetime, Mendel is now known as the first geneticist. His research and findings of how parents (plants, animals, and humans) pass down traits to their children is explained and diagrammed clearly.

Hidden Worlds: Looking Through a Scientist's Microscope by Stephen Kramer
The writer who brought us *Lightning, Tornado,* and *Caves* teams up with scientists/photographer Dennis Kunkel, whose life work has focused on exploring the unseen world of crystals, cells, algae, and other wonders. Fascinating, well-written infor-

mation and amazing photographs take us into the world of a practicing microscopist

How Come? by Kathy Wollard
This book answers common questions that kids ask and often no one knows the answers to, such as Why is space black? Great for text-lifting mini-lessons on finding answers to specific questions. Also see *How Come? Planet Earth.*

Ice Cream—The Full Scoop by Gail Gibbons
One of Gibbons' latest publications and formatted as her others. This is really fun. Book traces ice cream from the earliest hand-cranked to different ice cream makers to the origins of the ice cream cone to how a modern ice cream factory works!

In Your Face: The Facts About Your Features by Donna M. Jackson
This is "a guide to the human face!" Text explains how eyes, ears, mouth, and nose work; discusses the definition of beauty; notes various facial expressions; and includes lots of high-interest facts and authentic stories.

Looking at Glass Through the Ages by Bruce Koscielniak
A readable text that traces the origin (4,500 years ago) and processing of glass from hand blown to machine made and from stained glass to mirrors to lens.

Marvelous Mattie—How Margaret E. Knight Became an Inventor by Emily Arnold McCully
"Lady Edison," as she has been called, developed an early fascination with inventions and machinery when she inherited her father's toolbox. She eventually designed and patented a machine that cuts and glues together square-bottomed paper bags. Young scientists will especially enjoy the drawings from her notebooks.

A Million Dots by Andrew Clements
See what a million looks like! Readers of all ages will quickly be engaged in format, facts, and author's ability to put a "million" in perspective.

Mistakes That Worked by Charlotte Foltz Jones
A collection of accidents that resulted in surprising inventions such as Velcro, potato chips, and Post-it Notes. Kids love these unusual twists of events. A sequel, *More Mistakes That Worked,* is also available.

My Brothers' Flying Machine by Jane Yolen
This well-researched narrative reveals the story of Wilbur and Orville, as told from the perspective of their younger sister, Katharine. Orville once said, "When the world speaks of the Wrights, it must include our sister. Much of our effort has been inspired by her." Text includes information about the brothers' lives, inventions, and work—up to and including their first flight.

My Light by Molly Bang
Molly Bang's distinct style will appeal to readers. The creation of electricity is traced, beginning with energy from the sun.

Odd Boy Out—Young Albert Einstein by Don Brown
Young Einstein loved math and music but was an oddball. This is a brief look at the ways of the strange child whose ideas eventually changed the way we know and understand our world.

Outside and Inside Mummies by Sandra Markle
The cover photograph, alone, will attract readers. This is the kind of book that interested students will fight over to study the vivid (and graphic) photographs. Text updates readers on the latest technology and practices in solving mysteries about mummies.

Sea Clocks: The Story of Longitude by Louise Borden
The compelling story of John Harrison, an Englishman with no science training, who worked tirelessly for forty years to design the perfect clock. Before the time of Harrison, sailors could not calculate longitude and thus many people died at sea. A story of perseverance and determination.

Skyscraper by Susan E. Goodman
Statistics on the building of skyscrapers come to life with color photographs and readable text. Readers will gain a well-defined perspective on heights and weights of materials used.

Snowflake Bentley by Jacqueline Briggs Martin
The 1998 Caldecott winner and the story of Wilson Bentley's passion for photographing and studying snowflakes. He "loved snow more than anything else in the world" and developed the techniques of microphotography that allowed him to take thousands of photographs of exquisite snow crystals. A story of following one's passion and determination to document the wonders of nature.

Starry Messenger by Peter Sis
The story of Galileo told with illustrations and text of extraordinary beauty. A wonderful book to build background about Renaissance times and introduce the themes of the power of knowledge.

The Story of Salt by Mark Kurlansky
Salt is the only rock eaten by human beings! Text explains the history and evolution of salt's uses, processing, and role in ancient civilizations to the present time.

The Story of Science: Aristotle Leads the Way by Joy Hakim
Hakim traces the history of science beginning with the Greeks and the overriding influence of Aristotle on into the fifteenth century. The book ends, "There is something I want to be sure you understand before you close this book, science is not about certainty, it's about uncertainty . . . about trying ideas,

discarding those that don't work and building on those that do." Joy Hakim always keeps us thinking!

The Tarantula Scientist by Sy Montgomery
Traces the life and career of tarantula scientist Sam Marshall from the lab to the field as he studies the spiders he loves. Great photographs, scads of information about tarantulas, but most importantly insight into a truly passionate scientist.

Health

Guts—Our Digestive System by Seymour Simon is part of series that includes *The Brain, Bones, Eyes and Ears, The Heart,* and *Muscles*
Includes amazing photos (the inside of the esophagus is disgusting!), microscopic views, and x-rays to illustrate concepts.

Disasters: Man-made and Natural

Nonfiction

Avalanche by Stephen Kramer
A great nonfiction writer, Stephen Kramer gives the reader excellent content while at the same time painting vivid pictures with his words. Great for learning about avalanches as well as modeling strong nonfiction writing.

Bodies from the Ash by James M. Deem
This up-to-date source on Pompeii pieces together stories of peoples' lives using the plaster casts and artifacts that have mesmerized young readers for years. Deem reminds us, too, that Vesuvius is a sleeping giant, which adds to the suspense and power of the story.

The Buried City of Pompeii by Shelley Tanaka
Well-written history of Pompeii. Visually interesting with photographs and drawings, the book answers many student questions about how people died, what really happened, and how the city, lost for so many years, was rediscovered. Good for visualizing in reading and showing-not-telling in writing.

A Day That Changed America: Earthquake! by Shelley Tanaka
Eyewitness accounts from four young survivors tell the story of the 1906 San Francisco earthquake. Excellent historical photographs, maps, and pictures of artifacts complement the startling descriptions of what happened that day.

The Great Fire by Jim Murphy
The story of the great Chicago fire of 1871. The author includes personal accounts of survivors as well as an understanding of the history of the Chicago fire to tell a gripping story of the enormity of this event.

Hill of Fire by Thomas P. Lewis
An I Can Read Book based on reports of the eruption of

Paricutin volcano on February 20, 1943. This was one of only two eruptions in recorded history where the birth of a volcano has been seen by human eyes.

Story of the Titanic by Dr. Eric Kentley and Steve Noon
Readers will love to peruse this oversized book with double-paged illustrations. Cross-sections and cutaway details make it a great read on a high-interest topic.

Tsunami: Helping Each Other by Ann Morris and Heidi Larson
Amazing photographs and text tell the story of two young boys who survive the December 2004 tsunami. What their village was like before, during, and after the tsunami provides kids with many answers to their questions and ultimately is a story of how people, despite the tragic circumstances and with assistance from the rest of the world, have started to rebuild their lives.

Wildfire by Taylor Morrison
This is a great read for older readers interested in firefighting. Extensive text includes a story line as well as sequential, simple explanations. Covers the history of firefighting plus current practices.

Extraordinary Children

Nonfiction

Cracking the Wall: The Struggles of the Little Rock Nine by Eileen Lucas
An easy-to-read version of the story of the first black students to attend the all-white Central High School in Little Rock, Arkansas. The afterword provides background on what happened to the students when then-governor Faubus closed all the Little Rock public high schools rather than integrate the schools.

Heroic Children by Rebecca Hazell
A collection of short pieces telling the stories of amazing children through the ages, who come from many countries and cultures. These kids' stories of adventure, courage, and determination will inspire modern kids.

Kids at Work: Lewis Hine and the Crusade Against Child Labor by Russell Freedman
Photographs of children at work in factories, on the streets, and living in squalor are the same ones Lewis Hine used in his actual crusade against child labor many years ago. Excellent original sources and interviews allow students to use documents to learn about Hine's work.

Messages to Ground Zero: Children Respond to September 11, 2001 by Shelley Harwayne with the NYC Board of Education
A moving collection of children's poems, drawings, and memories that captures their questions and attempts to understand

this incomprehensible event. An important addition to any post–9/11 library.

Orphan Train Rider: One Boy's True Story by Andrea Warren
Beginning in 1854 trains carried orphaned children to new homes in the West and South. The story of Lee and his brothers, all adopted by different families, illustrates how the boys overcame grief and fear at losing their parents and being separated during their early years. Excellent information about this historical movement, tied together as the brothers are reunited as adults.

We Were There, Too—Young People in US History by Phillip Hoose
This remarkable resource tells the stories of over sixty children and young people who played a variety of fascinating roles in our nation's history. Their compelling stories, from Pocahontas in the 1600s to present-day young people fighting for civil rights and justice, jumpstart kids' interest in almost any important person or event.

Witnesses to Freedom: Young People Who Fought for Civil Rights by Belinda Rochelle
Recollections by students who organized sit-ins, integrated their schools, and participated in boycotts. The courageous behavior of these young people encourages others to work toward ending discrimination and injustice. In-depth information about the March on Washington, Freedom Schools, and other nonviolent aspects of the civil rights movement.

Sports

Amazing Athletes

Nonfiction

By My Brother's Side by Tiki and Ronde Barber
This is the childhood story about National Football League superstars Ronde Barber (Tampa Bay Buccaneers) and Tiki Barber (New York Giants). Their mother's influence lends to the theme of believing in oneself and "playing proud."

The Goalie Mask by Mike Leonetti
A "hockey" narrative that tells the story of Jacques Plante, a goalie who was the first to wear a mask during a game. He joined the Montreal Canadians in 1952 and ended up in the Hockey Hall of Fame. Interesting story for both hockey players and sports fans.

Joe Louis—America's Fighter by David A. Adler
Joseph Louis Barrow ends up in Detroit, circa 1930, and quits school to become a boxer. Without room to add "Barrow" on the sign-up for his first fight, he becomes Joe Louis, and eventually becomes the greatest heavyweight champion ever. During the

Depression, Louis is a hero for blacks; during WWII, he is a hero for Americans. Highlights of his life and author's notes are included at the end.

Perfect Timing—How Isaac Murphy Became One of the World's Greatest Jockeys by Patsi B. Trollinger
The artwork is astounding—each painting in this book is frameable. The story is amazing, too. Murphy (1861–1896) still holds the record for the highest percentage of racing wins (44 percent of all his races), including three Kentucky Derbies. The life of a jockey will intrigue readers of all ages.

Sixteen Years in Sixteen Seconds—The Sammy Lee Story by Paula Yoo
Although he grew up with limited amounts of practice time—in 1932, people of color were only allowed to swim in public pools on Wednesdays—Sammy Lee became the first Asian American to win an Olympic gold medal. His talent for diving, the inspiration gained from his father, and his determination to succeed led him to the 1948 Olympics at the age of twenty-eight.

Win One for the Gipper—America's Football Hero by Kathy-Jo Wargin
College Hall of Famer George Gipp played Notre Dame football not only with his body and mind, he also played with his heart. On his deathbed, he tells coach Knute Rockne to remind the team, when down, to go in there with all they've got and win just one for the Gipper. Moving, beautiful story of a short life well lived.

Series

A is for Axel—An Ice Skating Alphabet by Kurt Browning
Hat Tricks Count—A Hockey Number Book by Matt Napier
J is for Jump Shot—A Basketball Alphabet by Mike Ulmer
R is for Race—A Stock Car Alphabet by Brad Herzog
These are a few of the most recent titles in a series published by Sleeping Bear Press. Highly predictable format allows readers to enjoy the rhyming text and to digest the factual information provided on each page. Topics are of *high* interest. Struggling readers will appreciate an easy way to gain more information about the sports they love.

Baseball

Fiction

The Babe and I by David Adler
Babe Ruth's hitting streak helps one boy sell lots of newspapers as he tries to help his needy family during the Great Depression.

Baseball Ballerina by Kathryn Cristaldi
Much to her embarrassment, a young baseball-loving girl is

forced to take up ballet. All ends well when her team cheers her on at the dance recital, and she realizes that baseball and ballet are not mutually exclusive.

The Bat Boy and His Violin by Gavin Curtis
Reginald loves to practice his violin but his dad, the manager of one of the worst teams in the Negro leagues, needs a batboy. During downtime in the dugout, Reginald plays classical music and the team's luck begins to change.

Dirt on Their Skirts: The Story of the Young Women Who Won the World Championship by Doreen Rappaport and Lyndall Callan
Yeah! A book about *girls* playing baseball! This is about the 1946 championship game of the All-American Girls Professional Baseball League, as watched by a young girl in the stands. Black-and-white photos of team members are included on endpapers. Good model for writing blow-by-blow accounts of sporting events.

Girl Wonder—A Baseball Story in Nine Innings by Deborah Hopkinson
Told in the first person, this piece was inspired by Alta Weiss, born in 1890, who at seventeen pitched for a semipro, all-male team.

Hooray for Snail by John Stadler
Snail, the slowest member of the team, nails a home run that flies to the moon and back. Kids relate to Snail and love the story's humor.

Luke Goes to Bat by Rachel Isadora
A 1950s Brooklyn Dodgers/Jackie Robinson fan is too young to play stickball with the neighborhood kids. He strikes out when given the chance to play, yet ultimately learns that he can't give up. This simple story with lovely illustrations makes for a good read-aloud and will provide readers with many connections.

Play Ball, Amelia Bedelia by Peggy Parish
Everyone's favorite literal thinker joins a baseball team and, to the delight of young readers, takes the game's instructions literally.

Nonfiction

Ballpark—The Story of America's Baseball Fields by Lynn Curlee
Baseball fans will love this coffee-table-sized, chronologically organized history of baseball stadiums across the country. Extensive, narrative text is accompanied by illustrations, no photos.

Baseball, the American Epic series by Geoffrey Ward, Ken Burns, and Jim O'Connor
Two extremely well-written books based on the PBS series of the same name. The titles include *Shadow Ball: The History of the Negro Leagues in America* and *Who Invented the Game?* Great models for visualizing in reading and showing-not-telling in writing.

Baseball's Best: Five True Stories by Andrew Gutelle
The author tells the story of five of the greatest Hall of Famers of all time, including Babe Ruth, Joe DiMaggio, Jackie Robinson, Roberto Clemente, and Hank Aaron.

Baseball Saved Us by Ken Mochizuki
Based on the author's own experience, Japanese Americans interned during World War II organize a team and build a baseball diamond which provides a diversion during this sad period in their lives.

Hey Batta Batta Swing! The Wild Old Days of Baseball by Sally Cook and James Charlton
This well researched tribute to our nation's pastime includes a snappy collection of unusual facts and interesting stories about baseball since its inception. The charming illustrations combined with a running list of baseball terms and slang support kids to get a lot of information as they read the text. A great read for anyone who loves the game!

Lou Gehrig: The Luckiest Man by David Adler
A wonderful picture book that tells the story of one of baseball's greatest and his struggle with the disease that now bears his name.

Take Me Out to the Ball Game by Jack Norworth and Jim Burke
This book pays tribute to both Christy Mathewson, a pitcher for the New York Giants and one of the five first inducted into the Baseball Hall of Fame, and the 1908 hit song. Pages combine lyrics of the song, baseball trivia, and highlights of the 1908 game between the New York Giants and the Chicago Cubs.

Teammates by Peter Golenbock
The remarkable story of the friendship between Jackie Robinson and Pee Wee Reese during the period when Jackie broke the Major League color barrier. Thought provoking and rich in diverse themes.

Poetry

Baseball, Snakes and Summer Squash: Poems About Growing Up by Donald Graves
A collection of poems that describes the experiences and adventures of a young boy growing up.

Casey at the Bat by Ernest Lawrence Thayer
A recent edition of the classic story with soft acrylic illustrations that will capture the heart of any baseball fan.

The Arts: Fine Art, Music, Drama

Fine Art

Fiction

The Art Lesson by Tomie de Paola
Tomie de Paola's autobiographical story of a young boy who couldn't wait to start school and have real art lessons only to find that he had to draw what everyone else did. The story serves as an important reminder about individual differences.

Bonjour, Mr. Satie by Tomie de Paola
This clever story about a traveling cat in the 1920s Paris of Gertrude Stein addresses the notion that one person's art (Picasso's) is not necessarily better than another's (Matisse's), only different.

Children, A First Art Book by Lucy Micklethwait
Eighteen works of art illustrate activities throughout a child's day. Limited text; stimulating conversation piece to complement a classroom or library collection.

Hana in the Time of the Tulips by Deborah Noyes
Tulipomania struck Holland between 1634–1637 as tulips became the ultimate status symbol. The young girl in the story reminds her father of what is valuable in life, as he becomes overly greedy. Rembrandt appears, although he did not favor tulips as a subject.

Katie's Sunday Afternoon by James Mayhew
A playful way to promote interaction with fine art! While visiting an art museum, Katie "climbs" into different paintings and experiences quite an adventure. Five Pointillist paintings are featured. Information on artists (Seurat, Signac, Pissarro) is included.

Lucy's Picture by Nicola Moon
All the kids in class are painting pictures, but Lucy chooses to do a textured collage instead to give to her grandfather. The reader discovers that Lucy's grandpa is blind; he can feel the texture in Lucy's creation. The notion that it is all right to be different pervades this story.

The Squiggle by Carol Lexa Schaefer
Beautiful Chinese brush painting illustrations printed on stock that has the feel of rice paper. When the last little girl in line sees a red ribbon on the sidewalk, her imagination runs away with her. A true celebration of art and imagination that will ring true for kids everywhere.

When Clay Sings by Byrd Baylor
Baylor's homage to the early Native American art of pottery making and drawing. Terrific illustrations capture the early history and art of the Anasazi, Hohokam, and Mimbre. Kids love to draw these images and use them to visualize what life was like for these artistic people.

Nonfiction

Diego by Jonah Winter
The story of the famous Mexican muralist Diego Rivera, which speaks to his wonderful art as well as his love of country. The text is written in Spanish as well as English.

Georgia's Bones by Jen Bryant
As a child, shapes in nature please Georgia O'Keeffe; as an adult shapes grab her attention. Eventually, she finds her way to New Mexico, where she delights in all things natural—the sky, the hills, mountains and rivers, animal bones, and the ever-changing colors around her.

Grandma Moses by Alexandra Wallner
Insight into the life of Anna Mary Robertson, better known as the painter Grandma Moses. Illustrations done in the painter's style add to the authenticity of the story.

Josefina by Jeanette Winter
The author discovers Josefina Aguilar and her painted clay sculptures in Ocotlán, Mexico. This story about a remarkable woman and her folk art portrays Josefina's life as one steeped in art and tradition.

Leonardo: Beautiful Dreamer by Robert Byrd
A stunning biography with fetching illustrations not unlike Da Vinci's own notebook sketches and compelling text that gives us a true picture of the original Renaissance man. For those who want more, a bibliography and list of websites can be found at the end.

Leonardo da Vinci by Diane Stanley
The inspiring story of a poor, illegitimate child who grew up to be one of the most extraordinary minds the world has ever known. Diane Stanley's exceptional illustrations perfectly capture the time period in which he lived. A great book for research into the Renaissance.

Lives of the Artists by Kathleen Krull
One of a series of nonfiction books about writers, musicians, presidents, and athletes, containing interesting short biographies of visual artists.

My Name Is Georgia by Jeanette Winter
Written in the first person from the perspective of Georgia O'Keeffe, this book describes her individuality. She always saw the world differently and always knew she wanted to be an artist. Stunning illustrations fill the book, which lends itself to visualizing.

Talking with Artists (3 volumes) by Pat Cummings
Well-known children's book illustrators tell their personal stories

and answer questions about their artistic process. Each portrait includes photographs of the artist, a piece of art created by the artist as a child, and an example of the illustrations he or she does today.

Uncle Andy's: A Faabbulous Visit with Andy Warhol by James Warhola

Andy Warhol, among other pop artists of the 1960s, stretched the limits of art by portraying ordinary things that were popular in modern society. This glimpse at his life is written by his nephew, who remembers a visit to his uncle's home and studio in 1962. Great message about the fact that "art is all around us all of the time."

Series

Art Auction Mystery by Anna Nilsen

A great way to learn about art! The book lends itself to individual and/or partner study. Includes historical information about thirty-four paintings. *Art Fraud Detective* and *The Great Art Scandal* are other titles in the series.

Famous Artists series by Antony Mason

The series introduces young readers to the world's most celebrated painters and sculptors, including Cezanne, Leonardo, Michaelangelo, Monet, Picasso, and Van Gogh. Reproductions of famous works are included in each book.

Music

Fiction

Play, Mozart, Play! by Peter Sis

Illustrations are the draw to this book and will make for interesting and imaginative conversation. The very elementary, limited text focuses on Mozart and his father who made him practice (or *play*) all of the time. Readers will delight in Mozart's "play."

Summertime from Porgy and Bess by Ira Gershwin, George Gershwin, DuBose Heyward, and Dorothy Heyward

Beautiful illustrations by Mike Wimmer depict the artist's interpretation of the famous Gershwin song "Summertime." Readers will enjoy comparing their summertime experiences with the artist's and each other's.

What a Wonderful World by George David Weiss and Bob Thiele

The lyrics of Louis Armstrong's signature song are combined with illustrations of children from many different backgrounds in a celebration of diversity and unity.

Nonfiction

Ballet of the Elephants by Leda Schubert

This is the true story of a unique and surprising collaboration.

In 1942, John Ringling North (the owner of the Greatest Show on Earth), George Balanchine (the greatest choreographer of the twentieth century), and Igor Stravinsky (the famous composer) teamed up to present a ballet performed by elephants! Original black-and-white photographs are featured at the end.

Celia Cruz, Queen of Salsa by Veronica Chambers

"In the fabled land of Havana . . . there was a young girl who sang like a bird." Eventually, Cruz becomes the "Queen of Salsa" across the world. Illustrations complement the Afro-Cuban feel of her story. Glossary and Selected Discography included.

Charlie Parker Played Be Bop by Chris Raschka

Great illustrations and words like *boomba, bippity, boppity* fill this book for primary readers that celebrates the music of the great saxophonist Charlie "Bird" Parker. The rhythmic text is great for sensory imaging.

Dizzy by Jonah Winter

This inviting picture book honors Dizzy Gillespie's contribution to the jazz/bebop movement. Readers will be impressed by his strength of character and his penchant for fun. He got into a lot of trouble by having the courage to be himself. Author's note includes a brief biography.

Duke Ellington: The Piano Prince and His Orchestra by Andrea Davis Pinkney

Beautiful illustrations by Brian Pinkney complement a stunning text that traces the career and life of Edward Kennedy "Duke" Ellington, the piano player and bandleader extraordinaire.

If I Only Had a Horn: Young Louis Armstrong by Roxane Orgill

Based on a true event in the musician's life. Young Louis Armstrong's dream comes true when his neighbors pitch in to buy him a used cornet. A stunning lesson in community.

Lives of the Musicians by Kathleen Krull

One of a series of nonfiction books about artists, musicians, presidents, and athletes, this one includes interesting short biographies of musicians.

Mozart: Scenes from the Childhood of the Great Composer by Catherine Brighton

Written from the perspective of Mozart's sister, this book traces Mozart's childhood travels through Europe with his sister and his father. An excellent informational book for research on Mozart.

Sebastian: A Book About Bach by Jeanette Winter

"The first Voyager spacecraft was launched in 1977. On the spacecraft there is a recording of sounds from Earth. Should the spacecraft encounter any life beyond our galaxy, the first sound that will be heard is the music of Johann Sebastian Bach." So begins Jeanette Winter's stunning book about the life and work of Bach. Truly extraordinary illustrations make this one of her best.

Series

Bach's Goldberg Variations by Anna Harwell Celenza
Gershwin's Rhapsody in Blue by Anna Harwell Celenza
The Heroic Symphony by Anna Harwell Celenza
   Readable stories about how these musicians found inspiration for their compositions, the process involved in writing and performing them, and a few amusing personal accounts. CDs are included.

Poetry

Jazz by Walter Dean Myers
   Readers (and listeners) cannot help but feel the beat as they enjoy these fifteen poems celebrating the different styles of jazz. Striking, colorful artwork is full of movement, too. Fun for endless interpretations and performances; strong model for writing.

Woody Guthrie: Poet of the People by Bonnie Christensen
   This book celebrates the life and times of the famous folk musician. With lyrical words and artful illustrations, the text is both a biography of Woody Guthrie as well as an homage to American folk music.

Drama

Fiction

Macbeth by Bruce Coville
   A riveting rendition of one of Shakespeare's greatest plays. The eerie illustrations and the compelling text make this a story young readers will want to read over and over.

Nonfiction

The Bard of Avon by Diane Stanley
   Although little is known about the Millennium Man's background, Diane Stanley fills the reader in on what likely happened in the life of the Western world's greatest playwright. The illustrations give an accurate picture of life in Shakespeare's day.

Literacy

Fiction

Amber on the Mountain by Tony Johnston
   Amber's life high on a mountain has precluded school and reading. A girl moves in nearby, bringing the gift of reading and books to Amber, who returns the gift of a simple mountain life. Kids burst with questions when they read it, and the message that you can do anything you want to if you put your mind to it is a powerful one for children of all ages.

Amelia's Notebook by Marissa Moss
   Hand-lettered journal written by nine-year-old Amelia. Great for promoting journal writing, jotting thoughts and feelings, as well as selecting topics. The same author wrote *Rachel's Journal* and *Emma's Journal.*

Aunt Chip and the Great Tripple Creek Dam Affair by Patricia Polacco
   Aunt Chip, the librarian who understands the consequences of too much TV and not enough books, saves a town seduced by television from a terrible plight. An enjoyable book that inspires lots of questions as to the resolution.

The Chalk Doll by Charlotte Pomerantz
   Rose, sick in bed, gets her mother to tell story after story about growing up in Jamaica. One story leads to another—a great model for telling and writing family stories.

The Day of Ahmed's Secret by Florence Parry Heide and J. D. Gilliland
   This story, set in Egypt, shows a very different life for a six-year-old boy than most American kids are used to. Ahmed works rather than going to school. But at the end of the day, he reveals his most important secret: he has learned to write his name. Kids wonder about the secret as well as the foreign life of young Ahmed.

Edward and the Pirates by David McPhail
   Edward, who learned to read in McPhail's earlier *Santa's Book of Names,* now reads everything in sight. One night the pirates come to life in Edward's imagination, and after some harrowing moments he discovers that what they really want is to be read to. A great book for visualizing.

Emily by Michael Bedard
   The author's fictional account of a young girl who lives next door to the mysterious, "crazy" Emily Dickinson. Her meeting with the recluse changes her perspective. The poetic quality and striking language make the book effective for teaching visualizing. And readers have to infer the nature of this mysterious character from start to finish.

I Hate to Read! by Rita Marshall
   A good book to read to early readers, particularly those who are not that thrilled with reading, since Victor hates to read. The characters come to life and lure him into the adventure of reading.

I'm in Charge of Celebrations by Byrd Baylor
   The main character celebrates each day by keeping a notebook of natural occurrences and celebrating each one. A great model for showing how writers keep notebooks and write short descriptive entries.

Langston's Train Ride by Robert Burleigh
   "Poems are like rainbows—they escape if you're not quick,"

writes Langston Hughes, as he composes *The Negro Speaks of Rivers* (his first famous poem) on a train trip to Mexico in 1920. Illustrations are bold and inviting; poem is included in text.

The Library by Sarah Stewart

This book is an homage to book-loving librarians everywhere. Elizabeth Brown liked reading so much that she ran out of room for her books and donated them all to the public library in her ripe old age.

Library Lion by Michelle Knudsen

The emphasis is on library "rules"—until a well-meaning lion finds a good reason to break them. Librarians will appreciate discussion that can be generated from this one.

Max's Words by Kate Banks

Max's brothers collect stamps and coins, and will not share with him. He decides to collect words—and eventually has enough to tell a story. This is a *fun* book for writers (and would-be writers) of all ages, as they observe his process for telling a make-believe story.

Mr. George Baker by Amy Hest

Young Harry befriends Mr. George Baker—who is a hundred years old! Both are learning to read, and it's hard. Illustrations add to the charm of this story.

My Great-Aunt Arizona by Gloria Houston

Great-Aunt Arizona inspires her students to imagine by reading books about places far away, letting us in on one of the great joys of reading—that it can take you anywhere.

Read for Me, Mama by Vashanti Rahaman

Joseph loves library day at school, but when he asks his mom to read him one of his library books, he discovers she can't. A powerful story about community literacy and a loving relationship between a boy and his mom.

River Boy—The Story of Mark Twain by William Anderson

Traces the antics and adventures of a fun-loving boy turned author, Samuel Clemens. What a character! Chronology of his life is included at the end.

Santa's Book of Names by David McPhail

Edward is in first grade and struggling to read. His teacher suggests testing. His wise mom suggests waiting. Edward learns to read when he's ready and has a purpose. This book reminds us that readers learn to read at different times. Great for those kids who think they may never read.

Stella Louella's Runaway Book by Lisa Campbell Ernst

The most fun read-aloud ever! A must-have for all ages. Yikes! Stella Louella's library book has disappeared and is due at the library by five o'clock. Clever, cumulative tale has lots to offer observant readers.

A Story for Bear by Dennis Haseley

Sweet, rather calming story of the friendship that develops between a bear and the woman who reads aloud to him.

Superchicken by Mary Jane and Herm Auch

Henrietta, the chicken, loves to read. Because of this, she saves her "aunties" from becoming chicken soup. She rescues some pigs and cows along the way, too. Silly, but stresses the importance of learning to read. Fun read-aloud for younger students.

Thank You, Mr. Falker by Patricia Polacco

In this stirring account of her own learning disability in childhood, Patricia Polacco reminds all teachers of the importance of teaching and caring about students. Every child deserves a teacher like Mr. Falker. Great book to give kids an idea of how hard work and loving support make a difference in life.

Tomas and the Library Lady by Pat Mora

This book was inspired by the life of Tomas Rivera, who spent his early life moving from town to town in a migrant family. Tomas was befriended by a librarian who introduced him to the world of reading and books. Rivera eventually became a successful educator and the chancellor of the University of California at Riverside. His story is a testament to the importance of educators and librarians everywhere.

The Trouble with Henry—A Tale of Walden Pond by Deborah O'Neal and Angela Westengard

The townspeople of Concord are disgusted by Henry for, as one comments, he's "not like the rest of us." That sentiment does not bother Henry, who builds and moves to a one-room house on Walden Pond. Events occur that lead the townspeople to reconsider their priorities and appreciate the importance of nature and simple living. Concludes with additional information about Henry David Thoreau.

The Wednesday Surprise by Eve Bunting

In this touching book about teaching, learning, and adult literacy, Anna teaches her grandmother to read, surprising not only her dad for his birthday but also the reader. The reader bursts with questions and infers the surprise at the end from clues in the text.

Who's Afraid of the Big Bad Book? by Lauren Child

This is the story of a boy who fell into a book . . . of fairy tales. He meets a disgruntled Goldilocks, follows Hansel and Gretel, and discovers that Prince Charming is missing (due to his fault!) A fun and far-fetched read. Comprehension will be better if readers know original fairy tales.

Wild About Books by Judy Sierra

Molly McGrew, the librarian, accidentally drives her bookmobile into the zoo. She reads aloud and quickly attracts the attention of the animals, who not only learn to love to read, but also become writers. Written in rhyming verse, this was awarded the EB White Read Aloud Award. Engaging illustrations by Marc Brown.

Winston the Book Wolf by Marni McGee
Winston loves words. In fact, he thinks they are delicious and so he eats them! He is banned from the library until Rosie teaches him that "words taste better when you eat them with your eyes!"

Wolf! by Becky Bloom
A hungry wolf learns to read. His role models: a duck, a pig, and a cow who are pleased that he chooses reading over eating! A play on an old story, with an important message.

Nonfiction

The Boy on Fairfield Street: How Ted Geisel Grew Up to Become Dr. Seuss by Kathleen Krull
"Once upon a time, there lived a boy who feasted on books and was wild about animals. . . ." Ted Geisel actually lived three blocks from the library and six blocks from the zoo. He loved to doodle, fool around, and exaggerate things. A must-read for Seuss fans (and who isn't one?!) and great inspiration for young writers.

The Brontës by Catherine Brighton
This book invites the reader into the early lives of the four Bronte children, three of whom became world-famous writers. They recorded their childhood escapades in tiny elaborate books, some of which still survive today as early indications of the great novelists they would become.

Coming Home: From the Life of Langston Hughes by Floyd Cooper
The story of the early life of the renowned poet Langston Hughes, who grew up in poverty with absentee parents. Fortunately Langston lived with a loving grandmother who believed that everyone needs heroes, so she read to him and told him stories.

Grass Sandals: The Travels of Basho by Dawnine Spivak
The story of Basho, the most loved poet in the history of Japan, who traveled around his homeland on foot, observing nature and writing haiku. Characters of the Japanese alphabet fill the text.

The Librarian of Basra by Jeanette Winter
The inspirational story of Alia Muhammad Baker, the passionate chief librarian of the Basra National Library who at the advent of war in Iraq moved over 30,000 books to safety. Provides wonderful opportunities to talk about the horrors of war and the resilience of the human spirit. A strong message about the importance of libraries and books in the preservation of history and culture.

The Library Book—The Story of Libraries from Camels to Computers by Maureen Sawa
A must-read for librarians who can then share parts of the (extensive) text with students. This is a fascinating account of the history and evolution of libraries. Sidebars include facts and fun anecdotes.

Lives of the Writers by Kathleen Krull
One of a series of nonfiction books about artists, musicians, presidents, and athletes, this one includes interesting short biographies of nineteen writers.

Speaking of Journals: Children's Book Writers Talk About Their Diaries, Notebooks, and Sketchbooks by Paula Graham
A must-have book that allows readers and writers of all ages to take a peek at the journals of several dozen writers. Through interviews and written samples, the reader can explore the nature of journal and notebook writing.

Walking with Henry: Based on the Life and Works of Henry David Thoreau by Thomas Locker
Stunning illustrations illuminate this tranquil narrative of America's greatest nature writer, Henry David Thoreau, as he spends a day walking in the wilderness. The afterword reveals some of Thoreau's own words about nature and wilderness.

Walt Whitman—Words for America by Barbara Kerley
"Walt Whitman loved words" begins this narrative of the American poet from his early work as a printer to his travels as a poet to his response to the Civil War. Emphasis is on his passion for language and his desire to reflect the lives of common people in his writing. Notes on the Civil War are included at the end, as well as author and illustrator notes.

A Writer's Notebook: Unlocking the Writer Within You by Ralph Fletcher
The author describes how to keep a record of "dreams, feelings, and thoughts" that might someday turn into a written piece.

Poetry

Please Bury Me in the Library by J. Patrick Lewis
Fun collection of poems about reading. Poet/author offers a variety of forms, including an ode to other poets ("word wizards") who've inspired his own reading and writing.

Wonderful Words—Poems About Reading, Writing, Speaking, and Listening selected by Lee Bennett Hopkins
Content and writing of poems make this a must-have. Top-notch poets remind us about the magic and fun of language.

Short Text Collections

Fiction

The Blue Hill Meadows by Cynthia Rylant
Four short segments that each tell a story set in a different season about the simple adventures of Willie Meadow, a boy growing up in the Blue Hills of Virginia.

The Circuit: Stories from the Life of a Migrant Child by Francisco Jimenez
Award-winning collection of short stories and vignettes written from the point of view of a child in a migrant family. A portrait of a difficult but loving and interesting family life. Themes include family closeness, feeling alienated and lonely in school, and childhood struggles adapting to a new language and culture.

Dateline: Troy by Paul Fleischman
By juxtaposing newspaper clippings of modern day events with a retelling of the Trojan War story, the author points out many parallels between Homer's classic story and the present day.

Every Living Thing by Cynthia Rylant
A group of stories with animals at the center. Kids often connect these stories to their own experiences, making this an anchor text for the connection strategy.

Guys Write for Guys Read edited by Jon Scieszka
A charming collection of stories, essays, poems, and drawings written by world famous writers and illustrators and chosen by readers on the Guys Read website www.guysread.com A book that is practically guaranteed to get your middle school boys to read, read, read!

Not One Damsel in Distress: World Folktales for Strong Girls by Jane Yolen
Jane Yolen gives us a collection of stories of women from around the globe who will bowl you over with their cunning and bravery.

Out of the Dust by Karen Hesse
Written in free-verse poetry, this Newbery award-winning novel tells the story of Billie Joe, a strong heroine who confronts a life of misery during the Oklahoma Dust Bowl and begins to transcend it.

Owl at Home by Arnold Lobel
Five endearing stories about an owl who lives at home and gets mixed up in all kinds of predicaments. With simple vocabulary that young readers can read on their own.

The Stories Julian Tells by Ann Cameron
Julian is a heck of a storyteller and he can make everyone, especially his younger brother Huey, believe just about any-
thing he says. But these tall tales sometimes get Julian, Huey, and their best friend Gloria into big trouble. The sequel, *More Stories Julian Tells,* doesn't disappoint.

The Van Gogh Cafe by Cynthia Rylant
A girl and her father run a small cafe in Flowers, Kansas. Magic appears one day in the form of a possum, and things are never quite the same from that moment on. Each story stands alone but leads to the next with the last line of each chapter. This provides a great opportunity for readers to practice their inferential thinking skills.

Wachale! Poetry and Prose About Growing Up Latino in America by Ilan Stavens
Wachale is Spanglish for "Watch Out! Listen up!" This collection of memorable poems and prose celebrates Latino diversity. Available in both English and Spanish, the collection includes brief autobiographical essays, folk tales, and stories by both well-established and emerging authors.

Nonfiction

The Code: The 5 Secrets of Teen Success by Mawi Asgedom
Written by the motivational speaker and author of *Of Beatles and Angels* who made his way from a Sudanese refugee camp to a PhD at Harvard, this self-help book for teenagers shares five secrets the author believes can spur hope, happiness, and success in their lives.

Generation Fix: Young Ideas for a Better World by Elizabeth Rusch
The inspiring stories of more than fifteen young people who saw a problem in their community and did something to fix it.

Girls Who Rocked the World: Heroines from Harriet Tubman to Mia Hamm by Michelle Roehm
We all know about famous women who have rocked the world, but this book tells amazing stories about girls who shook things up while they were still teenagers. Oprah was seventeen when she broke into showbiz, and the Bronte sisters were teenagers when they wrote their novels. The message here is that you are never too young to go for it!

Mistakes That Worked by Charlotte Foltz Jones
Many things we use every day had haphazard beginnings. A collection of vignettes about some of them.

The Nobel Book of Answers edited by Bettina Stiekel
Since 1901, the Nobel Prize has been awarded to the world's most brilliant thinkers in our most important fields. This book shares answers that Nobel Prize winners gave to questions collected from kids throughout the world.

A Summer Life by Gary Soto
This series of short pieces and autobiographical vignettes explores life growing up in Fresno. Soto has recently written up some of these experiences in picture books like *Too Many Tamales.*

Top Secret: A Handbook of Codes, Ciphers, and Secret Writings by Paul Janeczko
A guide to secret writing. Details the history of code writing, famous codes, invisible ink recipes, as well as how to crack codes and make your own. Full of sketches, codes, and deciphering exercises. Kids will pore over this for hours.

Witnesses to Freedom: Young People Who Fought for Civil Rights by Belinda Rochelle
A collection of true stories of brave, young people in the sixties who integrated schools and fought for civil rights.

Women Writers of the West: Five Chroniclers of the American Frontier by Julie Danneberg
The author introduces us to five notable women who wrote about the West at a time when few women even thought about writing. They chronicled the hardships of the gold rush, Native Americans, and the lives and times of western expansion.

The World's Dumbest Criminals by Daniel Butler and Alan Ray
Draws on actual news clippings from around the world to present "a moron's gallery of would-be rogues, bumbling burglars, and foolish felons."

Poetry

19 Varieties of Gazelle: Poems of the Middle East by Naomi Shihab Nye
Naomi Shihab Nye has been writing about being Arab American, about Jerusalem, about the West Bank, and about family all her life. This collection of poems of the Middle East appear together here for the first time.

Neighborhood Odes by Gary Soto
Poems about growing up Latino in Fresno, California. Odes to sprinklers, tennis shoes, and raspados portray everyday life as seen through the eyes of a preadolescent boy.

Peacock and Other Poems by Valerie Worth
Accompanied by Natalie Babbitt's fine pencil drawings, "Peacock" is one of twenty-six elegant poems about things as various as pandas, steam engines, and icicles, in which, like in her earlier work, Worth "find[s] in ordinary things Blake's universe in a grain of sand."

The Place My Words Are Looking For selected by Paul Janeczko
Thirty-nine of our leading poets share their poems as well as their thoughts and recollections about their inspirations and their lives.

Seeing the Blue Between: Advice and Inspiration for Young Poets by Paul Janeczko
Janeczko compiled this collection of poems and letters to young writers from thirty-two well-known poets for children and young adults.

Waiting to Waltz: A Childhood by Cynthia Rylant
A collection of thirty poems about a girl growing up in a small Appalachian town.

Appendix B

Magazines, Newspapers, and Websites

Magazines and Newspapers for Kids

Name	Grade	Focus	Issues	Publisher	Phone	Website
Ask	2–4	Arts and science. Each issue focuses on one theme.	9/year	Cobblestone Publishing Group	800-821-0115	www.cobblestonepub.com
Calliope	4 +	World history. Each issue focuses on one theme.	9/year	Cobblestone Publishing Group	800-821-0115	www.cobblestonepub.com
Click	K–2	Science, exploration, nature, history, technology, and the arts.	9/year	Cobblestone Publishing Group	800-821-0115	www.cobblestonepub.com
Cobblestone	4 +	American history.	9/year	Cobblestone Publishing Group	800-821-0115	www.cobblestonepub.com
Cricket	4 +	Folktales, fiction, biographies, fantasy, poetry, science fiction, and history.	12/year	Cobblestone Publishing Group	800-821-0115	www.cobblestonepub.com
Dig	4 +	Archaeology. Each issue focuses on one theme.	9/year	Cobblestone Publishing Group	800-821-0115	www.cobblestonepub.com
Faces	4 +	Cultures of the world and geography.	9/year	Cobblestone Publishing Group	800-821-0115	www.cobblestonepub.com
Junior Scholastic	5–8	Current national and world events. Supports middle school social studies curriculum. Good features such as "Pro and Con" discussion prompts.	18/year	Scholastic, Inc.	800-724-6527	www.teacher.scholastic.com

Kids Discover	Elementary	Each issue focuses on one topic of either social studies or scientific nature. Can be ordered as a year's subscription or individually for specific content. Kids love this publication!	12/year	Kids Discover	212-677-4457	www.kidsdiscover.com
Muse	4 +	Smithsonian magazine for kids. Explores science, social studies, and discovery.	9/year	Cobblestone Publishing Group	800-821-0115	www.cobblestonepub.com
National Geographic Explorer	3–6	Focused on science, social studies, and geography. Great content and incredible photographs, of course! Great source of short text for instruction and practice. (Pathfinder Edition for intermediate grades, and Pioneer Edition for primary grades.)	7/school year	National Geographic School Publishing	800-368-2728	www.ngsschoolpub.org/ngexplorerweb
National Geographic Young Explorer	K–1	Science, social studies, and geography magazine for primary grades.	7/year	National Geographic School Publishing	800-368-2728	www.ngsschoolpub.org/ngexplorerweb
National Geographic Extreme Explorer	6–8	Another great magazine from NGS, this time with a focus on struggling readers.	7/year	National Geographic School Publishing	800-368-2728	www.ngsschoolpub.org/ngexplorerweb
National Geographic for Kids	3 +	Formerly known as *World Magazine*. Explores animals, entertainment, science, technology, current events, and cultures from around the world.	10/year	National Geographic Society	800-368-2728	www.nationalgeographic.com
Newsweek	7–12	The magazine also includes a feature great for middle and high school kids called "My Turn," which is an essay written on a different issue by a different writer every week.	53/year	Newsweek, Inc.	800-631-1040	www.newsweek.com
The New York Times Upfront	9–12	Published jointly by Scholastic and the NY Times. Created to make it easy for teachers to connect the news to the curriculum. Major national and world news features. History features, science features, and so on.	14/year	Scholastic, Inc.	800-724-6527	www.teacher.scholastic.com
Odyssey	4 +	Adventures in science.	9/year	Cobblestone Publishing Group	800-821-0115	www.cobblestonepub.com
Scholastic News	1–6	A curriculum-connected current-events news weekly. Available in Spanish at grades 1-3, and a good source of short text for instruction and practice. Available each week online.	32/year	Scholastic, Inc.	800-724-6527	www.teacher.scholastic.com
Science World	6–10	The latest science news and discoveries. Physical science, life science/health, earth and space science, environmental science, and technology.	14/year	Scholastic, Inc.	800-724-6527	www.teacher.scholastic.com
Sports Illustrated	7–12	*SI* concludes with Rick Reilly's essay. Always interesting and worth chewing on for middle and high school kids.	56/year	Time, Inc.	800-528-5000	www.si.com
Sports Illustrated for Kids	4 +	For those sports fanatics in your classroom. Interesting articles about sports figures, as well as issues facing sports.	12/year	Time, Inc.	800-992-0196	www.sikids.com
Time Magazine	7–12	The standard news magazine. Great for middle and high schoolers.	56/year	Time, Inc.	800-541-1000	www.time.com
Time for Kids	K–1, 2–3, & 4–6	Weekly news magazine that comes in three editions (K–1, 2–3, 4–6). Sold in class sets. Great for keeping up with world events, and a wonderful source of short texts.	30 or 26/year	Time, Inc.	800-777-8600	www.timeforkids.com

USA Studies Weekly	K–9	A weekly newspaper for students of U.S. history. Each issue focuses on a period or event in US history. Sold in class sets.	Every 1–2 weeks	Studies Weekly, Inc.	800-361-0502	www.studiesweekly.com
Weekly Reader	PreK–2	Weekly magazine that comes in four editions: PreK, K, 1, and 2. Sold in class sets.	28/year for PreK and K 32/year for 1 and 2	WRC Media	800-446-3355	www.weeklyreader.com
WR News	3–6	Weekly news magazine from Weekly Reader that comes in two editions, WR News Edition 3 for third graders and WR News Senior Edition for fourth, fifth, and sixth graders.	28/year	WRC Media	800-446-3355	www.weeklyreader.com
WR Science	3–5	An engaging classroom magazine from Weekly Reader that encourages students to think and read like scientists.	8/year	WRC Media	800-446-3355	www.weeklyreader.com

Good Reading on the Web

Ready-to-use short texts, engaging content and projects, and other valuable resources for kids and teachers are available just for the browsing.

www.nationalgeographic.com/kids	Visit this terrific site to explore geographic, scientific, and historical concepts, issues, and events. Extensive bibliographies and links to countless websites to explore a given topic in depth.
www.timeforkids.com/TFK	This site offers a variety of opportunities for kids and teachers including an archive link (http://www.timeforkids.com/TFK/magazines/archive) that allows you to print any or all of the *TFK* articles in English and Spanish!
www.nwf.org/kids	The kids' section of the website of the National Wildlife Foundation. Loaded with information about animal conservation and animals in general. Click on "Prowl the Past: *Ranger Rick* Index" to find the titles and locate any past articles in the *Ranger Rick* archives.
www.loc.gov	The official site of the Library of Congress. Click on "Kids, Families" to discover the compelling story of America's past as presented by the Library of Congress. Or explore this site endlessly for anything you can imagine.
www.nytimes.com/learning	The *New York Times* kids' edition. A truly fantastic site with news summaries, science Q&As, who's who and what's what features, as well as an opportunity to explore the *NY Times* learning network by subject.
www.thinkquest.org	A library created by students for students. The ThinkQuest Library is a free educational resource featuring 6,000+ websites created by students from around the world.
www.howstuffworks.com	A site that explains how just about everything in the world works. Kids will love this!
www.whyfiles.org	A site that gives us the science behind the news. Click on "The Why Files in Education" for an amazing array of information on scientific topics of all kinds.
www.nobelprize.org	This site offers Nobel speeches, history of winners and their prizes, simulations for kids, and more.
www.freedomcenter.org	The website of the National Underground Railroad Freedom Center in Cincinnati, Ohio. Click on "Learn" or "Educators" for historic information, narratives, and lesson plans related to the Underground Railroad.
www.ocean.com	Check this out for great information, photographs, and stories about anything pertaining to the ocean and to marine conservation.

www.ecokidsonline.com	EcoKids is Earth Day Canada's environmental education program for youth who care about the planet. This website is their interactive environmental site for children, their families, and educators in Canada and around the world.
www.nws.noaa.gov	The National Oceanic and Atmospheric Administration's National Weather Service provides up-to-date weather forecasts. Click on "Education/Outreach," and then "NOAA Education Page" for general educational information about the weather and a list of weather websites of interest to kids.
www.exploratorium.org	The site of the San Francisco–based Exploratorium Museum of Science, Art, and Human Perception. This is packed with scientific information and interactive possibilities on a wide range of topics.
www.learner.org	The site of the Annenberg Foundation to advance excellent teaching in America's schools. Information on school reform, professional development, teaching and learning, curriculum suggestions, and so on.
www.learner.org/students	The student section of the Annenberg Foundation's site with interactive exhibits that focus on extensions of a concept or theme explored on the site.
www.learner.org/biographyofamerica	The history of America from New World encounters to contemporary history with information, narratives, maps, and links to other relevant American history websites.
www.classicsforkids.com	A website dedicated to hooking kids on classical music. As they say on the site, "Classics for Kids is here to help you learn about classical music and have fun too!"
www.siforkids.com	*Sports Illustrated*'s website for kids. Full of sports information, articles, radio programs, survey questions, and more.
www.kidsdiscover.com	The website of *Kids Discover* magazine. Click on "Teach" and then click on "A Look Inside Every Title" and you will discover an amazing list of resources that includes a list of websites, children's books, adult books, and community resources related to the title topic.
www.si.edu	The "Kids" button on this Smithsonian Institution's website leads you to a selection of arts, science and nature, history and culture, and people and places resources that support both social studies and science curriculums.
http://edspace.nasa.gov	The National Aeronautics and Space Administration's education site. Check out the Site Map for an impressive array of space-based resources. The site's designed-for-kids games and activities pique interest in the universe beyond our planet.
www.pbs.org/teachersource	From PBS, an educator's resource that allows you to search for featured lessons and activities by curriculum area.
www.mos.org	The Boston Museum of Science website contains both student ("explore and learn") and teacher ("for educators") resources. The Virtual Exhibits provide great content for a variety of topic studies.
www.ushmm.org/education	With sections for students, teachers, and families, as well as for adults and scholars, the United States Holocaust Memorial Museum's website provides in-depth information about one of World War II's most shameful crimes.
www.sandiegozoo.org/teachers	In addition to local zoo events, the San Diego Zoo website offers a wealth of conservation and wildlife information, activities, and projects.

Professional Journals for Selection of Children's Books

Book Links: Connecting Books, Libraries, and Classrooms

American Library Association, 50 East Huron Street, Chicago, IL 60611–2795

Intended for librarians and teachers, the purpose of this journal is to connect children with high quality books. The articles contain information on children's books and ways to incorporate them into the curriculum and include annotated bibliographies of picture books, fiction, and nonfiction with recommended grade level. *Book Links* recently began including websites related to children's interests. The online version, accessed through ALA's website: www.ala.org has selected articles as well as an archived listing of *Book Links* articles beginning with the September 1998 issue. Six issues per year.

Booklist

American Library Association, 50 East Huron Street, Chicago, IL 60611–2795

Reviews more than 2,500 recommended fiction and nonfiction children's books and audiovisual materials a year. Feature articles include columns, author interviews, bibliographies, and book-related essays. "Editors' Choice," top picks of books and videos from the previous year, are published once a year. *Booklist Online* (www.booklistonline.com) includes a cumulative index not offered in print. Published semimonthly.

Bulletin, Center for Children's Books

Publications Office, Graduate School of Library and Information Science, University of Illinois at Urbana-Champaign, 501 East Daniel Street, Champaign, IL 61820–6211

Reviews feature critical annotations of selected new titles on content, reading level, strengths and weaknesses, and curricular uses. Titles are given one of four ratings, with outstanding books starred. Each issue is indexed by genre, subject, and curricular uses. "Bulletin Blue Ribbons," published annually, is a selection of the year's best books. The July issue includes an annual index arranged by subject, title, and author. Published monthly except August. Website: http://bccb.lis.uiuc.edu.

Children's Book Council

12 West 37th St., 2nd Floor, New York, NY. 10018–7490
This association encourages the enjoyment and use of children's books. Most notably, it copublishes several important book lists reviewing the notable trade books in science and social studies each year. With the National Science Teachers Association (see *Science and Children* below), it publishes short reviews in the list "Outstanding Science Trade Books for Students K–12." With the National Council for the Social Studies, it publishes "Notable Social Studies Trade Books for Young People" (see *Social Studies and the Young Learner* below). The CBC also reprints the "Children's Choices" reviews from *The Reading Teacher* (see below). Website: www.cbcbooks.org.

The Horn Book Guide to Children's and Young Adult Books

Horn Book, Inc., 56 Roland Street, Suite 200, Boston, MA 02129
Published by Horn Book, Inc., the Guide contains critical annotations of recently published children's hardcover books. Fiction books arranged by grade level and genre, nonfiction books arranged by Dewey classification. Annotated reviews are rated from 1 to 6, with 6 being the highest rating. Author, illustrator, subject, and series indexes make this a valuable resource for selection of children's books. Published twice a year and is also available online by subscription (www.hornbookguide.com).

Horn Book Magazine: Recommending Books for Children and Young Adults

Horn Book, Inc., 56 Roland Street, Suite 200, Boston, MA 02129
Features literary articles about and by children's authors and about issues related to children's literature. Signed critical reviews are of recommended fiction and nonfiction titles; all are subject to the qualifications in the notes. Annotated titles include fiction, arranged by genre, and nonfiction, arranged by Dewey classification. Titles that a majority of the reviewers believe to be outstanding are starred. Published six times a year. Website: www.hbook.com.

Language Arts

National Council of Teachers of English, 1111 W. Kenyon Road, Urbana, IL 61801–1096
Language Arts is a professional journal focusing on all aspects of language arts teaching and learning, preK through eighth grade. In addition to articles on teaching theory and practice, there are frequent reviews of children's and young adolescent literature, and a book review column—Reading Corner—is a focus in each issue. The yearly selection and review of outstanding nonfiction literature, the Orbis Pictus Award list, is a must-have. Published bimonthly. Website: www.ncte.org.

The Reading Teacher

International Reading Association, 800 Barksdale Road, P.O. Box 8139, Newark, DE 19714–8139
Professional journal with articles considering practices, issues, and trends in literacy education and related fields. Articles include bibliographies of children's books cited. Each issue features an annotated section on children's books, usually thematically selected. Especially useful is the "Children's Choices" October book review (reprinted by the Children's Book Council, see above). Published eight times a year. Website: www.reading.org.

School Library Journal: The Magazine of Children, Young Adults, and School Librarians

Reed Elsevier Business Information, 249 West 17th Street, New York, NY 10011; subscriptions to Box 57559, Boulder, CO 80322–7559
Feature articles on timely topics directed to public and school librarians. Numerous titles are reviewed in each issue. Reviewers are contracted by *SLJ*, and reviews are individual opinions subject to editor's approval. Titles are organized into preschool through fourth-grade fiction and nonfiction, and fifth-grade through eighth-grade fiction and nonfiction. Starred reviews are listed in each issue. The March issue features "Notable Books for Children," selected from books published the previous year. Published eleven times a year. Website: www.schoollibraryjournal.com.

Science and Children

National Science Teachers Association, 1840 Wilson Boulevard, Arlington, VA 22201–3000
Well-written articles are useful for teachers of science and include bibliography of books used with students. The March issue features "Outstanding Science Trade Books for students K–12" published the previous year. Annotated bibliography

categories include biography, life science, and earth science with suggested grade levels for each title. This list is also reprinted by and available from the Children's Book Council (see above). Published eight times a year. Website: www.nsta.org.

Social Education and Social Studies and the Young Learner

These two journals are published by the National Council for the Social Studies, 8555 Sixteenth St., Suite 500, Silver Spring, MD 20910

Social Education addresses all age levels and offers both practical ideas for the classroom as well as reviews of the latest research. *Social Studies and the Young Learner* focuses on K–6. Their "Social Studies Notable Trade Books for Young People," published each year, is a particularly good source of excellent trade books that match social studies standards. Lists of Notable Books from previous years are available on line. Website: www.socialstudies.org.

Voices from the Middle

National Council of Teachers of English, 1111 W. Kenyon Road, Urbana, IL 61801–1096

Journal for literacy and learning at the middle school level. Book reviews and columns include middle school students' reviews of adolescent literature and excellent monthly columns about thoughtful middle-level teaching practices. Each issue is focused on a topic or issue of concern to middle-level teachers. Published four times a year. Website: www.ncte.org.

Appendix D

Assessment Interview with Fourth Graders

Why This Assessment Interview?

This assessment interview was conducted with three fourth graders—Tiffany, Rachel, and Stuart—during reading workshop in the classroom. The purpose of this small-group discussion was to assess the children's ongoing thinking rather than checking for understanding after they had finished a story. Asking the students to think out loud as they read through the text together enabled Anne to observe and document those strategies the children used to understand the first few pages of the picture book *My Freedom Trip: A Child's Escape from North Korea*, by Frances Park and Ginger Park. The book portrays a family who tries to flee from North Korea to South Korea just as the Korean War begins. One interesting aspect of the book is that a character from the Korean alphabet is written at the top of each page, representing the theme of that page. Kids are drawn to these symbols, determined to figure them out.

Children view the interview as an opportunity to discuss their thinking with their peers as they read a story together, each with a copy of the book. Teachers can observe kids in action, documenting their strategy use in an authentic situation. The goal is to assess ongoing comprehension, not comprehension after the fact.

Logistically, this kind of short interview is best conducted during a time when the rest of the class is reading or writing independently. The following interview took about twenty-five minutes. Teachers may want to meet with small groups of children for these short interviews about once a month because the format is easy to implement and manage.

To prepare for the interview, Anne selected a compelling picture book that required a lot of interpretation. She knew that these three students had been introduced to questioning and inferring, and thought that the ambiguity in the story would provide many opportunities for them to practice these and other comprehension strategies. The goal was for the students to reason through the text together as they encountered the text for the first time. Anne wanted them to lead the discussion, so she did not prepare specific comprehension questions. She was ready with prompts if the group conversation lagged. Anne scripted their conversation to reflect on it later and evaluate their use of strategies.

Introducing the Think-Aloud

Anne first asked the children to explain which comprehension strategies they found themselves using most frequently. Rachel jumped in, saying, "I infer."

"Can you explain what you mean by inferring?" Anne asked.

"I make pictures in my head about what will happen next, with all the clues from the story." Anne scripted her comment and polled the other kids for ideas.

Tiffany added, "I ask questions when something's going on and I wonder what will happen next."

"Or if it's puzzling, I ask a question to try to figure it out," Stuart chimed in.

Next, Anne directed the kids in this way: "What I'd like you to do today is think out loud about the story as you read it together. I'm interested in what's going on in your heads—what you're thinking about that helps you understand the story. You just mentioned that inferring and asking questions are two strategies that you use a lot. As you read the story together, you might use questioning, inferring, or other strategies to better understand it, especially if you come to a part that's confusing. I'm interested in learning about what you think, so I'll just listen and write down what you say. Okay?"

Reading the Story and Thinking Aloud

Tiffany, Rachel, and Stuart looked over the cover and title pages of the book, discovering a list of the Korean characters translated into English. The English list, they noted, included words like *peace, fear, waiting,* and *love.*

Tiffany glanced at the cover and said, "It's about a Chinese family."

"No, Korean," Rachel noted. "It says so right in the title, 'A Child's Escape from North Korea.'"

Stuart flipped to the page with the translations, and then pointed to the first Korean character. "Look! This means peace!" he said.

Rachel said, "I'm inferring—they ran away for freedom. The little girl is telling her life story about when she ran away."

"Or traveling back in time in her memory," Tiffany added. She began paging through the book, wondering out loud if the Korean characters described what each page was about.

"Maybe it's what the page means," suggested Stuart.

Anne's comments: Rachel labeled her thinking as inferring. She predicted what she thinks the story will be about: "The little girl is telling her life story about when she ran away." Tiffany also inferred that "She's traveling back in time in her memory." Stuart and Tiffany discussed the Korean characters at the top of each page, correctly inferring that they help to enhance the meaning of the story. These inferences provide evidence that the children are thinking ahead about what will happen in the story.

Tiffany, Rachel, and Stuart next read the Introduction, written years later.

Many years have passed. I am no longer a little schoolgirl. But I still think about Mr. Han, my gentle guide, and about the soldier who set me free. Mostly, I think about my mother. When the evening is full of moon and warm winds, I can still hear her cry—Be Brave, Soo! Brave for the rest of my life!

"I wonder what 'brave for the rest of my life' means?" asked Stuart. "And who's the soldier?"

"So it is about her life story," Rachel added. Tiffany suggested that Soo (the little girl) may have some problems, wondering why she will have to "keep being brave."

Anne's comments: Rachel noted that the Introduction confirmed her prediction. Stuart asked, "I wonder what 'brave for the rest of my life means?'" He wondered about the soldier. Tiffany also wondered why Soo will have to "keep being brave." It's surprising that the kids didn't discuss the confusing introduction a little more, although they noticed and questioned the ominous tone of the text.

The children read Soo's words describing her home: "a peaceful sun shone down upon my village in North Korea, over rice paddies and pagoda roofs, on pink petals in ponds . . . and a soft breeze carried butterflies." Unfortunately, the peace and beauty were short-lived, because Soo's friends were leaving the country, and she found herself walking to school all alone. The next page in the story introduces the idea of leaving:

> *Then one night my father came to my room and gently woke me. It was so dark that I could not see his face. He spoke softly.*
>
> *"Tonight I must go on a trip. A man named Mr. Han will guide me to South Korea. He knows of a secret passage where I will cross the border at the shallow end of a river."*
>
> *"Apa," I wailed, "do not go!"*
>
> *My father stroked my hair. His fingers were trembling. "Soon, very soon, Mr. Han will return for you, too, Soo. And he will take you on your freedom trip. Then it will be your mother's turn."*

"Why is he only taking one person at a time?," wondered Tiffany.

No one seems to know, but Stuart is puzzled about how they leave.

"How do they leave? Do they go on a boat, a plane, walking, how?" he asked.

Rachel asked, "Will Soo really leave?"

Tiffany pointed to the Korean character at the top of the page. "I know why it says *whisper*," she commented. "It's because the dad spoke very softly."

They continued reading the story:

> *"But why can't we go together?" I pleaded.*
>
> *"Only one of us can go at a time," he tried to explain. "Less people means less danger of being captured by soldiers."*
>
> *What was danger? It sounded as deep and dark and cold as a river.*
>
> *My father kissed my cheek, then left my side. He stood in the doorway for a long time.*
>
> *"I will be waiting for you on the other side of the river," he promised.*

Stuart was puzzled. "I don't get it. Why did she ask what danger was?"

Rachel commented that maybe nothing bad had ever happened to her before. Tiffany concurred, suggesting that up until now, Soo had had a peaceful life. The children wondered again if Soo was going to leave and why each person had to go alone. Ever attentive to the Korean characters, Tiffany explained the symbol for promise saying, "I think it's telling us that the dad promises to wait for her on the other side of the river."

Anne's comments: Stuart consistently asked questions about what he doesn't understand, and both Tiffany and Rachel responded with explanations that help clarify his confusions. Questions propelled the kids' thinking and kept them engaged. Rachel asked if Soo would leave, Tiffany wondered why only one person could go at a time. Tiffany continued to explain each Korean character and its relation to the events and emotions in the story.

On the next page, Tiffany pointed out the Korean character for waiting, telling the group that "she's waiting to go see her father." In the story, mother and daughter wait nervously for word that Soo's father has made it to the freedom land. When word finally comes, they are relieved, but now it is Soo's turn to leave.

> *My mother quietly rejoiced, then began packing my knapsack with jelly candy, fruit, and clothing.*

"Tonight you go on your freedom trip, Soo," she carefully announced. "Now quickly, you must change your clothes."

"Oma," I begged, "come with me!"

She cupped my face and whispered, "Do not worry." Her breath was as warm and soothing as tea. "Mr. Han will return for me, and we will be reunited."

My mother hugged me. I could feel her heart beating against mine like a dying dove. "Be brave, Soo!" she cried.

"That's the symbol for love," Tiffany said, as she pointed to the character at the top of the page. "Because she's leaving her mom and she loves her very much."

Rachel added, "She's leaving, that's for sure. If you didn't know you could look at the picture and tell that."

"She's getting to freedom," added Tiffany. "Can you imagine how the mom would feel all alone in that house?"

"The family has to spread apart now, but someday they'll get to a new place together," said Rachel.

Stuart added, "They're moving like a little worm, first the dad, then the little girl, then the back part will go that is the mom."

Anne stopped the kids at this point and asked them to summarize what had happened so far, suggesting they try to tell what was going on in a few words.

Stuart mentioned that he thought there would be more soldiers, saying, "I'm wondering, is there a war, or what? And I still don't understand how they were leaving. Did they just walk all the way?"

Rachel summed up her version of the story, saying, "It's about a trip to the freedom land, they have to leave for freedom. But the little girl doesn't want to leave her mother, and I wonder if she meets her father. I wonder if something will happen."

Tiffany paged through the text, retelling the story according to the Korean character on each page, saying, "First there was peace, then the dad was whispering. On this page, Soo was afraid, and then there was love because the mother loves her, and she had to let her go away."

"They're like chapters," Stuart chimed in.

Tiffany added, "It's like the symbols tell what the people are thinking, or what's going to happen, through the whole story."

Anne's comments: When asked to summarize the story thus far, Stuart seemed unclear about what Anne was asking him to do and, determined to figure out what was going on, posed additional questions. Rachel thoughtfully summed up the story, but still wondered about what would happen. Tiffany once again discussed the Korean characters, compelled to try to understand these symbols and their relationship to the text. She explained that they "tell what the people are thinking, or what's going to happen."

Assessing the Children's Understanding

Hooked on the story and the fate of Soo and her family, Tiffany, Rachel, and Stuart raced off to read on their own. Anne jotted down comments about each child's thinking in an assessment notebook. It was clear that the children had used the strategies they mentioned—questioning and inferring—to reason through the text together. Based on the discussion, Anne realized that questioning and inferring enabled the kids to clarify confusions, better understand the characters, and anticipate story events and outcomes. Most important, however, inferences helped them think through and fill in gaps in the story, those things the authors left unsaid, or that would be resolved only at the end of the story.

Although all three children used the questioning and inferring strategies, Stuart primarily used questions to clarify what was going on or to ask his partners to explain something that confused him.

He asked important questions, such as "What does 'brave for the rest of my life' mean?" but didn't stop to try to answer them.

Rachel asked lots of questions and was able to sum up the important ideas in the story. She continued to wonder whether Soo would meet her father after all and described how it must be hard for the mother to allow her to leave.

Tiffany, intent on deciphering the Korean symbols, demonstrated considerable insight as she linked them to the people, emotions, and events in the story. She seemed particularly attuned to the feelings of the characters in the story, empathizing with the mother, all alone in the house after Soo and her father have gone.

The next day, after the children had finished reading the story on their own, Anne introduced them to the idea of inferring themes. She pointed out that many of their questions and inferences had focused on story themes, especially having to leave one's home and loved ones for freedom and a new life. She wanted to give the kids language, such as the term *theme*, to describe their thinking. The children also discussed the story's ending, because they had assumed the family would all escape. They were surprised that Soo was able to escape, but incredulous that she never saw her mother again. Paging back through the text, they searched for hints and evidence that the story would end this way.

Although Tiffany, Rachel, and Stuart were engaged with the content of the story, the point of the interview was not to assess their understanding of story events. Assessment interviews like these can be done at any point in a story. In fact, we tend to conduct these interviews early on in the story because we gain a more accurate picture of kids' ongoing thinking. That's when they have to fill in the gaps and figure things out, before the issues and problems that drive the story have been resolved. If kids only discuss the story after finishing it, they usually focus on the ending, and we don't have any idea what they were thinking all the way through. At that point it's difficult to tell if and how kids kept track of their thinking as they read. We want to capture kids' thinking throughout their reading, to check if they are monitoring their ongoing understanding. That's the only way to find out if and how students are using strategies on their own, when it matters most.

Anchor Charts for the Comprehension Strategies

MONITORING COMPREHENSION

When we monitor our comprehension we listen to the voice in our head speaking to us. We read Robin Cruise's <u>Little Mama Forgets</u>, the story of Lucy, a little girl who lives with her mom, dad, baby brother and her beloved grandmother. As her grandmother gets older, she forgets more and more things every day. But she never forgets how much she loves her little Lucy and the rest of the family.

After we read it, we wrote down what the story made us think about.

What the story makes us think about...

It reminds me of my favorite uncle who is really old but still loves to have fun.

It makes me think of my grandpa who forgets lots of stuff.

It makes me hungry when they eat all those tortillas for breakfast.

I don't like to take a nap either.

Why did she forget the stop light? That's dangerous.

I wonder why some people forget so much when they get old.

MAKING CONNECTIONS

OLIVER BUTTON IS A SISSY by Tomie de Paola

When we read stories we make connections to our own experiences = TEXT-TO-SELF CONNECTIONS (t-s) = and to other books we've read = TEXT-TO-TEXT CONNECTIONS (t-t). = These are some connections we made while reading Oliver Button is a Sissy:

(t-t) Oliver Button is a Sissy reminds me of Amazing Grace because they both liked to dress up. (Rosa)

(t-t) Oliver Button reminds me of when I tried out for Little League and couldn't hit the ball and kids teased me. (Ann)

(t-s) It reminds me of playing soccer because there are only two girls on our team. (Claire)

(t-s) In preschool there were some 5th graders who would pick on a little boy, just like the boys who picked on Oliver. (Lucas)

(t-s) It reminds me of when this boy took my sweater and ran away with it and passed it to his friends and wouldn't give it back to me. (Jacob)

(t-t) Oliver keeps practicing dance even though the boys teased him, just like in Amazing Grace when Grace kept practicing to be Peter Pan even though kids told her she couldn't. (McKenna)

(t-s) Kids teased me when I was little. (Jonathan)

(t-s) In my sister's dance class there is only one boy and he gets to be the main character in her recitals. (Claire)

Questioning

We read the story
ELISABETH, by Claire Nivola.

As we listened, we wondered about things that were happening in the story and asked lots of questions.

Is that turtle real?
Why did the soldiers watch their house?
Why did they have to leave everything behind?
Couldn't she have grabbed her doll?
Why did they have to leave so fast?
Did this really happen?
Was the doll really Elisabeth?
Why couldn't they ever go back?
Why, if the family was German, did they have to leave Germany?

NEXT, we checked to see if we had answered some of our questions. We could answer some of them, but we needed more information to answer others.

Question	Yes	No	We need more information
• Why did they have to leave so fast? The story didn't tell us — maybe because of a war because there were soldiers.			✔
• Did this really happen? We noticed on the front flap that there was a photograph of Ruth (the author's mother) with Elisabeth. That means it *did* happen.	✔		
• Was that doll really Elisabeth? The teeth marks from where the dog dragged it told us it was the same doll.	✔		

VISUALIZING

We read poetry out loud together. We listened to the words and created pictures in our minds to go with the words. Then we drew our pictures — and some of us wrote our own poem!

The white clouds and dark clouds are coming together. They all rain.

by Brayden

A shooting star
Flies through
The sky.
Over the world.
And it's gone
In a minute.

by McKenna

Inferring

REDCOATS AND PETTICOATS
by Katherine Kirkpatrick

Facts	Questions	Inferences
• The mother is acting funny — washing laundry all the time.	• Why? What's going on?	• Maybe the laundry
• father in prison		
• The mother went to her parents with a letter.	• What did the letter say? What was it for?	• Maybe the letter was a message to the British.
• Mother took a letter to the prison ship.	• Was father still OK?	
• The father was let go from the prison ship.	• Did they really trade vegetables for the father?	• At the end of the story we thought the letter from the mother's parents (Tories) probably helped save the father from prison.
	• What would happen to a spy if she was caught?	

Important things we learned from this book...

- Some families were Loyalist and Patriots.
- Spies had to be careful — mother kept the signals a secret.
- Kids like Thomas could help win the Revolutionary War.
- The British had prison ships for keeping prisoners.
- The father had to hide, even though he got out of prison.

DETERMINING   IMPORTANCE

As we read Dr. Robert Ballard's <u>Exploring the Titanic</u> we couldn't help but wonder what caused this "unsinkable" ship to sink. So we read to find an answer to that question. We had to pick out important information to help us understand.

Some things we noticed were:
- Iceberg warnings kept coming but they were ignored.

- The radio operators were tired and inexperienced.

- The sea was calm. It looked like clear sailing.

- The sky was clear and the sun was out.

- The captain was unconcerned.

- The captain knew that floating ice was not unusual at this time of year.

- "What danger could a few pieces of ice present to an unsinkable ship?"

★ All of this information combined can help us better understand why the ship sank. The people believed it was unsinkable and thus ignored all these danger signs.

Synthesizing

See the Ocean

When we finished reading **See the Ocean** by Estelle Condra we looked back at some of our post its. We put them in order (sort of) and we noticed that our thinking changed. It really changed when we finally figured out that Nellie was blind.

At first we asked questions...

> (Josh)
> Why does she spend so much time in the sand?

> (Marnie)
> Why didn't she complain that they got it first?

> (Bobbie)
> Why didn't she get car sick looking down?

Then we were confused...

> (Silva)
> When she asked, "What color is the ocean?" I thought why did she ask that question — couldn't she see for herself?

> (Elisabeth)
> In the pictures she covers her eyes. She does not look out the window She does not play the games. Why?

Then we understood... but still wondered...

> (Patricio)
> I think the mom and dad raised her on the beach so that she could feel and touch the things on the beach.

> (Tod)
> She's a good imaginer — maybe because her mom and dad and brother told her about the ocean and that's what it looks like to her.

> (Meg)
> Was she blind her whole life?

> (Jon)
> How did she become blind?

References

Children's Books

Abercrombie, Barbara. 1990. *Charlie Anderson.* New York: McElderry.

Adler, David. 1993. *A Picture Book of Anne Frank.* New York: Holiday House.

———. 1995. *A Picture Book of Ben Franklin.* New York: Holiday House.

———. 1997. *Lou Gehrig: The Luckiest Man.* San Diego: Harcourt Brace.

———. 1999. *The Babe and I.* San Diego: Harcourt Brace.

———. 2005. *Joe Louis: America's Fighter.* San Diego: Harcourt.

Aliki. 1989. *The King's Day.* New York: Crowell.

———. 1998. *Marianthe's Story: Painted Words/Spoken Memories.* New York: Greenwillow.

Allen, Thomas B. 2001. *Remember Pearl Harbor.* Washington, DC: National Geographic.

———. 2004. *George Washington, Spymaster: How the Americans Outspied the British and Won the Revolutionary War.* Washington, DC: National Geographic.

Altman, Linda. 1993. *Amelia's Road.* New York: Lee and Low.

Ancona, George. 1998. *Barrio: Jose's Neighborhood.* San Diego: Harcourt Brace.

Anderson, William. 2003. *River Boy: The Story of Mark Twain.* New York: HarperCollins.

Armstrong, Jennifer. 2000. *Spirit of Endurance: The True Story of the Shackleton Expedition to the Antarctic.* New York: Crown.

Asgedom, Mawi. 2003. *The Code: The Five Secrets of Teen Success.* New York: Little, Brown.

Ashby, Ruth. 2004. *The Amazing Mr. Franklin: Or the Boy Who Read Everything.* Atlanta, GA: Peachtree.

Aston, Dianna. 2006. *An Egg Is Quiet.* San Francisco: Chronicle.

Atkin, S. Beth. 1993. *Voices from the Fields.* Boston: Little, Brown.

Atkins, Jeannine. 1999. *A Name on the Quilt.* New York: Simon and Schuster.

Auch, Mary Jane, and Herm Auch. 2003. *Superchicken.* New York: Holiday House.

313

Bachrach, Susan D. 1994. *Tell Them We Remember.* Boston: Little, Brown.

Baillie, Allan. 1994. *Rebel.* New York: Tichnor and Fields.

Balit, Christina. 2003. *Escape from Pompeii.* New York: Henry Holt.

Ballard, Robert. 1988. *Exploring the* Titanic. New York: Scholastic.

Ballard, Robert, and Rick Archbold. 1998. *Ghost Liners: Exploring the World's Greatest Lost Ships.* Boston: Little, Brown.

Bang, Molly. 2004. *My Light.* New York: Scholastic/Blue Sky.

Banks, Kate. 2006. *Max's Words.* New York: Farrar, Straus and Giroux.

Barber, Tiki, and Ronde Barber. 2004. *By My Brother's Side.* New York: Simon and Schuster.

Bardoe, Cheryl. 2006. *Gregor Mendel: The Friar Who Grew Peas.* New York: Abrams.

Bartone, Elisa. 1996. *American, Too.* New York: Lothrop, Lee and Shepard.

Baylor, Byrd. 1972. *When Clay Sings.* New York: Aladdin.

———. 1986. *I'm in Charge of Celebrations.* New York: Charles Scribner.

———. 1994. *The Table Where Rich People Sit.* New York: Charles Scribner.

Bedard, Michael. 1992. *Emily.* New York: Doubleday.

Berger, Barbara. 1984. *Grandfather Twilight.* New York: Putnam and Grosset.

Berger, Melvin, and Gilda Berger. 1997. *The Strength of These Arms: Life in the Slave Quarters.* Boston: Houghton Mifflin.

———. 1998. *Do Stars Have Points?* New York: Scholastic.

Bernier-Grand, Carmen T. 2004. *Cesar: Si, Se Puede! Yes, We Can!* Tarrytown, NY: Marshall Cavendish.

Berry, James. 1993. *The Future Telling Lady.* New York: HarperCollins.

Bierman, Carol. 1998. *Journey to Ellis Island: How My Father Came to America.* New York: Hyperion.

Bisel, Sara. 1990. *The Secrets of Vesuvius.* New York: Scholastic.

Bjork, Christina. 1987. *Linnea in Monet's Garden.* New York: Farrar, Straus and Giroux.

Bloom, Becky. 1999. *Wolf!* New York: Orchard.

Blume, Judy. 1984. *The Pain and the Great One.* New York: Bradbury.

Bolden, Tonya. 2005. *Maritcha: A Remarkable Nineteenth-Century American Girl.* New York: Harry N. Abrams.

Bolotin, Norman, and Angela Herb. 1995. *For Home and Country: A Civil War Scrapbook.* New York: Dutton.

Borden, Louise. 1997. *The Little Ships: The Heroic Rescue at Dunkirk in World War II.* New York: McElderry.

———. 1998. *Good-bye, Charles Lindbergh.* New York: McElderry.

———. 1999. *A. Lincoln and Me.* New York: Scholastic.

———. 1999. *Good Luck, Mrs. K.* New York: McElderry.

———. 2000. *Sleds on Boston Common: A Story from the American Revolution.* New York: McElderry.

———. 2004. *The Greatest Skating Race.* New York: McElderry.

———. 2004. *Sea Clocks: The Story of Longitude.* New York: McElderry.

———. 2005. *The Journey That Saved Curious George: The True Wartime Escape of Margret and H. A. Rey.* Boston: Houghton Mifflin.

Borden, Louise, and Mary Kay Kroeger. 2001. *Fly High! The Story of Bessie Coleman.* New York: McElderry.

Bowen, Gary. 1994. *Stranded at Plimoth Plantation: 1626.* New York: HarperCollins.

Bradby, Marie. 1995. *More Than Anything Else.* New York: Orchard.

Brandenburg, Jim. 1995. *An American Safari: Adventures on the North American Prairie.* New York: Walker.

Bridges, Ruby. 1999. *Through My Eyes.* New York: Scholastic.

Brighton, Catherine. 1990. *Mozart: Scenes from the Childhood of the Great Composer.* New York: Doubleday.

———. 1994. *The Brontes: Scenes from the Childhood of Charlotte, Branwell, Emily, and Anne.* San Francisco: Chronicle.

Brinkloe, Julie. 1985. *Fireflies.* New York: Aladdin.

Brown, Don. 1997. *One Giant Leap.* New York: Scholastic.

———. 2004. *Odd Boy Out: Young Albert Einstein.* Boston: Houghton Mifflin.

Brown, Margaret Wise. 1992. *The Sailor Dog.* Racine, WI: Western.

Browning, Kurt. 2005. *A Is for Axel: An Ice Skating Alphabet.* Chelsea, MI: Sleeping Bear.

Bruchac, Joseph. 1994. *A Boy Called Slow: The True Story of Sitting Bull.* New York: Philomel.

———. 1996. *Between Earth and Sky: Legends of Native American Sacred Places.* San Diego: Harcourt Brace.

———. 1996. *The Circle of Thanks: North American Poems and Songs of Thanksgiving.* New York: BridgeWater.

———. 2000. *Squanto's Journey.* San Diego: Harcourt.

Bryant, Jen. 2005. *Georgia's Bones.* Grand Rapids, MI: Eerdman's Books for Young Readers.

Bullard, Sara. 1993. *Free at Last: A History of the Civil Rights Movement and Those Who Died in the Struggle.* New York: Oxford University.

Bunting, Eve. 1988. *How Many Days to America?* New York: Clarion.

———. 1989. *The Wednesday Surprise.* New York: Clarion.

———. 1990. *The Wall.* New York: Clarion.

———. 1991. *Fly Away Home.* New York: Clarion.

———. 1993. *Someday a Tree.* New York: Clarion.

———. 1994. *A Day's Work.* New York: Clarion.

———. 1994. *Smoky Night.* San Diego: Harcourt Brace.

———. 1994. *Sunshine Home.* New York: Clarion.

———. 1995. *Dandelions.* San Diego: Harcourt Brace.

———. 1996. *Going Home.* New York: HarperCollins.

———. 1998. *Some Frog!* San Diego: Harcourt Brace.

———. 1998. *Your Move.* San Diego: Harcourt Brace.

———. 1999. *A Picnic in October.* San Diego: Harcourt Brace.

———. 2001. *Gleam and Glow.* San Diego: Harcourt.

———. 2006. *One Green Apple.* New York: Clarion.

Burby, Liza. 1998. *Extreme Weather Series.* New York: Rosen.

Burg, Ann E. 2006. *Rebekkah's Journey: A World War II Refugee Story.* Chelsea, MI: Sleeping Bear.

Burleigh, Robert. 2004. *Langston's Train Ride.* New York: Orchard.

Burnett, Frances. 1938. *The Secret Garden.* New York: Lippincott.

Butler, Daniel, and Alan Ray. 1997. *The World's Dumbest Criminals.* Nashville, TN: Rutledge Hill.

Byrd, Robert. 2003. *Leonardo: Beautiful Dreamer.* New York: Dutton.

Caduto, Michael J., and Joseph Bruchac. 1988. *Keepers of the Earth: Native American Stories and Environmental Activities for Children.* Golden, CO: Fulcrum.

———. 1994. *Keepers of the Night: Native American Stories and Nocturnal Activities for Children.* Golden, CO: Fulcrum.

Cameron, Ann. 1981. *The Stories Julian Tells.* New York: Dell Yearling.

Campbell, Jim. 1992. *Baseball's Greatest Pitchers.* New York: Random House.

———. 1995. *Baseball's Greatest Hitters.* New York: Random House.

Cannon, Janell. 1993. *Stellaluna.* San Diego: Harcourt Brace.

Carlson, Lori Marie. 1998. *Sol a Sol.* New York: Henry Holt.

Carrick, Carol. 1988. *Left Behind.* New York: Clarion.

Cech, John. 1991. *My Grandmother's Journey.* New York: Bradbury.

Celenza, Anna Harwell. 2004. *The Heroic Symphony.* Watertown, MA: Charlesbridge.

———. 2005. *Bach's Goldberg Variations.* Watertown, MA: Charlesbridge.

———. 2006. *Gershwin's Rhapsody in Blue.* Watertown, MA: Charlesbridge.

Cha, Dia. 1996. *Dia's Story Cloth.* New York: Lee and Low.

Chall, Marsha Wilson. 1992. *Up North at the Cabin.* New York: Lothrop, Lee and Shepard.

Chambers, Veronica. 2005. *Celia Cruz, Queen of Salsa.* New York: Dial.

Chang, Ina. 1996. *A Separate Battle: Women and the Civil War.* New York: Puffin.

Charles, Veronika Martenova. 2006. *The Birdman.* Toronto, ON: Tundra.

Cherry, Lynne. 1990. *The Great Kapok Tree.* New York: Harcourt.

———. 1992. *A River Ran Wild.* San Diego: Harcourt Brace.

Cherry, Lynne, and Mark J. Plotkin. 1998. *The Shaman's Apprentice.* San Diego, CA: Harcourt Brace.

Child, Lauren. 2003. *Who's Afraid of the Big Bad Book?* New York: Hyperion.

Chin-Lee, Cynthia. 2005. *Amelia to Zora: Twenty-Six Women Who Changed the World.* Watertown, MA: Charlesbridge.

Christelow, Eileen. 1995. *What Do Authors Do?* New York: Clarion.

Christensen, Bonnie. 2001. *Woody Guthrie: Poet of the People.* New York: Knopf.

———. 2003. *The Daring Nellie Bly: America's Star Reporter.* New York: Knopf.

Clements, Andrew. 2006. *A Million Dots.* New York: Simon and Schuster.

Clinton, Catherine. 2005. *Hold the Flag High.* New York: HarperCollins.

Clyne, Densey. 1995. *Spotlight on Spiders.* St. Leonard's, Australia: Little Arc.

Coerr, Eleanor. 1993. *Sadako.* New York: Putnam.

Coffelt, Nancy. 1993. *Dogs in Space.* San Diego: Harcourt Brace.

Cole, Joanna. 1986. *Hungry, Hungry Sharks.* New York: Random House.

Coles, Robert. 1995. *The Story of Ruby Bridges.* New York: Scholastic.

Colman, Penny. 1995. *Rosie the Riveter.* New York: Crown.

Condra, Estelle. 1994. *See the Ocean.* Nashville, TN: Ideal.

Cooney, Barbara. 1982. *Miss Rumphius.* New York: Viking Penguin.

———. 1994. *Only Opal: The Diary of a Young Girl.* New York: Scholastic.

———. 1996. *Eleanor.* New York: Viking.

Cooper, Elisha. 1998. *Ballpark.* New York: Greenwillow.

Cooper, Floyd. 1994. *Coming Home: From the Life of Langston Hughes.* New York: Philomel.

Cooper, Michael L. 2004. *Dust to Eat: Drought and Depression in the 1930s.* New York: Clarion.

Corey, Shana. 2000. *You Forgot Your Skirt, Amelia Bloomer.* New York: Scholastic.

Coste, Marion. 2006. *Finding Joy.* Honesdale, PA: Boyds Mills.

Coville, Bruce. 1997. *Macbeth.* New York: Dial.

Cowley, Joy. 1980. *Mrs. Wishy Washy.* Chicago: Wright Group.

Cowcher, Helen. 1991. *Antarctica.* New York: Farrar, Straus and Giroux.

Crew, Gary. 2005. *Pig on the Titanic.* New York: HarperCollins.

Crist-Evans, Craig. 1999. *Moon Over Tennessee: A Boy's Civil War Journal.* Boston: Houghton Mifflin.

Cristaldi, Kathryn. 1992. *Baseball Ballerina.* New York: Random House.

Cromwell, Sharon. 1998. *Why Do My Feet Fall Asleep? And Other Questions About the Circulatory System.* Des Plaines, IL: Rigby.

Croswell, Ken. 2006. *Ten Worlds: Everything That Orbits the Sun.* Honesdale, PA: Boyds Mills.

Cruise, Robin. 2006. *Little Mama Forgets.* New York: Farrar, Straus and Giroux.

Crutchfield, James A. 1993. *It Happened in Colorado.* Helena, MT: Falcon.

Cummings, Pat. 1992. *Talking with Artists.* 2 vols. New York: Simon and Schuster.

———. 1999. *Talking with Artists.* Volume 3. New York: Clarion.

Cummings, Pat, and Linda Cummings. 1998. *Talking with Adventurers.* Washington, DC: National Geographic.

Curlee, Lynn. 2005. *Ballpark: The Story of America's Baseball Fields.* New York: Atheneum.

Curtis, Gavin. 1998. *The Bat Boy and His Violin.* New York: Simon and Schuster.

Danneberg, Julie. 2003. *Women Writers of the West: Five Chroniclers of the American Frontier.* Golden, CO: Fulcrum.

Davidson, Margaret. 1997. *I Have a Dream: The Story of Martin Luther King.* New York: Scholastic.

Davies, Jacqueline, and Melissa Sweet. 2004. *The Boy Who Drew Birds: A Story of John James Audubon.* Boston: Houghton Mifflin.

Davies, Nicola. 2005. *Ice Bear: In the Steps of the Polar Bear.* Cambridge, MA: Candlewick.

Day, Alexandra. 1985. *Good Dog Carl.* New York: Scholastic.

———. 1988. *Frank and Ernest.* New York: Scholastic.

———. 1989. *Carl Goes Shopping.* New York: Farrar, Straus and Giroux.

———. 1990. *Frank and Ernest Play Ball.* New York: Scholastic.

———. 1992. *Carl's Masquerade.* New York: Farrar, Straus and Giroux.

———. 1994. *Frank and Ernest on the Road.* New York: Scholastic.

de Paola, Tomie. 1978. *Nana Upstairs, Nana Downstairs.* New York: Puffin.

———. 1979. *Oliver Button Is a Sissy.* New York: Harcourt Brace.

———. 1981. *Now One Foot, Now the Other.* New York: Trumpet.

———. 1989. *The Art Lesson.* New York: Putnam.

———. 1991. *Bonjour, Mr. Satie.* New York: Putnam.

Dear America series. 1995+. New York: Scholastic.

Deem, James M. 2005. *Bodies from the Ash.* Boston: Houghton Mifflin.

Demi. 1991. *Chingis Khan.* New York: Henry Holt.

Dewey, Jennifer Owings. 1997. *Rattlesnake Dance.* Honesdale, PA: Boyds Mills.

Dolphin, Laurie. 1993. *Oasis of Peace.* New York: Scholastic.

———. 1997. *Our Journey from Tibet.* New York: Dutton.

Dorros, Arthur. 1991. *Abuela.* New York: Dutton.

Downey, Fran. 2006. "Freedom Readers." *National Geographic Explorer,* January/February.

Drez, Ronald J. 2004. *Remember D-Day: Both Sides Tell Their Stories.* Washington, DC: National Geographic.

Duggleby, John. 1995. *Artist in Overalls: The Life of Grant Wood.* San Francisco: Chronicle.

Duncan, Dayton. 1996. *People of the West.* Based on the public television series *The West.* Boston: Little, Brown.

Ehlert, Lois. 2005. *Leaf Man.* New York: Harcourt.

Erdrich, Liselotte. 2003. *Sacagawea.* Minneapolis: Carolrhoda.

Erickson, Paul. 1994. *Daily Life in a Covered Wagon.* New York: Puffin.

Ernst, Lisa Campbell. 1998. *Stella Louella's Runaway Book.* New York: Simon and Schuster.

Esbensen, Barbara Juster. 2000. *The Night Rainbow.* New York: Orchard.

Everett, Gwen. 1991. *Li'l Sis and Uncle Willie.* New York: Rizzoli.

———. 1993. *John Brown: One Man Against Slavery.* New York: Rizzoli.

Feelings, Tom. 1995. *The Middle Passage: White Ships/Black Cargo.* New York: Dial.

Feelings, Tom, comp. 1993. *Soul Looks Back in Wonder.* New York: Dial.

Fisher, Leonard Everett. 1986. *The Great Wall of China.* New York: Simon and Schuster.

———. 1987. *The Tower of London.* New York: Macmillan.

———. 1991. *Sailboat Lost.* New York: Macmillan.

Fitzpatrick, Marie-Louise. 1998. *The Long March.* Hillsboro, OR: Beyond Words.

Fleischman, Paul. 1988. *Rondo in C.* New York: Harper and Row.

———. 1993. *Bull Run.* New York: Scholastic.

———. 1996. *Dateline: Troy.* Cambridge, MA: Candlewick.

Fleming, Candace. 2003. *Boxes for Katje.* New York: Farrar, Straus and Giroux.

Fletcher, Ralph. 1997. *Twilight Comes Twice.* New York: Clarion.

Florian, Doug. 2007. *Comets, Stars, the Moon, and Mars: Space Poems and Paintings.* Orlando, FL: Harcourt.

Foreman, Michael. 1989. *War Boy.* New York: Little, Brown.

Fox, Mary Virginia. 1991. *The Story of Women Who Shaped the West.* Chicago: Children's Press.

Fox, Mem. 1985. *Wilfrid Gordon McDonald Partridge.* Brooklyn, NY: Kane/Miller.

———. 1988. *Koala Lou.* Orlando, FL: Harcourt Brace.

Fradin, Judith Bloom, and Dennis Brindell Fradin. 2004. *The Power of One: Daisy Bates and the Little Rock Nine.* New York: Clarion.

Fraser, Mary Ann. 1994. *Sanctuary: The Story of Three Arch Rocks.* New York: Henry Holt.

Freedman, Russell. 1980. *Immigrant Kids.* New York: Scholastic.

———. 1983. *Children of the Wild West.* New York: Clarion.

———. 1988. *Buffalo Hunt.* New York: Scholastic.

———. 1994. *Kids at Work: Lewis Hine and the Crusade Against Child Labor.* New York: Scholastic.

———. 1996. *The Life and Death of Crazy Horse.* New York: Holiday House.

———. 1997. *Lincoln: A Photobiography.* New York: Clarion.

———. 2002. *Confucius: The Golden Rule.* New York: Scholastic.

———. 2003. *In Defense of Liberty: The Story of America's Bill of Rights.* New York: Holiday House.

———. 2005 *Children of the Great Depression.* New York: Clarion.

———. 2006. *The Adventures of Marco Polo.* New York: Arthur A. Levine.

Friedman, Robin. 2005. *The Silent Witness: A True Story of the Civil War.* Boston: Houghton Mifflin.

Friedrich, Elizabeth. 1996. *Leah's Pony.* Honesdale, PA: Boyds Mills.

Fritz, Jean. 1973. *And Then What Happened, Paul Revere?* New York: Putnam and Grosset.

———. 1976. *Will You Sign Here, John Hancock?* New York: Coward McCann.

———. 1977. *Can't You Make Them Behave, King George?* New York: Coward McCann.

———. 1980. *Where Do You Think You're Going, Christopher Columbus?* New York: Putnam.

———. 1983. *Shh! We're Writing the Constitution.* New York: Putnam.

———. 1994. *Around the World in 100 Years: From Henry the Navigator to Magellan.* New York: Putnam and Grosset.

Garland, Sherry. 1993. *The Lotus Seed.* San Diego: Harcourt Brace.

Gershwin, Ira, George Gershwin, DuBose Heyward, and Dorothy Heyward. 1999. *Summertime from Porgy and Bess.* New York: Simon and Schuster.

Gherman, Beverly. 1992. *E. B. White: Some Writer.* New York: Atheneum.

Gibbons, Gail. 1995. *The Reasons for Seasons.* New York: Holiday House.

———. 2005. *Owls.* New York: Holiday House.

———. 2006. *Ice Cream: The Full Scoop.* New York: Holiday House.

———. 2007. *Galaxies, Galaxies.* New York: Holiday House

Gikow, L. 1993. *For Every Child a Better World.* Wave, WI: Golden Press.

Giovanni, Nikki. 2005. *Rosa.* New York: Henry Holt.

Golenbock, Peter. 1990. *Teammates.* San Diego: Harcourt Brace Jovanovich.

Goodman, Susan E. 2004. *Skyscraper.* New York: Random House.

Gourley, Catherine. 1999. *Good Girl Work: Factories, Sweatshops and How Women Changed Their Role in the American Workforce.* Brookfield, CT: The Millbrook Press.

Grace, Eric S. 1993. *Elephants.* San Francisco: Sierra Club.

Graham, Paula. 1999. *Speaking of Journals: Children's Book Writers Talk About Their Diaries, Notebooks, and Sketchbooks.* Honesdale, PA: Boyds Mills.

Graves, Donald. 1996. *Baseball, Snakes and Summer Squash: Poems About Growing Up.* Honesdale, PA: Boyds Mills.

Gray, Libba Moore. 1993. *Dear Willie Rudd.* New York: Simon and Schuster.

———. 1996. *Little Lil and the Swing-Singing Sax.* New York: Simon and Schuster.

Gray, Nigel, and Philippe Dupasquier. 1988. *A Country Far Away.* New York: Orchard.

Graydon, Shari. 2004. *In Your Face: The Culture of Beauty and You.* Toronto, ON: Annick.

Greenfield, Eloise. 1978. *Honey I Love.* New York: HarperCollins.

Greenfield, Eloise, and Lessie Jones Little. 1979. *Childtimes.* New York: HarperCollins.

Grindley, Sally. 1997. *Why Is the Sky Blue?* New York: Simon and Schuster.

Grodin, Elissa. 2006. *Everyone Counts: A Citizen's Number Book.* Chelsea, MI: Sleeping Bear.

Grutman, Jewel H., and Gay Matthai. 1994. *The Ledgerbook of Thomas Blue Eagle.* Charlottesville, VA: Thomasson-Grant.

Gunning, Monica. 2004. *America, My New Home.* Honesdale, PA: Boyds Mills.

Gutelle, Andrew. 1989. *Baseball's Best: Five True Stories.* New York: Random House.

Hacker, Carlotta. 1998. *Explorers. Women in Profile Series.* New York: Crabtree.

Hakim, Joy. 1995. *A History of US: The Story of America.* New York: Oxford University.

———. 2004. *The Story of Science: Aristotle Leads the Way.* New York: Smithsonian.

Hamilton, John. 1998. Mission to Mars Series. Edina, MN: Abdo and Daughters.

Hansen, Joyce. 1997. *I Thought My Soul Would Rise and Fly: The Diary of Patsy, a Freed Girl.* New York: Scholastic.

Harness, Cheryl. 2004. *Franklin and Eleanor.* New York: Dutton.

Harper, Isabelle. 1995. *My Cats Nick and Nora.* New York: Scholastic.

Harrison, David. 2005. *Mountains: The Tops of the World.* Honesdale,PA: Boyds Mills.

Harshman, Marc. 1993. *Uncle James.* New York: Cobblehill.

Harvey, Brett. 1988. *Cassie's Journey: Going West in the 1860s.* New York: Holiday House.

Harwayne, Shelley, with the NYC Board of Education. 2002. *Messages to Ground Zero: Children Respond to September 11, 2001.* Portsmouth, NH: Heinemann.

Haseley, Dennis. 2002. *A Story for Bear.* San Diego: Harcourt.

Haskins, James. 1992. *The Day Martin Luther King, Jr., Was Shot: A Photo History of the Civil Rights Movement.* New York: Scholastic.

———. 1995. *Freedom Rides: Journey for Justice.* New York: Hyperion.

Haskins, James, and Kathleen Benson. 1999. *Bound for America: The Forced Migration of Africans to the New World.* New York: Lothrop, Lee and Shepard.

Hatkoff, Isabella and Craig. 2006. *Owen and Mzee: The True Story of a Remarkable Friendship.* New York: Scholastic.

Hazell, Rebecca. 1996. *Heroes: Great Men Through the Ages.* New York: Abbeville.

———. 1996. *Heroines: Great Women Through the Ages.* New York: Abbeville.

———. 2000. *Heroic Children.* Cambridge, MA: Barefoot.

Hazen, Barbara Shook. 1979. *Tight Times.* New York: Viking.

Heard, Georgia. 1992. *Creatures of the Earth, Sea, and Sky.* Honesdale, PA: Boyds Mills.

Hearne, Betsy. 1997. *Seven Brave Women.* New York: Greenwillow.

Hehner, Barbara. 1999. *First on the Moon: What It Was Like When Man Landed on the Moon.* New York: Hyperion.

Heide, Florence Parry, and J. D. Gilliland. 1990. *The Day of Ahmed's Secret.* New York: Lothrop, Lee and Shepard.

———. 1992. *Sammy and the Time of Troubles.* New York: Clarion.

Henkes, Kevin. 1987. *Sheila Ray the Brave.* New York: Mulberry.

———. 1990. *Julius, the Baby of the World.* New York: Mulberry.

———. 1991. *Chrysanthemum.* New York: Mulberry.

———. 1993. *Owen.* New York: Greenwillow.

Herzog, Brad. 2006. *R Is for Race: A Stock Car Alphabet.* Chelsea, MI: Sleeping Bear.

Hesse, Karen. 1999. *Out of the Dust.* New York: Scholastic.

———. 2004. *The Cats in Krasinski Square.* New York: Scholastic.

Hest, Amy. 1995. *How to Get Famous in Brooklyn.* New York: Simon and Schuster.

———. 1997. *When Jessie Came Across the Sea.* Cambridge, MA: Candlewick.

———. 2004. *Mr. George Baker.* Cambridge, MA: Candlewick.

Heydlauff, Lisa. 2005. *Going to School in India.* Watertown, MA: Charlesbridge.

Heyward, DuBose. 1939. *The Country Bunny and the Little Gold Shoes.* Boston: Houghton Mifflin.

Hilliard, Richard. 2006. *Godspeed, John Glenn.* Honesdale, PA: Boyds Mills.

Hochain, Serge. 2004. *Building Liberty: A Statue Is Born.* Washington, DC: National Geographic.

Hoestlandt, Jo. 1993. *Star of Fear, Star of Hope.* New York: Walker.

Hoffman, Mary. 1991. *Amazing Grace.* New York: Dial.

Hooper, Meredith, and Lucia deLeiris. 2004. *The Island That Moved: How Shifting Forces Shape Our Earth.* New York: Viking.

Hoose, Phillip. 2001. *We Were There, Too: Young People in US History.* New York: Farrar, Straus and Giroux.

Hopkins, Lee Bennett. 1994. *Hand in Hand: An American History Through Poetry.* New York: Simon and Schuster.

———. 2004. *Wonderful Words: Poems About Reading, Writing, Speaking, and Listening.* New York: Simon and Schuster.

———. 2006. *Got Geography!* New York: Greenwillow.

Hopkinson, Deborah. 1993. *Sweet Clara and the Freedom Quilt.* New York: Knopf.

———. 2003. *Girl Wonder: A Baseball Story in Nine Innings.* New York: Atheneum.

———. 2005. *Saving Strawberry Farm.* New York: Greenwillow.

Hopkinson, Deborah, and James E. Ransome. 2002. *Under the Quilt of Night.* New York: Simon and Schuster.

Houston, Gloria. 1992. *My Great-Aunt Arizona.* New York: HarperCollins.

Howard, Elizabeth Fitzgerald. 1991. *Aunt Flossie's Hats (and Crab Cakes Later).* New York: Clarion.

Hudson, Wade. 2004. *Powerful Words: More than 200 Years of Extraordinary Writing by African Americans.* New York: Scholastic.

Hulme, Joy. 2005. *Wild Fibonacci: Nature's Secret Code Revealed.* Berkeley, CA: Tricycle.

Hunter, Sara Hoagland. 1996. *The Unbreakable Code.* Flagstaff, AZ: Northland.

Innocenti, Roberto. 1985. *Rose Blanche.* San Diego: Harcourt Brace.

Isadora, Rachel. 2005. *Luke Goes to Bat.* New York: GP Putnam's Sons.

Jackson, Donna M. 2004. *In Your Face: The Facts About Your Features.* New York: Viking.

Janeczko, Paul. 1988. *The Music of What Happens.* New York: Orchard.

———. 1990. *The Place My Words Are Looking For.* New York: Bradbury.

———. 1998. *The Sweet Diamond: Baseball Poems.* New York: Atheneum.

———. 2002. *Seeing the Blue Between: Advice and Inspiration for Young Poets.* Cambridge, MA: Candlewick.

———. 2004. *Top Secret: A Handbook of Codes, Ciphers and Secret Writing.* Cambridge, MA: Candlewick.

January, Brendan. 2002. *The CIA.* New York: Watts Library.

———. 2003. *Witness to History: September 11, 2001.* Chicago: Heinemann.

Jenkins, Alvin, and Steve Jenkins. 2004. *Next Stop Neptune: Experiencing the Solar System.* Boston: Houghton Mifflin.

Jenkins, Steve. 1997. *Biggest, Strongest, Fastest.* Boston: Houghton Mifflin.

———. 1998. *Hottest, Coldest, Highest, Deepest.* Boston: Houghton Mifflin.

———. 1999. *The Top of the World: Climbing Mount Everest.* Boston: Houghton Mifflin.

———. 2003. *Looking Down.* Boston: Houghton Mifflin.

———. 2004. *Actual Size.* Boston: Houghton Mifflin.

———.. 2005 *Prehistoric Actual Size.* Boston: Houghton Mifflin.

Jenkins, Steve, and Robin Page. 2001. *Animals in Flight.* Boston: Houghton Mifflin.

———. 2005. *I See a Kookaburra! Discovering Animal Habitats Around the World.* Boston: Houghton Mifflin.

Jimenez, Francisco. 1997. *The Circuit: Stories from the Life of a Migrant Child.* Albuquerque: University of New Mexico.

———. 1998. *La Mariposa.* Boston: Houghton Mifflin.

Johnson, Dolores. 1993. *Now Let Me Fly: The Story of a Slave Family.* New York: Macmillan.

———. 1994. *Seminole Diary: Remembrances of a Slave.* New York: Macmillan.

Johnston, Tony. 1994. *Amber on the Mountain.* New York: Dial.

———. 1999. *The Wagon.* New York: Morrow.

———. 2002. *Sunsets of the West.* New York: G.P. Putnam's Sons.

———. 2004. *The Harmonica.* Watertown, Mass: Charlesbridge.

Johnstone, Michael. 1997. *The History News: Explorers.* Cambridge, MA: Candlewick.

Jones, Charlotte Foltz. 1991. *Mistakes That Worked.* New York: Doubleday.

Jones, Thomas D., and June A. English. 1996. *Mission: Earth, Voyage to the Home Planet.* New York: Scholastic.

Joyce, William. 1999. *Baseball Bob.* New York: Harper Festival.

Junior Scholastic. 1999. "Should Cities Sue Gunmakers?" *Junior Scholastic* 101 (February 8): 5.

Kamensky, Jane. 1995. *Colonial Mosaic: American Women 1600–1760.* New York: Oxford University.

Kaplan, William, with Shelley Tanaka. 1998. *One More Border.* Toronto: Douglas and McIntyre.

Karr, Kathleen. 2004. *Exiled: Memoirs of a Camel.* London: Marshall Cavendish.

———. 2005. *Mama Went to Jail for the Vote.* New York: Hyperion.

Katz, William. 1995. *Black Women of the Old West.* New York: Simon and Schuster.

Kentley, Dr. Eric, and Steve Noon. 2001. *Story of the* Titanic. New York: DK.

Kerley, Barbara. 2004. *Walt Whitman: Words for America.* New York: Scholastic.

Khalsa, Dayal Kaur. 1986. *Tales of a Gambling Grandma.* New York: Clarkson Potter.

Kids Discover Magazine. 1999. "In Sickness and in Health." *Kids Discover Magazine.* April.

King, Martin Luther Jr. 1997. *I Have a Dream.* New York: Scholastic.

Kinsey-Warnock, Natalie. 2005. *Nora's Ark.* New York: HarperCollins.

Kirkpatrick, Katherine. 1999. *Redcoats and Petticoats.* New York: Holiday House.

Knight, Margy Burns. 1992. *Talking Walls.* Gardiner, ME: Tilbury House.

Knox, Bob. 1993. *The Great Art Adventure.* New York: Rizzoli.

Knudsen, Michelle. 2006. *Library Lion.* Cambridge, MA: Candlewick.

Kodama, Tatsuharu. 1995. *Shin's Tricycle.* New York: Walker.

Koscielniak, Bruce. 2006. *Looking at Glass Through the Ages.* New York: Houghton Mifflin.

Kramer, S. A. 1995. *Baseball's Greatest Hitters.* New York: Random House.

Kramer, Stephen. 1992. *Avalanche.* Minneapolis: Carolrhoda.

———. 1992. *Lightning.* Minneapolis: Carolrhoda.

———. 1992. *Tornado.* Minneapolis: Carolrhoda.

———. 1997. *Eye of the Storm.* New York: Putnam.

———. 2003. *Hidden Worlds: Looking Through a Scientist's Microscope.* Boston: Houghton Mifflin.

Krensky, Stephen. 2001. *Shooting for the Moon: The Amazing Life and Times of Annie Oakley.* New York: Farrar, Straus and Giroux.

———. 2005. *Dangerous Crossing: The Revolutionary Voyage of John Quincy Adams.* New York: Dutton.

Kroeger, Mary Kay, and Louise Borden. 1996. *Paperboy.* New York: Clarion.

Kroll, Steven. 1994. *Lewis and Clark: Explorers of the New American West.* New York: Holiday House.

———. 1998. *The Boston Tea Party.* New York: Holiday House.

Krulik, Nancy. 1991. *My Picture Book of the Planets.* New York: Scholastic.

Krull, Kathleen. 1992. *Lives of the Artists.* San Diego: Harcourt Brace.

———. 1993. *Lives of the Musicians.* San Diego: Harcourt Brace.

———. 1994. *Lives of the Writers.* San Diego: Harcourt Brace.

———. 1996. *Wilma Unlimited.* San Diego: Harcourt Brace.

———. 2003. *Harvesting Hope: The Story of Cesar Chavez.* San Diego: Harcourt Brace.

———. 2004. *The Boy on Fairfield Street: How Ted Geisel Grew Up to Become Dr. Seuss.* New York: Random House.

———. 2004. *A Woman for President: The Story of Victoria Woodhull.* New York: Walker.

Kumin, Maxine. 2006. *Mites to Mastadons: A Book of Animal Poems.* Boston: Houghton Mifflin.

Kurlansky, Mark. 2006. *The Story of Salt.* New York: Putnam.

Kuskin, Karla. 1975. *Near the Window Tree: Poems and Notes.* New York: Harper and Row.

Lamb, Nancy. 1996. *One April Morning.* New York: Lothrop, Lee and Shepard.

Lasky, Kathryn. 1993. *Monarchs.* San Diego: Harcourt Brace.

———. 1994. *Day of the Dead.* New York: Hyperion.

———. 1994. *The Librarian Who Measured the Earth.* Boston: Little, Brown.

———. 1995. *She's Wearing a Dead Bird on Her Head.* New York: Hyperion.

———. 2003. *The Man Who Made Time Travel.* New York: Farrar, Straus and Giroux.

———. 2003. *A Voice of Her Own: The Story of Phillis Wheatley, Slave Poet.* Eastsound, WA: Turtleback.

Lawlor, Laurie. 2005. *Shadow Catcher: The Life and Work of Edward S. Curtis.* Lincoln, NE: Bison.

Lawlor, Veronica. 1995. *I Was Dreaming to Come to America.* New York: Viking.

Lawrence, Jacob. 1993. *The Great Migration.* New York: HarperCollins.

Leedy, Loreen. 1992. *Postcards from Pluto.* New York: Scholastic.

Leedy, Loreen, and Andrew Schuerger. 2006. *Messages from Mars.* New York: Holiday House.

Lees, Stewart. 2004. *Runaway Jack.* New York: Barron's.

Leon, Vicki. 1998. *Outrageous Women of Ancient Times.* New York: John Wiley.

Leonetti, Mike. 2004. *The Goalie Mask.* Vancouver: Raincoast.

Lesser, Carolyn. 1999. *Spots: Counting Creatures from Sky to Sea.* San Diego: Harcourt Brace.

Lester, Julius. 1998. *From Slave Ship to Freedom Road.* New York: Dial.

———. 2005. *Let's Talk About Race.* New York: HarperCollins.

Le Tord, Bijou. 1995. *A Blue Butterfly: A Story of Claude Monet.* New York: Doubleday.

Levenson, George. 2004. *Bread Comes to Life: A Garden of Wheat and a Loaf to Eat.* Berkeley, CA: Tricycle.

Levine, Ellen. 1989. *I Hate English!* New York: Scholastic.

Lewis, J. Patrick. 2005. *Please Bury Me in the Library.* San Diego: Gulliver/Harcourt.

Lewis, Paul Owen. 1995. *Storm Boy.* Hillsboro, OR: Beyond Words.

Lewis, Thomas P. 1971. *Hill of Fire.* New York: Harper and Row.

Lin, Grace, and Ranida T. McKneally. 2006. *Our Seasons.* Watertown, MA: Charlesbridge.

Little, Jean. 1986. *Hey World, Here I Am!* New York: HarperCollins.

Littlechild, George. 1996. *We Are All Related.* Vancouver, BC: Polester.

Littlesugar, Amy. 2001. *Freedom School, Yes!* New York: Philomel.

Livingston, Myra, and Leonard Everett Fisher. 1998. *Space Songs.* New York: Holiday House.

Lobel, Arnold. 1970. *Frog and Toad Are Friends.* New York: Harper and Row.

———. 1982. *Owl at Home.* New York: Harper Trophy.

Locker, Thomas. 1985. *The Mare on the Hill.* New York: Dial.

———. 1990. *Snow Toward Evening.* New York: Penguin.

———. 2002. *Walking with Henry: Based on the Life and Works of Henry David Thoreau.* Golden, CO: Fulcrum.

London, Jonathan. 1996. *Into This Night We Are Rising.* New York: Puffin.

———. 1998. *At the Edge of the Forest.* Cambridge, MA: Candlewick.

———. 1998. *Dream Weaver.* San Diego: Harcourt Brace.

———. 1998. *Hurricane.* New York: Lothrop, Lee and Shepard.

———. 1998. *Like Butter on Pancakes.* New York: Puffin.

———. 1999. *Baby Whale's Journey.* San Francisco: Chronicle.

———. 1999. *The Condor's Egg.* San Francisco: Chronicle.

———. 1999. *Puddles.* New York: Puffin.

Lorbiecki, Marybeth. 2006. *Jackie's Bat.* New York: Simon and Schuster.

Lourie, Peter. 1991. *Amazon: A Young Reader's Look at the Last Frontier.* Honesdale, PA: Boyds Mills.

———. 1992. *Hudson River: An Adventure from the Mountains to the Sea.* Honesdale, PA: Boyds Mills.

———. 1992. *Yukon River: An Adventure to the Gold Fields of the Klondike.* Honesdale, PA: Boyds Mills.

———. 1997. *Erie Canal: Canoeing America's Great Waterway.* Honesdale, PA: Boyds Mills.

———. 1998. *Everglades: Buffalo Tiger and the River of Grass.* Honesdale, PA: Boyds Mills.

———. 1999. *Lost Treasure of the Inca.* Honesdale, PA: Boyds Mills.

———. 1999. *Rio Grande: From the Rocky Mountains to the Gulf of Mexico.* Honesdale, PA: Boyds Mills.

———. 2007. *Lost World of the Anasazi.* Honesdale PA: Boyds Mills.

Lucas, Eileen. 1997. *Cracking the Wall: The Struggles of the Little Rock Nine.* Minneapolis: Carolrhoda.

Lunn, Janet. 1998. *Charlotte.* Plattsburgh, NY: Tundra.

Lyon, George Ella. 1999. *Book.* New York: DK.

———. 2003. *Mother to Tigers.* New York: Atheneum.

MacGill-Callahan, Sheila. 1991. *And Still the Turtle Watched.* New York: Dial.

MacLachlan, Patricia. 1991. *Journey.* New York: Bantam Doubleday Dell.

———. 1994. *All the Places to Love.* New York: HarperCollins.

Madrigal, Antonio Hernandez. 1999. *Erandi's Braids.* New York: Putnam.

Maestro, Betsy, and Giulio Maestro. 1996. *The New Americans.* New York: Lothrop, Lee and Shepard.

Mann, Elizabeth. 1996. *The Brooklyn Bridge.* New York: Mikaya.

Markle, Sandra. 2005. *Outside and Inside Mummies.* New York: Walker.

———. 2005. *Snakes: Biggest! Littlest!* Honesdale, PA: Boyds Mills.

Markun, Patricia Maloney. 1993. *The Little Painter of Sabana Grande.* New York: Simon and Schuster.

Marshall, James. 1972. *George and Martha.* Boston: Houghton Mifflin.

———. 1973. *George and Martha Encore.* Boston: Houghton Mifflin.

———. 1976. *George and Martha Rise and Shine.* Boston: Houghton Mifflin.

Marshall, Rita. 1993. *I Hate to Read!* New York: Creative Company.

Martin, C. L. G. 1991. *Three Brave Women.* New York: Macmillan.

Martin, Jacqueline Briggs. 1995. *Washing the Willow Tree Loon.* New York: Simon and Schuster.

———. 1998. *Snowflake Bentley.* Boston: Houghton Mifflin.

Mason, Antony. 1994/95. Famous Artists Series. Hauppauge, NY: Barron's Educational Series.

Mayhew, James. 2005. *Katie's Sunday Afternoon.* New York: Orchard.

McCann, Michelle, and Luba Tryszynska-Frederick. 2003. *Luba: the Angel of Bergen-Belsen.* Berkeley, CA: Tricycle.

McCully, Emily Arnold. 1992. *Mirette on the High Wire.* New York: Putnam.

———. 1996. *Ballot Box Battle.* New York: Knopf.

———. 1996. *The Bobbin Girl.* New York: Dial.

———. 2004. *Squirrel and John Muir.* New York: Farrar, Straus and Giroux.

———. 2006. *Marvelous Mattie: How Margaret E. Knight Became an Inventor.* New York: Farrar, Straus and Giroux.

McDonald, Megan. 1991. *The Potato Man.* New York: Orchard.

McGee, Marni. 2006. *Winston the Book Wolf.* New York: Walker.

McGill, Alice. 1999. *Molly Bannaky.* Boston: Houghton Mifflin.

McGrath, Barbara Barbieri. 2006. *The Storm: The Students of Biloxi, Mississippi, Remember Hurrican Katrina.* Watertown, MA: Charlesbridge.

McKee, Tim, and Anne Blackshaw. 1998. *No More Strangers Now.* New York: DK.

McKissack, Patricia, and Fredrick McKissack. 1995. *Red-Tail Angels: The Story of the Tuskegee Airmen of World War II.* New York: Walker.

McMahon, Patricia, and Conor Clarke McCarthy. 2005. *Just Add One Chinese Sister: An Adoption Story.* Honesdale, PA: Boyds Mills.

McPhail, David. 1993. *Santa's Book of Names.* Boston: Joy Street.

———. 1997. *Edward and the Pirates.* Boston: Little, Brown.

Merk, Ann, and Jim Merk. 1994. Weather Report Series. Vero Beach, FL: Rourke.

Merrill Earth Science. 1993. Seventh-grade textbook. Westerville, OH: Macmillan/McGraw Hill.

Micklethwait, Lucy. 2006. *Children, A First Art Book.* London: Frances Lincoln.

Miller, William. 1994. *Zora Hurston and the Chinaberry Tree.* New York: Lee and Low.

———. 1995. *Frederick Douglass: The Last Day of Slavery.* New York: Lee and Low.

———. 1997. *Richard Wright and the Library Card.* New York: Lee and Low.

Mills, Lauren. 1991. *The Rag Coat.* Boston: Little, Brown.

Milner-Halls, Kelly. 2005. *Wild Dogs: Past and Present.* Columbus, OH: Darby Creek.

Mitchell, Rita. 1993. *Hue Boy.* New York: Puffin.

Mitton, Jacqueline. 2004. *Zodiac: Celestial Circle of the Sun.* London: Frances Lincoln.

Mitton, Jacqueline, and Christina Balit. 2001. *Kingdom of the Sun: A Book of Planets.* Washington, DC: National Geographic.

Mochizuki, Ken. 1993. *Baseball Saved Us.* New York: Lee and Low.

———. 1997. *Passage to Freedom: The Sugihara Story.* New York: Lee and Low.

Montgomery, Sy. 2004. *The Tarantula Scientist.* Boston: Houghton Mifflin.

Moon, Nicola. 1995. *Lucy's Picture.* New York: Dial.

Mora, Pat. 1997. *Tomas and the Library Lady.* New York: Knopf.

Morris, Ann, and Heidi Larson. 2005. *Tsunami: Helping Each Other.* Minneapolis, MN: Millbrook.

Morrison, Taylor. 2002. *The Buffalo Nickel.* Boston: Houghton Mifflin.

———. 2006. *Wildfire.* Boston: Houghton Mifflin.

Morrison, Toni. 2004. *Remember: The Journey to School Integration.* New York: Houghton Mifflin.

Moss, Marissa. 1995. *Amelia's Notebook.* Middleton, WI: Pleasant Company.

———. 1998. *Rachel's Journal.* San Diego: Harcourt Brace.

———. 1999. *Emma's Journal.* San Diego: Harcourt Brace.

———. 1999. *True Heart.* San Diego: Harcourt Brace.

Munoz, Pam Ryan. 2002. *When Marian Sang: The True Recital of Marian Anderson.* New York: Scholastic.

Murawski, Darlyne A. 2005. *Animal Faces.* New York: Sterling.

Murphy, Claire Rudolf, and Jane Haigh. 1999. *Children of the Gold Rush.* Boulder, CO: Roberts Rinehart.

Murphy, Jim. 1990. *The Boys' War.* New York: Clarion.

———. 1995. *The Great Fire.* New York: Scholastic.

———. 1996. *A Young Patriot: The American Revolution as Experienced by One Boy.* New York: Clarion.

Murphy, Nora. 1997. *A Hmong Family.* Minneapolis: Lerner.

Murray, Peter. 1994. *The Space Shuttle.* Chicago: Child's World/Encyclopedia Britannica.

Myers, Walter Dean. 1991. *Now Is Your Time! The African–American Struggle for Freedom.* New York: HarperCollins.

———. 1998. *Angel to Angel.* New York: HarperCollins.

———. 2004. *I've Seen the Promised Land: The Life of Dr. Martin Luther King, Jr.* New York: HarperCollins.

———. 2006. *Jazz.* New York: Holiday House.

Napier, Matt. 2005. *Hat Tricks Count: A Hockey Number Book.* Chelsea, MI: Sleeping Bear.

National Geographic for Kids. 2001. "Humpbacks Make a Comeback." *National Geographic for Kids,* September.

National Wildlife Federation. 1988. *The Unhuggables.* Reston, VA: National Wildlife Federation.

Navasky, Bruno, ed. 1993. *Festival in My Heart: Poems by Japanese Children.* New York: Harry N. Abrams.

Nevius, Carol. 2006. *Building with Dad.* Tarrytown, NY: Cavendish.

Nilsen, Anna. 2005. *Art Auction Mystery.* Boston, MA: Kingfisher.

Nivola, Claire. 1997. *Elisabeth.* New York: Farrar, Straus and Giroux.

Norworth, Jack, and Jim Burke. 2006. *Take Me Out to the Ball Game.* Boston: Little, Brown.

Notorious Americans and Their Times Series. 1999. Woodbridge, CT: Blackbirch.

Noyes, Deborah. 2004. *Hana in the Time of the Tulips.* Cambridge, MA: Candlewick.

Nye, Naomi Shihab. 2002. *19 Varieties of Gazelle: Poems of the Middle East.* New York: Greenwillow.

O'Connor, Jane. 2004. *If the Walls Could Talk: Family Life at the White House.* New York: Simon and Schuster.

O'Neal, Deborah, and Angela Westengard. 2005. *The Trouble with Henry: A Tale of Walden Pond.* Cambridge, MA: Candlewick.

Oppenheim, Shulamith. 1992. *The Lily Cupboard.* New York: Harper and Row.

Orgill, Roxane. 1997. *If I Only Had a Horn: Young Louis Armstrong.* Boston: Houghton Mifflin.

Osbourne, Mary Pope. 1998. *Standing in the Light: The Captive Diary of Catharine Carey Logan.* New York: Scholastic.

Parish, Peggy. 1995. *Play Ball, Amelia Bedelia.* New York: HarperTrophy.

Park, Frances, and Ginger Park. 1998. *My Freedom Trip: A Child's Escape from North Korea.* Honesdale, PA: Boyds Mills.

Parker, Nancy Winslow. 1998. *Locks, Crocs, and Skeeters: The Story of the Panama Canal.* New York: Philomel.

———. 2001. *Land Ho! Fifty Glorious Years in the Age of Exploration.* New York: HarperCollins.

Partridge, Elizabeth. 1998. *Restless Spirit: The Life and Work of Dorothea Lange.* New York: Viking.

Paterson, Katherine. 1977. *Bridge to Terabithia.* New York: Crowell.

Peacock, Louise. 1998. *Crossing the Delaware: A History in Many Voices.* New York: Simon and Schuster.

Perspectives on History Series. 1991+. Carlisle, MA: Discovery Enterprises.

Peters, Russell M. 1992. *Clambake: A Wampanoag Tradition.* Minneapolis: Lerner.

Philip, Neil, ed. 1997. *In a Sacred Manner I Live: Native American Wisdom.* New York: Clarion.

Pinkney, Andrea Davis. 1994. *Dear Benjamin Banneker.* San Diego: Harcourt Brace Jovanovich.

———. 1996. *Bill Pickett: Rodeo-Ridin' Cowboy.* San Diego: Harcourt Brace.

———. 1998. *Duke Ellington: The Piano Prince and His Orchestra.* New York: Hyperion.

Polacco, Patricia. 1988. *The Keeping Quilt.* New York: Simon and Schuster.

———. 1991. *Some Birthday!* New York: Simon and Schuster.

———. 1992. *Chicken Sunday.* New York: Putnam and Grosset.

———. 1992. *Mrs. Katz and Tush.* New York: Bantam.

———. 1993. *The Bee Tree.* New York: Philomel.

———. 1994. *My Rotten Red-Headed Older Brother.* New York: Simon and Schuster.

———. 1994. *Pink and Say.* New York: Philomel.

———. 1996. *Aunt Chip and the Great Cripple Creek Dam Affair.* New York: Philomel.

———. 1998. *Mrs Mack.* New York: Philomel.

———. 1998. *Thank You, Mr. Falker.* New York: Philomel.

———. 2000. *The Butterfly.* New York: Philomel.

Pomerantz, Charlotte. 1989. *The Chalk Doll.* New York: Lippincott.

Poole, Josephine. 2005. *Anne Frank.* New York: Knopf.

Prap, Lila. 2005. *Why?* La Jolla, CA: Kane/Miller.

Prince, April Jones. 2005. *Twenty-One Elephants and Still Standing.* Boston: Houghton Mifflin.

Provensen, Alice. 2005. *Klondike Gold.* New York: Simon and Schuster.

Rabin, Straton. 1994. *Casey Over There.* San Diego: Harcourt Brace.

Rahaman, Vashanti. 1997. *Read for Me, Mama.* Honesdale, PA: Boyds Mills.

Rappaport, Doreen. 2005. *In The Promised Land: Lives of Jewish Americans.* New York: HarperCollins.

———. 2006. *Freedom Ship.* New York: Hyperion/Jump at the Sun.

Rappaport, Doreen, and Lyndall Callan. 2000. *Dirt on Their Skirts: The Story of the Young Women Who Won the World Championship.* New York: Dial.

Raschka, Chris. 1992. *Charlie Parker Played Be Bop.* New York: Orchard.

Raven, Margot Theis. 1999. *Angels in the Dust.* New York: Troll.

———. 2002. *Mercedes and the Chocolate Pilot.* Chelsea, MI: Sleeping Bear.

———. 2005. *America's White Table.* Chelsea, MI: Sleeping Bear.

———. 2005. *Challenger: America's Favorite Eagle.* Chelsea, MI: Sleeping Bear.

———. 2005. *Let Them Play.* Chelsea, MI: Sleeping Bear.

———. 2006. *Night Boat to Freedom.* New York: Melanie Kroupa.

Ray, Delia. 1991. *Behind the Blue and Gray: The Soldier's Life in the Civil War.* New York: Penguin.

Riggio, Anita. 1997. *Secret Signs.* Honesdale, PA: Boyds Mills.

Ringgold, Faith. 1992. *Aunt Harriet's Underground Railroad in the Sky.* New York: Crown.

———. 1993. *Dinner at Aunt Connie's House.* New York: Hyperion.

Rochelle, Belinda. 1997. *Witnesses to Freedom: Young People Who Fought for Civil Rights.* New York: Puffin.

Rochman, Hazel, and Darlene McCampbell. 1997. *Leaving Home.* New York: HarperCollins.

Roehm, Michelle. 2000. *Girls Who Rocked the World: Heroines from Hariet Tubman to Mia Hamm.* Hillsboro, OR: Beyond Words.

Rosen, Michael. 1992. *Home.* New York: HarperCollins.

Rumford, James. 2004. *Sequoyah.* Boston: Houghton Mifflin.

Rusch, Elizabeth. 2002. *Generation Fix: Young Ideas for a Better World.* Hillsboro, OR: Beyond Words.

Russell, Barbara Timberlake. 2006. *Maggie's Amerikay.* New York: Melanie Kroupa.

Rylant, Cynthia. 1982. *When I Was Young in the Mountains.* New York: Dutton.

———. 1984. *Waiting to Waltz: A Childhood.* New York: Simon and Schuster.

———. 1985. *Every Living Thing.* New York: Aladdin.

———. 1994. *Something Permanent.* San Diego: Harcourt Brace.

———. 1995. *The Van Gogh Cafe.* San Diego: Harcourt Brace.

———. 1996. *An Angel for Solomon Singer.* New York: Scholastic.

———. 1997. *The Blue Hill Meadows.* San Diego: Harcourt Brace.

———. 2006. *The Journey: Stories of Migration.* New York: Blue Sky.

Salkeld, Audrey, 2003. *Climbing Everest: Tales of Triumph and Tragedy on the World's Highest Mountain.* Washington, DC: National Geographic.

San Souci, Robert. 1997. *A Weave of Words.* New York: Orchard.

Sawa, Maureen. 2006. *The Library Book: The Story of Libraries from Camels to Computers.* Toronto, ON: Tundra Books.

Say, Allen. 1988. *A River Dream.* Boston: Houghton Mifflin.

———. 1993. *Grandfather's Journey.* Boston: Houghton Mifflin.

———. 1999. *Tea with Milk.* Boston: Houghton Mifflin.

Schaefer, Carol Lexa. 1996. *The Squiggle.* New York: Crown.

Schanzer, Rosalyn. 2004. *George vs. George: The American Revolution as Seen from Both Sides.* Washington, DC: National Geographic.

Schertle, Alice. 1999. *A Lucky Thing.* San Diego: Harcourt Brace.

Schmidt, Cynthia. 1984. *Colorado Grassroots.* Phoenix, AZ: Cloud.

Scholastic News. 2006. "Be a Better Test Taker." *Scholastic News,* November 13.

Schroeder, Alan. 1996. *Minty: A Story of Young Harriet Tubman.* New York: Dial.

Schubert, Leda. 2006. *Ballet of the Elephants.* New Milford, CT: Roaring Brook.

Scieszka, John. 2005. *Guys Write for Guys Read.* New York: Viking.

Seidensticker, John, Susan Lumpkin, and Christer Ericksson. 1995. *Dangerous Animals.* New York: Orchard.

Seuss, Dr. 1954. *If I Ran the Zoo.* New York: Random House.

———. 1991. *The 500 Hats of Bartholomew Cubbins.* New York: Random House.

Sewell, Anna. 1941. *Black Beauty.* New York: Dodd, Mead.

Seymour, Isobel. 1997. *I Am Mexican American.* Our American Family Series. New York: Rosen.

Shange, Ntozake. 1994. *I Live in Music.* New York: Welcome.

Shea, Pegi Deitz. 1995. *The Whispering Cloth.* Honesdale, PA: Boyds Mills.

Shore, Diane Z., and Jessica Alexander. 2005. *This Is the Dream.* New York: Amistad.

Sidman, Joyce. 2005. *Song of the Water Boatman and Other Pond Poems.* Boston: Houghton Mifflin.

———. 2006. *Butterfly Eyes and Other Secrets of the Meadow.* New York: Houghton Mifflin.

Sierra, Judy. 2004. *Wild About Books.* New York: Knopf.

Simon, Seymour. 1985. *Saturn.* New York: Morrow.

———. 1986. *The Sun.* New York: Mulberry.

———. 1993. *Autumn Across America.* New York: Hyperion.

———. 1998. *Destination: Jupiter.* New York: Morrow.

———. 2003. *The Moon.* New York: Simon and Schuster.

———. 2004. *Cats.* New York: Harper Collins.

———. 2005. *Guts: Our Digestive System.* New York: HarperCollins.

Simon, Seymour, ed. 1995. *Star Walk.* New York: Morrow.

Sis, Peter. 1995. *Starry Messenger.* New York: Farrar, Straus and Giroux.

———. 1998. *Tibet: Through the Red Box.* New York: Farrar, Straus and Giroux.

———. 2003. *The Tree of Life.* New York: Farrar, Straus and Giroux.

———. 2006. *Play, Mozart, Play!* New York: Greenwillow.

Sisulu, Elinor Batezat. 1996. *The Day Gogo Went to Vote: South Africa, April 1994.* Boston: Little, Brown.

Smith, Lane. 2006. *John, Paul, George and Ben.* New York: Hyperion.

Sneve, Virgina Driving Hawk. 1989. *Dancing Teepees.* New York: Holiday House.

———. 1993. *The Navajos.* New York: Holiday House.

———. 1995. *The Hopis.* New York: Holiday House.

———. 1995. *The Iroquois.* New York: Holiday House.

———. 1996. *The Cherokees.* New York: Holiday House.

Sorenson, Henri. 1995. *New Hope.* New York: Lothrop, Lee and Shepard.

Soto, Gary. 1991. *A Summer Life.* New York: Dell.

———. 1992. *Neighborhood Odes.* San Diego: Harcourt Brace.

———. 1993. *Too Many Tamales.* New York: Putnam and Grosset.

Spinelli, Eileen. 2004. *Feathers: Poems About Birds.* New York: Henry Holt.

Spivak, Dawnine. 1997. *Grass Sandals: The Travels of Basho.* New York: Atheneum.

Stadler, John. 1985. *Hooray for Snail.* New York: Harper Trophy.

Stanley, Diane. 1990. *Good Queen Bess.* New York: Macmillan.

———. 1992. *The Bard of Avon.* New York: Morrow.

———. 1996. *Leonardo da Vinci.* New York: Morrow.

———. 1998. *Joan of Arc.* New York: Morrow.

Stanley, Jerry. 1992. *Children of the Dust Bowl.* New York: Crown.

Stavens, Ilan. 2001. *Wachale! Poetry and Prose About Growing Up Latino in America.* Chicago: Cricket.

Steig, William. 1969. *Sylvester and the Magic Pebble.* New York: Trumpet.

———. 1971. *Amos and Boris.* New York: Farrar, Straus and Giroux.

Stein, R. Conrad. 1993. *The Trail of Tears.* Chicago: Children's Press.

Stelson, Caren Barzelay. 1988. *Safari.* Minneapolis: Carolrhoda.

Stevenson, Robert Louis. 2006. *The Moon.* New York: Farrar, Straus and Giroux.

Stewart, Sarah. 1995. *The Library.* New York: Farrar, Straus and Giroux.

Stiekel, Bettina, ed. 2001. *The Nobel Book of Answers.* New York: Atheneum.

Stock, Catherine. 1993. *Where Are You Going, Manyoni?* New York: HarperCollins.

Stowell, Penelope. 2005. *The Greatest Potatoes.* New York: Hyperion/Jump at the Sun.

Stroud, Bettye. 2005. *The Patchwork Path: A Quilt Map to Freedom.* Cambridge, MA: Candlewick.

Sullivan, George. 2005. *Built to Last: Building America's Amazing Bridges, Dams, Tunnels, and Skyscrapers.* New York: Scholastic.

Swanson, Diane. 1998. *Animals Eat the Weirdest Things.* Vancouver, BC: Whitecap.

Swinburne, Stephen. 1999. *Safe, Warm, and Snug.* San Diego: Gulliver Books.

———. 2006. *Wings of Light: The Migration of the Yellow Butterfly.* Honesdale, PA: Boyds Mills.

Tanaka, Shelley. 1997. *The Buried City of Pompeii.* New York: Hyperion/Madison.

———. 2004. *A Day That Changed America: Earthquake!* New York: Hyperion.

Thaher, Ernest Lawrence. 1995. *Casey at the Bat.* New York: Aladdin.

Thomas, Joyce Carol. 1993. *Brown Honey in Broomwheat Tea.* New York: HarperCollins.

Time for Kids. 2002. "Could You Survive a Week Without TV?" *Time for Kids* 7 (22). April 12.

Tompert, Ann. 2004. *Saint Valentine.* Honesdale, PA: Boyds Mills.

Toupin, Laurie Ann. 2002. "What's the Fuss About Frogs?" *Odyssey,* May.

Trollinger, Patsi B. 2006. *Perfect Timing: How Isaac Murphy Became One of the World's Greatest Jockeys.* New York: Viking.

Tsuchiya, Yukio. 1988. *Faithful Elephants: A True Story of Animals, People, and War.* Boston: Houghton Mifflin.

Tunnell, Michael O., and George W. Chilcoat. 1996. *The Children of Topaz: The Story of a Japanese–American Internment Camp.* New York: Holiday House.

Turbak, Gary. 1993. *Survivors in the Shadows.* Flagstaff, AZ: Northland.

Turner, Ann. 1987. *Nettie's Trip South.* New York: Aladdin.

———. 1992. *Katie's Trunk.* New York: Simon and Schuster.

———. 1997. *Red Flower Goes West.* New York: Hyperion.

———. 1999. *The Girl Who Chased Away Sorrow: The Diary of Sarah Nita, a Navajo Girl.* New York: Scholastic.

Turner, Glennette Tilley. 2006. *An Apple for Harriet Tubman.* Morton Grove, IL: Whitman.

Uchida, Yoshiko. 1993. *The Bracelet.* New York: Philomel.

Ulmer, Mike. 2005. *J Is for Jump Shot: A Basketball Alphabet.* Chelsea, MI: Sleeping Bear.

Van Allsburg, Chris. 1986. *The Stranger.* New York: Houghton Mifflin.

Van der Rol, Ruud, and Rian Verhoeven. 1993. *Anne Frank: Beyond the Diary.* New York: Penguin.

Van Leeuwen, Jean. 1992. *Going West.* New York: Dial.

———. 1998. *Nothing Here But Trees.* New York: Dial.

Viorst, Judith. 1971. *The Tenth Good Thing About Barney.* New York: Aladdin.

———. 1972. *Alexander and the Terrible, Horrible, No Good, Very Bad Day.* New York: Scholastic.

———. 1974. *Rosie and Michael.* New York: Aladdin.

———. 1990. *Earrings.* New York: Trumpet.

Vogt, Gregory. 1999. Explore Space Series. Mankato, MN: Bridgestone.

Volavkova, Hana, ed. 1993. *I Never Saw Another Butterfly: Children's Drawings and Poems from Terezin Concentration Camp, 1942–1944.* 2nd ed. New York: Schocken.

Waber, Bernard. 1972. *Ira Sleeps Over.* Boston: Houghton Mifflin.

Wallner, Alexandra. 2004. *Grandma Moses.* New York: Holiday House.

Ward, Geoffrey, Ken Burns, with Jim O'Connor. 1994. *Shadow Ball: The History of the Negro Leagues.* Baseball, the American Epic series. New York: Knopf.

Ward, Geoffrey, Ken Burns, with Robert Walker. 1994. *Who Invented the Game?* Baseball, the American Epic series. New York: Knopf.

Wargin, Kathy-Jo. 2004. *Win One for the Gipper: America's Football Hero.* Chelsea, MI: Sleeping Bear.

Warhola, James. 2003. *Uncle Andy's.* New York: G.P. Putnam's Sons.

Warren, Andrea. 1996. *Orphan Train Rider: One Boy's True Story.* Boston: Houghton Mifflin.

———. 2004. *Escape from Saigon: How a Vietnam War Orphan Became an American Boy.* New York: Farrar, Straus and Giroux.

Waters, Kate. 1989. *Sarah Morton's Day: A Day in the Life of a Pilgrim Girl.* New York: Scholastic.

———. 1991. *Tapenum's Day: A Wampanoag Indian Boy in Pilgrim Times.* New York: Scholastic.

———. 1993. *Samuel Eaton's Day: A Day in the Life of a Pilgrim Boy.* New York: Scholastic.

Weber, Belinda. 2006. *The Best Book of Nighttime Animals.* Boston: Kingfisher

Weiss, George David, and Bob Thiele. 1995. *What a Wonderful World.* New York: Simon and Schuster.

Wells, Rosemary, and Tom Wells. 2002. *The House in the Mail.* New York: Viking.

Wheeler, Lisa. 2006. *Mammoths on the Move.* New York: Harcourt.

Whelan, Gloria. 2005. *Friend on Freedom River.* Chelsea, MI: Sleeping Bear.

White, E. B. 1952. *Charlotte's Web.* New York: Harper and Row.

White, Linda Arms. 2005. *I Could Do That! Esther Morris Gets Women the Vote.* New York: Melanie Kroupa.

Whitman, Sylvia. 1993. *V Is for Victory: The American Home Front During World War II.* Minneapolis: Lerner.

Wick, Walter. 1997. *A Drop of Water: A Book of Science and Wonder.* New York: Scholastic.

Wiesner, David. 1988. *Free Fall.* New York: Lothrop, Lee and Shepard.

———. 1992. *June 29, 1999.* New York: Clarion.

Wilkes, Sybella. 1994. *One Day We Had to Run.* Brookfield, CT: Millbrook.

Williams, Laura E. 2006. *The Best Winds.* Honesdale, PA: Boyds Mills.

al-Windawi, Thura. 2004. *Thura's Diary.* New York: Viking.

Winnick, Karen. 1997. *Mr. Lincoln's Whiskers.* Honesdale, PA: Boyds Mills.

———. 2000. *Sybil's Night Ride.* Honesdale, PA: Boyds Mills.

———. 2005. *Cassie's Sweet Berry Pie, A Civil War Story.* Honesdale, PA: Boyds Mills.

Winter, Jeanette. 1988. *Follow the Drinking Gourd.* New York: Trumpet.

———. 1991. *Diego.* New York: Knopf.

———. 1996. *Josefina.* San Diego: Harcourt Brace.

———. 1998. *My Name Is Georgia.* San Diego: Harcourt Brace.

———. 1999. *Sebastian: A Book About Bach.* San Diego: Harcourt Brace.

———. 2005. *The Librarian of Basra.* San Diego: Harcourt Brace.

———. 2007. *The Tale of Pale Male: A True Story.* Orlando: Harcourt.

Winter, Jonah. 2006. *Dizzy.* New York: Arthur A. Levine.

Wollard, Kathy. 1993. *How Come?* New York: Workman.

Woodson, Jacqueline. 2001. *The Other Side.* New York: GP Putnam's Sons.

———. 2002. *Our Gracie Aunt.* New York: Hyperion/Jump at the Sun.

———. 2004. *Coming on Home Soon.* New York: GP Putnam's Sons.

Worth, Valerie. 1987. *All the Small Poems.* New York: Farrar, Straus and Giroux.

———. 2002. *Peacock and Other Poems.* New York: Farrar, Straus and Giroux.

Wright, Alexandra. 1992. *Will We Miss Them? Endangered Species.* Watertown, MA: Charlesbridge.

Wright, Courtni C. 1994. *Journey to Freedom: A Story of the Underground Railroad.* New York: Holiday House.

Wright-Frierson, Virginia. 1996. *A Desert Scrapbook: Dawn to Dusk in the Sonoran Desert.* New York: Simon and Schuster.

———. 1998. *An Island Scrapbook: Dawn to Dusk on a Barrier Reef.* New York: Simon and Schuster.

Yin. 2001. *Coolies.* New York: Philomel.

———. 2006. *Brothers.* New York: Philomel.

Yolen, Jane. 1992. *Encounter.* San Diego: Harcourt Brace.

———. 1992. *Letting Swift River Go.* Boston: Little, Brown.

———. 1994. *Granddad Bill's Song.* New York: Putnam and Grosset.

———. 2000. *Not One Damsel in Distress: World Folktales for Strong Girls.* San Diego: Harcourt Brace.

———. 2003. *My Brothers' Flying Machine.* Boston: Little, Brown.

Yolen, Jane, and Heidi Elisabet Yolen Stemple. 1999. *The Mary Celeste: An Unsolved Mystery from History.* New York: Simon and Schuster.

———. 2003. *Roanoke: The Last Colony: An Unsolved Mystery from History.* New York: Simon and Schuster.

Yolen, Jane, and Jason Stemple. 2006. *Count Me A Rhyme: Animal Poems by the Numbers.* Honesdale, PA: Boyds Mills.

Yoo, Paula. 2005. *Sixteen Years in Sixteen Seconds: The Sammy Lee Story.* New York: Lee and Low.

Young, Ed. 2005. *Beyond the Great Mountains: A Visual Poem About China.* San Francisco: Chronicle.

Yurkovic, Diana Short. 1998. *Meet Me at the Water Hole.* Denver, CO: Shortland.

Zalben, Jane Breskin. 2006. *Paths to Peace: People Who Changed the World.* New York: Dutton.

Zaunders, Bo. 2004. *Gargoyles, Girders and Glass Houses: Magnificent Master Builders.* New York: Dutton.

Zhensun, Zheng, and Alice Low. 1991. *A Young Painter: The Life and Paintings of Wang Yani.* New York: Scholastic.

Zimet, Sara Goodman. 2005. *Hannah and the Perfect Picture Pony: A Story of the Great Depression.* Denver: Discover.

Zolotow, Charlotte. 1972. *William's Doll.* New York: HarperCollins.

———. 1992. *The Seashore Book.* New York: HarperCollins.

References

Professional References and Adult Resources

Abbey, Edward. 1991. *Desert Solitaire.* New York: Ballantine.

Abeel, Samantha. 1993. *Reach for the Moon.* Duluth, MN: Pfeifer-Hamilton.

Ackerman, Diane. 1990. *A Natural History of the Senses.* New York: Vintage.

Alicea, Gil. 1995. *The Air Down Here.* San Francisco: Chronicle.

Allen, Janet, and Kyle Gonzalez. 1998. *There's Room for Me Here: Literacy Workshop in the Middle School.* Portland, ME: Stenhouse.

Allington, Richard. 1994. "The Schools We Have. The Schools We Need." *The Reading Teacher* 48, 1: 14–29.

———. 2005. *What Really Matters for Struggling Readers: Designing Research-Based Programs.* 2nd ed. Boston: Allyn & Bacon.

Allington, Richard L., and Peter H. Johnston. 2002. *Reading to Learn: Lessons from Exemplary Fourth-Grade Classrooms.* New York: Guilford.

Ambrose, Stephen. 1997. *Undaunted Courage: Meriwether Lewis, Thomas Jefferson and the Opening of the American West.* New York: Touchstone.

American Association for the Advancement of Science. 2000. Annual report. Washington, DC: American Association for the Advancement of Science.

Anderson, R. C., C. Chinn, M. Commeyras, A. Stallman, M. Waggoner, and I. Wilkinson. 1992. The Reflective Thinking Project. In *Understanding and Enhancing Literature Discussion in Elementary Classrooms.* Symposium, 42nd Annual Meeting of the National Reading Conference, San Antonio, Texas.

Anderson, R. C., and P. D. Pearson. 1984. "A Schema-Theoretic View of Basic Processes in Reading." In *Handbook of Reading Research,* ed. P. D. Pearson. White Plains, NY: Longman.

Atwell, Nancie. 1987. *In the Middle: Writing, Reading, and Learning with Adolescents.* Portsmouth, NH: Boynton/Cook.

Baker, Linda. 2002. "Metacognition in Comprehension Instruction." In *Comprehension Instruction: Research-Based Best Practices,* ed. Cathy Collins Block and Michael Pressley. New York: Guilford.

Barber, Jacqueline, Kristin Nagy Catz, and Diana Arya. 2006. "Improving Science Content Acquisition Through a Combined Science/Literacy Approach: A Quasi-Experimental Study." Paper presented at the American Educational Research Association Annual Convention. April.

Barrett, Andrea. 1996. *Ship Fever.* New York: W. W. Norton.

Barry, Dave. 1991. *Best Travel Guide Ever.* New York: Fawcett.

Bartley, Paula, and Cathy Loxton. 1991. *Plains Women.* New York: Cambridge University.

Beane, James A. 2005. *A Reason to Teach: Creating Classrooms of Dignity and Hope.* Portsmouth, NH: Heinemann.

Beck, Isabel, Margaret McKeown, Rebecca Hamilton, and Linda Kucan. 1997. *Questioning the Author: An Approach for Enhancing Student Engagement with Text.* Newark, DE: International Reading Association.

Bentley, W. A., and W. J. Humphreys. 1962. *Snow Crystals.* New York: Turtle.

Block, Cathy Collins, and Michael Pressley, eds. 2002. *Comprehension Instruction: Research-Based Best Practices.* New York: Guilford.

Block, Cathy Collins, Linda B. Gambrell, and Michael Pressley, eds. 2002. *Improving Comprehension Instruction: Rethinking Research, Theory, and Classroom Practice.* San Francisco: Jossey-Bass.

Block, Cathy Collins, Joni L. Schaller, Joseph A. Joy, and Paolo Gaine. 2002. "Process-Based Comprehension Instruction: Perspectives of Four Reading Educators." In *Comprehension Instruction: Research-Based Best Practices,* ed. Cathy Collins Block and Michael Pressley. New York: Guilford.

Boyd, Robert S. 1999. "Moonstruck Scientists Count 63 and Rising." *Denver Post,* January 3.

Brantley, Ben. 1996. "Flying Feet Electrify the Sweep of History." Review of *Bring in da Noise, Bring in da Funk. New York Times,* April 26.

Britton, James. 1970. *Language and Learning.* Harmondsworth, UK: Penguin.

Broad, William. 1997. "Misunderstood Sharks, Not Just Feeding Machines." *Denver Post,* December 7.

Brown, A. L., and J. D. Day. 1983. "Macrorules for Summarizing Texts: The Development of Expertise." *Journal of Verbal Learning and Verbal Behavior* 22: 1–4.

Brown, Dee. 1991. *Bury My Heart at Wounded Knee: An Indian History of the American West.* New York: Henry Holt.

Buckner, Aimee. 2005. *Notebook Know-How: Strategies for the Writer's Notebook.* Portland, ME: Stenhouse.

Buhrow, Brad, and Anne Upczak Garcia. 2006. *Ladybugs, Tornadoes, and Swirling Galaxies: English Language Learners Discover Their World Through Inquiry.* Portland, ME: Stenhouse.

Busching, Beverly, and Betty Ann Slesinger. 2002. *"It's Our World Too": Socially Responsive Learners in Middle School Language Arts.* Urbana, IL: NCTE.

Buzan, Tony, and Barry Buzan. 2005. *The Mind Map Book: How to Use Radiant Thinking to Maximize Your Brain's Untapped Potential.* New York: Plume.

Calaprice, Alice. 1996. *The Quotable Einstein.* Princeton, NJ: Princeton University.

Calkins, Lucy, Kate Montgomery, Beverly Falk, and Donna Santman. 1998. *A Teacher's Guide to Standardized Reading Tests: Knowledge Is Power.* Portsmouth, NH: Heinemann.

Charlton, James. 1991. *The Writer's Quotation Book: A Literary Companion.* New York: Barnes and Noble.

Cisneros, Sandra. 1991. *Woman Hollering Creek and Other Stories.* New York: Vintage Contemporary.

Conroy, Pat. 1994. *Prince of Tides.* New York: Bantam.

Cruise, Robin. 1999. Personal interview.

Crutchfield, James A. 1993. *It Happened in Colorado.* Helena, MT: Falcon.

Cullinan, Bernice E. 1981. *Literature and the Child.* San Diego: Harcourt Brace.

Cunningham, Anne, and Keith Stanovich. 2003. "What Principals Need to Know About Reading." *Principal* 83 (2): 34–39.

Daniels, Harvey. 2002. *Literature Circles: Voice and Choice in Book Clubs and Reading Groups.* 2nd ed. Portland, ME: Stenhouse.

Daniels, Harvey, and Marilyn Bizar. 2004. *Teaching the Best Practice Way: Methods That Matter.* Portland, ME: Stenhouse.

Daniels, Harvey, and Steven Zemelman. 2004. *Subjects Matter: Every Teacher's Guide to Content-Area Reading.* Portsmouth, NH: Heinemann.

Davey, Beth. 1983. "Think Aloud: Modeling the Cognitive Processes of Reading Comprehension." *Journal of Reading* 27: 44–47.

Del Calzo, Nick. 1997. *The Triumphant Spirit: Portraits and Stories of Holocaust Survivors, Their Messages of Hope and Compassion.* Denver: Triumphant Spirit.

Diamond, Jared. 1999. *Germs, Guns, and Steel: The Fates of Human Societies.* New York: W. W. Norton.

Dillard, Annie. 1989. *The Writing Life.* New York: HarperCollins.

Dole, Jan. 1997. Public Education and Business Coalition Reading Comprehension Workshop. Denver, CO. April.

Dreifus, Claudia. 1997. *Interview.* New York: Seven Stories.

Duke, Nell K. 2000. "3.6 Minutes per Day: The Scarcity of Informational Texts in First Grade." *Reading Research Quarterly* 35 (2), 202–224.

Durkin, Dolores. 1979. "What Classroom Observations Reveal About Reading Instruction." *Reading Research Quarterly* 14: 481–533.

Edlin, John. 1992. "Rhino Dehorned by Rangers." *Denver Post,* January 10.

Eggen, Dan, and Shankar Vedantam. 2006. "More Questions Than Answers." *Washington Post,* May 1.

Epstein, Norrie. 1993. *The Friendly Shakespeare.* New York: Penguin.

Esquibel, Curtis L. 1999. "Frigid Weather Teases State." *Denver Post,* March 13.

Feynman, Richard. 1985. *"Surely You're Joking, Mr. Feynman!"* New York: Bantam.

———. 1988. *What Do You Care What Other People Think? Further Adventures of a Curious Character.* New York: Bantam.

Fielding, Linda, and P. David Pearson. 1994. "Reading Comprehension: What Works?" *Educational Leadership* 51, 5: 62–67.

Fletcher, Ralph. 1996. *A Writer's Notebook: Unlocking the Writer Within You.* New York: Avon.

Frasier, Charles. *Cold Mountain.* 1997. New York: Atlantic Monthly Press.

Gallagher, Margaret C. 1986. Knowledge Acquisition in the Content Area Classroom: Exploring the Consequences of Instruction. Doctoral dissertation, University of Illinois. Dissertation Abstracts International Vol. 47 01A.

Gardner, Howard. 1991. *The Unschooled Mind: How Children Think and How Schools Should Teach.* New York: Basic.

Gilbar, Steve. 1990. *The Reader's Quotation Book.* New York: Barnes and Noble.

Glovin, David, and David Evans. 2006. "How Test Companies Fail Your Kids." *Bloomberg Markets.* December: 126–142.

Goldberg, Natalie. 1986. *Writing Down the Bones.* Boston: Shambhala.

Goudvis, Anne, and Stephanie Harvey. 2005. *Reading the World: Content Comprehension with Linguistically Diverse Learners* (video). Portland, ME: Stenhouse.

Grafton, John, ed. 1991. *Abraham Lincoln: Great Speeches.* New York: Dover.

Graves, Donald. 1991. *Build a Literate Classroom.* Portsmouth, NH: Heinemann.

Greene, Maxine. 1982. "Literacy for What?" *Visible Language* 16.

Guthrie, J.T. 2003. "Concept Oriented Reading Instruction." In *Rethinking Reading Comprehension,* ed. C.E. Snow and A.P. Sweet. New York: Guilford.

Hagerty, Pat. 1992. *Reader's Workshop: Real Reading.* Ontario: Scholastic Canada.

Hall, Susan. 1990. *Using Picture Storybooks to Teach Literary Devices.* Phoenix, AZ: Oryx.

Hansen, Jane. 1981. "The Effects of Inference Training and Practice on Young Childrens' Reading Comprehension." *Reading Research Quarterly* 16: 391–417.

Harrer, Heinrich. 1997. *Seven Years in Tibet.* New York: Putnam.

Harvard College Library. 2007. "Interrogating Texts: 6 Reading Habits to Develop in Your First Year at Harvard." Harvard University. http://hcl.harvard.edu/research/guides/lamont_handouts/interrogatingtexts.html.

Harvey, Stephanie. 1998. *Nonfiction Matters: Reading, Writing, and Research in Grades 3–8.* Portland, ME: Stenhouse.

Harvey, Stephanie, and Anne Goudvis. 2001. *Strategy Instruction in Action* (video). Portland, ME: Stenhouse.

———. 2003. *Think Nonfiction! Modeling Reading and Research* (video). Portland, ME: Stenhouse.

———. 2004. *Strategic Thinking: Reading and Responding, Grades 4–8* (video). Portland, ME: Stenhouse.

———. 2005a. *The Comprehension Toolkit: Language and Lessons for Active Literacy.* Portsmouth, NH: Heinemann.

———. 2005b. *Read, Write, and Talk: A Practice to Enhance Comprehension* (video). Portland, ME: Stenhouse.

Harvey, Stephanie, Sheila McAuliffe, Laura Benson, Wendy Cameron, Sue Kempton, Pat Lusche, Debbie Miller, Joan Schroeder, and Julie Weaver. 1996. "Teacher Researchers Study the Process of Synthesizing in Six Primary Classrooms." *Language Arts* 73, 8.

Harwayne, Shelley. 1992. *Lasting Impressions: Weaving Literature into the Writing Workshop.* Portsmouth, NH: Heinemann.

———. 1999. *Going Public: Priorities and Practices at the Manhattan New School.* Portsmouth, NH: Heinemann.

———. 2000. *Lifetime Guarantees: Toward Ambitious Literacy Teaching.* Portsmouth, NH: Heinemann.

Hawking, Stephen. 1988. *A Brief History of Time.* New York: Bantam.

Heard, Georgia. 1995. *Writing Toward Home.* Portsmouth, NH: Heinemann.

Hearne, Betsy. 1993. *The Known and the Unknown: An Exploration into Nonfiction by Jean Fritz.* The Zena Sutherland Lectures, 1983–1992. New York: Clarion.

Hindley, Joanne. 1996. *In the Company of Children.* Portland, ME: Stenhouse.

Housen, A., P. Yenawine, and A. Arenas. 1996. *Visual Thinking Curriculum.* Unpublished. New York: Museum of Modern Art.

Hughes, Langston. 1994. *The Collected Poems of Langston Hughes,* ed. Arnold Rampersad. New York: Vintage.

Hyde, Arthur. 2006. *Comprehending Math: Adapting Reading Strategies to Teach Mathematics, K–6.* Portsmouth, NH: Heinemann.

Johnson, Cynthia, and Drew Johnson. 2000. *Kaplan Parent's Guide to the Virginia SOL Tests for Grade 3: A Complete*

Guide to Understanding the Tests and Preparing Your Child for a Successful Test-Taking Experience. New York: Kaplan.

Johnston, Peter. 2004. *Choice Words: How Our Language Affects Children's Learning.* Portland, ME: Stenhouse.

Keating, Kevin. 1998. "This Is Cruising." *Hemispheres Magazine.* March.

Keene, Ellin Oliver. 2002. "From Good to Memorable: Characteristics of Highly Effective Comprehension Instruction." In *Improving Comprehension Instruction: Rethinking Research, Theory, and Classroom Practice,* ed. Cathy Collins Block, Linda B. Gambrell, and Michael Pressley. San Francisco: Jossey-Bass.

Keene, Ellin Oliver, and Susan Zimmermann. 1997. *Mosaic of Thought: Teaching Comprehension in a Reader's Workshop.* Portsmouth, NH: Heinemann.

Kobrin, Beverly. *The Kobrin Letter,* 732 Greer Road, Palo Alto, CA 94303.

Krakauer, Jon. 1997. *Into Thin Air.* New York: Villard.

Lamb, Brian. 1998. *Booknotes: America's Finest Authors on Reading, Writing, and the Power of Ideas.* New York: Random House.

Lamb, Charles, and Mary Lamb. 1996. *Illustrated Tales from Shakespeare.* North Dighton, MA: World.

Lamont, Anne. 1994. *Bird by Bird: Some Instructions on Writing and Life.* New York: Anchor.

Lawlor, Laurie. 1994. *Shadow Catcher: The Life and Work of Edward S. Curtis.* New York: Walker.

Levstik, Linda. 1993. "I Wanted to Be There: The Impact of Narrative on Children's Historical Thinking." In *The Story of Ourselves,* ed. M. Tunnell and R. Ammon. Portsmouth, NH: Heinemann.

Levstik, Linda, and Keith G. Barton. 2001. *Doing History: Investigating with Children in Elementary and Middle Schools.* Mahwah, NJ: Lawrence Erlbaum.

Lopez, Barry. 1986. *Arctic Dreams.* New York: Charles Scribner.

Lord, Walter. 1997. *A Night to Remember.* New York: Bantam.

Lynton, Michael. 2000. Keynote address at the Mid-Atlantic Venture Fair, Philadelphia. Oct. 25.

MacNeil, Robert. 1990. *Wordstruck: A Memoir.* New York: Penguin.

McCullough, David. 1983. *The Great Bridge: The Epic Story of the Building of the Brooklyn Bridge.* New York: Simon and Schuster.

McKenzie, Jamie. 1996. "Making Web Meaning." *Educational Leadership* 54 (3): 30–32.

McPhee, John. 1966. *Oranges.* New York: Farrar, Straus and Giroux.

Mehler, Carl. 1998. *Satellite Atlas of the World.* Washington, DC: National Geographic.

Miller, Debbie. 2002. *Reading with Meaning: Teaching Comprehension in the Primary Grades.* Portland, ME: Stenhouse.

Miller, Debbie, and Anne Goudvis. 1999. "Classroom Conversations: Young Children Discuss Fairness and Justice, Intolerance and Prejudice." In *Teaching for a Tolerant World,* ed. Judith Robertson. Urbana, IL: National Council of Teachers of English.

Miller, Sue. 1993. *For Love.* New York: HarperCollins.

Nafisi, Azar. 2003. *Reading Lolita in Tehran.* New York: Random House.

National Reading Panel. 2000. *The Report of the National Reading Panel: Teaching Children to Read.* Washington, DC: National Reading Panel.

Nelson, George. 1999. Quoted in "Heavy Books Light on Learning: Not One Middle Grades Science Text Rated Satisfactory by AAAS's Project 2061." September 28. Press release by the American Association for the Advancement of Science available online at http://www.project2061.org/about/press/pr90928.htm.

The New York Times. 2006. "Schools Cut Back Subjects to Push Reading and Math: Responding to No Child Left Behind, Thousands Narrow the Curriculum." *The New York Times.* March 26.

Nofi, Albert, comp. 1995. *A Civil War Journal.* New York: Galahad.

Nordstrum, Ursula. 1998. *Dear Genius: The Letters of Ursula Nordstrum.* New York: HarperCollins.

O'Brien, Tim. 1989. *The Things They Carried: A Work of Fiction.* New York: Broadway.

Ondaatje, Michael. 1992. *The English Patient.* New York: Vintage.

Palincsar, A. S., and A. L. Brown. 1984. "Reciprocal Teaching of Comprehension-Fostering and Monitoring Activities." *Cognition and Instruction* 1: 117–175.

Paris, S. G., M. Y. Lipson, and K. K. Wixon. 1983. "Becoming a Strategic Reader." *Contemporary Educational Psychology* 8: 293–316.

Paterson, Katherine. 1995. *A Sense of Wonder: On Reading and Writing Books for Children.* New York: Penguin.

Pearson, P. David. 1995. Personal Interview.

———. 2006. "Roots of Reading/Seeds of Science." Presented at the National Geographic Literacy Institute, Washington, DC.

Pearson, P. David, and Nell K. Duke. 2001. "Comprehension Instruction in the Primary Grades." In *Comprehension Instruction: Research-Based Best Practices,* ed. Cathy Collins-Block and Michael Pressley. New York: Guilford.

Pearson, P. David, and M. C. Gallagher. 1983. "The Instruction of Reading Comprehension." *Contemporary Educational Psychology* 8: 317–344.

Pearson, P. David, J. A. Dole, G. G. Duffy, and L. R. Roehler. 1992. "Developing Expertise in Reading Comprehension: What Should Be Taught and How Should It Be Taught?" In *What Research Has to Say to the Teacher of Reading,* ed. J.

Farstup and S. J. Samuels, 2nd ed. Newark, DE: International Reading Association.

Pearson, P. David, Stephanie Harvey, and Anne Goudvis. 2005. *What Every Teacher Should Know About Reading Comprehension* (video). Portsmouth, NH: Heinemann.

Pearson, P. David, and R. J. Tierney. 1984. "On Becoming a Thoughtful Reader: Learning to Read Like a Writer." In *Becoming Readers in a Complex Society,* ed. A. Purves and O. Niles. Chicago: National Society for the Study of Education.

Pennac, Daniel. 1999. *Better Than Life.* Portland, ME: Stenhouse.

Perkins, David. 1992. *Smart Schools: Better Thinking and Learning for Every Child.* New York: Free Press.

Pinker, Steven. 1997. *How the Mind Works.* New York: W. W. Norton.

Plimpton, George. 1988. *Writers at Work.* Eighth Series. New York: Penguin.

Pressley, Michael. 1976. "Mental Imagery Helps Eight-Year-Olds Remember What They Read." *Journal of Educational Psychology* 68: 355–359.

———. 2002. *Reading Instruction That Works: The Case for Balanced Teaching.* 2nd ed. New York: Guilford.

Proulx, E. Annie. 1993. *The Shipping News.* New York: Charles Scribner.

Quindlen, Anna. 1998. *How Reading Changed My Life.* New York: Ballantine.

Reutzel, D. R., J. A. Smith, and P. C. Fawson. 2005. "An Evaluation of Two Approaches for Teaching Reading Comprehension Strategies in the Primary Years Using Science Information Texts." *Early Childhood Research Quarterly* 20: 276–305.

Rief, Linda. 1992. *Seeking Diversity: Language Arts with Adolescents.* Portsmouth, NH: Heinemann.

Ritchhart, Ron. 2002. *Intellectual Character: What It Is, Why It Matters, and How to Get It.* San Francisco: Jossey-Bass.

Rosenblatt, Louise. [1938] 1996. *Literature as Exploration.* New York: Modern Language Association of America.

Routman, Regie. 2003. *Reading Essentials: The Specifics You Need to Teach Reading Well.* Portsmouth, NH: Heinemann.

Roy, Arundhati. 1997. *The God of Small Things.* New York: Random House.

Ruddell, Robert B., and Norman J. Unrau, eds. 2004. *Theoretical Models and Processes of Reading.* Newark, DE: International Reading Association.

Rudloe, Jack, and Anne Rudloe. 1994. "Sea Turtles in a Race for Survival." *National Geographic Magazine* 185: 94–121.

Schwarz, Patrick. 2006. *From Disability to Possibility: The Power of Inclusive Classrooms.* Portsmouth, NH: Heinemann.

Shaara, Michael. 1974. *The Killer Angels.* New York: Ballantine.

Shefelbine, John. 1999. "Reading: Voluminously and Voluntarily." In *Scholastic Reading Counts! Research and Results Report.* New York: Scholastic.

Shenk, David. 1997. *Data Smog: Surviving the Information Glut.* New York: Harper Edge.

Sibberson, Franki, and Karen Szymusiak. 2003. *Still Learning to Read: Teaching Students in Grades 3–6.* Portland, ME: Stenhouse.

Simmons, Ruth. 2001. Interview on *60 Minutes.* June 24.

Sobel, Dava, and William J. H. Andrewes. 1998. *The Illustrated Longitude: The True Story of a Lone Genius Who Solved the Greatest Scientific Problem of His Time.* New York: Walker.

Stamberg, Susan. 1993. *Talk: NPR's Susan Stamberg Considers All Things.* New York: Random House.

Strunk, William J., and E. B. White. 1999. *The Elements of Style.* 4th ed. New York: Allyn and Bacon.

Suskind, Ron. 1998. *A Hope in the Unseen: An American Odyssey from the Inner City to the Ivy League.* New York: Broadway.

Szymusiak, Karen, and Franki Sibberson. 2001. *Beyond Leveled Books: Supporting Transitional Readers in Grades 2–5.* Portland, ME: Stenhouse.

Trabasso, Tom, and Edward Bouchard. 2002. "Teaching Readers How to Comprehend Text Strategically" In *Comprehension Instruction: Research-Based Best Practices,* ed. Cathy Collins Block and Michael Pressley. New York: Guilford.

Tatum, Alfred W. 2005. *Teaching Reading to Black Adolescent Males: Closing the Achievement Gap.* Portland, ME: Stenhouse.

Tishman, Shari, David N. Perkins, and Eileen Jay. 1994. *The Thinking Classroom: Learning and Teaching in a Culture of Thinking.* Boston: Allyn & Bacon.

Tovani, Cris. 2000. *I Read It, but I Don't Get It: Comprehension Strategies for Adolescent Readers.* Portland, ME: Stenhouse.

———. 2004. *Do I Really Have to Teach Reading? Content Comprehension, Grades 6–12.* Portland, ME: Stenhouse.

Trelease, Jim. 2006. *The Read-Aloud Handbook.* 6th ed. New York: Penguin.

Ueland, Brenda. 1987. *If You Want to Write.* 2nd ed. Saint Paul: Graywolf.

Watson, James D. 1991. *The Double Helix: A Personal Account of the Discovery of the Structure of DNA.* New York: New American Library.

Webster's New World Dictionary. 1991. New York: Simon and Schuster.

Welty, Eudora. 1983. *One Writer's Beginnings.* Cambridge, MA: Harvard University.

Wiesel, Elie. 1982. *Night.* New York: Bantam.

Wild Outdoor World. 1999. "Howling Again." *Wild Outdoor World* 3, January/February.

Wilhelm, Jeffrey. 1996. *"You Gotta Be the Book" Teaching Engaged and Reflective Reading with Adolescents.* New York: Teachers College.

Williams, Terry Tempest. 1992. *Refuge: An Unnatural History of Family and Place.* New York: Vintage.

Wills, Garry. 1992. *Lincoln at Gettysburg: The Words That Remade America.* New York: Simon and Schuster.

———. 1994. *Certain Trumpets: The Call of Leaders.* New York: Simon and Schuster.

Zemelman, Steven, Harvey Daniels, and Arthur Hyde. 2005. *Best Practice: Today's Standards for Teaching and Learning in America's Schools.* 3rd ed. Portsmouth, NH: Heinemann.

Zimmermann, Susan, and Chryse Hutchins. 2003. *7 Keys to Comprehension: How to Help Your Kids Read It and Get It.* New York: Three Rivers.

Zinsser, William. 1976. *On Writing Well.* New York: HarperCollins.

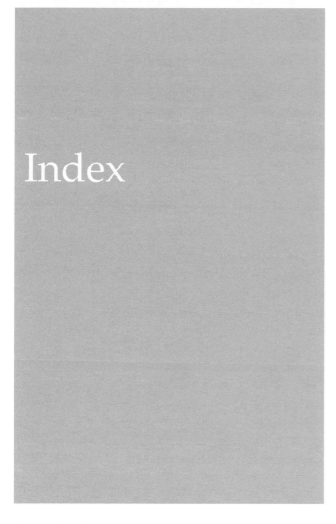

Index